GUIDES of the ADIRONDACKS
A History

A Short Season • Hard Work • Low Pay

by

Charles Brumley

North Country Books, Inc.
Utica, New York

Guides of the Adirondacks
A History

Copyright © 1994
by Charles Brumley

ISBN 0-925168-32-7

Library of Congress Cataloging-in-Publication Data

Brumley, Charles.
    Guides of the Adirondacks : a history / by Charles Brumley.
        p.   cm.
    Includes index.
    ISBN 0-925168-32-7 cloth; ISBN 0-925168-36-X paper
        1. Adirondack Mountains (N.Y.)—History.   2. Tour guides
(Persons)—New York (State)—Adirondack Mountains—History.
    I. Title.
    F127.A2B69   1994
    974.7'5—dc20   94-10561
                                                                              CIP

North Country Books, Inc.
PUBLISHER—DISTRIBUTOR
18 Irving Place
Utica, New York 13501

Dedicated to

THE ADIRONDACK GUIDES

"Everything depends in the Adirondacks
upon your guide."
    —Author *Henry Van Dyke* (1852-1933)

and to

A DOG NAMED BEAR
1981-1993

He loved the woods and waters as much
as any man. He was a boon companion.

TABLE OF CONTENTS

Preface v

Acknowledgements vii

PART ONE: The Guide Through the Years 1
    Beginnings 1
    The Guide: Oarsman, Hunter and Fisherman 6
    A Reputation in Decline; A Reputation Regained . . . 18
    Guides in the Mountains 25
    The Professional Guides Associations 28
    The Role of the State 36
    Private Preserves and Commercial Hunting Camps . . 47
    Guides in Adirondack Literature and Art 52
    Sometimes Things Go Wrong 61

PART TWO: Biographies of Adirondack Guides 91

PART THREE: Nine Interviews and a Diary 193
    Brian McDonnell 194
    Clarence Petty 198
    Carl Hathaway 209
    Dan and Bill Frayne 223
    Wayne Failing 233
    Dick Emperor 238
    Sandy and Fred Fountain 244
    Dave Cilley 252
    Reginald Whitney 263
    Frank M. Wardner Diary 272

PART FOUR: Two Trips to Hamilton County 278

Appendix A: A List of Guides 310

    Number of Guides Licenses Issued by Year
    1924-1963 312

Appendix B: Some Quotations by and about Guides 364

Index 369

PREFACE

"Since taxidermy appears to be out of the question, we must resort to prose." -- Author Pieter W. Fosburgh, wishing to preserve guides, in The Natural Thing, 1959.

The Adirondack guiding tradition is now about one-hundred and fifty years old. Most of the guides who served in that span have faded into oblivion. In most of the 1800's the supposition was any native Adirondack male of teen years or older could guide a vacationer hunting or fishing. For decades many natives were hired as guides, and there were hundreds of them; the 1893 Forest Commission Report lists 626 -- ranging from part-timers to those booked in advance for the entire summer and fall. Perhaps because there have been so many, an attempt to gather and publish the history of Adirondack guides has never been tried, to my knowledge.

But of all the categories of people that enrich the evolving tapestry of Adirondack history -- lumberman, settlers, hotel keepers, tourist, artists and writers, and more -- the guides can lay as strong a claim as any to uniqueness, to indispensability in the saga. They were the catalysts, the bridge between the wilderness and the people.

However, the guides have gotten peculiarly short shrift in Adirondack history. Most enthusiastic accounts of guided Adirondack outings written by tourists stress they couldn't have done it without their guides. But as the tourists -- the writers, the authors, the others -- made their own interpretations of their experiences, their guides were pushed, or faded, into the background. What did the guides think about their own work; about the wilderness; about their customers, or "sports"; about the totality of their own lives? With the exception of what a few guides such as Orson Phelps and John Cheney (who were treated somewhat as curiosities) thought about some aspects of the wilderness, the historical record is antiseptically mute.

The guides kept few diaries (indeed, many guides couldn't read or write very well), they were the subjects of few interviews, and of little, if any, academic attention in the days of the "great men" theories of history. The contemporary interviews in this account include some sociological commentary on the guide and his sport, and the guide-caretaker and employer relationship. A leap of faith, but perhaps not a very big one, is needed to believe similar relationships extend back to the beginnings of the Adirondack guiding tradition.

One problem with this history is that many of the old guides' obituaries read more or less the same: "He was a well-known guide in the area and guided many famous people." Period. Nothing is said about who he guided, or why he was well-known, and no other information can be found. Thus some of the biographical sketches, drawn from such information, are pitifully scant. *Sic transit gloria.* I tried to piece a picture together from the book literature of the Adirondacks, microfilms, scrapbooks of old newspapers, and periodicals, especially one little-known today, the *Spirit of the Times*, going back to the 1830's. The resource material is so scattered I am at a loss to suggest a bibliography, normally a task I would welcome. In spite of all my disclaimers, I think a picture emerges of the essential nature of Adirondack guides and their profession. But we must remember that -- while we think of the nineteenth century in the Adirondacks, particularly, and the Adirondacks in general, as a tableau frozen in time, with nothing to disturb the cycles of the seasons -- if there is one thing that is true about the guides and what they did, it is that their profession was never static.

The masculine pronoun "he" is used most of the time, a sensitive subject in these politically correct days. While interpretations of history change, certain irreducible essentials often remain. Guiding was almost an all-male field. I looked hard and long for female guides and found two important earlier ones: Lottie Tuttle and Ann Telfer. Their biographies are included. Recently the situation has changed and men and women are intermixed and mostly interchangeable in their roles as guides.

But by no means did I uncover all the guides, or everything about them. Some readers may look in vain here for Uncle, Aunt, or Grand Pa So-and-so, and be disappointed not to find them, not even in the appendix list of 2,700 names. No doubt other omissions, and errors, exist. (I know better now why authors often waffle with a title that starts, "A Preliminary History of ...")

Even though revised editions of books such as this are rare, I would appreciate hearing from people who can offer corrections or additional material.

Charles Brumley
Saranac Lake

ACKNOWLEDGEMENTS

The following people, in addition to those listed in the interview section, helped make this book possible:
Dave Ames, James Bailey, Vernon Bailey, Iris Barcomb, Charles Beahan, Bob Bedford, Muriel Benson, Marjorie Berger, Edward "Bud" Betters, Laura Bick, Harriet Bigelow, Marvin Bissell, Phyllis Bogle, Elizabeth Squires Botten, Gene Brooks, Beverly Burchill, A. Carmen Clark, Ted Comstock, Matthew "Joe" Conway, Frank Cross, Shirley Daily, Janet Decker, Bob Dickers, Noelle Donahue, Dave Dudajek, Horton Duprey, John Duquette, Roy Early, Margaret Edwards, Bing Faxon, Edna Finn, Alice Freeman, Claude Freeman, Maybelle Gregory, Judd Groff, Joe Hackett, Anne and Dick Hallock, Harold Harter, Maude Haskell, Caroline Hotaling, Mary Hotaling, Ruth and Gould Hoyt, Nona LeClair, Jay O'Hern, Dave Hunt, Reid Larson, Mrs. Lawrence, William Lawson, Mr. and Mrs. Jack Leadley, Jack Leadley, Jr., Vernon Lee, Jim Meehan, Helen Miller, Rita Mitchell, Nancy Montville, SSJ, Edith Morcy, Tony Munn, Lillian Nolette, Maurice Otis, Janet Parent, Jane Parrott, Joan Patton, Janice Peasley, Jerry Pepper, Susan Perkins, Leon Perry, Don Perryman, Clarence Petty, Edith Pilcher, John Plumley, Emma Remington, Carol Rogers, Helen Rogers, Richard Roth, Jean Russell, Harry Schrader, Frances Seaman, Addie Shields, Louis Simmons, Gill Slater, Mr. and Mrs. Percy Stanton, Linda Thomas, Breck Turner, Newell Wagoner, Carolyn Walker, Anita Washburn, Clifton West, William Wharton, H. Whitlock, Jeffrey Whittemore, Naj Wikoff, Paul Wilbur, and Alan Woodruff.

The interviews were among my greatest personal rewards from the project, and owe their success to their cooperative subjects:

Dave Cilley, Dick Emperor, Wayne Failing, Dan and Bill Frayne, Carl Hathaway, Fred and Sandy Fountain, Brian McDonnell, Clarence Petty, and Reginald Whitney.

Special thanks are due Warder Cadbury, Adirondack historian and author, and Chris Jerome, editor and Adirondack author, for reading and critiquing my manuscript in an early version -- if you think it's convoluted now, you should have seen it before; they are blameless. Also Mary MacKenzie, Historian for the Town of North Elba and the Village of Lake Placid, who treated my project as well as if it were her own; Sheila Orlin and the rest of the folks at North Country Books, for publishing the book; Cheryl Ploof and Teresa Bordeau for transcribing the interviews; Barb Young for typing "Two Trips to Hamilton County" the first time; Frank Cross of Saranac Lake for a computerized alphabetical list of guides and "area codes" derived from the 1893 Forest Commission Report; Edith Pilcher for permission to include her list of Ausable Lake guides from her book *Up the Lake Road*; and computer wizard Paul Moriarty (also a guide) for assembling the appendix list of guides and typing the entire manuscript. Grateful appreciation is given to the Adirondack Museum for permission to reproduce approximately two dozen guide-related photographs, many of which have never been published before. Some of the concepts in the literature section originated with Richard Roth.

Heartfelt thanks to my wife Karen for explicating our computer, serving as an in-house editor in spite of her own time-consuming commitments as a college student, and sharing many miles of tramping and canoeing. Being on the waters and in the woods with her and the parties I have guided helped me to understand why guides are so important.

I extend a profound apology to anyone who may have assisted me whose name I inadvertently omitted. All errors of fact, omission, emphasis, or any other type remain entirely my own.

PART ONE:
The Guide Through the Years

Beginnings

"The edges of this enormous wilderness are thinly inhabited by hunters and trappers, who pierce its deepest recesses in their light boats, and act as guides to visitors in summer." -- Woods and Waters: or, The Saranacs and Racket, by Alfred B. Street, 1860.

The period between 1836 and 1865 has been described as the "golden years" of the Adirondacks. In a part of the country becoming rapidly civilized, the area was an island of wilderness. By 1850, the population of the large outer portion of the present Adirondack Park was almost as great as it is today. But some of the interior townships were barely formed; for example, North Elba, which includes Lake Placid, wasn't established until 1849. These golden years of the wilderness were also the golden years of the guides. The guide was the catalyst that first brought together client or "sport," scenery, and hunting and fishing adventures.

Some think of the Adirondack guide as a product of the 1890's, part of the heyday of the grand hotels, with their verandahs and parasols. But the guides at the end of the century were the literal or figurative grandsons of the real pioneer Adirondack guides. Even three of the region's most famous guides, ones we think of as real old-timers, just barely made it as true pioneers: Orson "Old Mountain" Phelps, Bill Nye, and Alvah Dunning. By a quirk of fate they were all born in 1816, and were mere teenagers when the Adirondack guiding tradition got under way. That tradition started in the 1830's, and continued to the end of the century with many of the same practices unchanged. But the tradition didn't spring up without precedents; people, opportunity, and traditional skills all came together in the golden era.

One's first impulse when looking for the origins of the guiding tradition in the Adirondacks is to say "Indians." Evidence of their pre-historic presence, as shown by pottery shards, pestles, pipes, honing stones, and projectile points has been found near waterways throughout much of what is now the Adirondack Park. There is no question they used the area for hunting and fishing; their ability to traverse the forests on the fringes of the Adirondacks was legendary. This came to light in the French and Indian War, when the primary role of the Indians in the Champlain Valley was scouting for the French and British to gather intelligence.

In 1756, the French officer Louis Antoine de Bougainville remarked that the Iroquois could tell from tracks the number of people who had passed, whether they were Indians or Europeans, healthy or sick. He said they possessed "an instinct superior to all reasons." Indians from French-held Fort Carillon spied on the British as far south as Albany. In the process they had to by-pass the British vanguard at Fort William Henry at the south end of Lake George, going behind enemy lines.

In peacetime, Indians with such skills would seem to be the natural ones to fill the role of guides in the nearby Adirondacks; however, a combination of factors worked against this. First, almost no evidence of permanent Indian settlements of any size exist in the Adirondack interior. The Adirondacks were apparently never "home" to many Indians, especially from the war-torn eighteenth century on. And almost from the minute white men got anywhere near the Adirondacks, the Indians' rights to their own land disappeared. Many so-called "peace treaties" were made by whites with the Iroquois of the area, which included the Mohawks and some Oneidas. The treaties were designed, and sometimes broken, to gain land. In some cases Indians who couldn't read or write didn't know what they were signing; they sold land they had no right to sell, land that could only be sold with full native council approval.

Soon after the Revolutionary War virtually all of the lands in the Adirondacks were in the hands of whites. The state briefly owned most of the land, which was sold to land speculators. Eventually much of it ended up back in the hands of the state. The few Indians scattered in the region had come from a variety of tribes in addition to those of the Iroquois, including many Canadian tribes such as the St. Regis, Abenaki, and Penobscot. The Indians who did become guides -- Mitchell Sabattis is the most well-known -- kept their woods skills but assimilated white ways of living and doing business. They also didn't begin living in the Adirondack interior in any numbers until whites did. In Long Lake, for example, that was as late as 1830.

George Marshall, in the 1920's one of the first three Adirondack Forty-Sixers, has stated an evolutionary chronology that begins with a caveat: "It is difficult to give a precise definition of a guide. When did the Indian first take men of European background through the mountains? When did the frontier scout become hunter and woodsman? When did the hunter-woodsman become the guide? ... These were not clear cut stages."

In Marshall's outline the Indian gave way to the frontier scout. This is true, but it was not a friendly passing of the torch. Many examples in the literature of the Adirondacks show mutual hatred between Indians and scouts. This schism eventually dictated who would be guides. In the beginning there would be a few Indians, but more whites. Part of the problem was the legacy from the French and Indian, and Revolutionary Wars. The Indians were caught in the middle both times; their ideas of cowardice and bravery were different from Europeans. Sometimes they switched sides depending on who was winning. After the wars, some Indians pursued trapping, competing economically with whites.

One example in the second step of Marshall's chronology is scout Nick Stoner, a Revolutionary War veteran who turned to trapping after the war. He was just as skillful in the woods as any Indian. It was said of him that he could "kindle a fire, climb a tree, cook a dinner, empty a bottle, shoot a deer, hook a trout, or scent an Indian" quicker than any man known. He was troubled by Indians robbing his traps, and once after checking them returned home with what he called, sardonically, a "spare rifle."

Nat Foster, another frontiersman, was born in Vermont about 1767, and moved to the Adirondacks ten years after the Revolution. He could load and fire a muzzle-loading flintlock rifle six times a minute, an unheard-of speed. Like Stoner, he had a veiled way of discussing his Indian dealings. For instance, "The best shot I ever made, I got two beaver, one otter, and fifteen marten skins; but I took the filling out of a blanket to do it!" And, "I was once in the woods, and saw an Indian lay down to drink at a brook; something was the matter; he dropped his face into the water and drowned; I thought I might as well take his fur, gun, blanket, &c., as leave them there to spoil." He was tried for murder and acquitted in 1834 in Herkimer County for shooting a St. Francis Indian named Peter Waters.

Former scouts such as these and others who were hunters and trappers took to the deep Adirondack woods for their own reasons. They guided the adventurers who came to the wilderness, taking the role of guide a step farther. For example, every writer who visited Raquette Lake in the 1840's and '50's mentioned a pair of hunters, William Wood and Matthew Beach. Originally from Vermont and Massachusetts, respectively, they were the first settlers at Raquette Lake. They bridged the roles of hunter/trappers, and guides, hiring out themselves and Wood's hunting dogs. In one of those classic tales prescient of Yukon sourdough cabin fever, the two had an argument -- Wood moved out of their wilderness cabin and lived for five years in his own hut less than a quarter mile away.

One winter around 1835, Wood lost both feet from freezing after he fell, perhaps drunk, into the icy Independence River near Old Forge. His matches wet and legs frozen, he lay alone until found by Nat Foster. Indians helped amputate his legs below the knees. Wood got around almost as well as before on heavy leather knee pads. Guide Alvah Dunning said Wood went seventy-five miles to Elizabethtown in the 1850's on his pads, with his boat and a pack.

Before their falling out, Wood and Beach had built a hut so crude that in 1849 journalist Charles Webber said that few would imagine it a human habitation -- it was merely a hunter's bark shanty, but with a huge fireplace of spruce bark and a rough floor. Gradually they domesticated their acreage -- or their separate acreages -- and raised vegetables, cattle, berries, and fruit trees.

In 1835, the well-to-do Constable brothers, John and Will, went to Raquette Lake. They were guided by two trappers, "Old Johnson" and Daniel Chase. In 1843, with their brother Stevenson, the boys returned with William Higby, known as Higby the hunter.

The Constables and Higby hiked to First Lake after staying one night at the home of Otis Arnold, who had moved into the abandoned Herreshoff Manor near what is now Old Forge.

"We soon reached the First Lake of the Fulton Chain where we found our boat (snugly hid in the reeds) which was to convey us to our camping ground 25 miles further. This boat, which was built by Higby himself, in the woods, with no other tools than a hatchet, drawing-knife, hammer, and nails, was made as light as possible, 90 pounds, in order to carry it from lake to lake (portages of one to three miles) and yet was capacious enough to carry all our party with dog, gun, rods, provisions, etc. Higby carries the boat by means of a yoke rigged across the gunwales, turned upside down, with his head inside."

Kenneth Durant, author of *The Adirondack Guide-boat,* calls this description "the earliest specific report we have giving some details about a portable (Adirondack) boat." At night Higby paddled in pursuit of deer "without taking his paddle out of the water, and so slowly as not to make a ripple at the bow, for the slightest noise of water is sure to startle a deer."

These particulars make Higby one of the first full-fledged Adirondack guides, the culmination of the skills of the Indian, the frontier scout, and the hunter-woodsman. At the same time similar men had assembled the same kinds of skills in other places in the Adirondacks, and accounts of their abilities followed closely on Higby's heels. The golden years were under way.

The Guide: Oarsman, Hunter and Fisherman

"There is a breed in the Adirondacks today that calls itself guide. Let the outlander beware. The last genuine article passed over the hills ... years ago ... around 1900 he disappeared from the landscape with the earlier wolf and the panther, and the woods never saw his like again." -- Lake Placid Historian Mary MacKenzie.

In the 1840's, the demand for guides increased rapidly. Part of the reason was the new attention the Adirondacks were getting. "*The Spirit of the Times*" was the leading weekly sporting newspaper in the United States. Its editor, William Porter, visited Hamilton County in the central Adirondacks in 1840 and after. In his paper he extolled the hunting and fishing as "immense," the fish of "prodigious size," and compared moose hunting in the Adirondacks with the excitement of hunting buffalo out West. He gave column space to many who wanted to send in descriptions of their own travels. Surprisingly well-written accounts poured in, mostly from vacationing professionals.

All Adirondack sport depended on a guide, Porter said. When he came to Lake Pleasant the "first important step" was to hunt up Nat Morrill, Tim Skidmore, Randall or Cole. Readers of "*The Spirit*" and other papers were quick to get the message. Some came, stayed at local hotels, and hired guides by the day. Groups of a dozen or so formed fishing clubs such as the Lake Piseco Trout Club in Hamilton County, and hired guides by the week or season. The Trout Club's fishing was done in a week or slightly more each summer. From 1842 to 1847 the club took more than two tons of trout. The members noticed that for some reason the fishing had become very poor, and moved on to other waters, leaving behind their guides.

By the middle of the nineteenth century, the mutual roles of guides and clients were well established. When Murray's *Adventures in the Wilderness* came out in 1869, various types of guides were so stereotyped that Murray could easily devote a whole chapter to them. He put his readers on notice what to look for in a guide, describing the independent guide, "models of skill, energy, and faithfulness," and the hotel guide, "inferior, and given to drunkenness." In any class of guide, he said, could be found the witty guide, "forever talking; the braggart; and the lazy guide." The last group could be spotted by their "fleshy, lymphatic, and dirty appearance, and they are often advanced in years."

But the independent guides, he said, depend for future business on their present success, and as a whole were a capable and noble class of men. Most of the guides, in fact, met Murray's approval. Always eloquent, he waxed especially so about guides:

"I cannot let this opportunity pass unimproved of testifying to the capacity, skill, and faithfulness of a great majority of the guides through the Adirondack region. With many I am personally acquainted, and rejoice to number them among my friends. I have seen them under every circumstance of exposure and trial, of feasting and hunger, of health and sickeness, and more honest, cheerful, and patient class of men cannot be found the world over. Born and bred, as many of them were, in this wilderness, skilled in all the lore of woodcraft, handy with the rod, superb at the paddle, modest in demeanor and speech, honest to a proverb, they deserve and receive the admiration of all who make their acquaintance. Bronzed and hardy, fearless of danger, eager to please, uncontaminated with the vicious habits of civilized life, they are not unworthy of the magnificent surroundings amid which they dwell. Among them an oath is never heard, unless in moments of intense excitement. Vulgarity of speech is absolutely unknown, and theft a matter of horror and surprise. Measured by our social and intellectual facilities, their lot is lowly and uninviting, and yet to them there is a charm and fascination in it. Under the waters of these overhanging mountains they were born. Upon the waters of these secluded lakes they have sported from earliest boyhood. The wilderness has unfolded to them its mysteries, and made them wise with a wisdom nowhere written in books. This wilderness is their home. Here they were born, here they have lived, and here it is that they expect to die. Their graves will be made under the pines where in childhood they played, and the sounds of wind and wave which lulled them to sleep when boys will swell the selfsame cadences in requiem over their graves. When they have passed away, tradition will prolong their virtues and their fame."

Sixty-five years after Murray, Gurth Whipple, who wrote *Fifty Years of Conservation in New York State, 1885-1935*, called the guides a "gnarled and woolly coterie (that) never could be mistaken for anyone else." He might have had in mind Lake Pleasant guide Elijah Cowles, who in 1853 stood six feet seven inches in his stockings. When urged, Cowles, a modest man, would tell of capturing panthers, moose, and deer. He may have been even more effective as deputy sheriff and jail keeper than as a guide. He sometimes brought prisoners along on his hunts; the story goes that one prisoner got so weary on a moose hunt that he threatened to return to the jail. Cowles threatened to shoot him on the next outing if he did. Or Whipple may have had in mind Steve Turner, a Paul Smiths guide, who was once accused to his face of being round-shouldered. He snapped back, "Who the blazes wouldn't be round-shouldered after carrying boats for forty years or more?"

Some of the best of them could not measure up to the physical image of a Cowles. The legendary John Cheney, for example, with his "almost whining, high-pitched voice," didn't fit the mold, nor did the famous Orson Phelps, small of build, with a "small, high-pitched half-querulous voice (that) easily rises into the shrillist falsetto." Guide Julia Preston from Hamilton County was remembered recently by one woman as "about four feet nine, each way. I don't think I ever saw her in a skirt. She always wore breeches; she was a darling."

A picture of a fully-equipped nineteenth-century guide getting ready to shove off on to a lake would show a guide-boat, a pack basket, fishing tackle and at least one gun, a jacklight, an axe, provisions, and hounds. Shoehorned in would be the customer, or sport. Only the guide-boat and maybe a snatch of the background scenery would brand the setting as truly Adirondack; the rest could be found in other places.

THE GUIDE-BOAT

The guide-boat originated as the workboat of hunters and trappers, and then became the guide's most essential piece of equipment. He and his sports needed it for transportation, fishing, hunting and occassional shelter. Guide-boats are indigenous to the Adirondacks, and different in construction from both the birch bark canoe and the canvas canoe.

Guide-boat construction begins by fastening spidery ribs to a flat bottom board, an elongated oval. The boat gets much of its strength and lightness from the ribs which are sawn from spruce (sometimes tamarack) roots, following the natural curve of the tree's trunk where it flares out just above and below ground. (The stump and roots have to be dug up for this purpose.) The grain of the wood follows this curve, making the rib much stronger than a rib of identical shape sawn across grain, as from a wide straight-grained board.

The outside of a guide-boat is usually planked with pine or cedar. In a sense the planking is clapboard, as on a house -- many of the early boats looked just this way. But this evolved to where the tops, bottoms, and ends of each plank are beveled to fit the one next to it. The result is a smooth side. The planks are screwed to the ribs, and tacked together with hundreds of copper tacks to make the boat watertight. Guide-boats weigh 75 pounds, more or less, depending upon length and finesse of construction.

In the vernacular they are called "cranky," (or tippy) and are rowed with oars whose handles are long for greater leverage; the handles overlap. A person by himself usually sits in the middle to row; if there is a passenger in the back of the boat, the rower moves closer to the bow, using a different set of oarlocks. Two can row in unison, but this is rare. When jacklighting, the boat was paddled from the stern and not rowed because oarlocks make noise.

The seats are caned, and the center one is removable so the boat can be overturned and carried on the shoulders of one person by means of a carved wood yoke, similar to a milk-bucket yoke. The yoke fits between the sides of the boat on braces. Most of the early boats were painted in a type of camouflage -- dark blue or black outside and green inside. The varnished boat, unpainted and varnished to show the natural wood, probably came later as a result of tourist's desires. By 1900, the guide-boat had lost most of its original raison d'etre as jacklighting and hounding were banned and fewer men were pursuing subsistence hunting and fishing.

Today some builders still make traditional boats at a cost of up to $10,000. Others have incorporated modern materials and techniques, such as epoxied laminated ribs, and fiberglass or Kevlar for the hull. Old or new, guide-boats can go very fast -- once you get past the knuckle-banging stage of rowing.

Hallock's 1877 *Gazetter* carried an extensive section on sporting boats, and called the guide-boat the "Adirondack boat." He described it as "a round-bottom, lap streak cedar boat," neglecting any mention of smoothsidedness. Among the builders he listed were C. J. Chase of Newcomb, Reuben Cary and Henry Stanton of Long Lake (these three were all guides), and W. E. Martin, E. Peck, and G. Philboots of Saranac Lake. Other boats of the age included the Colvin Canvas Boat, made by R. C. Scott of Albany, named after Adirondack surveyor Verplanck Colvin. Colvin improvised such a boat in the Adirondacks for his own use, calling it a "boat without a frame." The ribs, keelson, and gunwales were cut in the woods from branches, as needed.

HUNTING

Judging by the number of enthusiastic accounts, hunting deer from a guide-boat by jacking struck sports as the most unusual Adirondack hunting technique. Jacking is done by shining a light into an animal's eyes, which will mesmerize it long enough to be shot. An early description said,

"Jacks are made either of tin or bark, resembling in shape a large sugar scoop (imagine the scoop standing on its handle, with two or three candles stuck in the bottom or end that holds the handle, and you have a jack.) This, when used, is fitted on a staff about four feet long ... the hunter lights the jack noiselessly, it is turned towards where the deer was heard ... a deer seen in the light of a jack appears much larger than it really is, and the novice, firing as he supposes at the shoulder, will almost invariably shoot over its back. The aim should be very low."

Some nineteenth-century guide-boats still show evidence of the jack lantern pole by a hole in the bow deck. Soon the bark lantern was replaced with a lantern worn on the head -- one was "Boudren's Patent Combination Reflecting Fishing, Jack and Dash Lamp." Made by the White Manufacturing Co. of Bridgeport, Conn., it was advertised for night hunting of deer, spearing fish, lighting camps and landings. Most head lamps burned kerosene or turpentine. One of the advantages of the head lamp was the rear sight of the gun was now more visible, which meant a rifle could be used rather than shooting wide-fanning buckshot. Some jackers used a small lantern mounted on the rifle itself.

In both jacking and hounding the odds were in the sport's favor. An account from 1848 describes hounding:

"When followed by dogs or wolves, deer always take to the water for escape, and so well do the hardy hunters understand the habits of these wary animals, that they know to a certainty, when they see where, and at what time of day a deer is started, for what water he will run; and though sometimes he may be ten miles from a lake, and there are many others nearer, yet the backwoodsman immediately heads for the lake near which it is accustomed to sleep and drink. His knowledge of the ground, and his acquaintance with the 'walks' of the animal, learn him to do it with unfailing accuracy. Then, if he can launch his boat before the deer reaches the lake, he has him almost in his power the moment he has swam so far from shore as to be incapable of returning, and to despatch him with spears and guns is the hunter's only effort."

The dogs used for the most part in the Adirondacks were called spaniel-hounds, or northern fox hounds, and weighed about 35 pounds. But the type of dog used in hounding did vary. On one hunt in the Elizabethtown area in 1855 two dogs were used, one a half-mastiff and half-greyhound "not much on scent, but capital with other dogs," and the other a black and white hound whose nose "never failed the track." (Also along on the hunt was "Three-Legs," a tan-colored hound who had given up a limb to a bear-trap. Caught and starving, she gnawed off her leg and returned home to hunt once again, with a leather boot on the shortened limb.)

Another method of killing deer in the water was withing. A withe was described as a "forked sapling, with a noose or rope or grape vine at the end, to throw over a wounded deer's horns when your shot does not stop his swimming." Once the deer was caught in a withe, its throat could be slit or it could be clubbed or shot.

In winter deer ordinarily congregate in "yards," sometimes miles in length, and were hunted by "crusting." Their sharp hooves would break through the crust of the snow, but the snowshoes of the hunter and the paws of the dogs wouldn't. Deer travel along deep paths they have made, and won't leave them unless forced to do so by dogs or man. Impeded in the snow, the deer won't run far, choosing to stand and fight. They are easy prey for a hunter with a gun, or even a club or axe. Adirondack residents, including guides, were accused of practicing "crusting" to the detriment of the game available to the summer sports.

Two other methods of hunting still practiced today, when there is little or no snow, are driving deer on their runways and still-hunting. Driving deer means drivers or beaters march forward making noise, such as barking like dogs, and chase the deer to hunters already stationed ahead. Still-hunting, usually done alone, means walking as silently as possible through the woods in search of deer. Modern guide Bill Wharton, Jr., prepares for his deer hunters by provisioning a camp accessible only by water. His clients include muzzleloaders and handgunners. Wharton prefers positioning his hunters in ground blinds near well-used deer trails that lead to water.

Various techniques have been used to attract deer, including "bleating," salt licks, and scents. Newell Wagoner, of Boonville, recently recalled the efforts of the Duane brothers, guides from Speculator around the 1920's. "They used to try to get camp meat and hope the doe was in 'heat.' They salvaged the bladder and used the contents to treat their clothes, pinning the bladder on the back of their hunting coats. My Dad said that after two weeks in the woods it was nice that they had two tents."

Some guides specialize in bear hunting. There are three ways to get a bear, according to guide Bob Bearor: surprising one when deer hunting, chancy at best; hounding bear, which is permitted in certain areas; baiting bear and shooting them from an elevated stand. In the early 1980's, baiting bear was inadvertently outlawed -- a bill designed specifically to stop the hunting of deer at salt licks was written to include all "big-game animals." While baiting is permitted in neighboring states, in New York the practice has been reduced to watching corn fields and apple orchards, permissable but unrewarding practices.

When baiting was in full swing, modern bear hunting guide Bill Leege would arrange a series of stands a quarter mile apart, facing away from each other. The hunters were instructed to stay in the stands after shooting, regardless of results. Leege, waiting in the center of the wide circle, would head toward any stand that shot, preferring to deal with a possible wounded bear himself. Leege's success rate for hunters was well over fifty percent.

When more than one hunter had a hand in killing the game, the bounty had to be divided. One custom for dividing game has continued in some places to this day. The carcass is divided into as many pieces as there are persons in the party, the antlers and skin belonging to the one who first drew blood. One member turns his back, and to the question, "Who shall have this pile?" calls out the names of the rest of the party by chance. Another custom followed by sports was to give their guides the remaining provisions at the end of their trip. These could include not only what was bought locally, but what was brought from out of the area. In 1864, such provisions left for the guides of one party included "preserves, both potted and pickled, the jellies, buffalo tongues, dried mutton, hams, biscuit and pastry, Java, green tea, etc., (the sports) reserving only the wine and segars."

When game was hunted for market the object was quantity, not sport. In New York City in the 1840's, well-known restaurants such as the Shakespeare, the Cornucopiae, Windust's, Sandy Welch's, Clarke and Brown's, the Globe, and Delmonico's featured fish and game from the Adirondacks, all taken "for market."

The books and sporting periodicals of the times listed or described these practices, and recommended equipment. One of the most comprehensive publications of the era on the subject of sporting equipment was Charles Hallock's *The Sportsman's Gazetter and General Guide*, first published by Forest and Stream Publishing Co. in 1877. Hallock founded, edited, and published the influential sporting weekly "Forest and Stream," a figurative successor to "The Spirit of the Times." He wrote on sports, exploration and travel, and visited the Adirondacks frequently from about the time of the Civil War to the end of the century. (His article "The Raquette Club," in Harper's for August 1870, is a satire on the rush of "Murray's Fools")

Hallock believed modern American breech loading rifles did not fire a large or heavy enough projectile to kill "an old buck deer" and that the ball lacked velocity because the cartridges had too much twist and spin but not enough powder. The older muzzle loaders avoided the problem of twist, imparted by the rifling, or grooves, inside the barrel, but their calibre was often too small because "in those days a hunter had to prepare his own ammunition, and he liked to make it go as far as possible."

Hallock believed the muzzle loading rifle could still hold its own with the breech-loader, but the muzzle loading shotgun could not. Some old muzzle loaders which could be bought cheaply were altered to breech loaders for the sake of convenience and safety, but the expense could equal the cost of a new breech loader, and required the services of a gunsmith. For this reason many guides still used a muzzle-loader long after the coming of the breech loader. "Choice of guns depends upon the habits of the shooter," Hallock said.

The early repeaters, a form of rifle that carries a magazine of cartridges as opposed to a single shot, got "out of order at critical moments," as Hallock put it, "their pet vice being a tilting of the ball just as it entered the breech, whence arose jammings and rammings." Hallock recommended the new Winchester repeaters as more dependable, and thought them a good deer gun in spite of the relatively small powder charge. Adirondack Murray touted the Ballard or Maynard among breech loading guns, and thought shotguns a "nuisance and a pest." (His own double muzzle loading rifle was a Lewis he called "Never Fail.") Guide Freeland Jones, who was active near the turn of the century at Raquette and Blue Mountain Lakes, used an 1894 repeating Winchester. The "old meat gun" of Saranac Lake guide Les Hathaway was an 1894 Model 38-40, according to Gill Slater who now owns it. Julia Preston, one of the first female Adirondack guides, used a Winchester 25-20 with a trimmed-down stock.

In 1840 William Porter wrote quixotically, "You had best take your rifle, or double-barrelled Westley Richards with you, and if you have one of Colt's revolving pistols take that along -- (there's fine dog shooting on the road.)" In 1868, it was said "All through the Adirondacks the guides and hunters swear by and believe in the Henry rifle as the old prairie trappers used to in 'Jake Hawkins.'"

Charles Holt, a descendant of the venerable Keene Valley Holt clan which included a number of guides, says regarding the calibre of rifles that his grandfather's favorite rifle was the 45-90, also a choice of Teddy Roosevelt's. Holt's father preferred a 33 Winchester; Holt himself started with a Savage 30-30 and then switched to a Remington 250-3000. The new cartridges are charged with a modern, more powerful powder; certain new cartridges will fit the old guns but shouldn't be used. Holt says, in *Adirondack Frontier -- Stories of Keene Flats After 1776*:

> "The debate really centers around the large slow moving bullet that cuts through small brush with little deflection and produces much shocking power but is short ranged, and the small fast traveling bullet that is deflected by brush but reaches 'out there a far piece.' The good old dependable 30-30 was the first of the so-called high velocity bullets and has probably been the downfall of more Adirondack deer than any other one caliber.
>
> Before the Savage Rifle made its debut, most guns had an exposed hammer which also acted as a safety at halfcock position. Many old timers called the Savage a 'mulie' because it had no horns or to be exact no exposed hammer. My father tried my Savage out once, and though he had a good chance at a buck, he never got the shot off; for he was reaching for the hammer which he was used to and it just wasn't there. By the time he had released the safety the buck just wasn't there either."

In the mid-1850's, the Caswell Company in Lansingburgh was said by one writer to be "the only manufacturer Northern hunters thought capable of boring a decent barrel." One marksman was challenged to hit a small bird ten rods distant with his Caswell. "I'll not kill him, but I'll cut his legs off," he said. "The bird plied his little wings as he fired, flew around and around, tried in vain to alight, but could not, and at last, wearied and bleeding, fell to the earth, both legs missing."

In 1859, a sport spotted a deer and was urged by his partner to shoot it. He declined, saying they were sadly in want of venison, and wished one of the guides would go, who was sure to kill. Their guide John offered to go after the deer, taking the sport's rifle. The partner told John he would surely miss the deer, "for the gun pulled off so hard that John could not keep his aim when he fired." It was a government rifle, with a lock that according to the partner, would "not go off at any little jar. It required a pull to bring the hammer down, such as I knew no backwoodsman was accustomed to. Such a pull as was necessary to fire it would break an ordinary lock." John missed the deer, and returned to much ribbing.

Guides were forbidden to carry rifles or shotguns after 1924, when mandatory state licensing of guides took effect. Behind the law was the long-established practice of guides shooting deer for their "sport," or client, which was illegal. Guides could, however, carry pistols. Gene "The Judge" Brooks of Speculator related the story of guide Dave Page, who in the 1940's got seven buck for his party with a 765 Luger pistol with a 4" barrel.

FISHING

Fishing equipment varied at least as much as hunting equipment. Fishing reels were classified into three types -- salmon, trout, and trolling, the first two being large in diameter relative to their width. For years the preference in fishing lines was for linen waterproof laid lines, or in some cases silk, or a tapered braid of silk and hair. A braided cotton line would suffice for trolling. Fishing rods also fell into three types, the long, slender, elastic fly rod, the shorter, stiffer trolling rod, and the baitrod, a compromise between the first two. (The rod of the guide John Cheney might have been considered a compromise of them all. In 1849, one author wrote "Cheney fishes a good deal in the stream where I took my trout, but can never be persuaded to accept a joint rod. He adheres with pertinacity to the 'stout ash pole.'")

Some of the artificial fishing flies recommended by Murray and others were gaudy and imaginative, little resembling any naturally occuring food fish were likely to eat. Some anglers tied their own flies, believing the ones sold in tackle shops were too bushy and the masses of feathers prevented the trout from hooking themselves. Certain flies, especially for salmon, used feathers of exotic birds some of which today are on the endangered or protected list. Feathers from the peacock, wood duck, pin tail, jungle cock, red ibis, parrot, and macaw were used; feathers from some of these have been replaced today with artificial materials. Certain artificial flies were considered good for certain months -- a Black Gnat, or Midge for

April, Cow Dung for May, Hawthorne for June, Little Egg for July, and Grey Coffin for August and September -- but flies "good at any time," according to Hallock, included: Ibis No. 8, Peacock Palmer, Grey Palmer, Professor, Queen of the Water, Grizzly King, Blue Bottle, Abbey, and March Brown.

Adirondack Murray included small salmon flies in his assortment. He admitted this would "astonish some," as there were no true salmon in the Adirondacks. But he defended their inclusion because they caught fish. (Salmon-trout, a common name in the nineteenth century for lake trout [and steelhead], were sometimes fished over a buoy baited with cut-up fish, such as shiners and suckers.) Often two or more flies were tied a distance apart on the same line, and it was not unusual to get multiple strikes. This two-or-more fly rig often resulted in disaster, as one hook snared weeds or two fish swam in opposite directions and parted the line. A triple-decker worked in 1847: "After my second or third fish had been caught, my second dropper, a bright blue Martin Kelly fly, was engulfed by one hungry fish, another Martin Kelly by a second, while my stretcher, a large gaudy salmon fly was appropriated by a third..." Such luck was the exception, and fishing usually called for more work and skill. One sport observed that his guide always kept him "at the top of his throwing," as far as possible from the hole, and knew to move off as soon as a fish was hooked.

A guide could put a live shiner on a hook in such a way it would still be swimming briskly after an hour's trolling. He could row noiselessly, the boat's wake closing ahead of the bait. (Trolling did have its unexciting side. One sport complained of his "basting limbs" in the heat, and guessed he caught no fish because they would "scald their noses" if they came near enough to the surface to strike.)

Guides counted on fish and game for camp fare. Most advice to sports up until about 1870 was that tea, flour, ham, salt pork, soda powder, and salt and pepper were the only food you needed to bring (not counting whiskey and wine). With these spartan essentials a tasty meal could be prepared. In one account a meal of fish was prepared as follows:

"A circular hole of three feet across, by four inches deep, was soon dug in the ground, and filled with clean stones from the brook. On these a rousing fire was kindled, and left to burn nearly out. The guide made an incision down the whole length of the back of the two-pound trout, nearly as deep as the back-bone. Into this was laid a thin slice of raw pork; if you can add a squeeze of lemon to the pork, all the better. The belly was stuffed with the soft part of a loaf of rye and Indian-bread, mixed with say a gill of Madeira wine. His troutship was then carefully and tightly rolled up in the half of a clean newspaper, and laid in the embers to bake."

The rest of the camp would be arrayed around such a "troutship." "A Time at Cranberry Lake" gave a description of camp life in 1852:

"Think of stout, thick, swarthy men, in dusky cotton duck, stout, short-legged nailed stogies, with coarse, shining rifle grain, suspended in stout flasks, with thick hemp cords; big heavy black rifles, wicked at the muzzle, their winding bore radiant with a caststeel polish. Think of knapsacks filled with pork, coarse rye and Indian, salt, onions, some coarse strong tea; think of big long knives in coat pockets; stout tin cups, dangling at each right side, and at the left a tin box or vessel, cartridge shaped, but twice as big, and made to leak only at the top; a serviceable camp kettle and frying-pan cover, and a chunked sheet-iron thing, with handle and spout; these latter shifting from one to another as the party get up to leave a spring or resting place. At the shanty, think of vast sheets of peeled bark, supported by poles and stakes over a big pile of hemlock boughs; light coarse woolen blankets depending, airing at the sides; a long clean sheet of spruce bark, inside up, with bread, salt, cups, whittled forks, long knives; on the pole across the fire a kettle of venison ribs, and a chunk of pork boiling; on the coals, the pan sputtering with pork, and trout and venison steak; beside the table, a jug of whiskey and a pot of onions."

Dozens of tasks around camp called for the guide's ingenuity: rigging a cooking pot over a fire; building a smudge to keep bugs away; patching a new hole in his boat; skinning and gutting game; storing the food away from big or little mauraders; finding good firewood; keeping his sports dry, warm and well-fed; predicting the weather; suggesting the right fishing lures; building the shanty, etc. For these tasks the guide wore many figurative hats, including cook, chore-boy, raconteur, woodsman and philosopher. His best technique, improvisation, had to be ready on a moment's notice -- there was no telling what a city sport might do or what might be needed. The guide did all that for two or three dollars a day.

A Reputation in Decline;
A Reputation Regained

"They were illiterate. After a certain point in their lives they were the town bums." -- Dr. Gail Rogers Rice, President of North Country Community College in Saranac Lake, and a native Adirondacker, on guides.

The seeds of the demise of the guiding profession's reputation were sown early in its history. Among the initial causes were the differences between independent guides and hotel guides. The independents had everything to gain or lose: repeat business, reputation, and word-of-mouth advertising by satisfied sports. But the hotel guides had nothing to lose and little to gain. A. Judd Northrup, in *Camps and Tramps in the Adirondacks* (1880), described the tactics of the hotel guides:

> "... it was impossible for us to reach Osgood Pond before night-fall. Our most excellent hypocrites, the hotel guides, knew that before we started, but we had been left in blissful ignorance ... our guides displaying a mastery of the art of rowing, on our return, which, with excessive modesty on their part, had been concealed from us until then ... don't trust the word of a Boniface of the woods as to where the good fishing is, if it happens to be beyond the range of his dinner horn, and don't employ a 'hotel guide' if you can help it. The 'independent guides' have a reputation to make and keep, and their employment depends on that; but a man paid by a hotel keeper so much for the season, prefers whittling under the woodshed to rowing and roughing it, for the same money."

The hotels often employed young inexperienced guides and older ones who had never established a personal following. The hotels' clientele was a constantly revolving group of employers; a dissatisfied customer would be replaced the next day or week with a new unsuspecting one. The shabby treatment of sports by hotel guides began as early as 1847. George Howland, proprietor of the Lake House at Lake Pleasant, was accused of condoning his guides taking newcomers to fished-out spots where they would have little success. Good fishing holes still existed, it was reported, but "the guides have their favorites, and as a stranger, unless you choose to submit to heavy extortions, they purposely keep you from these reserved places. The rascally guides will endeavor to make you believe that the fishing is good at these places all summer."

Howland and his guides were accused of excluding other guides from employment. His guides were charging for "every day of their attendance upon the sport -- if that merely amounts to the little form of asking him in the morning what he is going to do today! The sport may expect to find 'unusual extras' staring him in the face at every turn, and if he dares to protest, the rascals wink at each other and begin to talk loftily among themselves about 'Gentlemen who don't dispute charges, etc.'" The criticisms were countered by other sports who said anglers coming to Hamilton County already knew how to fish, and would discharge an unsatisfactory guide. But soon some hotel guides were reported as too lazy to make even smudges, preferring to be bitten by insects.

The problem some guides had of drinking too much alcohol is mentioned throughout the nineteenth century. The causes and extent of the problem are difficult to pinpoint, but the incidence of excessive drinking does appear to be higher than the general population. (One psychological explanation suggests that guides were caught in a conflicting and uncomfortable role as both servant and leader.) But a guide, when drunk, had to some extent abandoned his party. An Englishman, F. French Townshend, describes in 1869 the plight of sports dependent on their guides yet fearful of them. In this case one of the guides is one of the ubiquitous Moodys:

"Daylight on the morning of September 1st, found us quite ready to leave our not too luxurious couches. To our disgust, we discovered that our keg of whiskey, which we had left in Moody's hut, had been nearly emptied during the night. To add to our chagrin, our host became so surly under the effects of the liquor which he had so freely consumed, that he refused to allow us to hire his dogs to hunt for us, as he had agreed to do the previous evening. However, as the more we argued, the surlier he became, we had no alternative but the disagreeable one of going down to our boats, minus the whiskey and the dogs ... (A)s a rule the guides are not at all communicative, but seem rather to have adopted the silent habits of the Indian. Ya and Na for yes and no, being the only answer one can generally extract from them. They are, however, good rifle shots, and can find their way through the forest nearly as well as the red man. Like men accustomed to depend on themselves, they can cook well, and manage the crank boats admirably. If civilly spoken to they are tolerably obliging, but they resent anything offensive in the manner or bearing of the traveller who is compelled to avail himself of their services. I heard of a traveler who abused his guide in rather strong language while out on one of the lakes, whereupon the man in revenge upset the boat and nearly drowned the gentleman. Having been told the story before starting, we were particularly careful not to use any irritating language to men who are not accustomed generally to put any restraint on their feelings."

The guides of certain areas -- Blue Mountain Lake, Saranac Lake, Long Lake, Fulton Chain, St. Regis, Raquette -- had formed small, sometimes loose associations to bar outsiders. A guide "cannot depend upon a cordial reception" if he goes outside his own area, it was reported. A Saranac Lake guide, for example, who had taken a sport to be dropped off in Old Forge would not dare solicit a customer for the return trip. (But he would demand return fare from his sport.)

Reverend John Lundy, who had spent most of the winter of 1877-78 at Saranac Lake, wrote of both hotel and independent guides:

"The Saranac guide is the wonder of humanity. He has the doubtful reputation of being the best guide in the woods, saving few exceptional cases. He sits and watches every coach load of tourists and sportsmen like a hawk, and selects his victim with unerring precision. He is all smiles and promises before going to camp; all glumness and apology in camp ... He knows all the best fishing and hunting grounds in the wilderness, but seldom finds them. He boasts of his great hunting prowess and success, but the camp is often without venison ... Faithful and true, he is all you own to do and dare, but he is full of ingenious tricks, practical jokes, and long-winded stories. He takes you fishing and dumps you in the mud. He takes you partridge shooting, and tears you and your clothes to pieces in dense thickets of briars and young evergreens. He sends you after a bear, and has made impressions in the soft sand with a claw which he carries for the purpose ... He is very industrious and enterprising, and there is never enough wood for a big campfire at night. He is incapable of fatigue, and lounges around camp for hours together. He anticipates all your wants and wishes, and must be specially told what to do and when to do it. He is the very soul of honor, and cannot be trusted out of your sight ... He is honest and careful of your property; but guns, pistols, camp-stores, watches, pocket knives, pelts, and other possessions disappear, and are only found when the law and penalty are invoked."

Lundy admitted not all guides were like that, but it took "long experience" to find a good one. This problem existed even though a customer presumably had a wide field to chose from, for as early as 1842 guides were thought to be in abundance, "hundreds having nothing to do but hunt and fish after the lumbering season is over."

The predilection for alcohol produced ingenuity. Joel Headley, author of *The Adirondack; or, Life in the Woods*, was the victim of a trick in 1847 by guides to force him to give up his brandy. In 1849, Richard Henry Dana, Jr., author of *Two Years Before the Mast*, recorded in his journal his Adirondack trip of two years before, that Headley's guides, near the village of Adirondac, had

> "exhausted their brandy and he (Headley) had a large bottle of his own which he kept drinking from, without offering them any, although it was a cold night. The guides were indignant, & after various hints to no purpose, they consulted together & determined to burn Headley out. Accordingly they moved the fire close to the mouth of the tent, & piled on the wood until the heat became intolerable. One after the other they crawled out, & at length H. had to come out too, leaving his bottle behind. One of them then reached in & got it, & pretending to think it was common property, they drank all around. Whether Headley ever discovered the design I don't know, but the camp is called 'Burn out camp' to this day."

In 1883 Lester Beardslee complained that when he sought to hire a guide and boat for a few hours at Raquette Lake he was told by the guides at Bennett's Hotel -- with "derisive grins ... and sardonic chuckles" -- that they didn't do business that way. Not only would they only hire out for a minimum of one day, but the guides involved, although then at Raquette Lake, were from Blue Mountain Lake. They would demand one day's pay each way from there in addition to the day spent at Raquette Lake. He pleaded his case to the hotel proprietor, who lent him a boat for free, as hiring boats without a guide was forbidden. Beardslee found he could row quite well by himself, and determined to dispense with a guide in the future. Some hotel keepers showed less consideration. In 1880 one writer drew a comparison between a party that was outfitted by their guide for a two-month trip at less than $3 a day, and a party outfitted by a hotel at a cost closer to $6.50 a day. In both cases the charge for the guide was the standard $2.50 a day, but the hotel charged, among other things, an additional fifty cents a day for the use of a bait fishing rod, with line and hooks, "that could not have cost over $3 at the most ... I advise all those who are not millionaires to keep clear of such sporting houses." Another writer acknowledged that a person could be eminent in the professional world without being able to distinguish between good guides and poor ones.

Soon the well-respected guide book author Seneca Ray Stoddard began omitting lists of guides in his annual books, saying the title "guide" was no longer an indication of fitness for the position. He thought a guides' union or some other authority could rectify this; he did restore his lists after the Adirondack Guides Association formed in the early 1890's. But the biggest problem was that there were not enough qualified guides to go around; sports had to accept almost anybody. The would-be guides included a "beardless youth in faultless sailor attire," in actuality an amateur yachtsman from Narragansett who evidently thought guiding for a summer would be quite the lark. In 1906, "picking lillies" was facetiously described as "one of the most important functions of the Adirondack guide ... the requisites of the lily-picking operation are a guide-boat and the knowledge necessary to convey visitors to the outlet of the lake or to the bay where water lilies abound and bring them safe again to the hotel."

Photographs of guides in their boats from the waning years of their popularity about 1900 show the dramatic change. Gone was the spotted spaniel hound, the pack basket, the recumbent glazed-eye buck, the satisfied Edwardian-looking sport. In their place were women with bustles and parasols, children, and hubby, wearing the expression of a bookkeeper in blissful domestic conformity. But the guides looked most out of place, ill at ease, left over from a by-gone era. Their hands and wrists, once capable of surging the boat after a swimming deer, rest languidly on the oars. Their expression is of people with nowhere to go, overtaken by an alien world.

What had happened to them? The reasons for the decline of guiding, especially after the turn of the century, include the development of motor boating, the introduction of automobiles, the launching of steamers, the organization of clubs for shooting and golf, the development of the highways, the improvement of the trails, the creation of maps for canoeing and hiking, the construction of permanent camps, the demise of the big hotels, more people putting pressure on less fish and game, and trends toward less physically strenuous vacations.

In the 1950's the Adirondack Guides Association, barely a vestige of the old-time organization, faded away. The depression had curtailed vacations and two world wars had siphoned away many of the guides and sportsmen. A handful of guides still catered to big gregarious hunting parties in the fall, such as at Whitehouse in Hamilton County, forty men housed dormitory style. But now hunters were staying in motels, rather than in old-time hunting camps. They wanted to get their buck and go home. A few guides, hardly enough to make the case, made good money working on retainer for the season for the wealthy. Others, aging, hunted out of nostalgia in their camps each fall with their equally aging but loyal downstate sportsmen; everybody had become more like family through the years. They spent more time in camp now, and for those guides accepting money was something of an embarrassment. The old days were gone.

By the middle of the twentieth century much of the vigorous, organized Teddy Roosevelt-like outdoor recreation had slipped away. Many summer camps had closed; the Boy Scouts had lost numbers. Those who did come paddled, or hiked, or hunted for themselves. What did they need a guide for? There was little chance of getting lost, a hunting party could drive its own deer, families could climb their own mountains. But beginning in the 1960's and '70's a new movement recognized the fragility and magic of the environment. Mother Nature made a comeback. Earth Day, hippies, homesteading and communes, backpacking, environmental concerns, folk music -- all combined in a back-to-nature trend that spawned lighter equipment, improved physical fitness, and a desire to see the backcountry. Some of the movement was more cerebral than actual, hiking boots that trod only city streets and college campuses. But much was real. Leisure time, money, and a desire to see the woods and waters spawned a need for canoe trips for the newly-inspired urban family, or executive retreats to the woods, or physical challenges for ghetto kids and students of exclusive private schools alike.

Who would lead them? A new kind of guide stepped forward, almost as though he -- or she -- had been waiting in the wings. Perhaps they'd been through Scouts or Outward Bound, or a college wilderness recreation program. The new guide understood and saw the need for the new conservation ethic. The days of fresh balsam bough beds and shanties were gone, dismissed as too destructive. The new guide saw specialized niches for guides, activities the old days never offered -- white water sports, rock climbing, nature and photography trips, recreational snowshoeing, cross-country skiing, outdoor sessions in search of one's lost soul. The new guides were still part servant, cook, and chore-boy, but added to the old sports of hunting, fishing, and camping, all the new pursuits made a formidable list. The state had begun to regulate the new activities with an eye toward safety, education, and professionalism. New regulations, new challenges, and new ideals had together redefined the profession as it headed for the twenty-first century.

Independent, resourceful, demi-god, bum -- historically descriptions of Adirondack guides run the gamut. He was Everyman -- the guide could not be otherwise in a profession that through the years numbered in the thousands. The Adirondack guide is in the middle of one of those concentric rings conjured up by historians. What was his place in the grand scheme of things? Was his influence only local, as for example in the St. Regis area? Yes, if he ventured no farther. Did he have significance throughout the Adirondacks? Yes, as a regional species. Was he a national or international figure? No, by definition of being "Adirondack," yes, by virtue of having world-wide clientele.

The guide had opened the Adirondack wilderness by leading in everyone from artists to industrialists, preservationists to developers. "Everyman" had taken everybody to see it all, and then been set aside. In the epilogue to Joseph Grady's book published in 1933 about the Fulton Chain-Big Moose region, an old woodsman who could be speaking as a guide rows his guide-boat to the dock, pursued by the thoughtless waves of a motorboat:

> "Damn 'em," he snarled. "The white-livered imbeciles ain't got gumption enough to pull a pair of oars! They have to run an engine to haul their lazy carcasses a mile or two upstream and spoil the lakes for men who know how to use them! They've plumb ruined the woods ... First they wanted a railroad in here, and they got it. Then they wanted steamboats and motorboats, and they got them. And now what have they got? They ain't got nothing!"

At that point the guides felt they, too, now had nothing. But in spite of the changes the profession lives on, some of it in the old way. The new guides don't want to let go of the old myths. They wear quaint hats and suspenders, carry packbaskets, tell tall tales, and reincarnate the old guides. "There I was!" their tale begins. Gathered imaginations poise in expectation; a simmering blue enameled coffee pot murmurs agreement. The fragrant smoke of birch wood curls away, and the sun sinks just beyond the trees, ushering in a fine and satisfying late-summer chill. Mother nature see all this, smiles, and understands. The tradition of the Adirondack guide lives on. Long live the Adirondack guide!

Guides in the Mountains

"It makes a man feel what it is to have all creation under his feet. There are woods there which it would take a lifetime to hunt over, mountains that seem shouldering each other to boost the one whereon you stand, up and away Heaven knows where. Thousands of little lakes are let in among them so light and clean. Old Champlain, though fifty miles away, glistens below you like a strip of white birch when slicked up by the moon on a frosty night, and the Green Mountains of Vermont beyond it fade and fade away until they disappear as gradually as a cold scent when the dew rises." -- Guide John Cheney

Most of the first tourists in the Adirondacks came to hunt and fish, but a few came to climb some of the hundreds of mountains scattered throughout the region. The greatest concentration of mountains, the High Peaks, is mostly in Essex County, roughly between Lake Placid and Lake Champlain. Here on a clear day the tallest, almost fifty over four-thousand feet, beckon the hiker to panoramic views of Lake Champlain and Vermont's Green Mountains to the east, Canada to the north, and the far expanses of the west and south. Guides had taken the first explorers to these mountains, and blazed the first trails.

In the 1920's Russell M. L. Carson, a Glens Falls insurance executive and one-time president of the Adirondack Mountain Club, became acquainted with a number of the older guides whose memories went back to the 1870's or earlier. From them he obtained information on first ascents and the naming of many of the peaks; in 1927 he wrote *Peaks and People of the Adirondacks*. Carson's inquiries not only turned up new information, but challenged some prevailing folklore; for example, he believed Orson Phelps' son Ed to have been not only a greater guide than his father, but the greatest guide in the history of the Adirondacks -- a rather heretical revision.

Carson knew that mining men, lumbermen, scientific explorers, and writers came to the Adirondacks between 1800 and 1837. He wrote, "With two execeptions it was from the last two groups that the names of the lofty peaks originated." The scientific explorers tended to apply names rather straightforwardly, such as Mt. Marcy for New York's Governor William Learned Marcy, who served from 1832-1838. Writers, on the other hand, were prone to flights of fancy, such as Charles Fenno Hoffman's calling Mt. Marcy "Tahawus," which means "cloud splitter," an Indian-derived name apparently never used before in the region. Alfred Street undoubtedly transplanted the Seneca Si-non-do-wanne meaning "great hill" to the mountain Santanoni.

George Marshall, one of the first to climb all the Adirondack peaks over 4,000 feet, has pointed out that there were one or more guides in the parties that made thirty-one of the first ascents of the forty-six High Peaks. Both Marshall's guide Herb Clark and the earlier mountain guide Orson Phelps, among others, had an often commented upon ability to head out seemingly willy-nilly and emerge exactly on the desired mountain peak. The early guides led "bush whacks," or trailless trips; they established, blazed and cleared trails to the summits as well.

Mount Marcy, at 5,344 feet the highest Adirondack peak, has gotten the lion's share of notoriety, starting with the first recorded ascent in 1837. The purpose of that first climb was scientific in nature; under the leadership of Ebenezer Emmons, a geologist and professor at Williams College, a group of ten urbanites were guided to the peak by Harvey Holt of Keene and John Cheney -- the hunter at the ironworks at Tahawus --with five unidentified woodsmen as assistants. Holt and Cheney carved out life-long reputations as expert guides.

On the second ascent of Marcy, mountain climbing for its own sake might be said to have begun. In 1849, Orson Phelps, with Almeron Oliver and George Estey, climbed Marcy from Elk Lake. This ascent, like the first one, was a bushwhack, but in about 1861 Phelps cut a trail from the southeast (abandoned for a new route selected by Verplanck Colvin in 1873) that began between the Ausable Lakes, went around Haystack, and through Panther Gorge (still a popular repository of lost Marcy hikers) to the summit. Phelps, accompanied by six Keene Flats guides, led three women up Marcy in the 1860's; three days were needed to reach the top.

The pioneering efforts of the women hikers signaled recreational Adirondack mountain climbing was in full swing. In 1860, a guide named Hickok cut a trail up Whiteface from the Wilmington side. He made a crude shelter there and touted the trip as a good way to see the sun set and rise. Around 1865, Bill Nye cut another trail up Whiteface at his own expense. (Whiteface, which sits off by itself from the other peaks, could later claim the dubious distinction of being the only High Peak climbed on horseback, a usual method of ascent there for about 25 years before 1900.)

In 1866 David Hunter of Tahawus (the Indian name was also given to the settlement at the iron works near Newcomb) was one of two who made the first ascent of Santanoni -- he was fifteen at the time; six years later he guided Colvin to the top. Other first ascents were recorded in the 1860's and '70's, and the popularity of the pastime grew with the increasing numbers of tourists. In a climb that typified the era, well-known Keene Valley guide Mel Trumbull led Arthur H. Wyant on the first ascent of Macomb in 1872. Wyant was one of a group of artists who began coming to Keene Valley about 1868. Artists and "physical culture" afficianados figured in many early ascents, the first group already drawn there for the scenery, and the second group attracted by the challenge of mountain climbing.

As important and romantic as these literally trail-blazing first efforts were, from the standpoint of the guides' role mountain climbing was significantly more specialized and one-dimensional than other contemporary guiding. Their trips were relatively short and specific in nature, and lacked the ebb and flow of protracted hunting, fishing, and camping trips. Most of the early High Peaks guides were from Keene Valley, and got their bread-and-butter income from camps on the Ausable Lakes and vicinity.

Once started, however, the pursuit of mountain climbing never faltered. The establishment of the Adirondack Forty-Sixers, inspired by the feat of the Marshalls and Herb Clark with their completion of the climbing of the High Peaks in the 1920's, has resulted today in about 100 people per year totalling up identical climbs, and earning the coveted two-and-a-half-inch patch saying "Adk 46-R." The challenge of "bagging" the forty-six appeals to climbers of all ages -- the youngest recorded are twins Fred and Phelps Turner, of Lake Placid, who completed their appointed rounds in 1983 at age five; John Corrados was eighty-one when he finished them all in 1985. About half the routes are considered trailless, without markers, although worn "herd paths" lead the way, sometimes in confusing abundance. Occassionally these days a guide will be hired to lead the way on a trailless peak, but most people seeking such summits are aspiring Forty-Sixers who would rather do it themselves. More often a guide is hired for safety and companionship, even up such a well-used route as the Van Hoevenberg trail to Marcy. Even greater specialization in the mountains has resulted in teaching the skills of ice and rock climbing, for which a guide's license is required.

The Professional
Guides Associations

"That such Association was organized for the purpose of preserving the forest and game in the Adirondacks and the enforcement of the game laws and the regulation of the charges and conduct of the guides of the Adirondacks." -- from the Certificate of Incorporation of the Adirondack Guides Association, 1897.

The Adirondack Guides Association, begun in 1891; the Brown's Tract Guides' Association, begun in 1898; and the New York State Outdoor Guides Association (NYSOGA), begun in 1983, have been the three major guides organizations in the Adirondacks. The goals of all three have been similar: to provide reliable guides, ensure respect of existing laws regarding the outdoors and serve as fraternal organizations. Other smaller organizations have existed through the years. The Independent Guide Club, for example, was a forerunner of the first big professional group, the Adirondack Guides Association. The Club published a broadside in 1868 that listed twenty-six guides, most from Saranac Lake: the full name was the Independent Guide Club of the Saranac and Raquette. The broadside touted the club's guides as "old and experienced woodsmen who thoroughly understand their business." The guides could be contacted through four Saranac Lake hotels, but it was emphasized that "all contracts made with and wages paid to the Guides."   The independents wanted to distance themselves from the hotel guides, and the broadside served as an advertisement in advance of such guidebooks as Stoddard's and Wallace's, which began in the 1870's.

The Adirondack Guides Association was the first group to set professional standards and represent the entire Adirondacks. The first Article of its Constitution stated the organization's purpose:

"The object of this association shall be to promote and facilitate travel in the Adirondacks; to secure to the public competent and reliable guides, thus assuring the welfare of tourists and sportsmen; to aid in the enforcement of the Forest and Game Laws of the State; to secure wise and practical legislation on all subjects affecting the interests of the Adirondack region; to maintain a uniform rate of wages of guides; and to render financial assistance to its members in case of sickness or other disability or to their families in case of the death of such members."

The Adirondack Guides Association was lucky to have quality leadership from the start. Fitz Greene Hallock, who guided Dr. Edward Livingston Trudeau (the originator of the tuberculosis cure industry in Saranac Lake) and who was later superintendent at Seward Webb's Nehasane Park, was elected President. The Honorary President was Verplanck Colvin, Superintendent of the Topographical Survey of the Adirondack. (The Survey started about twenty years before; even before that Colvin had campaigned tirelessly for the creation of an Adirondack Park.) The elected secretary was J. Herbert Miller, from Saranac Lake, who was or had been town clerk, town supervisor, Democratic party leader and postmaster. He had the confidence of the guides and knew how to promote the organization. Right away he began a mailing campaign to enlist associate members.

Among local guides present at the Association's formation were Lute Evans, Steve Martin, Ed Sumner, Eugene Allen, George Fayette, Marshall Brown, Ben Moody, Hiram Benham, Walter Rice, Alonzo Dudley, John Slater, Sim Torrence, Tom Healy, and Peter Solomon. Membership was contingent on: being a citizen and permanent resident of New York State; at least twenty-one years old and an Adirondack resident at least 15 years; an Adirondack guide with at least three years experience; a well-equipped, competent, and in every way reliable guide. Local committees were to be established in the Adirondacks, made up of the "old, original established resident guides of at least 20 years standing." The Association would present names of applicants, recommended by three Association members, to the Local Committee. An applicant had to be approved by at least two-thirds of the Local Committee. There was a two dollar election fee and dues of one dollar per year.

Membership cards were issued stating the bearer was a "reliable and competent guide." On the back was the statement that the rate of pay for guides was three dollars a day and their expenses. Associate members could enroll for the same fees, but had no vote; they were not licensed to guide. Members were expected to assist each other in obtaining employment "in preference to those who are not members," and to respect each others rights to camps owned or built by members. The Association evidenced many of the practices of a labor union by fixing wages, excluding non-members, and offering sickness, disability and death benefits.

Secretary Miller, who died in 1896, was succeeded by Ed Sumner. Sumner was instrumental in getting the Association's exhibit at the Sportsmen's Exposition in Madison Square Garden in New York City for a number of years. In 1897 the Association incorporated.   The number of directors was set at twelve, and at incorporation included Warren Slater, Saranac Lake; Thomas Healy, Saranac Lake; C. W. Blanchard, Blue Mountain Lake; O. A. Covill, Saranac Lake; A. H. Billings, Lake Placid; E. L. Scafford, Old Forge; Douglas Martin, Paul Smiths; J. W. Hinkson, Childwold; Warren Cole, Long Lake; James McBride, Tupper Lake; E. E. Sumner, Saranac Lake; and C. C. McCaffrey, Saranac Lake.   Vice-presidents included Thomas Redwood, Paul Smiths; Peter Solomon, Saranac Lake; Ernest Johnson, Tupper Lake; Miles Kennedy, Lake Placid; Isaac Sabattis, Long Lake; Richard Crego, Fulton Chain; Halsey Sprague, Meacham Lake; Jerome Wood, Racquette (sic.) Lake; C. W. Blanchard, Blue Mountain Lake; H. B. Marden, Childwold; Charles McCaffrey, Saranac Inn.

A glance at the list will show that most of the men lived in the northern Adirondacks. Members from other areas to the south, east and west didn't feel fairly represented. Soon the Adirondack Guides Association began to lose members, those from far away complaining of bad roads and the heavy hotel and traveling expenses of attending meetings. The Secretary reported that, "The faraway branches feel their views are disregarded and voted down by members who can with little difficulty and expense attend the annual convention ... these things ... have resulted in the withdrawal from the organization of several of the branches, so that now it can scarcely be called in truth the Adirondack Guides Association in respect to representing the entire territory."

The Brown's Tract Guides' Association formed in 1898; many of its original members had belonged to the Adirondack Guides Association. Their organizational meeting was held in the Boonville boat shop of guide-boat maker Dwight Grant, who would be credited with being the father of the organization, and included Garry Riggs, Peter Rivett, Ira Parsons, Nelson Chandler, John Cummerford, Artie Church, Frank Williams, George Barber, Merril White, Robert Roberts, William Cummerford and Richard Crego. Crego was chosen as President, Garry Riggs, Vice-President, and Artie Church, Secretary and Treasurer.   Church was to serve for twelve years, almost the entire life of the organization, which lasted until 1913. The organization's purposes were similar to those of the Adirondack Guides Association:

"To aid and secure a better enforcement of the game and forest laws of the state, to secure wise and practical legislation on all subjects affecting interests of the game regions of the state; to secure to the sportsmen who visit the Brown's Tract region competent and reliable guides, and to maintain a uniform rate of wages for guides."

The membership requirements were less stringent than those of the Adirondack Guides Association -- in addition to U.S. citizenship, a member need only live in the Adirondack region for five years and have been a reliable and well equipped guide for three.

Three years after its formation the group urged a ban on buoy or anchor fishing, recommended a closed season on deer from November 1 to August 31, and a closed season on bear from May 1 to September 30; they protested the cutting of timber on state lands, and the sale of deer, partridge, woodcock, quail and trout. They noted, as had the Adirondack Guides Association, that they believed the game protectors appointed by the state inadequate in number and "by reason of their manifest unfitness and training as woodsmen and lack of endeavor to perform their duty." (Some didn't know a "salt lick from a lily pad.") The guides cited their "practical and personal knowledge of the rapid destruction of the fish and game both in and out of season in this region ... by irresponsible persons, pot and market hunters." In 1906 the Brown's Tract Guides' Association had released for the Fish and Game Commission 1,600,000 whitefish fry, 250,000 lake trout fry and 10,000 brook trout fry.

One year after the Association's organization, Governor Theodore Roosevelt, a sportsman and devotee of Adirondack camp life, invited the Association to send a committee of guides, including Church, to Albany to meet with him regarding proposed amendments to conservation laws. In addition to Church the committee included Dwight Grant, Garry Riggs, Merrill White, Bill Dart, Henry Covey and Bill Cummerford.

Perhaps the most interesting, but probably not the most profitable, responsibilities assumed by the Brown's Tract guides were their efforts to stock the Central Adirondack region with moose, beaver, and wapiti (a variety of deer, erroneously called "elk," which can be as tall at the shoulder as five feet and weigh nine hundred pounds.) Moose had entirely disappeared forty years before, beaver were virtually extirpated and wapiti had never been known in the region.

In 1902, the city of Binghamton offered the Brown's Tract Guides' Association five wapiti to be used as parent stock in establishing the species as native game animals in the Adirondacks. Four cows and one bull were crated and shipped by rail to Big Moose Station. From there they were hauled in wagons to Dart's Lake where Bill Dart had improvised winter quarters to feed and shelter them until spring. They wintered well and were set free in March.

The Brown's Tract Guides' Association voiced a public appeal on their behalf, asking that they not be harmed. Newspapers reported on their condition and whereabouts. But the wapiti refused to "go native." They were tame moochers, and sought handouts from local households all too willing to oblige.

In the late autumn, the five wapiti were found dead in the woods at the foot of Moss Lake. The rumor was they had been shot by a disgruntled guide who was in disagreement with the Association over some matter; since there was no conclusive proof, nothing could be done against the perpetrator. The antlered head of the bull was put in Dart's camp. Secretary Artie Church, a taxidermist, had mounted it. At the winter guides' banquet the following year guide David Charbonneau, who possessed a "distinctive, curt and emphatic vocabulary," was called on to give his opinion of "the man who shot the elk." He said "I don't care to mention the matter at this time for the reason that what I think of that fellow is not fit for public expression."

In 1901, the Legislature passed a bill appropriating $5,000 for the purchase and transportation of wild moose to be released in the Adirondacks, and then-Governor Odell signed it. The first shipment -- a bull, a cow, and a bull calf -- arrived in 1902. They were consigned to Game Protector John (Ned) Edwin Ball, an active member of the Brown's Tract Guides' Association. (He had begun coming to the Fulton Chain in 1879, and in 1886 built a permanent camp near Bullhead Rock on the river between Old Forge Lake and First Lake of the Fulton Chain, where he lived until his death in 1927.)

The three moose had been captured in Canada, but while in captivity they, too, had become tame. Other moose, at least fifteen, were imported and set free. Their tame ways did them in. One innocently approached a woman hunter who shot and killed it from fear. None of the others survived, most shot wantonly.

The Association, along with the young and fanatical preservationist Harry Radford, next turned its efforts to beaver. Creating what came to be called an "Army of Liberation," the guides volunteered to keep seven beaver at Old Forge during the winter of 1904-05 for the State Forest, Fish and Game Commission. The Commission had ended up with some well-traveled beaver -- they had come from Canada via St. Louis where they had been guests of the Louisiana Purchase Exposition as exhibits of the Canadian

Government. They wintered over in captivity on a bushel of vegetables a week and cut brush. In the spring the guides let two beaver go on Otter Brook, where a lone beaver still lived. It had escaped from Lt. Governor Woodruff's estate at Lake Kora in 1902. Four were let go at Big Moose Lake. The seventh one had been set upon and killed by his kin in the winter. All the surviving beaver prospered.

In 1906, the Forest, Fish and Game Commission purchased from the Federal Department of the Interior twenty-five more beaver which had been captured in Yellowstone National Park. These were released between the Fulton Chain and Tupper Lake; altogether, thirty state-owned beaver were released by the "Army." These, joined by the approximately twenty already in the wild, including escapees from private preserves, brought the number available to breed to about fifty. A survey conducted in 1915 put their numbers at between fifteen and twenty thousand. (Beaver have two to eight, usually four, young each year.) In 1924 and again in 1925, a trapping season was instituted.

As did the Adirondack Guides Association in Saranac Lake, the Brown's Tract group held an annual winter gathering, "The Guides Banquet." At these meetings "fraternal regards" were sent to the Adirondack Guides Association, which were usually reciprocated, evidencing the basic good will between the two groups. In 1913 the Brown's Tract Guides' Association disbanded; the Adirondack Guides Association disbanded in 1952; each faded away from a lack of interest. By the 1980's, which brought a new and different interest in the outdoors, the time was ripe for a new style of guide and a new private organization. The state was getting ready to license guides with a vengeance now, with the most stringent licensing requirements ever. The new organization would be NYSOGA, the New York State Outdoor Guides Association, and it would try to play an instrumental role in developing the new licensing requirements.

"I helped start NYSOGA on a fluke, you might say." said Ray Brook resident Joe Hackett. "In the late 1970's I wanted to begin guiding for a living. I didn't know how to go about it. I thought you had to undergo an apprentice program, and/or be recommended by other guides. When I looked around to find out how to learn the profession, there was no one who knew. There were people who know woods skills, but no one who could explain insurance, rates, the business end of it. In the summer of 1977, I was charging $25 a day, including food, working on my days off from lifeguarding. One day I took out eight people and ended up twelve dollars in the hole. So about 1982 I went with Howard Riley and Mike O'Malley to Tom Monroe, Region 5 Director of DEC (Department of Environmental Conservation) in Ray Brook. We wanted to host a gathering of guides at the Lake Placid Club to discuss these matters, maybe organize. Mark Brown, a DEC wildlife biologist, was instrumental in tieing in DEC. Mark, my wife Maria and I licked envelopes and mailed out notices. We held a Woodsman's Workshop, had a meal with venison, turkey and trout. It was great; a fellow had a pet raccoon that followed him around, there was a fishing contest.

There was a lack of credibility about guides then. Let me give you an example -- I was hiking in the High Peaks and met a family from Schenectady or Albany -- mom, dad, two kids, a dog -- and they all had guide's badges. Even the dog. That hit me between the eyes. I'd been struggling since '78 to get my business going, and found out even a dog could get a guide's license.

At the convention there wasn't total agreement by any means. There were fellows from Albany, Troy, New York City and the Catskills who wanted to be involved, and some of the old-time Adirondackers were offended by these outsiders who wanted to be guides. We wanted to make it state-wide, not just the Adirondacks. Later we were criticized for working with the state -- it was seen as more regulation. The state had a Guides Advisory Committee, in the early 1980's, at least. DEC knew there had to be some changes, they saw the need for licensing. The state was getting requests for lists of guides, and they really didn't know anything about the people on the lists. The backpacking craze and the Green Movement of the 1970's had brought this new interest about. There were more people in the woods all the time.

The move toward licensing was about fifty-fifty, the state and the guides each wanting it. We formed NYSOGA in '83, I think, and the state came to NYSOGA for some direction. Our committees came up with the test questions for the licensing exam. We figured if one guide can get a little press, a hundred guides can get a lot more. I knew there should be a clearing house for information. There were guys like me who wanted to know. Now, with NYSOGA, it's easy to get this information. We're looking ahead to an apprentice program."

Brian McDonnell, a former NYSOGA president, remembers those times:

In NYSOGA the big push was to get the legislation. We knew if we didn't regulate ourselves, DEC or somebody else would. They were talking about Civil Service doing it. DEC went into moratorium and stopped issuing licenses, then they issued temporary licenses for two or three years.

DEC said 'We'll take your information, but we'll do it on our own.' They gleaned a lot of information we sent them. When I was president I'd talked to Jacoby (Col. Edward Jacoby, Superintendent, Forest Protection and Fire Management; his department administers licensing of guides) about upgrading the standards even more, but the budget crunch has knocked that out.

Partly NYSOGA was formed for the social angle, guys who were 'into the woods.' And the licensing, wages, etc. Joe Hackett did the first conference; he was one of the 'founding fathers.' We've been on and off about training -- there's a whole market there. Maybe the Wilderness Education Association could provide that; it's based right here at North Country Community College."

The three major Adirondack guides organizations formed at different times for different reasons. The first two, the Adirondack Guides Association and the Brown's Tract Guides' Association, had much in common. They formed partly in response to more tourists creating a demand for more qualified guides, a need unqualified guides tried to meet. The increase in tourism came from improvements in transportation, new leisure time created by the industrial revolution, and publicity about the area. More sportsmen meant more pressure on less and less fish and game. The net result near the turn of the century was the inevitable end of the old ways of guiding, and the eventual end of the first associations. Not until the 1980's and a new way of thinking about the outdoors was there a need for another association, the New York State Outdoor Guides Association.

What challenges must be met in the future by a guides organization is impossible to predict, of course. Certainly increased population, the economics of leisure, and the stress of increasingly technological modern life will all be involved. Both regulations by the state and practices adopted by professional groups such as NYSOGA are becoming increasingly strict -- these restrictions seem necessary as the wilderness gets loved almost to death by hordes of people. How NYSOGA or any professional organization deals with these and other critical factors will determine not only the group's future, but the future of guiding.

The Role of the State

"The lands of the state, now owned or hereafter acquired, constituting the forest preserve as now fixed by law, shall be forever kept as wild forest lands. They shall not be leased, sold or exchanged, or taken by any corporation, public or private, nor shall the timber thereon be sold, removed or destroyed ..." -- Article XIV of the New York State Consitution.

The State of New York affects Adirondack guides in three major ways: fish and game regulations, registration and licensing, and laws controlling the use of public state-owned land. Fish and game regulations impact both the guides and sportsmen by dictating when, by what means, and to what extent fish and game can be taken -- and have often involved controversy. Voluntary guide registration by the state began in 1919, and mandatory licensing, which continues today, in 1924. The third area, laws controlling use of public state-owned land in the Adirondacks, has probably affected the guiding profession the most.

For almost a hundred years the state, and before that the Crown, held Adirondack lands they literally could not give away. Free land had been offered to military veterans when they left the service; it was often refused in favor of more tillable land in warmer climates. Sales of huge tracts of land at pennies an acre to absentee land speculators had resulted in some sparse settlement. But much land ended back in the lap of the state, followed by the widespread practice of lumber companies buying the land, cutting the timber, and then letting the land revert to the state for non-payment of taxes. The lands were considered waste lands.

In 1885, New York became the first state in the nation to set up a lasting mechanism to preserve state forest lands by creating the Forest Preserve. The law at the Forest Preserve's inception read in part: "The lands now or hereafter constituting the Forest Preserve (in eleven Adirondack and three Catskill counties) shall be forever kept as wild forest lands. They shall not be sold, nor shall they be leased or taken, by any corporation public or private." Most of the reasons for the creation of the Forest Preserve were pragmatic rather than esthetic, such as a concern from people downstate for a watershed.

At the same time the Preserve was created, a three-man Forest Commission was also created and given funds for the Preserve's surveillance and protection. This state agency evolved as follows:

1885 -- Forest Commission
1895 -- Fisheries, Game and Forest Commission

1900 -- Forest, Fish and Game Commission
1911 -- Conservation Commission
1926 -- Conservation Department
1970 -- Department of Environmental Conservation

In the beginning of the Forest Commission era, the total state-owned acreage in the Adirondacks was about 681,000 acres. The boundaries in many areas were obscure, and the long-established practice of timber poaching continued. In 1885, the Forest Commission went on record in an attempt to stem the flow of timber from state land: "Trespass ... shall be deemed to include ... cutting ... any tree or timber standing within the forest preserve, or any bark thereon ... with intent to remove such tree or timber ... or bark ... from the said forest preserve."

A guide, as such, was not in the timber or bark business, so this regulation posed no threat. But the commission went on:

"The practice of tree cutting and tree destroying, prevalent about camps, is too often considered harmless, from an idea that nature is so lavish in her bounty that what is taken will not be missed. These rules call direct attention to many of these evils, and propose a simple means of remedying them, there being no escape from others except in positive prohibition. There is so much tending to destroy, and so little to conserve, that the Commission feels constrained to throw around the remnant of forest lands belonging to the State, all the protection that ingenuity and the counsel of many minds can suggest:

... fires are permitted in or near the forest for cooking, warmth and insect smudges, but all other fires are absolutely prohibited ... clear away all combustible material for a space of six feet around.

Peeling or girdling trees of their bark for covering camps or shanties is hereby prohibited. For such purpose the tree must be felled, and all bark removed therefrom before another tree is cut down. The trees thus felled, and such fallen timber as lies in the vicinity, must be used for firewood or in camp construction before any standing timber is cut for that purpose."

In case anyone was still tempted to steal trees, the penal code was revised to set a fine of twenty-five dollars for each tree removed from state land, the equivalent of about eight days' wages. The guides' resentment at this restriction can well be imagined -- didn't the Commission know if you cut down a green tree for the bark, except for perhaps birch, it won't burn as firewood? And if it lays there on the ground it will soon rot and become useless, but if you peel it and leave it standing, it will eventually dry and then be good for firewood?

The Commission appointed "special agents" who toured the Adirondacks to announce the existence of the little-known new Forest Commission and solicit local opinions, in particular regarding forest fires and the dying of the spruce that was prevalent at the time. Among the comments gathered was the suggestion that guides be licensed by state law, and charged with the responsibility of putting out fires when built by camping parties. (Mandatory state licensing would not follow for thirty-nine years.) The Commission recommended a law be passed making it "presumptive evidence of guilt if the origin of a fire can be traced to the operations of a guide or tourist whether any malicious intention existed or not."

The Commission openly attempted to curry favor with the guides from the start, describing their role in flattering terms, but made it clear the state now had control of public lands. The Commission dealt with the problem of the construction of bark shanties by suggesting canvas tents in their place, or at least the following of more economical cutting practices. Guides and tourists alike were "requested to give it careful thought."

In 1899, the Commission heard the report of Forester Henry Studor of Herkimer County with regard to the practice of building shanties: "I find people who visit the woods are very careful in regard to fires and also the girdling of trees. Several years ago it was a rare thing to find a camp covered with shingles; and now it is just as rare to find one covered with bark." But the Commission also noted that in Hamilton County "small trespasses have been committed on State lands to obtain timber for firewood, barns, houses, and boat building. Cedar and pine are used in the construction of the Adirondack skiffs, which are a necessity and almost the only means of conveyance in that wilderness." The state felt no trees could be spared, not even for the construction of guide-boats.

In 1892 the Adirondack Park was established. A line on a map, a "blue line" was drawn around 2.8 million acres of a mix of public and private land. For over twenty years the Park legally consisted of only the Forest Preserve lands within the Blue Line. The Park boundaries were enlarged in 1912, 1931, 1956, and again in 1972, resulting in a total of 5,927,600 acres. Historian Philip Terrie has pointed out that:

> "The clear original intent of the park law was to demonstrate the state's interest in what happened to all the land inside the new

park's boundaries ... both legislators and Governor Flower appeared
to have been assuming that the state would eventually own all the
land in the newly defined park ... The 1892 park legislation ... was
the last effort of the state before the 1970's to realize the dream of
region-wide conservation."

Near the end of the nineteenth century large parcels of private
land were posted against trespass, barring guides and sportsmen alike.
The practice of posting continues. Today the Park is slightly less
than half state-owned; the rest is in private hands. Such a mix of
ownership has caused constant and on-going problems regarding use
and management that would not exist if the lands were all public or
all private. The difference between the Adirondack Park and the
Forest Preserve has always been confusing: There are Forest
Preserve lands outside of the "blue line," but they are not part of the
Adirondack Park. The state lands within the "blue line" are parts of
both the Preserve and the Park. The private lands within the "blue
line" are parts of the Park, but not of the Preserve.

In 1893, the Forest Commission and legislators approved timber
sales, the sale and lease of more state land and road building in the
Park. These laxities in Preserve protection were opposed by many
New York City business associations; in 1894 a Constitutional
Convention was convened and resulted in state constitutional
protection for the Forest Preserve. The protection took the form of
the famous Article XIV (originally it was known as Article 7) of the
New York State Constitution, sometimes called the "Magna Carta" of
the Forest Preserve: "The lands of the state, now owned or hereafter
acquired, constituting the forest preserve as now fixed by law, shall
be forever kept as wild forest lands. They shall not be leased, sold
or exchanged, or taken by any corporation, public or private, nor
shall the timber thereon be sold, removed or destroyed ..."

The law was now clear and had teeth in it regarding timber use -
- "not to be sold, removed, or destroyed." The guides and sportsmen
weren't being "requested to give it careful thought." You could not
build a shanty or a camp on state land and not destroy timber.
Perhaps it wasn't being destroyed if it was put to good use as a
camp? It was no use -- guides and sportsmen soon learned "dead and
down" timber was really all that was legally available for their use,
and that no permanent structures were permitted in the Forest
Preserve. By 1975, even the leased tent platform sites on state land,
beloved of up to four generations of campers, were banned. At about
the same time, fire towers and interior Ranger cabins were removed
and high-altitude or shore-line lean-to's were burned or moved.

Those who had always known these things, such as the old-time guides, saw an emotional and irretrievable loss; those who hadn't known them saw the biggest parcel of wilderness east of the Mississippi getting a little wilder again.

At the end of the nineteenth century, major changes having to do with game laws were on the state's mind. In the winter of 1884-1885 the state legislature had passed the Curtis Hounding Law, prohibiting the hounding of deer. In 1886, after being widely ignored, the law was repealed. But sentiment against this practice and jacking was mounting. In the Fisheries, Game and Forest Commission Report for 1895 the state aired the controversy about the time-honored practices of hounding and jacking, building its case against them:

"There are three methods of hunting practiced in the Adirondack woods: night-hunting, hounding, and still hunting .. (n)ight hunting (is) permissable all season, but practicable only during the warm nights in the earlier part of the hunting season (with the) lantern and reflector higher than the head of the hunter when seated ... (m)ost sportsmen would willingly see it discontinued by law ... many (deer) are wounded and lost. The guides say four are wounded and lost for every one taken. Four-fifths of the deer taken are does. They are nursing does, thin and poor, their venison inferior. The venison cannot be kept, and spoils ... deer should not be killed before September 20 (the season ran August 16 to October 31) -- after that the fawns can care for themselves, the does' meat is better ..."

The 1895 report asserted that "no other State or Canadian Province permitted the killing of deer in those early months. It was reserved for New York to frame a law based on personal interests instead of the dictates of humanity and the ethics of sport."

The state sought the opinions of various hotelkeepers, guides, and sportsmen regarding the proposed changes:

Ernest H. Johnson, Tupper Lake guide: "Stop the hunting and fishing (out of season) for market, and pass an act making it unlawful to buy or offer for sale any venison in the Adirondacks. It is not the deer and fish caught by sportsmen and tourists that are exterminating them; but those that are taken out of season by pot-hunters and sold to hotels."

Charles Bennett, Raquette Lake, hotel proprietor, former guide: "The idea of dictating how a person shall kill a deer, once the season is open, seems to me, and always has, absurd. Open the season

when the animals are fat, and let each man kill a deer in whatever manner he chooses, provided he does not use traps or salt licks."
Charles Wood, North Elba, guide: "Shorten the hounding season."
D. E. Farrington, Indian Lake, guide: "More hounding."

Under the new laws of 1895 the hounding season ran from September 10 to October 10 in 1895, then changed to fifteen days, October 1 to 15 in 1896, cutting the season in half. In 1897 the laws changed again and the deer season expanded, from August 15 to November 15, with a limit of two deer. But after June 1, 1897 there was to be no jack-lighting and no hounding for five years. A period of lax enforcement followed; this was the period of the incompetent game wardens the guides complained so bitterly about. But hounding and jacking deer were never legal again.

In 1913, the Conservation Commission began permitting construction of open camps (before only tents had been permitted) under certain conditions: The builder must have Commission permission and the camp must have a sign stating "Property of the State of New York and open to the public." State employees fighting fires were to get first claim to occupancy.

In 1918, the Conservation Commission proposed registration of guides, and recognized the pressure to break the law put on guides by some hunters, as well as the economic benefits of registration to guides:

"The better opinion is in favor of such a system of registration so successful in Maine, Canada, and some of the western states. Only those men should be registered who are thoroughly competent in woodcraft, and well versed in the knowledge of fish and game. This would not prevent an unregistered man from guiding, but would result in vacationists choosing, in most instances, the registered guides. If the guides be registered and be clothed with some legal authority and be subject to forfeiture of their registration certificates if they violate the law, or permit their parties to violate it, the guides would be in a much better position as a class and as individuals, to take an independent attitude with those who do not wish to observe the law. The Commission believes no registration fee should be charged. A list of guides should be published."

In 1919, voluntary state registration of guides began. The Conservation Commission was authorized to maintain a register of guides in the Forest Preserve counties, and to issue a license and distinguishing badge to qualified persons; the badge showed the state seal and an open camp. It was believed this would bring better protection against fires, result in more effective game protection, and give "more complete enjoyment by vacationists of the State's great Forest Preserve."

The Forest Preserve counties were divided into eight districts, and in each of these districts a guides' committee of three men was appointed by the Commission until such time as the guides themselves could meet and elect their own committees. Many applications were received from persons not engaged in the business of guiding, who desired "registration as a testimonial of their ability as woodsmen." They were turned down.

The first year the Commission registered 176 guides, with 54 applications on file for submission to district guides' committees. The next year 314 guides registered, and 6,200 copies of the Register of Guides were distributed.

One of the problems with voluntary registration was that registered guides were subject to more severe penalties for violations of fish and game laws than unregistered guides, thereby discouraging registration. The state decided that, beginning in 1924, registration and licensing would be mandatory, a function of the Department of Fish and Game within the Conservation Commission. The new licenses cost $2 (a fee that would stay fixed for years), required that the holder be 21, a citizen, and "safe and competent to guide." Guides were prohibited from shooting or killing any game, and could carry only a pistol or revolver. The guides were vested with the powers of game protectors, except for making a search without a warrant. The state reasoned that hunters, unable to depend on their guides to shoot their deer for them, would stay in the woods longer, benefitting not only the guides but the camps and hotels catering to hunters. The state pointed out that the practice of a client offering his guide a bonus for shooting a deer was possibly three violations: the guide in killing more than the legal number of deer allowed, the guide selling game, and the hunter buying game.

The Commission also required that guides have skill in small boat handling, including the ability to swim. This resulted in a few amusing cases of summer visitors trying to teach their guides to swim. Fines for guiding without a license could range from $10 to $100; in the first half of 1924, 415 guides were licensed.

In 1925, it was stated that, "A guide convicted of breaking any regulation of the Conservation Law or of the Commission is not only liable to the penalty fixed by law, but forfeits his license and is not eligible to receive another license for 2 years." In 1926 the department, now the Conservation Department, stated that, "During the past year 21 guides were prosecuted ... and surrendered their licenses to engage in guiding to the Commission." In 1927, the Department restated the reasons for licensing:

> "When the services of a guide could be cheaply bought little complaint was heard, but as time passed and guides were receiving pay more nearly commensurate with the value of the service they render, many persons from various parts of the State, and even from points without the State, moved into the deer country and hired out their services as guides, knowing nothing of the country, possessing little knowledge of the ways of the wild, and in general unskilled in the art of guiding. It was not uncommon for a 'guide' to get lost. From this came the belief that the activities of guides should be regulated ..."

In 1928, the Department stated that, "Protectors were instructed to examine the credentials of all persons found guiding last fall, and in only two instances were persons apprehended who were not licensed ... each paid $12.50 in settlement of their offense." In 1930 the Department stated that, "This is the first year (since mandatory registration) that the number of applications received was less than the number received in the previous year. The falling off is mostly accounted for by the refusal of the Department to issue guide licenses to 24 persons licensed in previous years who violated the provisions of the Conservation Law." During the subsequent Depression years Department reports were issued, but mention of guides disappears; the numbers of licenses issued annually fell to about half what it had been in 1924.

In 1941 the Conservation Department began putting on each license the exact territories for which the guide was licensed and for which type of guiding: hunting, fishing, camping, or any combination of the three. Guides were required to attend an annual meeting called by the District Game Protectors to go over fish and game laws, conservation activities and mutual concerns. At year end guides were asked to submit a brief report of the season's work; people employing guides could do the same.

For the next twenty years, the number of guides licenses issued each year stayed at about 500. After World War II, according to Town of Arietta historian Helen Rogers, "most of the old-timers were gone. The hunting and need for guides passed with them."

In 1980, Don Perryman was a District Ranger, Assistant to the Superintendent of the Department of Forest Protection and Fire

Management, within DEC (Department of Environmental Conservation.) In 1991, now as Regional Forest Manager, he recalled his role in the formulation of the present licensing requirements of New York State guides:

"I wrote the original legislation, the rules and regulations. It took so long to get the legislation in place, some of the organizations we wanted to control had lobbied themselves out of it. Children's camps, for example -- we had so many search and rescues of children. The camps, through their camp associations, were able to secure exemptions form needing guides. But we were also having more search and rescues, particularly in the Adirondacks, of groups accompanied by a so-called guide who the State of New York licensed. We were saying they were qualified without knowing if they knew what they were doing.

The state formed a committee to advise on the new licensing, they had a lot of input. Tom Monroe here in Region 5 started the committee. The licensing program was moved from Fish and Wildlife because they didn't have the staff or interest. It went to the Rangers in Forest Protection and Fire Management. The Rangers had to search, and have abilities parallel to what guides should have. Rangers can say who is capable. But even now the laws regarding guides remain in Fish and Wildlife under Article 11, instead of Article 9 of Forest Protection and Fire Management. Originally you had to violate the law regarding your guide's license to have your license revoked. Now, any DEC law violation can result in revocation.

NYSOGA (New York State Outdoor Guides Association) wanted to participate in the regulations for licensing -- they became more organized than the state, earlier. I was a speaker at one of their meetings. -- they put me through the wringer, which was good. They wanted input, wanted to be professional. At one point they wanted to do it themselves, but they could see the state was going to do it. Their recommendations were very seriously considered. The state hired Fred Oettinger, the retired Assistant to the Division Director, with a private firm, Cloud Nine Associates, as a consultant. He put the finishing touches on when we got short-handed. Up until the new licensing there wasn't even a list of guides.

It took from 1978 or '79 until 1986 before we gave the first test and got the program in place. Too long -- we had contingency licenses, temporary licenses. The new law was enacted in 1985, if you had a contingency license, you had to take and pass the exam.

When Norm Van Valkenburg was Division of Lands and Forests Director, the direction regarding guidelines was to license all the lands and waters in the state.

If you offer services to the <u>public at large</u>, you need a license. But if you are a confined group, such as campers, or members of a club, you don't need it. So if the Adirondack Mountain Club goes up Mt. Jo, they don't need a licensed guide. Non-licensed guides we catch with undercover operations.

So far I think it's a good program. I could count the search and rescues on one hand. The guides are properly tested, we know they have the ability. And I'm not sure we really missed the children's camps and Boy Scouts. The counselors say, 'We mess up one more time and we'll have more regulations.' Because we showed interest they came up with the Voyageur's Program, for example. And the Health Department has control over children's camps -- they can control how children are supervised. There are regulations over who's eligible to take people out, and how."

In the 1970's author Anne La Bastille (an Adirondack Park Agency Commissioner at the time of this writing), was told that to become a guide she would need "to know a certain section of the woods pretty well, most of a topographic map quadrangle. An already licensed guide must vouch for you, and then a State game warden must sign your application. Both swear you know your way around in the woods. If they decide you're competent, they grant you a guide's license."

Under the new regulations as of 1987 a guide must: Have a physician's statement certifying good health; hold current Red Cross CPR, First Aid, and Basic Water Safety status; take a general basic exam, and an exam in each category in which one wants to guide -- hunting, fishing, camping, hiking, white-water rafting and/or canoeing and/or kayaking, and rock climbing and ice climbing.

Following the inital exams in August of 1987, approximately 30 percent of the 989 licensed guides were residents of the Adirondacks. License enforcement followed soon after; a woman who met all DEC requirements to receive a whitewater rafting guide license, but had not obtained it, was fined $250 for guiding a raft down the Hudson.

In 1935, after mandatory licensing was well established in New York, Gurth Whipple, wrote:

"The latter-day guides are like the latter-day saints; they can't compare in genuineness with the old orthodox patriarchs; they are a different race. Their hunting ground is no longer a free domain; they can no longer take game at will and build camps wherever their fancy dictates. They are all regimented, registered, licensed and badged, which proclaims to the public that they are qualified persons. The old-timers would rest uneasy in their graves if they knew this. No member of that gnarled and woolly coterie could ever be mistaken for anyone else. He needed no badge and no government mandate to designate his business or support his qualifications."

Private Preserves and Commercial Hunting Camps

"The guides were reported as 'entertaining feelings of complacency.'" -- Dr. Walter Lowrie, a summer resident of Keene Valley in 1887.

Most guides worked either for themselves or for hotels in the early years of the guiding profession. But the coming of private clubs or preserves and commercial hunting camps created jobs for a number of guides. By about 1895 there were almost 50 private preserves in existence in the Adirondacks owning or controlling a million acres of land. While most did not employ guides, the Adirondack League Club near Old Forge and the Adirondack Mountain Reserve in the Keene Valley area are both examples of large private preserves that did; they date back to the nineteenth century. An example of a commercial hunting camp is Whitehouse in Hamilton County.

The Adirondack League Club was founded in 1890. At its greatest extent, in 1897, the club owned 128,000 acres and leased 63,000 more. From the beginning, members were entitled to the use of club land held in common and to individual parcels of land for their exclusive use. In 1904 the club had twenty-three guides on staff, and individual members hired many more. The club was the single greatest employer of guides in the southwest Adirondacks. In 1911 the club guides, hoping to add a dollar a day to the going rate of three dollars, where it had been for twenty years, joined with the better paid guides in the Brown's Tract Guides' Association. Club membership, made up almost entirely of wealthy, resisted the increase. The members told the guides they intended to publish the existing rate in the next club yearbook, furthering the rate for at least another year. In 1919, perhaps as a tardy concession, the guides were provided with new dwelling quarters at each of the club's three lodges, complete with reading room, bathroom, and individual beds.

The Adirondack League Club was in some ways in the forefront of game conservation. On its property in 1892, no deer were to be killed before September 1, two weeks after the state's season opened. The club made an effort to get jacking outlawed state-wide, but failed. (In different years before 1897 a bill passed either the Assembly or the Senate, but not the required both.) But the club allowed hounding because the members "enjoyed it."

As early as 1892 club guides were issued badges saying "Police Guide." The guides functioned as game constables and fire wardens. One guide, while employed by a club member, was caught by a state game warden and fined for fishing in an illegal manner on state land. The guide was also reprimanded by the club officials.

Other club guides rose to positions of higher esteem. Club guide John Commerford became both a fish culturist and Club Superintendent. He later served as a character in William Boardman's novel, *Lovers of the Woods.* Guide Dwight Grant also served as Club Superintendent, as well as being a prominent guide-boat builder, a founder of the Brown's Tract Guides' Association and a member of the New York State Assembly. His son Lewis, also a guide-boat builder, guided briefly at the club before replacing his father as Club Superintendent. On its property the club had rustic outlying camps for a night or two of "roughing it," usually with a guide. These camps and family traditions of employing a guide prolonged the use of guides at the club longer than elsewhere; some club guides today are fourth generation. But after World War II most club guides had shifted into caretaker roles.

Diagonally across the Park from the Adirondack League Club is the Adirondack Mountain Reserve (AMR). This 25,000 acre preserve was established in the Keene Valley area in 1887. Before that the Thomas and Armstrong Lumber Company, the previous owners, had given the local guides permission to build semi-permanent camps on the Upper Ausable Lake. They believed the guides' presence would discourage illegal lumbering and guard against forest fires. The guides agreed not to cut green timber, and were paid to fight fires and improve trails.

Most of the early guide's camps on the Upper Ausable Lake were built in the 1870's and '80's, and numbered almost two dozen. But some were built before that. One who built much earlier was the famous Orson "Old Mountain" Phelps. He began climbing Mt. Marcy in 1849, and in 1861 cut the first trail from the Upper Ausable Lake over Bartlett Ridge. Along with the Holt's and Beede's, who supplied generations of guides to AMR members, Phelps helped begin the distinctive look of the Upper Lake open camps, lean-to's joined at gentle angles and modestly filigreed, with small out buildings close by. In the early days the guides were reported as "entertaining feelings of complacency," as they held sole possession of the one possible route to Mt. Marcy from the east. When a man named Walter Lowrie and his son Adrian re-established the Orson Phelps trail to Marcy in 1886 after a hurricane had obliterated it,

Lowrie's canoe, "moored at the Lakes, was duly sunk beneath the waves by the guides."

After the AMR took over only certain guides were permitted on their property; hunting was prohibited, and fishing restricted to members and guests of the AMR. Hikers and campers on the property were required to have a guide who belonged to the Keene Valley Guides Association, and rules for a set number of guides per party were in place. But overall the new AMR regulations eliminated much of the local guides' business.

The Keene Valley Guides Association, a chapter of the Adirondack Guides Association, had formed the same year as the AMR; most of the members worked on AMR property. These Keene Valley guides were required to be at least twenty-one, U.S. citizens, Adirondack residents for at least 15 years, and have a minimum of three years experience as assistant guide -- a handy way to welcome in sons and relatives. The Keene Valley group, with Arthur Trumbull as president, quickly numbered nineteen. The Association attempted to monitor the actions of its members, rather than having infractions handled by the Reserve officials. Coincidentally, the Keene Valley Bicycle Association formed the same year as the Guides Association and the AMR. The guides adopted bicycles as a method of transportation to get from the Ausable Club at St. Huberts to the lakes. The next year author Katherine McClellan wrote that of all the changes in the Adirondacks, the most startling was the sight of a "Keene Valley guide on a wheel."

By 1906, AMR management considered the open guide camps too primitive, and began buying them up and tearing them down. They also ceased to authorize new guides. By 1907 the construction of closed camps began on the Upper Lake, and ownership of the old sites began passing into the hands of AMR members. Many of the guides shifted into guide-caretaker roles for the new owners. Today some of the guide-caretakers and their employers are third or fourth generation.

In contrast to the exclusiveness of the private clubs and preserves, large commercial hunting camps offered an opportunity for groups of men of lesser means to be in the woods during hunting season. In Hamilton County one of the best-known was at Whitehouse, on the West Branch of the Sacandaga River, sometimes called the West River.

The Whitehouse hunting camp was about seven miles from the village of Wells, south of Speculator. The building complex had originally been a logging camp with 16 buildings, and later served as a boy's camp. The camp's own 350 acres adjoined thousands of acres of state land. After a succession of owners -- John Seever, Abe Lawrence and Lee Fountain -- Millo Kniffen, a Cobleskill attorney, and Ed Richard, a Fort Plain Chevrolet dealer, bought the property in 1950.

Richard got his start in 1932 guiding hunting parties with Lyman Avery at Avery's Hotel, also on the West Branch of the Sacandaga in the Town of Arietta. He boasted he had the only guide's license good throughout the Park, although it has been pointed out that at that time one's license merely reflected what you wrote down as to where you wished to guide. Educated with a military background, and with the bearing of a British Cavalry officer, he saw to it strict rules were followed: no drinking (this rule was bent behind his back) or swearing (also bent), and the guide's words were law. These strictures paid off -- Richard and Kniffen owned the property for twelve years, accomodating 30 to 50 men at a time, and never had a hunting accident or a seriously lost hunter.

Richard, described in one reminiscence as confident "bordering on arrogance," kept meticulous records for more than ten years, of every buck, its weight and rack size. Almost 300 deer were taken. The average was slightly under 140 pounds, about the same as at the turn of the century. Richard wrote a booklet called "Deer Production vs. Doe Reduction," and distributed thousands of copies to fish and game clubs. He documented the harmful effects of doe hunting.

Guides at Whitehouse included one-time Hamilton County Sheriff "Pants" Lawrence, Fred Coluton, Les Danferd, Irv Clouthier, and near the end of the camp's existence, Jim Craig and Pat Conway. On a typical day of a deer drive the guides would post the hunters on specific "watches." They marked the watches on topo maps, and gave them names such as Barkstack, White Deer, Barkpile, Picnic Grounds, Lean-to, 10-point, and Priest's Vly. The guides would then go around with other hunters to the start of the drive and start the deer. At Whitehouse horses were used to carry deer and the occassional bear out of the woods. The horses ran away at least twice.

Don Wharton, writing in "The Barkeater," recalls

"one did not necessarily have to be a crack shot to be able to go home with a good buck. Whitehouse guides could handle that part of the hunt if required to. Before the season officially opened a guide's hunt was held that was both a source of venison for the lodge and a source of eight and ten point bucks for the right customer. One especially large buck had a tag of $75 on it -- a lot of money in the Thirties. Bucks that were taken under these circumstances were said to have been taken with a 'silver bullet.'"

The Whitehouse inspired at least one folksong, by Archlus (Pete) Craig. Titled "West River Valley," one verse describes the fate of the great old hunting camp: "Now it's maintained for the wandering litterbugs; the State finally owns that whole tract."

In 1962 the property was offered for sale. No one but the state was interested, and the Whitehouse was sold for $17,500. The Northville-Lake Placid Trail runs by the site, crossing the river on a suspension bridge. In the old days hikers had to holler across in hopes of getting ferried over in a boat. Wading was the only alternative if no one responded.

Avery's, where Richard got his start, was both a hunting camp and a hotel. One dodge employed in the restaurant was serving trout and venison -- the sale of wild fish and game is illegal -- as a "free side dish" with the purchase of a chicken dinner. In 1960 Avery's hunters had a banner year, killing 63 buck and 11 bear. Most years about 45 deer were taken. One hunting party numbered just over a hundred; driving two mountain ranges at once, they shot seven buck and a bear. Guides employed at Avery's included Dutch Smith, Bob Porter, and "Albany Sam" Clafin.

A hunting camp at Stony Creek, near Luzerne, run by Jack Baker, was similar to the Whitehouse. In the 1940's Baker could accomodate up to 20 hunters, and with his wife raised cattle, sheep, cows and chickens to help feed them. Baker served as a guide, but employed additional guides to dress the deer and other game. He advertised "deer, bear, wolf, and rabbit hunting." Hunters followed cut trails and marked trees, and were transported on one of the first snow toboggins, a primitive version of snowmobile. Guides at these large hunting camps have always been aware of the dangers posed by excited and, in some cases inexperienced, hunters. Special precautions, such as keeping rifles unloaded until hunters were in position, were followed.

Guides in Adirondack
Literature and Art

"The incidents recorded in the following pages have been neither invented nor exaggerated to any appreciable degree."
-- A. Judd Northrup, in the preface to his book *Camps and Tramps in the Adirondacks (1880.)*

LITERATURE

In a treatment of "literature" that includes guides, the problem arises of where to place the cut-off line through a continuum that runs from newspaper articles to magazines, then book-length travel narratives, and finally novel-length works wholly fiction. Fiction, as opposed to factual writing, recommends itself for analysis because the author creates his characters, and can portray them as he sees fit. He can make them the essence of a role, mirroring the distilled traits of a whole segment of society, rather than attempting to render actual people objectively.

This assumption lies behind the often-held tenet in literature that ficitional portrayals are sometimes more "true" than factual ones. True or not, when one looks at the Adirondack Bibliography through 1965 only about one-hundred and seventy entries are works of fiction out of a list of over ten-thousand titles. And none of the fictional works were written by guides or deal primarily with guides. But some of the fictional works include guides, and are important because they sum up the image of guides in the popular imagination, and place the guides in what is a usually romanticized and idealized Adirondacks.

These portrayals are mostly in keeping with the rest of Amercan literature at the time. Literature in America in the nineteenth century often portrayed simple, rough-hewn men whose future success lay not in the vagaries of fate but in their wits, their own two hands, and their capacity for work. Thoreau said, "I believe that Adam in paradise was not so favorably situated on the whole as is the backwoodsman in America." This tenet first materialized in American fiction in James Fennimore Cooper's immortal series of Leatherstocking novels from 1823-1841. Five of these featured the woodsman-guide Natty Bumpo; however, only one, *The Last of the Mohicans*, is set in the Adirondacks. The book came out in 1826, and sure enough, reality soon began to imitate art -- real people were compared to Bumpo. Charles Fenno Hoffman's book *Wild Scenes in the Forest and Prairie*, which included a large section on the

Adirondacks, appeared in 1839. In it the guide John Cheney, who had been on the first ascent of Mt. Marcy in 1837, was depicted as a Leatherstocking type. In a chapter called "A Mountaineer of the Hudson" Hoffman says,

> "I was lately looking over Cooper's 'pioneers,' and, re-reading it after the lapse of years, found myself as much delighted as ever with the best character he ever drew -- 'The Leather-stocking.' If it did not involve an anachronism, I would swear that Cooper took the character of Natty Bumpo from my mountaineer friend, John Cheney. The same silent, simple, deep love of the woods; the same gentleness and benevolence of feeling toward all who love his craft; the same unobtrusive kindness toward all others; and, lastly, the same shrewdness as a woodsman, and gamesomeness of spirit as a hunter, are common to both; and each, while perhaps more efficient, are wholly unlike the dashing swashbuckler of the far-west, the reckless ranger of the prairies ... I saw that this formidable Nimrod carried with him, as his only weapons and insignia of his art, a <u>pistol and a jack-knife</u>!"

In 1855 the Leatherstocking tradition of reality mimicking art still lived on in the Adirondacks in "A Deer Hunt on the Bouquet" by Paul Martindale:

> "John Archibald was <u>the</u> character of the county. In the vigor and prime of his manhood, he possesed many traits of character to remind one of Cooper's Leather-Stocking. An excellent hunter, cool, keen, and sagacious -- loving his dog and his gun more than he did most of his family -- like "Leather-Stocking," fearing the face of no man, but unlike him, fearing also neither God nor the devil. He was honest, because it was his nature to be so, and perfectly good-tempered, unless his dog or his rifle were abused; then his anger and his profanity knew no bounds. But the over-ruling trait of his character was an unbounded love of fun and frolic."

Modern author Paul Jamieson, recalling the Thoreauvian idea, has described Natty Bumpo as:

> "a kind of backwoods angel who totes a gun. He is the one man whom power does not spoil. Though a lord in the forest, he is incorruptible in his innocence. He is Adam before the Fall living in a wild, shaggy American Eden and holding the key to it ... This lovely fiction was the party's ideal for his guide. The guides

themselves did not read Cooper. If they had, they might have criticized Natty Bumpo's woodcraft."

Once the guides had surpassed Bumpo in woodcraft and were established in their own right, they began to be treated in literature less as Bumpo replicas, and more as Adirondack guides. The guides' woodsman skills, simplicity, naivety, and basic integrity are the traits most often portrayed.

William Murray's *Adventures in the Wilderness* (1869) is arguably the most well-known book in the literature of the Adirondacks. It hit the market at an absolutely perfect time, unlike its important predecessor, *The Adirondack; or, Life in the Woods*, by Joel Headley, published in 1849. People were ready by 1869 to accept what Murray offered. After the Civil War, America had shifted from a society dominated by agriculture to one of industrialization and urbanization. The book triggered a new and different interest in the Adirondacks, and was said to have "kindled a thousand camp fires and taught a thousand pens how to write of nature." Murray's book has some fictional flights of fancy, but it is far from a novel. It includes sections on "Why I go to the Wilderness, What it costs in the Wilderness, Where to buy Tackle, Hotels," etc.

Murray eulogizes his guide "Honest John" Plumbley as:

"... the prince of guides, patient as a hound, and as faithful, -- a man who knows the wilderness as a farmer knows his fields, whose instinct is never at fault, whose temper is never ruffled, whose paddle is silent as falling snow, whose eye is true along the sights, whose pancakes are the wonder of the woods, -- honest, patient, and modest John Plumbley, may he live long beyond the limit so few of us attain, and depart at last full of peace as he will full of honors, God bless him!"

In the reaction following the flood of tourists triggered by Murray's book, the guide "Uncle" in *The Modern Babes in Woods*, by H. Perry Smith (1872), is described, curiously, as "not a scientific guide of John Plumbley order." Perhaps "Uncle" thought Plumbley was scientific because he pondered why trees a hundred and fify feet high often fell "when there was not wind enough to float a feather."

An Adirondack novel that achieved great popularity was *Silas Strong*, by Irving Bacheller (1859-1950), published in 1906. The protagonist, Strong, was modelled loosely after Cranberry Lake guide Philo (Fide) Scott. (Scott, who had assisted Bacheller in procuring a 4,000-acre tract for his camp Robinwood, near Long Lake West, later even started writing his own biography, dictating it to a stenographer.) In the book, Strong is driven from his woods haunts by a not-entirely evil lumber company. The fictional conflict is drawn to show the powers of larger, societal forces. Such things did not actually happen to Scott; in fact, he actually derived some livelihood from working in lumbering. The character Strong is painted as much more stern than the humorous and talkative Scott. Bacheller says of Strong: "He was what they called in the country a 'one-wordman.' The phrase indicated that he was wont to express himself with all possible brevity. He never used more than one word if that could be made to satisfy the demands of politeness and perspicacity ... he was never profane."

When he is handed an eviction notice from the Migley Lumber Company, Strong, who stammers slightly, "broke the silence of more than forty years," and rose to his most eloquent:

> "N-no, no," he said, "it can't be. Ye 'ain't no r-right t' do it, fer ye can't never put the w-woods bac agin. My God, sir, I've w-wandered over these hills an' flats ever since I was a little b-boy. There ain't a critter on 'em that d-don't know me. Seems so they was all my b-brothers. I've seen men come in here nigh dead an' go back w-well. They's m-med'cine here t' cure all the sickness in a hundred cities; they's f-fur 'nough here t' c-cover their naked -- they's food 'nough t' feed their hungry -- an' they's w-wood 'nough t' keep 'em w-warm. God planted these w-woods an' stocked 'em, an' nobody's ever d-done a day's work here 'cept me ... Y-you 'ain't no right t'git together down there in Albany an' make laws as'in' the will o' God ... you d--- bullcook!" (A bullcook was a chore-boy in a lumber camp.)

Strong is a clearly defined character who doesn't believe in hounding deer, is careful with fire, and respects nature. He is capable of wry observation, classifying sports into swishers, pouters, and paunchers. Rather than effeminates, sulkers, and the obese, Strong believed a "swisher was one who filled the air within reach of his cast, catching trees and bushes, but no fish; a pouter, one who baited and hauled his fish as if it were no better than a bull-pout; a pauncher was wont to hit his deer 'in the middle' and never saw him again."

But Bacheller, said by critic Charles Samuels to have made a "hopeless muddle" of realism, veritism, romanticism, and local color, also undermines the effectiveness and convictions of his novel with a distracting sub-plot involving a pretty girl and a would-be politician. The sub-plot, coupled with Strong's rather stilted dialogue, relegated the work to a minor niche in American literature. Batcheller intended the novel to be a muckracking story of land abuse, but it was too weak to achieve this.

William H. Boardman (1846-1914) was editor and president of the *Railroad Gazette*, as well as a president of the Adirondack League Club. In 1901 he wrote *Lovers of the Woods*, in which the guide John is modelled after ALC guide John Commerford. The fictional John is something of a connoisseur of the woods:

"John was cooking a supper of bacon, trout, and tea. It was not an elaborate bill of fare, and his working kit was a two-quart pail and a frying pan, but the quantities were enormous and the quality the best in the world. Everything was clean. The supper-table was the leathery surface of the inner side of a sheet of spruce bark ... there was a dainty neatness and precision in his way of camp-fire cooking."

Perhaps because food plays such a central role in camp, H. L. Ives, in *Reminiscences of the Adirondacks* (1915), also portrayed the cooking of his guide, Moses St. Germain, in lyrical terms:

"When I use the term 'guide cook' it means something more than an ordinary cook. It is no great art for a person who can read and understand to go into a modern kitchen, furnished with a modern range and everything used in the art of cooking, take a cook book and make things. But to build a fire on the ground, arrange your back logs and fore sticks, lug poles, kettle hangers, etc., and construct a fire suitable to do cooking, and then mix a Johnny-cake that would melt in your mouth, bake it in a tin oven, cook a venison steak smothered in onions, fry a pan of trout to a turn, make a pot of coffee that will cast its aroma through the woods for miles around, and, last but not least, a stack of pancakes that would have to be weighed down to keep them from floating right off on the light Adirondack air -- that's what I call a guide cook. And Mose could fill the bill."

The Great Adirondack Novel has yet to be written. The Adirondacks as a whole are thought by critics not to have a truly distinct regional literature, on a par with the South or West. When a definitive literary work is done for the region, it will of necessity include one or more Adirondack guides, regardless of the era or its setting.

ART

American Romanticism, which emerged in the 1820's and continued until about the Civil War, was enthusiastic for "the strange, remote, solitary, and mysterious." The paintings of the era are mostly lumped into the Hudson River School. One would think literature and art in the same movement would stand on a par. But critic James Fosburgh has said of the paintings that they were dominated by literary romanticism: "(The artists') ambition was to paint heroic landscapes, a literary conception rather than a visual one, and although they painted every leaf on every tree, they never painted the actual details of the landscape itself." Any signs of human activity were usually left out of the heroic panoramas as insignificant.

There were exceptions, however, such as Frederic Rondel and William Stillman, who zeroed in on Adirondack camp life -- Rondel in his painting "A Hunting Party in the Woods/In the Adirondac (sic.), N. Y. State, 1856," and Stillman's "The Philosopher's Camp in the Adirondacks," 1858. In these, each of which includes guides, the artist's focus narrows down from the panoramic. How the people are arranged; what they are shown doing, and how they are dressed are an attempt at both realism and commentary. The guides are shown at camp chores, the sports in play or contemplation. Later, painting gave way to photography. In a group photo of mixed sports and guides, the guides can usually be picked out. The differences are subtle ones -- the guides' cock of the hat, gauntness of cheekbone, and penetration of gaze. The sports usually look paunchy and Edwardian, the guides physically hardened.

These works of Rondel and Stillman are almost documentary in their preciseness, but somewhat lifeless; when we come to the artists A. F. Tait and Winslow Homer we see the same journalistic focus re-enthused with artistic energy -- a sense of "the moment," but with greater action and tension. Tait (1819-1905) was the artist who did as much as anyone to popularize the Adirondacks. He is most well-known for the eleven Adirondack scenes he produced for Currier and Ives. He was an Englishman who began coming to the region soon after he settled in New York City in 1850. When he got to America he was already established as an artist in England, primarily as a lithographer of animals. By 1852 Tait had built a shanty on Upper Chateaugay Lake and painted a picture of it. In 1854, his painting "Arguing the Point" showed three men in spirited, though non-hostile, discussion. The three are guides from the Chateaugay Lake area -- Anthony Sprague, Jonathan Bellows, and Francis Bellows. A few years earlier three untutored backwoodsmen gathered near a woodpile would have been unworthy of art. Suddenly they were dignified by the attention; Currier reproduced the painting, and it elevated the common man to a place in the mainstream of rural life.

"A Good Time Coming" (published as a print by Currier and Ives in 1862) depicted what Tait called a "shanty scene." Tait shows a lean-to with all the needed camping accoutrements. The sport is dressed in jacket and tie; one guide tends the campfire, while another is bringing a stringer of fish to the camp. Through the depictions of dress, manner, and activity, the economic and social distinctions are apparent. "Going Out Deer Hunting in the Adirondacks," done in 1862, includes guide Captain Calvin Parker, of Long Lake. A work done in 1881 shows an older Parker, in "Still Life in the Snow," with his dog, coming upon a dead deer. Whether he shot it or simply happened on it is unclear; slice-of-life realism, with all its unanswered questions, is both unsettling and satisfying after viewing the dominating but dull or incredulous landscapes of prior eras.

Another of the foremost artists of the age who painted in the Adirondacks was Winslow Homer (1836-1910), usually cited for his "Americanism," localism, and realism. He was born in Boston, and at nineteen was a lithographer's apprentice, but quit on his twenty-first birthday to become a free-lance magazine illustrator. During the Civil War he was a pictorial reporter for *Harper's Weekly*. His localism was, and is, sometimes negatively viewed as provincialism, as though his subjects were too narrow in universal meaning to give his art stature. On the other hand, Homer scholar Lloyd Goodrich believed him to be "our greatest pictorial poet of outdoor life in America," and even a forerunner of French impressionism.

Homer began coming to the Adirondacks in 1870, and continued sporadically until 1908. Here he painted outdoors, mostly in watercolors. In his early years in the Adirondacks he stayed at an artists' colony in Keene Valley, and then began staying in Minerva. In the late 1880's, with his brother, he became a charter member of the North Woods Club, between the Hudson and Boreas Rivers, about ten miles from Minerva. One paradox in the accusation that Homer's work is provincial is that his choice of subject matter was original, painting people and actions not dealt with before. He was thought provincial compared to the prevailing wisdom, that if a subject wasn't grand and romantic, it was necessarily mundane -- a state of mind that had to be unlearned.

"Two Guides," one of Homer's most famous Adirondack paintings, done about 1875, depicts a bearded, wizened old-timer with a packbasket, pointing out something across the mountains to a younger, strapping man holding an axe insouciantly. With a little imagination one feels the painting could just as easily be called "The Lesson," or "Remembrance of Things Past," or even "Showing the Route." As models Homer used Orson Phelps for the old-timer, and Monroe Holt, grandson of early (1806) Keene Valley settler Smith Holt, as the younger man -- two true examples of guides if there were any. Unlike the other Hudson River School artists, Homer never painted a panoramic landscape -- a startling contrast. His subjects are a magnified telescopic field out of a broader background, and give intimacy and detail to pictures of "man in nature."

While at the North Woods Club, Homer used two guides frequently, both separately and together -- Michael Francis "Farmer" Flynn, about 20, and Rufus Wallace, an older bachelor resident of Minerva. While both are identified as guides in writings about Homer, neither show up in the 1893 Forest Commission list of guides, which suggests they may have been part-timers engaged in other activity, such as posing for Homer. "Adirondack Guide," probably done in 1876, before Homer's North Woods Club residency, shows a long-legged young man with his hat at a jaunty angle and his rifle cradled ready for use. The background is indistinct, so the painting is essentially a portrait. "Adirondack Woods, Guide and Dog," is just that, the leashed dog and the guide contrasted with a huge, shaggy-barked tree. "The Guide" shows an older man paddling a guide-boat-like skiff. "End of the Hunt" depicts a dead buck already in the stern of a scow rowed by a younger man, while an older man is in the process of assisting two dogs into the boat.

"Hound and Hunter" is even more graphic, the hunter laying prone out across the deck of a guide-boat, trying to tie a painter rope on a swimming, or perhaps dead buck, as a hound swims closer. The picture gives a tremendous sense of tension and the moment, as all possibilities are present -- for the buck to sink or swim away, the dog to grapple with the buck, or even the boat to turn over. "Huntsman and Dogs" shows not only the somewhat-gory remains of a dressed deer, but dogs animated by the whole business, and a lumbered-over landscape.

"Guide Carrying a Deer" shows how twisted and grotesque a lifeless deer can look. Many of Homer's other works don't have 'guide' in their title, but leave little doubt one or more guides are shown. His sense of verisimilitude is so strong it creates a tendency to see his paintings as historical references, which they might well be. Interestingly, Homer's frequently used technique of setting his figures off against a rising hillside in the background is attributed by some historians to Homer's knowledge of Japanese woodcuts by Hiroshige. Because we have to some extent come to think of the Adirondacks in the way Homer depicted them, the notion our perception is influenced by Japanese art is a tantalizing one.

For the most part Adirondack literature and art portrayed the guide realistically, but with a touch of romanticism born from envy of the guide as "natural man."

Sometimes Things Go Wrong

"He was a sorry sight to see. Not a single garment was left in its integrity...the old broad-brimmed beaver, which served as hat, umbrella, drinking cup, and landing net...had been floated off and sunk." -- A Deer Hunt on the Bouquet, 1855.

Someone once said the adventure doesn't begin until something goes wrong. In the Adirondacks what would most likely go wrong on a guided trip in the early days -- not counting the inconvenience of spoiled or nonexistent provisions -- was getting lost, or botching the killing of a deer or bear. When a gun suddenly won't fire or a wounded deer won't die without a fight, odds between hunter and hunted begin to even up. In many cases such misadventure becomes -- in hindsight -- the highlight of the trip. In modern times, with fewer guided hunting trips, guiding mishaps are more likely to involve bears or raccoons getting into the food bag, no matter how carefully it is hung, capsized canoes, and the occasional turned or broken ankle. Accidents in the relatively new pursuits of winter hiking and camping, ice and rock climbing, and skiing can have even greater consequences.

Sometimes the misadventures could start before you even got to your destination. In 1850, one stage took ten and a half hours to make the 34 mile trip from Elizabethtown to Harrietstown. The stage driver, Caleb Burton, drove safely past "yawning gulfs," but eventually an embankment gave way and a wheel jammed against a rock. "The horses stood stock still, as if endowed with reason." Everything was spilled out with no loss except some gingerbread. The hoped-for climax of hounding, chasing down a swimming deer in a guide-boat, was a scaled-down version of pursuing whales with a whaleboat, and the chase could have similar disastrous results.

The last thing one sport remembered in 1848 was the crash of timber as a swimming buck kicked in a guide-boat with both front feet. Next the sport heard "pleasant voices...and I thought I was at home, and I clasped my cousin's white hand on my cheek, and I dreamt a pleasant dream." When he woke up he had a broken arm, and the guide's dog Hector was licking the blood from the face of a nearby stag, the perpetrator of the mayhem.

In 1852 a guide named Jerome learned that deer don't like to be stabbed. When he stooped to cut the throat of one he'd shot, it kicked him, his headlamp, and gun into the "mud and mire." In 1853 Saranac Lake guide Cort Moody and his wife discovered a huge bear crawling out on a dead tree that overhung the lake two miles from Baker's Hotel. Moody shot him seven times, killing him, but not until their boat was overturned in three feet of water. On their return they were in "a terrible plight, mudded from top to toe, but in capital spirits, for all that." The bear weighed nearly 500 pounds, the biggest in the oldest inhabitant's memory, its tusks and grinders worn. One paw measured eight by four and a half inches, and weighed over two pounds.

That same year a sport guided by Elijah Cowles of Hamilton County longed for a bear fight. When they came on a bear Cowles instructed the sport to shoot all the buck shot into it he could, then stand with his back to a pine tree and stab the bear if it hugged him. The sport shot, and Cowles urged him to "Go -- in! -- lemons -- and -- get squeezed!" The sport got his left arm broken in two places. Hand-to-hand combat with a deer could have similar consequences. In 1855 a deer was shot in the Bouquet River. The hunter, an old guide, went in to cut its throat, but the deer lunged at the hunter, who tried to catch him by the horns and force his nose under water:

"He next attempted to hold him by one horn, and use the knife on the back of his neck. The result of this experiment was that he was landed about six feet off, with the whole front part of his clothing torn from his body, and his knife lost. The deer made another spring at him, with the intent to put his fore-feet on top of him as he lay in the water, and trample him. This he evaded by a sudden spring, and again succeeded in grasping him by both horns. Thus they struggled and floundered, sometimes one under water, and then the other, for some twenty minutes. Meantime the dogs had run in, and the mastiff at once came to the rescue."

But the water was too deep for the dogs to stand, and they were almost useless. At last another hunter waded in and cut the deer's hamstrings. As for the first hunter, "He was a sorry sight to see. Not a single garment was left in its integrity, while the old broad-brimmed beaver, which had served him for years as hat, umbrella, drinking cup, and landing net, as occassion required, had been floated off and sunk."

But when the ineptness is total, the results could be harmless, as in this 1857 account by "H.G.H.":

"(While jacking deer) soon a white-looking object was seen among the trees, and the boat's head was silently turned, as I supposed, to throw light upon the game. Again I took careful aim and fired, but contrary to my former experience, it neither fell nor ran away [he had fired at a deer earlier, missed, and fallen backward in the boat.] My astonishment was soon dispelled by Lutes (the guide) asking: 'What the devil you firing at?' 'Firing, why a deer, of course!' 'The only deer thing you will find will be paying Dunning for a dozen buckshot holes in his tent.' But, best of all, upon getting to it, I had missed again." One sport said he had seen the light of a deer's eyes plainly, and he had fired both barrels at them; but, on going to the spot the deer were "non est inventus." Later his guide said privately it was a star shining through the bushes.

Guide-boats demand respect in their handling. One sport with a companion in his guide-boat jumped up wildly for a good shot, and over went what he later called "the crank little shell," spilling out fish, rods, guns and hunters. "Wall," said Tony, their Tahawus guide, on shore, "I've seed deer hunted in all sorts of ways, but never afore hev I seed two gentlemen try to ketch one by simmin' arter him."

In 1848 the last moose shot in the Adirondacks had not yet met its demise. But moose were getting to be scarce, possibly worth more alive than dead -- but perhaps more trouble that way. That year it was reported that some lucky hunter had captured a couple of moose, and sold them to a menagerie company for a "round sum." This set all the hunters in a fury to catch a live moose. The yard of a bull was discovered, the snow was very deep, and the moose was soon brought to stand by dogs. The hunters threw slip-nooses among the moose's feet, hoping it would step into them, and that they would then be able to throw it. "They caught one foot only, when the hunter attempted to jerk the foot from under it, it made one tremendous surge at him, snapped the rope about its horns like a whip cord, knocked him heels over head, and ran off into the snow. The bruised and crippled hunter seized his gun, limped up close to the moose, and shot it dead in his rage."

Dogs bred to hunt game usually try to avoid trouble, but even the best of hunting dogs can get in a fix. In the middle of the nineteenth century "Old Sound" encountered a deer that beat him down in the snow with his forepaws, and then stood on his prostrate body. Old Sound emerged unhurt after the deer was shot.

Hunting is probably the most dangerous activity in which a guide can engage. Many a guide has given up leading hunting parties or driving deer for hunters because of the perils inexperienced hunters present. In 1859 William Moody of Tupper Lake was shot beneath the shoulder-blade by a sport named Lockwood. Moody's doctor decided to leave the bullet where it was. Guides represented a danger to themselves, too. One reporter, describing how a guide named

Dechine shot himself by removing his rifle by the muzzle from his boat and catching the hammer on one of the boat's ribs adds, "It is passing strange that men accustomed to the use of fire-arms should be so indiscreet in their handling."

In 1898 guide Ernest Coulson, of Tupper Lake, was on the road to Saranac Inn with a fellow guide, Zeke Westcott. They had been out all night looking for deer.

> "They had heard a rustle in the woods, and imagined it was a deer. Just then their attention was attracted by a sound further up the road. Before Westcott could discern the newcomers there was a crack of a rifle and Coulson fell among the bushes along the roadside, dead. Westcott said he was able to distinguish the shadowy forms of two men, who took to their heels and disappeared among the trees."

In September of 1910, a traveling salesman named Timothy Healy was shot by his guide, who mistook his brown coat for a deer; the same year, in Herkimer, Charles Dodge of Springfield, Mass., was killed just as he was about to go on a runway to watch for deer. He was shot by Sam Brakey, who was guiding the party of hunters. In the same year, of those wounded but surviving, Truman Haskell, a hotel keeper and guide in Wilmurt, had the closest call. A gun in the hands of one of the hunters in Haskell's deer hunting party was discharged, the bullet shattering Haskell's shoulder blade and lodging in his back.

Examples of deliberate shootings involving guides are rare in the Adirondacks. On November 25, 1925, Eula Davis, guide and caretaker for the Brooks hunting camp on Whitaker Lake, in Hamilton County, was getting ready to head out and visit his sister in the Town of Wells. The day before, in Speculator, Davis had let be seen a roll of bills, amounting to $144, he intended as the final payment on his sister's property. Four days later, Thanksgiving Day, Ernie Duane, who had guided boxer Gene Tunney, left Speculator on a hunting trip to Whitaker Lake. Duane came out of the woods and told the State Police he had found Davis dead in his cabin. The officers went to the cabin and found it a slaughter house -- Davis had been shot and dragged himself helplessly around before he died. He had been shot in the hip, the bullet going through his wallet; seventeen pieces of money were driven into his body. But the bills themselves were missing. Two days later Ernie Duane went in a local store, bought some articles, and paid for them with a ten dollar bill with a small round hole in it. Duane was charged with murder, convicted and sentenced to death. Governor Franklin Roosevelt commuted his sentence to life imprisonment.

In 1906, guide Dave Arnold discovered a brutal murder at the Klondike House, on the old road between Wells and Lake Pleasant. There was a trial; during Arnold's testimony he said the bathroom of the Klondike House was on the left as he entered the hotel.

"Then the bathroom was on the right when you left," the assistant district attorney affirmed.

"No, sir," replied Arnold.

"But you just said it was on the left when you went in," the district attorney protested.

"I backed out," Arnold replied.

The author L. E. Chittenden, to whom we owe so much for his reminiscences of guide Mitchell Sabattis, once got rid of two teenage boys who had joined his party -- "unmannerly cubs who would not obey their father, and passed their time when awake in howling like untamed hyenas" -- by telling their father that Sabattis, the Indian guide, "would certainly contrive to rid the camp of them by accident or design." Chittenden once had a minister in his party who promised he would not make a sound while night floating for deer. Sabattis cautioned the minister that the slightest sound would destroy all their chances, and after his repeated promises of absolute silence they took him along. At the moment they sighted a deer, the minister boomed out: "Great and wonderful are Thy works, O ---"

"Why don't you shoot his fool head off?" Sabattis asked Chittenden. "How many kinds of a fool do you suppose you are, anyway?" Chittenden asked the minister. The minister was profuse in apologies. He had not heard any sound, he was so overcome by the glories of the starlit sky that he quite forgot himself, the words escaped from his mouth involuntarily, and so forth. If they could go on he was certain he could keep quiet.

"There is no deer within two miles of Long Lake now," said Sabattis. "That sound would scare the devil. We go home -- no use for waste time tonight." Using the same scare tactic that had worked with the teenagers, Chittenden told the minister that Sabattis "was of an unforgiving nature, that he was angry and might be dangerous." Chittenden loaned the minister guide Lon Wetherby to row him through Catlin Lake to Newcomb. The minister was "much frightened and very grateful."

Guide Arch Giffin was chaperoning a tame night canoe trip with some young girls when a deer got in one of the boats. They next:

"witnessed an Adirondack drama. The deer untangled itself from the blankets and pillows and bobbed hair in a wild scramble. The boat capsized; as the quiet of Adirondack peacefulness at midnight once more settled down over the scene, those in the rear saw two young ladies dazedly seated in a boat that was completely out of sight, one of them on a nice cork cushion buoyant enough so that she seemed to be in a constant eruption, the other 'sitting pretty,' visible upward from a little above the waist line."

H. L. Ives described what happened about the turn of the century when a deer was shot and wounded in the water:

"They paddled up to him. The man who had the paddle said: 'I will hold the boat while you cut his throat.' He got out his knife and put his hand on the deer's head, and then he said: 'I can't cut this deer's throat, I never cut a deer's throat in my life.' So they turned the boat around in position for the man in the stern to do the cutting. While they were turning the boat the deer began to make another struggle and before they could get around he had succeeded in getting partly up the bank. The man could not then reach his head, and commenced to hit him over the rump with his paddle. This seemed to make the deer more active, and at last when he got his hind feet on the bank, the man made a jump out of the boat and caught him by the tail, and away they went through the briar bushes, man and deer, the man with his paddle in one hand and hold of the deer's tail with the other, and the deer making for the tall timbers...he lost his hold and, returning, looked like a bundle on the back end of a tin peddler's cart, his clothing badly battered and torn."

Ives told one tale on himself. Shooting at a deer five times from his boat, he thought he was out of bullets, but he remembered he had two more in his hip pocket, and he "rolled over in my chair on one side to get them. I do not suppose I made this move very gently, as I was getting somewhat excited, and as a result of changing my weight so suddenly to one side of the boat it turned bottom up about as spry as a trick monkey can take off his cap." Ives lost his gun, his guide nearly drowned, and he added, "While it is not a pleasant admission for me to make, I am obliged to say for the benefit of the reader that the deer escaped and we never found hair or blood."

Startled or wounded deer, angry bears and moose, and the carelessness, greed, or myopia of hunters and fishermen -- all these and more contributed to things going wrong on a guided trip in the Adirondacks. Sometimes the guide had to try to straighten out these tangles for the sport. Other times the guides were tangled, too. But by the next season the guides would probably tidy up the tales and have them ready for telling around a campfire, good stories for fresh sports.

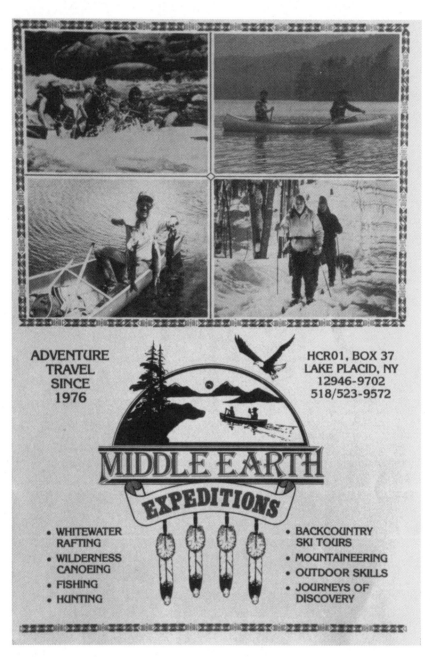

Guide Wayne Failing of Lake Placid operates Middle Earth Expeditions. Failing is one of the few Adirondack guides who works year-round.

Ann Telfer (l.) guided in the Speculator and Indian Lake areas in the mid-twentieth century. She is shown with her daughter, stretching pelts of beaver she trapped.

Francis Coburn (r.) guided from Palmer's Pond off the Blue Ridge Road near North Hudson with Ed Gereau (l.).

Guide William LeBeau, the grandfather of Saranac Lake-area historian, John Duquette, at his camp on Lower Saranac Lake.

Nineteenth-century guides at Blue Mountain Lake in 1885. L-R: Harry Graves, Ernest Carter, Ed Graves, Mitchell Sabattis, Herbert Carter, Farrand Austin, Robert Adams, and Johnnie Keller.

Photographer Seneca Ray Stoddard captured his own feet as well as a classic profile of a guide rowing a guide-boat in the late nineteenth-century. Note the overlapping oar handles for greater leverage.

The dock at the Sagamore Hotel on Long Lake held many guide-boats in this nineteenth-century Stoddard photo.

Guide Alvah Dunning, holding a grouse or "partridge," could lure a mink out of hiding by a "peculiar chipper," and bring a deer to water by bleating and making the noise of wading.

Lake Placid guides Dan Frayne, Jr. (l.), and his brother Bill (r.).

State-issued guide badges through the years. A badge for voluntary registration was first issued in 1919 (upper left), followed by button badges (lower left). The hexagonal badge (upper right) was issued from 1941 to 1962 and the current badge (lower right) came with new licensing regulations in the mid-1980's.

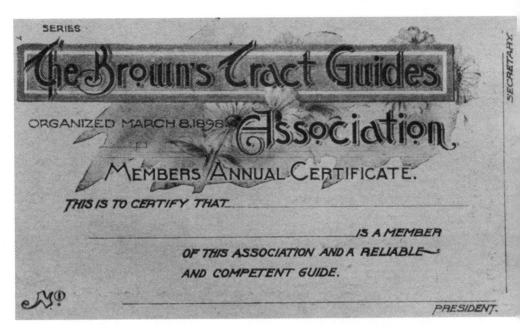

The Brown's Tract Guides Association

ORGANIZED MARCH 8, 1898

MEMBERS ANNUAL CERTIFICATE.

THIS IS TO CERTIFY THAT_____

_____ IS A MEMBER

OF THIS ASSOCIATION AND A RELIABLE

AND COMPETENT GUIDE.

PRESIDENT.

The Brown's Tract Guides' Association, 1898-1913, issued cards to members stating "Guides' wages are Four Dollars per day and their expenses."

Shown at Brandreth Lake, c. 1915, are Curtis Hall (l.), son-in-law of guide Reuben Cary, and guide Jeremiah Plumley, brother of author William Murray's guide, John Plumley.

Orson "Old Mountain" Phelps, born in 1816, is shown here at his home in Keene Valley with his wife, Lorinda.

Guide "Honest John" Plumley shown here in his later years; he died in 1900.

ORIGINAL BASS DEVIL BUG

One evening -
From a guide boat a solitary fisherman watches a dark Bug land upon the water. A wild splash of a Bass, and the Bug is gone! Many an evening the fisherman waits, until one of these strange Bugs lands in his boat - his patience rewarded!

(ACTUAL SIZE 1/0) 60¢ EA.

Out of deer hair he fashions a Bug to resemble it and thus O.C. Tuttle made the first <u>deer hair Bug</u> to be marketed. Mrs. Tuttle, saying the Bug looked like the "Devil" - suggested the Trade Name that has been world famous for over 30 years - "DEVIL BUGS".

(This lure is "tops" for <u>Pike</u> when attached to a spinner and trolled.)

No. 1 Black
2 Red & Gray
3 Yellow & Gray

No. 4 Brown & Gray
5 White & Red
6 Green & Gray

Guide Orley Tuttle of Old Forge began fashioning "Devil Bug" fishing lures from deer hair in 1919. With the help of his wife Lottie, one of the first Adirondack woman guides, Tuttle also ran the Bay View Hotel on Fourth Lake.

Reginald Whitney of Keene worked as a guide and caretaker on the Upper Ausable Lake in the Adirondack Mountain reserve from 1966 to 1976.

No. 724

STATE OF NEW YORK

GUIDE LICENSE FOR 1928

This is to certify that *Arthur Farmer*

Age 51 Weight 142 Height 5 - 7 Hair Blk Eyes Brn

residing at *St Regis Falls*, N. Y., is hereby

licensed to act as a guide in the forest preserve counties.

This license is not transferable and expires December 31, 1928.

Dated *Oct 11* 1928

CONSERVATION COMMISSION

By *Francis C. Disney*

Commissioner

No. 607

STATE OF NEW YORK

GUIDE LICENSE FOR 1929

This is to certify that *Arthur Farmer*

Age 50 Weight 145 Height 5 - 8 Hair Black Eyes Brown

residing at *St Regis Falls* N. Y., is hereby

licensed to act as a guide in the forest preserve counties.

This license is not transferable and expires December 31, 1929.

Dated *October 8* 1929

CONSERVATION DEPARTMENT

*Arthur Farmer lived and guided in the St. Regis Falls area. The
description on his guide licenses for 1928 and 1929 suggest he gained
three pounds and grew an inch in one year; perhaps he did.*

CONSERVATION DEPARTMENT

STATE OF NEW YORK

_____

APPLICATION FOR GUIDE LICENSE FOR THE YEAR 192......

_____

DIRECTIONS — Read Carefully

1. Read § 188 of the Conservation Law printed on this blank form.

2. Use great care in making out this application as the applicant is required to swear that the statements made are true.

3. The application must be sworn to before a Notary Public or other officer authorized to administer an oath.

4. The character, ability and experience of the applicant must be vouched for by at least three citizens of the United States, of full age, of good character and standing in the community where they reside, and who have been personally acquainted with the applicant for at least one year.

5. The application must be approved by an Inspector or Game Protector of the Conservation Department.

6. The application and accompanying certificates when properly filled out should be forwarded to the Conservation Department, Albany, N. Y.

7. _Two dollars must be sent with this application._

_____

To the Conservation Department:

I hereby apply for a license as a guide for the year ending December 31, 192........, and in support of this application make the following statements:

1. What is your name? _Harold N Thomas_

2. Where is your home? _Saranac Lake_ County _Essex_

3. What is your postoffice address? _"_ County _"_

4. How long have you lived in the State of New York? _23 years_

5. What is your age? _44_ Weight? _200_ Height? _5'11"_ Color of Hair? _Brown_ Color of Eyes? _Blue_

6. Where were you born? _Andover Maine_

7. Are you a citizen of the United States? _yes_

8. If you were admitted to citizenship by naturalization, when and where were you naturalized? _X_

9. What other occupation have you besides guiding? _Boating & teacher_

10. How long have you guided for fishing parties, receiving pay? _10 years_

11. How long have you guided for hunting parties, receiving pay? _" "_

12. In what counties have you guided? _Franklin & essex_

11. Can you swim? _yes_

Harold Thomas of Saranac Lake never completed this application for a guide's license in the 1920's. Only page one of four is shown.

BITS OF ADIRONDACK LIFE

Three of the best-known Adirondack guides (l. to r.): Alvah Dunning, Orson Phelps, and Mitchell Sabattis. Some of their fame came as a result of Stoddard's photography.

Many hotels furnished guides for their clientele, as advertised on this envelope from the Blue Mountain Lake House in 1880.

Students in North Country Community College's Wilderness Recreation Leadership Program, 1992.

Descending toward a peak named Elizabethtown #4 in the Dix Range above the Boquet River, students from North Country Community College.

Jacklights for hunting deer evolved from birch bark and pine knot torches to headlamps such as shown in this 1886 ad in the weekly "Forest and Stream."

Nineteenth century artist Arthur F. Tait depicted one version of jacklighting Adirondack deer in this drawing.

Meacham Lake guides with dogs used to "run" deer. Lyme Debar, extreme left, Lute Trim, extreme right, and Zeke Perkins, third from right.

Guides at Paul Smith's Hotel boathouse, probably 1880's.

Certain nineteenth-century guides had special privileges on the Upper Ausable Lake near Keene Valley, building permanent camps with covered stoves and tables such as these.

Guides organized their own associations and issued badges long before the state did.

The Ricketson guide-boat shop in Bloomingdale near Saranac Lake furnished guide-boats with all the accessories: yokes, paddles, oars and seats.

Most of the guides in this c. 1885 photo are holding lever action rifles.

This classic Stoddard photo shows the results of hounding deer. The guide is probably Pete O'Malley from the Saranac Inn; the sport in the stern, Charles Oblenis, Stoddard's brother-in-law.

"The Lazy Guide" was depicted in a spoof of William Murray's best-seller in 1869. Called "The Raquette Club," the satire appeared in Harper's New Monthly Magazine, August 1870.

Dick Emperor of Saranac Lake, a retired Game Protector, was a guide in his youth.

Clarence Petty, the son of a guide, grew up and guided in the Corey's area, between Saranac Lake and Tupper Lake.

Orley Tuttle and his wife, Lottie, guided in the Old Forge area beginning about 1912.

Members of the Adirondack Guides Association in front of Saranac Lake's newspaper, the "Adirondack Enterprise," February 1898 at the winter Pontiac Carnival.

Artist Homer Dodge Martin's wood engraving "A Carry on the Raquette River," from "Every Saturday."

In his painting, "Two Guides," Winslow Homer used as models guides Orson Phelps (r.) and Monroe Holt.

Sanford McKenzie was a watchmaker and jeweler in Lake Placid in the 1890's. He also guided, selling this picture postcard to promote his services.

PART TWO:
Biographies of Adirondack Guides

HARVEY ALFORD and his four brothers were all guides. They were the sons of Ruel and Climena Alford, who moved from Peasleeville with their family to a farm in Averyville, Town of North Elba, in 1880. At one time the Alford family owned most of the farmland in Averyville. In adulthood all the sons but Harvey had their own farms and guided on the side.

Harvey was born December 4, 1870, and lived in Lake Placid for 72 years. He worked for the John Prall family for 50 years, and was associated with Calvin and Ario Pardee as a guide and caretaker. For a short time he owned part of Whiteface Mountain, according to his obituary, selling it in 1900 to the Pardee family, who in turn sold it to the state for inclusion in the Park. A different source says he owned, instead, the property Camp Woodsmoke is now on. Harvey also was a builder and contractor, and built the camp Eagle's Eyre, subsequently becoming its caretaker. With his brothers he ran a large maple sugar works along the Averyville Road.

Harvey's guiding was not confined to the Adirondacks; some of the wealthy people he guided took him to Canada and out west. Harvey was the father of Climena Wikoff, who founded the Mirror Lake Inn in Lake Placid. According to Harvey's great-grandson, Naj Wikoff, Harvey was a market hunter: "He killed deer for restaurants in New York. At the early part of the century deer were extremely plentiful. His record, I believe, was around 160 deer in one day (each individually shot) - he killed over 7,500 in his lifetime. [Note: this would exceed the record of Elijah Simonds, called "the greatest hunter and trapper the Adirondacks ever produced," by 5,500 deer.] Back then you could find herds of deer. He would butcher them on the spot, load the carcasses on his wagon and haul them to the train (Westport, I believe) for shipping to New York." Harvey died in July, 1955, at 84. His brothers died as follows: FRANK died in June 1960, at 94; GEORGE died in August 1933, at 70; OLIE died in November 1961, at 88; RUFUS died in August 1919, at 58. Two years before his death one of his brothers shot him in his arm while hunting, resulting in amputation of the arm.

EUGENE ALLEN was born in Vermont, the son of Hiram and Clarissa Swan Allen. The Allen family came to the Adirondacks in the 1870's. The elder Allens died at Lake Placid. Their son Henry, Eugene's brother, owned the famous Grand View Hotel. Eugene lived in Lake Placid a short time and moved to Saranac Lake before

1885. He married Adeline Wells; they had three children -- Henry, Mildred, and Evelyn. There he took up guiding and lived until his death in 1936.

BYRON POND AMES was an uncle to Daniel II and William Ames (See). He was born July 28, 1858, at the Ames farmhouse in Ray Brook, and died November 12, 1913, at Lake Lila, Nehasane Park, where he was superintendent for Dr. William Seward Webb. He died "in harness," guiding Mrs. Webb. She shot a buck; Ames died from overexertion in sacking it out.

DANIEL E. AMES was born in Ray Brook, November 22, 1870, and lived in Lake Placid for approximately 34 years. In 1959, he was reported as having been born in the house then occupied by "Hike" Tyrell, the professional at the Saranac Lake Golf Club; his family later moved beyond the tracks on the Old Ray Brook Road. His father, Edward, farmed, lumbered, and did mill work, employing 10 to 15 men. Daniel Ames was a millwright and installed sawmills in the area. He had been employed as a manager of the Oseeta Dairy off Ray Brook Road; at one time he was supervisor of the Town of North Elba. In the 1893 Forest Commission report he is listed as a Ray Brook guide. He died at 88 in May, 1959.

DANIEL AMES II (see William Ames) was born November 22, 1870 in the Ames farmhouse, built in the late 1840's, in Ray Brook. He worked as a guide in his youth and entered into the lumber and sawmill business with his father at Ray Brook.

WILLIAM AMES was born July 5, 1872, in the old Ames farmhouse in Ray Brook, still standing opposite the Saranac Lake Golf Course. His parents, Daniel and Jane Ames, were the first permanent settlers of Ray Brook. Daniel made Ray Brook navigable for logs, floating the timber into the Saranac and on to Plattsburgh. William Ames guided in his youth and became a leading businessman of Ray Brook and Saranac Lake in lumbering, dairy farming and road construction. He was also president of Saranac Lake Troy Laundry, as well as a member of the Village Board. He married Agnes Mary Smith of Lake Placid; they had a son, Stanley, and a daughter Ruth. Ames and his brother Daniel (see) probably guided at the old Ray Brook House, owned and run by their uncle Duncan Camerson. Ray Brook was famous in those days for trout fishing.

EDWIN ARNOLD was the oldest child of Otis Arnold, who had moved in 1837 from a farm in Boonville to the abandoned Herreshoff Manor in what is now Thendara. Ed, born in 1829, guided with his father, sold venison and furs in Boonville and, with the rest of the family, by 1846 had created one of the first hotel businesses in the Adirondacks. In 1857, Ed and Otis killed one of the many 'last' moose in the Adirondacks; the last one killed before that was by Ed, and Sanford Sperry along the North Branch of the Moose River in 1855. (Alvah Dunning claimed to have killed one in 1862.)

Ed Arnold had an insatiable appetite for fish. A former guide declared Ed had devoured enough trout in his life "to re-stock the entire Adirondacks with mature fish." In his later years near the turn of the century, Arnold worked as a handy man at the Cohasset, on Fourth Lake. He had an 18-foot guide-boat built by Parsons and Roberts of Old Forge, into the middle of which he put an old armchair with the legs off. He fished for lake trout at buoys in water 45-60 feet deep, using foot-long wooden bobbins wound with a heavy linen line with a lead sinker and a large-ringed hook at the end. The buoys were baited with cut-up fish caught in a minnow trap baited with pancakes. For fly fishing he used a Scarlet Ibis for the tail fly, a Grizzly King in the middle, and a Brown Hackle for the dropper. Another set had a Montreal, Cowdung, and Black Gnat in the same order; a Yellow Sally was also used. In his later winters he went to Utica to stay with his sister, saying, "I'm gettin' too old to waller around in the snow." He died about 1906.

ANDREW BAKER was the owner of the house in Saranac Lake where Robert Louis Stevenson resided in 1888. The Bakers continued to live in a wing of the house while Stevenson was there.

JOHN EDWIN "NED" BALL was born in England in 1854, came to America in 1874, and married Flora Burke of Boonville in 1890. He was one of the first settlers in the Old Forge area; when he built his log cabin the only other buildings were the Forge House and the Arnold house at Thendara. He built a road to Little Moose, now on the Adirondack League Club property. Ball served 16 years as game protector, until 1915, and was the tax collector for the Town of Webb. (See Brown's Tract Guides' Association.)

SAMUEL MERRIFIELD BARTON lived in Lake Placid for almost fifty years, and was almost 80 when he died in 1923. An extensive reminiscence, and obituary, capture memories of Barton:

MEMORIES OF SAM BARTON, BY GENERAL HUGH W. ROWAN

When I first visited Lake Placid in the summer of 1901 and for several years thereafter, one of the most popular picture postcards on sale in the village was a photograph of a handsome man in late middle age with grey hair and moustache, dressed in woodman's costume with a packbasket on his back. At the bottom of the picture was the caption: "Sam Barton, Civil War Veteran and Famous Adirondack Guide."

Sam's fame must have been built up in the '80's and '90's. I don't recollect his ever being very active as a guide in my day, and even as early as the turn of this century, he was getting a bit old for the rugged work of guiding as a steady diet, especially since his physique was never more than average. He was more of an odd job specialist when I first knew him, and he delighted in helping to put on the frequent outdoor parties that were so characteristic of those old days.

Though many years older, Sam was an intimate pal of our caretaker, Orrin Fay. The two men were attracted to each other by their great love of the woods and their passion for hunting and fishing. Sam would often appear at our camp an hour before Orrin's quitting time and wait for him, and then the two of them would go off together fishing or on some other late afternoon project.

While waiting for Orrin, Sam would often tell me stories, usually about the Civil War or life in the woods. He was a born story teller with a delightful, whimsical sense of humor. His stories were always told as personal experiences and I accepted them as gospel truth at the time, but upon looking back I suspect that a certain amount of embellishment crept in from time to time.

In 1909 I killed my first and only deer. It happened to be a buck of unusually large size and so the carcass was hung from a tree back of our boat-house on exhibition for a day. Sam was the first of about a dozen visitors that day and took elaborate measurements of the entire animal.

Late in his career, about 1913, Sam was appointed either a Town Constable or a Deputy Sheriff. He attended to all the duties expected of such a law enforcement officer, but he developed a specialty as a process server. Some of the schemes he concocted to serve papers on unwilling recipients were marvels of ingenuity.

One of Sam's last public appearances was at the Lake Placid Yacht Club on Labor Day, 1916. For a number of years the Yacht Club held guide contests on Labor Day. These consisted of guide-boat races, log riding, chopping, sawing and the others. Sam was too old to enter most of the contests, but in that year he did enter the fly casting contest, the object of which was to determine who could cast a fly the longest distance. Sam's artistry with a fly rod was a beautiful thing to behold and he soon left all competitors except one way behind. Sad to relate, however, Sam, as good as he was, finished only second. The winner was Harvey Alford (father of Mrs. Climena Wikoff). Harvey's technique was no better than Sam's but it was on a par with his, and being much younger, Harvey had the extra strength of arm and snap of the wrist to bring him to victory.

But my most vivid memory of Sam concerns the great fireworks debacle at Whiteface Inn. It was around 1905 or 1906 that Whiteface Inn decided to put on a really elaborate exhibition of fireworks on the night of July 4th. The plan was to set them off from a swimming float anchored about 50 yards north of the dock and an equal distance from the shore so as to give a good view of the show from the front porch of the Inn.

Donovan, the head boatman, was in charge of the project. Sam was engaged as his assistant. Donovan conceived a faulty and dangerous plan in an endeavor to avoid frequent trips back to the dock to bring out more fireworks with consequent delays. He rowed Sam and half the entire supply of fireworks out to the float, unloaded them on to the floor of the float and covered the fireworks with a rubber blanket to protect them from sparks. Then, leaving Sam on the float, he returned to the dock, picked up the second half of the fireworks and rowed them out. He got out of the boat but left the second load in it, which was also covered with a rubber blanket, and as an added precaution, the boat was tied to the float by a rope some ten feet long so it would drift well away from harm.

The program began very pleasantly and auspiciously. After three or four fireworks had been set off, however, a mass of incandescent material fell out of the air on to the rubber blanket on the float and quickly burned a hole in it. This was unobserved by the two men until their attention was called to it by an ominous hissing noise under the blanket. As soon as he heard this, Donovan panicked, made a flying leap for the boat, came down short, landed on the gunwale and upset the boat, dumping himself and the entire second half of the fireworks into the lake. Sam, on the other hand, remained at his post. Apparently he had a greater fear of cold water than of pyrotechnics.

In a moment all Hell broke loose. Rockets zipped between Sam's legs, he was pelted on all sides by Roman candles, sprayed by pinwheels and illuminated by ghastly flares of all colors, while bombs burst loudly over his head. It was a lurid and highly impressive exhibition, although a highly condensed one, and in trying to dodge the missiles coming at him, Sam put on a dance that a teenager of the present day would have greatly admired.

In a few minutes it was all over, and except for numerous burns in this clothing, Sam was miraculously uninjured. Halsey Wood, the Inn caretaker, went out in another boat to rescue Sam and Donovan, still clinging to the upset fireworks boat. Sam got into Halsey Wood's boat in complete silence, but when safely seated he smiled and said, "Well, the troops fought noble!" He told me several days later that the Civil War was a tame affair compared to his experience on the Whiteface Inn float.

(Reprinted from "Lake Placid News," December 28, 1923)

COMMUNITY SADDENED BY PASSING OF PIONEER

Samuel Barton Was Widely Known
and Universally Loved

A VETERAN OF CIVIL WAR

Kindly Disposition and Keen Sense of Humor Made Him Friends and Admirers Everywhere -- As an Adirondack Guide He Will Be Kindly Remembered by Many Who Loved the North Woods in the Past Generation.

The passing of an old resident brings a note of sadness into the Holiday season in Lake Placid. Samuel Merrifield Barton, widely known Adirondack guide and one of the pioneers of this place, died suddenly at 4 o'clock Sunday morning, December 23, at his home on Main Street. Born at Black Brook, Clinton County, in March, 1845, Mr. Barton, familiarly known as Uncle Sam, was in this seventy-ninth year.

Saw Nineteen Battles

Mr. Barton was one of the few remaining Civil War veterans in Lake Placid. In the latter part of the year 1861, at the age of sixteen he enlisted at AuSable Forks in Company I of the 97th [Note: Should read 77th] New York State Volunteers. He was mustered in with other Adirondack volunteers at Saratoga and it is recalled that he weighed just 108 pounds in his uniform at that time. Altogether during his term of enlistment, Mr. Barton was in nineteen battles. Showing skill in marksmanship from the start, he was early detailed as a sharpshooter in which capacity he distinguished himself throughout the war. In the course of the war he was serving in a special capacity in Grant's army. His old captain, Martin Leonard, is buried near Bloomingdale.

Lived at AuSable Forks

At the expiration of his enlistment term Mr. Barton returned to AuSable Forks where he made his home for nearly twenty years. He was for a long time employed in one of the old nail mills of that place. These mills, it will be recalled, manufactured the old-fashioned "cut" nail which eventually gave place to the modern steel wire nail.

Married 52 Years

At the age of 27 Sam Barton married Miss Lucy Wood of AuSable Forks. Incidentally, the couple had been married almost 52 years at the time of Mr. Barton's death. Two sons born at AuSable Forks, Frank and Sam, Jr., died in early childhood.

40 Years in Lake Placid

It was 40 years ago that Sam Barton came to Lake Placid. The present site of Lake Placid village and the section about Mirror Lake were practically a wilderness then. It was about this same time that the Stevens brothers, George A. and John Stevens, founders of the Stevens House, located at Lake Placid. Mr. Barton was associated with the Stevens House project from its beginning, and helped in the construction of the first hotel building. For years he guided during the summer season from the hotel and during the winter months was employed by the hotel company.

Mr. Barton watched the development of this resort town from its infancy. For a number of seasons he guided from the old Mirror Lake House which stood on the west side of Main Street just south of the present Grand View property.

Popular at Sportsmen's Shows

Endowed with a keen sense of humor and a gift at narrative, Mr. Barton had made during his lifetime a wide circle of friends and acquaintances. He attended the first and second Sportsmen's Shows at Madison Square Garden in New York and also the first Boston Show as representative of the Adirondack Guides Association. It is said that Mr. Barton's quiet humor and entertaining anecdotes and reminiscences constituted one of the chief attractions at these shows.

Keen Woods Lover

A keen lover of the woods and mountains, Mr. Barton, except for his enlistment period during the Civil War, spent his entire life within view of the summit of Whiteface. He held this fine old peak in veneration and always maintained that it affords the best view of all the Adirondack peaks.

Sam Barton was a member of the local Episcopal Church and the F.M.Bull Post G.A.R. He is survived by a widow, Lucy Wood Barton, a son, Earl H. Barton, and daughter, Miss Maude M. Barton, all of Lake Placid; also a sister, Mrs. F.H. Adams of Taunton, Mass.

The funeral was held Wednesday at 2:00 P.M. from the Episcopal Church, Rev. S.T. Ruck officiating, with M.B. Clark in charge of funeral arrangements. Interment was in North Elba cemetery. Four Civil War veterans, residents of Lake Placid, James Littlejohn, John Walton, James Colby and Moses Dashnaw, were in attendance, and the local post of the American Legion sent a firing squad.

GILES BECRAFT, born in 1850, grew up on the East Branch of West Canada Creek, and guided for the Adirondack League Club at Honnedaga. He died on the Piseco Lake road of a heart attack in 1893.

CHARLES BEEDE was a resident of Keene Valley where he guided, and a nephew of Smith Beede and a son-in-law of Orson Phelps. He died April 28, 1933.

DELL BELLINGER of Forestport, guided for internationally famous wild life photographer Hobart Roberts, of Utica, for 25 years. On moonless nights they would stalk game with a camera.

FRANK BENHAM died in 1943 at 67 at Saranac Lake.

ED BENNETT, after guiding for about six years, built "Under the Hemlocks," the first modern hotel on Raquette Lake. It operated from 1880 to 1882 and was destroyed by fire. Bennett guided George Thatcher, the mayor of Albany, and once said, describing his experience while lost in a snowstorm, "I had no compass, and would not have known how to use it if I had." His brother Charles Bennett began the "Antlers" hotel in 1885. Ed Bennett went to Saranac Lake in 1887, and met Robert Louis Stevenson, who inquired about renting a cottage on Raquette Lake.

"He asked me to call again, and I did. He would always fix up a hot scotch for us. He was a very pleasant and interesting man. Instead of coming to Raquette Lake the next season, he went to the Samoa Islands and died."

In 1891, Bennett was unjustly suspected of the murder of Mrs. Josephine Barnaby, who was poisoned by a physician named Thomas Graves. Bennett spent seven weeks in Denver, Colorado, during Graves' trial. Graves was convicted in 1893, and committed suicide by taking poison.

CHARLES BIGELOW was a native of Ausable Forks and lived and guided at Paul Smiths. He was a resident of Malone at the time of his death at 76 in Ogdensburg.

ALBERT BILLINGS was born in Windsor, Vermont, in 1853, son of Alonzo Billings. With his older half-brother George, Albert came to what is now Lake Placid in the 1870's. In 1871 Benjamin Brewster built a small hotel known as Brewster's, just north of the present Mirror Lake Inn and hired Billings as a guide. In 1875 George married Benjamin Brewster's daughter Elsie, and shortly afterward Albert married Brewster's daughter Ella. As a wedding present Brewster gave Albert and Ella a piece of land he owned on the east shore of Mirror Lake, now part of the Lake Placid Club complex. The couple occupied the property for some years, building a rather large house near the lakeshore and farming on a small scale. Albert continued guiding and also worked as a carpenter.

In the late 1880's he began building Adirondack guide-boats in the winter in his boathouse on Mirror Lake. In 1897 Billings established a boathouse-marina on Lake Placid he called Billings Landing. Here he ran a boat livery, and continued building guide and other boats, as well as doing boat repairing and refinishing. He enlarged the boathouse in 1899 and 1902. After Billings died in 1903, two of his employees, Thomas H. George and C. Herman Bliss (his chief boat-builder), ran the business for Mrs. Billings for a year.

ABNER BLAKEMAN was killed at age 60 in 1925 when a tree fell on his car.

ERNIE BLANCHARD lost the record of his birth, but remembered walking to the Church of the Transfiguration in Blue Mountain Lake to be baptized in 1884, when he was four or five. Walking along the Moose River at the age of ten, he shot his first deer with a 38-55 calibre Ballard rifle. In 1894 he earned more than $2,000 trapping. Blanchard once tried to train Scottish staghounds for a Colonel Beecher, but they were accustomed to hunting by sight in the open Scottish Moors and were helpless in the dense Adirondacks. In 1919 he made almost $4,000 trapping and guiding; fisher or otter skins brought as high as $165. Guides pay had risen to $10 a day.

JESSE BOULA was born in Canada and became a guide and boat builder in the late 1850's. He died at Saranac Lake at 88.

RICHARD BRADY was born at Seeley's Bay near Lansdowne, Ontario, in May 1864, but came to the U.S. at 13 and lived near Lafargeville. He guided for over 60 years, dying in 1947 at 83.

BENJAMIN BREWSTER (see Albert Billings) probably guided the author Richard Dana, who wrote *Two Years Before the Mast*, along with a guide Dana had brought from Vermont, up Whiteface in 1849. Brewster would have been about 20 at the time.

MARTIN BREWSTER (see Albert Billings and Benjamin Brewster) was born August 29, 1865, in Lake Placid, the son of Benjamin T. and Julia Brewster. He moved from Jay to North Elba with his parents in 1841. At the age of 17, Martin purchased the Lake Placid House from his father, running it for four years (1884-88) before selling back the contract. This hotel was between Lake Placid and Mirror Lake where the old Lake Placid Inn (which burned) stood. He guided in his early years. Later he traded in real estate, and sold Tableland Farm to the Lake Placid Club. He was a village assessor for 16 years after the village was incorporated in 1900. He was also a director of the Bank of Lake Placid, President of the Sewer Commission, a Village Trustee, honorary member of the Shore Owners Association, Saseganiga Fish and Game Club and Masons from 1886. As a child he went to the Red School House, taught by Bidney Conoboy Brewster. His wife was the former Margaret O'Neill. Martin's brother EDWARD also guided. Martin Brewster died in 1953 at 87.

CHARLES BROWN, a guide, shot George A. Berkeley in 1888. Berkeley was a bartender at the Riverside Inn in Saranac Lake on Lake Flower. He refused to sell Brown any more drinks, and forcibly ejected him from the inn. Brown got a gun and waited an hour outside until Berkeley came out, shot and killed him, and fled. It was reported Brown's "whereabouts and ultimate fate were not a complete mystery to his friends."

REUBEN BROWNELL was born in Barnes Corners, New York, on April 17, 1873. At 27 he went to Nehasane Park, where he spent seven years as a guide and caretaker for Dr. William Seward Webb. In 1907, he came to Twitchell Lake and took over the operation of Skilton's Lodge, until 1944, when failing health forced him to retire. He died August 21, 1948, at 74 in Phoenix, Arizona.

WARREN BRYANT died in 1934 at 83.

JOSEPH O.A. BRYERE was born in 1859 in St. Anne de la Parade, Quebec. His father, Pierre, went out on the California gold rush and never returned. Bryere married Mary Gooley in 1884 at Ed Bennett's "Under the Hemlock's" Hotel, and lived in the boathouse of Charles Durant's Camp Fairview, where he was a caretaker. The Bryere's built Brightside on Raquette Lake, opening it to guests in 1891. Bryere, who was alleged in his youth in Canada to have wrestled a

1,200 pound moose and cut its throat, was a guide, caretaker and carpenter. Examples of rustic furniture he made are in the Adirondack Museum. He died in 1941.

FREE BURLEY was born at Cape Vincent in 1874, the youngest of fourteen. About 1902 he joined the John Robbins circus and came to North Creek as the driver of four horses, pulling the cook tent and equipment. He quit the circus at North Creek. Burley was a guide at Thirteenth Lake Lodge for a number of years, and held guide license #1, of which he was very proud. He worked at Low's Horse Shoe Pond making maple sugar, Cedar Lakes for Ed Brooks, Blue Mountain Lake for George Hall, and the North Woods Club for Robert Bibby. Someone observed of him that, "I never saw him with a hat that seemed to be large enough. They just did not seem to make them that large." After Burley stopped guiding, part of his meager income was the $16 a month he made working on the Weverton-North Creek Road. In retirement he lived as caretaker in a camp owned by Cleon Hall at North Creek. The camp and all Burley's possessions burned, injuring him and putting him in the hospital for three months. He then lived in a camp owned by Guy Alexander. Burley had taught himself to read, and enjoyed Zane Grey's *Cimmarron* and Whitman's *Leaves of Grass*. He died in 1959.

CLIFFORD BURLINGAME guided doctors and dentists in the Beaver River area, according to his daughter, Beverly Burchill, of Norwich. During hunting season he moved the whole family there, to land rented from Frank Rice of Frankfort. The children attended a one-room school; their temporary home was accessible only by train.

REUBEN CARY was born about 1844 at Long Lake, the oldest of five children. He went on his first guiding trip in 1864. He guided the artist A.F. Tait (His wife's brother was named Arthur Tait Stanton), and was also credited with inventing the open car lock, a questionable attribution at best. He worked for several seasons for the Benedicts from New York City, then William Constable of Constableville, N.Y., going with him to the Marguerite River in Canada for salmon. Cary also guided Stevenson Constable (See "Beginnings"), James Blandford, and Dr. Benjamin Brandreth. He once guided General John J. Pershing, and helped him get a buck. In 1880, Cary became gamekeeper and caretaker on the Brandreth

Park Reserve, where he worked until 1930. He hunted with a breech loading Maynard rifle. He was quoted as saying, "Arnold and Sam Dunnigan and Clark Farmer got 25 or 30 panther skins on a trip one winter down Brown's Tract -- that's how panthers came to be exterminated." Cary claimed to have trapped the last timber wolf in 1893. When Cary's teeth bothered him, he was asked why he didn't go to a dentist: "Ain't no use in doing that -- it's too near sunset." Cary died in 1933 at 89.

JOHN CHENEY is remembered today as being on the first ascent of Mt. Marcy in 1837, and guiding a succession of writers of that era and beyond who immortalized him. They included William Redfield, Ebenezer Emmons, Charles Fenno Hoffman, Charles Lanman, and Farrand Benedict. These authors helped put Cheney on every historical list of the Adirondacks' top half-dozen guides.

But when he was his most active he was known as "Cheney the hunter," at the ironworks at Tahawus, rather than Cheney the guide. As a hunter he took some short cuts that made Adirondack history.

One of the more complete biographical sketches of Cheney comes from Masten's *The Story of Adirondac*: "John Cheney (was born) in New Hampshire June 26, 1800, (and) died in Newcomb June 1, 1877...At one time he lived at Adirondac, but afterward built a house about half a mile east of the Lower Works, on the road to Schroon, where in 1849 a farm of 100 acres was given him by the proprietors."

In the winter of 1838 Cheney carried a box of fresh trout and moose meat from the iron works to owner Archibald McIntyre in Albany, who shared part of it with Governor Marcy. Some was forwarded to David Henderson in Jersey City, who had a party, including David Colden, Charles Fenno Hoffman, and Charles Ingham.

He once went to New York City. Coming out of Grand Central Station into the ordinary traffic of the day he said, "Don't you think we ought to wait for the parade to go by before crossing the street?" At the zoo he saw a giraffe and remarked it was "the tormentingest great varmit that ever he did see. But he guessed a moose would run it off its haunches."

He tired of New York City in a few hours, and before the second day of his visit was half over impatiently started for home.

"For a time Cheney and his family occupied the Company's boarding house at the Lower Works, where they kept a hotel called the Tahawus House. In October, 1874, Cheney's son, who was mentally defective, set fire to this house, and stood guard, armed with a shotgun, until it was destroyed." Tahawus was made a post office in May, 1873, with Cheney as postmaster.

Masten quotes an unidentified source as saying in his late years Cheney had an "almost whining, high-pitched voice...but one never felt that his whine was more than throat deep and that he had a quiet sense of humour no one could doubt...he had that form of rheumatism which disappears under the prospect of a good time, and to him a good time meant a tramp through the woods, setting out his dog, a rapid making for a runway to watch..."

Cheney himself said, "Even from childhood, I was so in love with the woods that I not only neglected school, but was constantly borrowing a gun, or stealing the one belonging to my father...I...was always called the black sheep of the family."

Seneca Ray Stoddard's first edition of *The Adirondacks Illustrated* in 1874 is in narrative form and includes a visit to the hotel (boarding house). Stoddard learned from Cheney's wife that Cheney lived at Ticonderoga until about age 30, "when finding that game was growing scarce, he shouldered his rifle, and calling his faithful dog, set out for the then almost unknown wilderness." Mrs. Cheney said, "If he is 73 years old, he can run in the woods now and beat most of 'em when he feels like it; if you could see him and he happens to feel all right, you could find out a good deal, but he's awful changeable, either awful good or awful bad."

Later Cheney sent Stoddard a letter, saying, "...(I) have had a great many narrow escapes from being torn to pieces by bears, panthers, wolves and moose...I had a pistol made expressly for my use. The stock was made out of a birch root, the barrel was eleven inches long and carried a half ounce ball."

The pistol rates further discussion, as, in addition to great amounts of game, Cheney managed to shoot himself with it. An outside, though doubtful, chance exists it was also the gun that accidentally killed David Henderson, one of the principles with the original iron mine at Tahawus.

In "Original Letters from a Sporting Naturalist," from the *Spirit of the Times* for November 3, 1849, it is recounted:

"The only weapon he (Cheney) has used for many years is a very plainly mounted, but no doubt accurately shooting, heavy twelve inch pistol, which carries forty bullets to the pound. On my requesting him to show it to me, he brought his favorite shooting iron from its resting place, together with its case of leather in which, strapped about his shoulders and waist, he always carries it, and which besides its great convenience, protects it from being wet. I should think the weight of the pistol was about three pounds, and though remarkably plain looking, and apparently having seen long and hard service, yet Cheney prizes it highly. On taking it back from my hands he remarked, at the same time giving it a glance of affection: 'that pistol has killed 22 moose, and how many deer I certainly could not tell you.'

I asked him how far he could shoot with certainty with it. He remarked -- 'Twelve rods, with a sure chance of bringing my game to the ground; but I have killed deer much farther. And, he continued, 'a pistol is a very bad thing to shoot with on the jump, and when I do bring down game with it on the jump, I feel as if I had done something.' He assured me he had several times succeeded in that difficult feat."

(In 1930 it was reported this pistol was in the collection kept in the State Geological rooms in the Educational Building in Albany. Mr. S.E. Stimson, of Albany, who often hunted with Cheney, had raffled it off to obtain funds for him, and it went on exhibit about 1874. It brought one hundred dollars and the pistol was presented by the winner to the collection. However, a letter of inquiry in 1955 to the New York State Museum and Science Service in Albany elicited the reply that the pistol wasn't there.)

Cheney himself related:

"I never was so badly hurt in hunting any animal as I was in chasing a buck on Cheney Lake (which was named after me by Mr. Henderson in commemoration of my escape.) I was in a canoe and had laid my pistol down by my side, when as I was pressing hard upon the animal my pistol slipped under me in some queer way and went off, sending a ball into my leg just above the ankle and which came out just below the knee. Being fourteen miles from any habitation and alone, I only stopped long enough to see what harm it had done, then seized my oars and started for the deer again as I thought I might need that deer now more than ever. I caught up with him and killed him, took him ashore, dressed and hung him up. I soon perceived that if I ever got out of the woods, I must lose no time as my boot was full of blood and my ankle began to pain me very badly. I cut two crotched sticks and by their help managed to get out of the woods in eight hours. I only stopped to sit down once, it was so hard to start again. I succeeded in walking fourteen miles to my house where I was confined to my bed from October until April. My leg got entirely well, and is now as good as ever."

Cheney had a near miss when he camped out with Dr. John McIntyre, the son of Archibald McIntyre, who owned the iron works. They heard animal screams in the night, Cheney got up to investigate, and McIntyre opened fire, just missing Cheney.

The same sang froid that enabled Cheney to continue for the deer after he accidentally shot himself occurs again and again in various accounts. Joel Headley, author of *The Adirondack; or, Life in the Woods* got a taste of it when,

> "I asked him how he felt when he saw the animal (a panther) crouching so near. 'I felt,' he said coolly, 'as if I should kill him.' I need not tell you that I felt a little foolish at the answer, and concluded not to tell him that I expected he would say that his heart suddenly stopped beating, and the woods reeled around him; for the perfect simplicity of the reply took me all aback -- yet it was rather an odd feeling to be uppermost in a man's mind just at that moment -- it was, however, perfectly characteristic of Cheney."

Cheney may have simplified the story for Headley somewhat, because in an obscure account by George Shaw of Long Lake, who knew him, Cheney admitted his hair stood on end as he grasped the situation, and that he felt the perspiration start on his face when the panther left the tree after being shot. Cheney had prepared to do battle by treading down the snow around him, cutting a club, and shooting from behind a tree. His trusty .32 calibre pistol shot true the first time, however, and the expected combat never materialized. On the same day, supposedly, he shot a moose and had to sleep for the night inside the gutted hide. He was forever starting out on hunting excursions unprepared by normal standards; his last questions to his companions were, "Got your pork? Got your matches? All right! Let's go!"

Historian Alfred Donaldson calls Cheney and a few similar others "the type that could face daily the primitive hardships and dangers of the woods, and yet survive. Surprise, agitation, fear were virtually unknown to them. They looked upon dangers and emergencies not as detached possibilities but as the woof and web of every hour...For them the unforseen was never the unexpected, and they reacted to it as normally as other men do to the commonplace."

Cheney's battle with a wolf showed how he reacted to the unforseen. Headley tells it:

> "His fight with a wolf was a still more serious affair (than that with a panther.) As he came upon the animal, ravenous with hunger, and

floundering through the snow, he raised his rifle and fired; but the wolf, making a spring just as he pulled the trigger, the ball did not hit a vital part. This enraged her still more; and she made at him furiously. He had now nothing but an empty rifle with which to defend himself, and instantly clubbing it, he laid the stock over the wolf's head. So desperately did the creature fight, that he broke the stock into fragments without disabling her. He then seized the barrel, which, making a better bludgeon, told with more effect. The bleeding and enraged animal seized the hard iron with her teeth, and endeavored to wrench it from his grasp -- but it was a matter of life and death with Cheney, and he fought savagely. But, in the meantime, the wolf, by stepping on his snow-shoes as she closed with him, threw him over. He then thought the game was up, unless he could make his dogs, which were scouring the forest around, hear him. He called loud and sharp after them, and soon one -- a young hound -- sprung into view: but no sooner did he see the condition of his master, then he turned in affright, and with his tail between his legs, fled into the woods. But, at this critical moment, the other hound burst with a shrill savage cry, and a wild bound, upon the struggling group. Sinking his teeth to the jaw bone in the wolf, he tore her fiercely from his master. Turning to grapple with this new foe, she gave Cheney opportunity to gather himself up, and fight to better advantage. At length, by a well directed blow, he crushed in the skull, which finished the work. After this he got his pistol made."

Cheney admitted to Charles Fenno Hoffman, regarding the wolf fight, that "I ought, by rights, to have waited for my dogs." As for the young hound that fled, Cheney said, "Had I one shot left I would have given it to that dog instead of dispatching the wolf with it."

Another time Cheney clubbed a bear with his pistol, but the bear knocked it away. Once again one of Cheney's dogs came to the rescue and distracted the bear. As far back as Redfield's visit in 1836 one sees references to Cheney's dogs. "August 19. (We) made with John Cheney, our huntsman, the circuit of Lake Colden, having in (our) course beaten up the quarters of a family of panthers, to the great discomfiture of Cheney's valorous dog." Cheney said,

"You may not believe it, but I have seen a good many men who were not half as sensible as that very dog (Buck.) Buck is now four years old, and though he's helped me to kill several hundred deer, he never lost one for me yet...Buck is of great use to me, when I am off hunting, in more ways than one. If I happen to be lost in a snow storm, which is sometimes the case, I only have to tell him to go home, and if I follow his tracks I am sure to come out in safety;

and when sleeping in the woods at night, I never have any other pillow than Buck's body."

Cheney's penchant for taking on big game in close quarters continued on into his old age. Cheney's wife wrote a letter on July 16, 1875, that was published in "*Forest and Stream*" on August 5, of that year:

"Dear Friend W--: Pa got his old bear trap fixed, set it, and caught a large bear. He went up to the pond fishing and thought we would look at the trap, and there was Mr. Bear. He happened to have the hatchet, so he cut a club and struck him on the head, and when he struck the bear struck too, tearing his shirt just below the stomach, taking a chunk nearly out with his paw, at the same time taking hold of his wrist and chewing it pretty badly. He got hurt in several places -- taught him a lesson in his old age -- but he went at him again and made him lie still. He had a small jacknife with him, so he sawed away on his neck with it until he thought he had surely killed him, and then left him in the trap. When David got up there he was still alive and quite active, and he had to kill him over again. Pa had a pretty bad leg and arm, but they are getting well now.
I think this is doing right smart for an old man, and my only regret is that I was not there to have a finger in the pie."

Cheney's "life list" of killed animals is impressive (however, by comparison, see Elijah Simonds' elsewhere): six hundred deer, four hundred sable, nineteen moose, twenty-eight bears, six wolves, seven wildcats, thirty otter, one panther, and one beaver.

Many of the deer were destined for market, thus they represented not sport, but a livelihood. Of the sole beaver, Cheney says, "He was the last, from all that I can learn that was ever taken in the State." Beaver have since been successfully reintroduced, and the extirpated species of moose and "wild cats" or lynx, are also being reintroduced in recent times.

After dispatching such a quantity of game, Cheney had derived a personal hunting and conservation ethic. The jacklighting vs. hounding vs. still-hunting for deer controversy raged in the nineteenth century -- the first two were outlawed in 1897 -- and Cheney was resolute in his convictions. He saw jacklighting or calling a deer by "bleating at her" as wrong, but viewed hounding as "natural," involving a chase and a sporting chance. (It was a still-hunter that eventually shot Cheney's dog that had been in the wolf fight.)

Although he hunted deer for subsistence and market, their beauty was apparent to him: "There isn't a creature in this whole wilderness that I think so much of as a deer. They are so beautiful, with their bright eyes, graceful necks, and sinewy legs...I wish I could get my living without killing this beautiful animal! -- But I must live, and I suppose they were made to die. The cry of the deer, when in the agonies of death, is the awfulest sound I ever heard..."

He made a similar clear-cut choice between "withes and tails" -- that is, the practice of lassoing a swimming deer from a boat versus grabbing it by the tail. "Well, if I know'd I could never tail another, an' I have thousands, the cretur might go free afore I'd be the man to drown him with a withe! Withing only does for those that don't know how to tail a deer."

Cheney faced each day in the woods with his pistol, his axe, and his dog. Perhaps from such simplicity can come humility before nature. Here is Cheney's description of the view from Mt. Marcy:

"It makes a man feel what it is to have all creation under his feet. There are woods there which it would take a lifetime to hunt over, mountains that seem shouldering each other to boost the one whereon you stand, up and away Heaven knows where. Thousands of little lakes are let in among them so light and clean. Old Champlain, though fifty miles away, glistens below you like a strip of white birch when slicked up by the moon on a frosty night, and the Green Mountains beyond it fade and fade away until they disappear as gradually as a cold scent when the dew rises."

Cheney's name is perpetuated by two ponds and a mountain near Lake Sanford.

HERB CLARK was born near Keeseville, N.Y., July 10, 1870. In 1896 he began work at the club on Bartlett's Carry, between Upper and Middle Saranac Lakes. He worked as a night watchman for two years, then for five summers rowed the freight boat to Ampersand Bay and back daily, once carrying a load of 2,200 pounds, and another time rowed 65 miles in one day, 24 of those miles in the freight boat. For three years he worked only as a guide.

In 1906, Clark began to work for the Marshall family on Lower Saranac Lake. Possessed of a fine sense of humor, he once told some greenhorns from Schenectady who were camped on an island in Middle Saranac (Round) that the woods were full of panthers, wild boars, rugarues, and snakes -- but none of these could swim, so the campers were safe. For the Marshall boys he made up the grandest fables, recounted by Bob Marshall: a rock on Lower Saranac with a peculiar dent was where Captain Kidd had bumped his head, the Ausable River below where the Olympic ski jump is now was where the Monitor and Merrimac had fought -- an old lady who came limping along as he told this tale was used as circumstantial evidence, for her shinbone had been taken off by a stray shell at the time of the conflict. Great heroes in his tales included Sliny Slot, a sort of reverse Paul Bunyan, who did everything poorer than you could imagine it could be done; Jacob Whistletricker, a man with many marvelous drugs; Joe McGinnis, who got the fantod, a disease in which one shrinks to the size of a baseball; Susie Soothingsyrup, a gay young lass of many virtues, and the grandfather pickerel with gold teeth and spectacles.

Clark coined the name 'cripplebrush' for the mountain balsam which can be so confining and frustrating on a mountain bushwhack. For years Clark's catch of an 18 1/2 pound pickerel was a local record over a six-year period. Beginning in 1918, Clark climbed the 46 Adirondack peaks over 4,000 feet with George and Bob Marshall. In 1921 only 12 of those peaks had trails to their summits. Bob Marshall wrote: "At the age of 51 he (Clark) was the fastest man I have ever known in the pathless woods. Furthermore, he could take one glance at a mountain from some distant point, then not be able to see anything 200 feet from where he was walking for several hours, and emerge on the summit by what would almost always be the fastest and easiest route."

FRANCIS N. COBURN was born in Ellenburg, N.Y., March 4, 1907. One of 12 children, he was "farmed out" to older brothers and sisters when his father died. While at the home of his sister Agnes and her husband, Frank helped farm from the age of seven. At 25 he married Beulah Bessey, and they farmed in Ellenburg. Coburn hunted with "Old Betsy," a gun he used for 50 years. (His daughter Maybelle, one of Coburn's five children, reports she hates venison to this day because she ate so much of it as a child.)

At 33 Coburn went to work as a miner at the National Lead Co. in Tahawus, N.Y. He had acquired the nicknames "Frank Buck," "Black and Tan," and "Shine," and began guiding regularly. He moved to Mineville in 1945, working for Republic Steel. With the help of his family he built a hunting camp on Palmer's Pond on the Blue Ridge Road near North Hudson, where he spent time with his family and friend Ed Gereau. At "Camp Bear Paw" Beulah cooked and cleaned for 20 men during hunting season. Coburn's system for finding lost hunters -- which on at least one occasion included his sons Ephrim, Bernard, and Lloyd, who sang "The Bear Went Over the Mountain" to bolster their spirits -- was for Coburn to shoot three times, after which the lost party was to follow the first river they came to downstream to a bridge, and stay put until help arrived.

Coburn was superstitious, always spitting on his fishing worm and saying "water go luck" before casting. One of his clients, Jay Janassee, gave Coburn his first spinning reel, and brought candy and gifts regularly for the children. Coburn claimed to have seen a deer that turned its head in a complete circle as it watched him. Talking on the phone after shooting an illegal deer he said, to avoid detection, "We got a d-o-e," spelling out the word.

One summer while on strike from the mines, Coburn worked as a blacksmith and stagecoach driver at Frontier Town. One of his son-in-laws held up the stage, and stole the dentures out of Coburn's mouth, returning them on the next trip. Caught on an ice flow once in a break-up on Lake Champlain, Coburn dashed to safety. "You must have really been running," a friend said later. "Hell no," Coburn replied, "but I passed a lot them that were!"

Coburn raised as many as 300 pigs at once, and became known as the Pig Doctor, performing such tasks as neutering and administering shots. He told his daughter Rita she was a P.D.D. -- a pig doctor's daughter.

When Coburn retired from the mines he went into gardening in a serious way, driving over 20,000 miles a year selling vegetables from a Coke-a-Cola cooler.

Coburn died April 12, 1990; his grandson BERNARD COBURN guides in the Blue Ridge Road area. (Information supplied by Maybelle Coburn Gregory and Rita Coburn Mitchell.)

EDISON CORBIN lived in Paul Smiths and died in Malone at 73.

JIM COUGHLIN guided in 1919 for both Harry L. Severance, a copper king who owned Deerwood near Saranac Inn, and the Rosenbaum Camp, Pine Brook; he earned about $4 a day. He served as police chief of Saranac Lake from 1933 to 1944.

CHRIS CRANDALL lost a leg in a hunting accident, but continued to guide in the Meacham Lake area. He lived in Jenning's Clearing on the Santa Clara Road about 1875, across from his estranged wife. He committed suicide by pulling the trigger of a rifle with a toe from his remaining leg.

JIM "BROCKIE" DALTON lived in Boonville and guided at the Adirondack League Club, as well as for Thomas R. Proctor of Utica. He died in Rome, N.Y. at 86 in 1945.

HENRY DAVIS guided out of Saranac Lake from 1885 to 1920, when he died. In 1885, with his brother Frank, Davis moved with his wife and four children to Saranac Lake after being injured in a dynamite accident at Lyon Mountain. Davis and his family stayed briefly at the home of a guide named Stephen Martin, then soon moved to Ampersand Bay on Lower Saranac Lake. Here Davis began to guide for the patrons of the Ampersand Hotel, and then gained a regular clientele, including David Stevenson, a New York City brewery owner. Together they hunted moose and caribou in Canada and fished for sea bass and marlin off the coast of California.

In the early 1900's Davis bought a camp on leased state land on Long Pond, now in the St. Regis Canoe Area. The camp, a tent colony, was nearly lost in the great fire of 1903. In 1911, Davis built a large canvas-covered log framework as a main building. It's location was known as Pine Point, next to Mineral Springs Bay, from which leads the carry to Nellie and Bessie Ponds. In 1914 this building had to be torn down and rebuilt to conform to new state regulations. To get materials a little closer to camp from the Floodwood Railroad Station, Davis devised a hand car he used illegally on the tracks.

Guide-boat builder Theodore Hanmer built Davis a boat about 14 feet long, weighing only about 45 pounds, named "Hattie." (A photocopy of a newspaper clipping from a 1970 *Adirondack Enterprise* has written on it, "The boat was named for Peacock's wife who was an old terror -- Margaret Davis.") Peacock had a camp in the narrow end of the Kettle Hole on Long Pond, according to Saranac Lake's Maurice Otis. It was later taken over by Henry's son FRANK, a guide and rural mailman in Saranac Lake who once guided Mark Twain. Son Nelson Davis, also a mail carrier, and son Al maintained the camp until 1975. With the little boat Davis could easily visit the many small ponds in the area. Davis died May 9, 1920, from peritonitis after ignoring a ruptured appendix, and is buried in Pine Ridge Cemetery in Saranac Lake.

GEORGE DeBAR guided in the Meacham Lake area. He claimed to have shot 400 deer, including a 24-pointer. He died at 86 on November 27, 1940.

ARCHIE DELMARSH went into the woods in 1891, and guided at Cedar Island in the middle of Fourth Lake. He ran the lodge there from 1902 to 1914. Once he rowed with guides Fred Kirch and Johnny Rarick to Saranac Lake, then turned around and rowed back to Old Forge. They had left at 3 a.m., and got back to Old Forge by 11 p.m., stopping twice to eat.

SAM DUNAKIN left school in New Jersey in 1849 and went to the former Herreshoff Manor in Thendara to live with the Arnold family. In 1862, he enlisted with the 220th New York Volunteers, serving three years as a sharpshooter. In 1872 he built a camp on the north shore of Fourth Lake by the outlet of Carry Pond. When Dr. William Seward Webb later bought the property (among much more), Dunakin was thought to be a squatter, but claimed he had been given a deed by the prior owner, Dr. Thomas Durant. Dunakin said that the deed was not only unrecorded, but had burned up when his camp burned. Webb declined to pursue the matter; the next owner, William Thistlewaite, gave Dunakin life tenancy.

In his later years Dunakin drank too much and became anti-social. He submerged one edge of his dock under water; when he rowed home he slid his guide-boat onto the dock and rolled out. Before his death in 1907 he was pictured on souvenir postcards as "Sam, the oldest guide on the Fulton Chain." When he died his material possessions consisted of a boat and fishing rod.

ALVAH DUNNING was one of the six most famous Adirondack guides of the last half of the nineteenth century. He stands out as the best combination hunter-naturalist, and the one who cared least for the civilized world. (The other famous guides were Orson Phelps, Mitchell Sabattis, John Cheney, John Plumley, and William Nye.)

Ed Bennett, a guide who built "Under the Hemlocks," the first modern hotel on Raquette Lake, said of Dunning, "He cared nothing for news of the outside world. A newspaper a year old was just as good to him as one a day old. He could not tell you who was governor of the state or who was president. But he did know how to hunt and trap."

Dunning wouldn't accept checks, and once turned down a $100 check from a prominent banker for ten otter skins until it was replaced with cash.

He believed the earth was flat, exclaiming, "What would become of the fellows on the other side of the ball? They would stand on their heads, and then would drop off."

The Bible was an additional source of perplexity. Once reading the Bible he was overheard to say "That's a damn lie. It says here the Lord opened the flood gates of Heaven and it rained down 40 days and 40 nights and drowned the earth to the tops of the highest mountains. Why, I've seen it rain here for 40 days and 40 nights and it never raised Raquette Lake more than a foot."

But he invoked the Bible and the Deluge when it came to the hydraulics of lakes, saying "each lake had an inlet and an outlet, but the ocean had only inlets; but it must have an outlet, otherwise the world would have seen a second deluge like Noah's." If you disagreed with him on matters such as this you fell into disfavor; agree, and you were friends.

But if he didn't understand some of the grander mechanics of the world, he certainly knew the day-to-day skills needed for survival. He could, by a peculiar chipper, call a mink from its hiding place in the rocks and shoot it, and bring a deer back into the water by bleating and making the noise of wading.

In a shooting match with Caleb Chase of Newcomb they agreed to shoot at a carpet tack in a plank forty yards away, each to have five shots. They each grouped their first four shots around the tack, then Dunning buried it with his fifth. Dunning, who was over sixty at the time, used a rifle made by C. Steward, of Painted Post, Pennsylvania.

At one time he had a three-barreled muzzle loader with two 16-gauge shot barrels on top, and a rifle barrel underneath. "She do throw buckshot wicked," he said.

He learned to throw buckshot and ball early. He shot his first moose right in the ear when he was twelve, leaving no mark his father could find at first. "This moose ain't been shot -- it's just been scared to death," his father said.

Once when Alvah wanted a cow moose to come out of the water where she was standing before he shot her, he deliberately shot her in the nostrils for provocation. After eleven shots between the eyes and nostrils she hadn't budged, so he killed her in the water and hauled her out.

Dunning was born at Lake Pleasant, Hamilton County, in 1816 (the same year Phelps and Nye were born.) His father, according to Donaldson's *History*, was "Scout" Dunning, a veteran who served under Sir William Johnson. This military service would have been in or soon after the French and Indian Wars about 1755, as Johnson died in 1774; thus, the senior Dunning would have been pushing eighty at the time of Alvah's birth. Perhaps an in-between generation has been left out of the historical record. But Dunning's father -- whoever and whenever he was -- turned to hunting and trapping, teaching his son the skills. Alvah lived in the Lake Pleasant and Piseco Lake area until be beat his young wife severely after an act of infidelity on her part, when he left to escape the law.

He moved first to Blue Mountain Lake, where he feuded with the writer Ned Buntline. In 1859 Buntline threatened to shoot Dunning -- he was probably as good a shot as Dunning -- and the tale, which is probably apocryphal, still circulates that Buntline shot Dunning's dog as it sat between Dunning's legs.

In 1865, Dunning moved to Raquette Lake for more privacy, where for years he was the only year-round resident. Here he lived alone as a hermit, although he began guiding in the summers. One of his early clients was William H.H. Murray, author of *Adventures in the Wilderness*. This book, which came out in 1869, is credited with starting one of the greatest tourist rushes the Adirondacks have ever seen. Generally Dunning was disgusted with the class of tourist that had begun to come to the Adirondacks, but he admired Murray. Of the rest Dunning said, "They pay me well enough, but I'd rather they stayed out of my woods. They come, and I might as well guide them as anybody, but I'd rather they stay to home and keep their money. I don't need it. I can get along without them. They're mostly darned fools, anyhow."

Dunning lived first on Indian Point, then moved in 1869 to the open camp (which he enclosed) on Osprey Island, which Murray had used for three summers.

After that burned in 1875 he rebuilt with a rough shanty -- described as "crude and unlovely" -- but his squatter's rights, such as they were, were bought off for $100 about 1880 by Dr. Thomas C. Durant, who actually owned the island and wanted to sell it to his nephew Charles Durant. Mrs. Thomas Durant had invited Alvah over for a cup of tea at Camp Pine Knot and charmed him into cooperation. As Dunning said, "Alvah can be coaxed, but he can't be druv."

Another time he was coaxed involved baking powder, which was invented about 1850. He had always used Royal Baking Powder and was asked why, since he was a Democrat -- at least in theory -- he didn't support the then-president, Democrat Grover Cleveland, whom he had guided. Dunning couldn't refute the logic of it, and switched to Cleveland Baking Powder. There was no connection between the President and the baking powder company. However, Dunning must have thought his allegiance conferred special privileges, as he wrote to Cleveland saying, "Some time ago Ike Kenwell asked me to catch you some lake trout. I done so. He offered to pay me but I did not take any pay. Just now I am out of baking powder and if you would send me some I would be very much obliged to you. A. Dunning." The President sent two cases of Cleveland Baking Powder. In addition to Cleveland, Dunning guided William West Durant, Collis Huntington and J. Pierpont Morgan.

Dr. Arpad Gerster, a summer visitor, said of Dunning,

> "He was the only guide I ever met that refused to be paid at the end of the engagement, because, 'he had not earned the money.' We had camped at Eighth Lake and had missed three deer through the stupidity of the other two guides. They took their pay, all right; Alvah declined it. I saw him in his 70th year carry a boat across to Eighth Lake, a distance of one and a half miles, with two rests only, and found him on one occasion at dawn on the beach of his lake, fast asleep, curled up like a woodchuck, dusted all over with snow which was falling."

Gerster was an artist of some talent. After Dunning lost his inexpensive but beloved pocket watch overboard, Gerster made a copper etching from the well-known Stoddard photo of Dunning. The photo captures the piercing gaze that earned Dunning the name Hawk-eye, as well as his aquiline nose and wrinkled, weatherbeaten face. Gerster sold proofs to the summer visitors on Raquette Lake. With the proceeds another watch -- this one gold -- was bought.

Dunning brought his myopic logic to bear on matters of game as well as gravity. Later in life he lamented the disappearance of the moose, saying, "What caused the moose to all leave in one season, right after the Civil War, is a mystery I never could solve. They were thick thirty years ago. I killed eight big ones in five days. My father, myself, and two others killed 100 moose one winter." Dunning claimed to have killed the last moose in 1862; conflicting claims abound. However, as Donaldson says, "To be told that Alvah did not kill the last moose, is like being told that St. George did not kill the last dragon."

He also claimed to have killed the last panther in the vicinity, and claimed or had attributed to him the killing of the unlikely total of 102 panthers in eight years.

Dunning paid little attention to game laws, and told Fred Mather, author of *My Angling Friends*, that in the old days nobody cared if a poor man wanted a little meat and killed it, but now the laws meant, "They're a-savin' it until the dudes get time to come up here an' kill it, an' some of 'em leave a deer to rot in the woods, an' on'y take the horns ef it's a buck, or the tail ef it's a doe, just so's they can brag about it when they go home, an' they'd put me in jail ef I killed a deer when I needed meat. I dunno what we're a-comin' to in this free country."

The concept of "mountain mutton," or out-of-season venison, applied to Dunning, and Mather was once offered some in the summer by the Adirondack canoeist and writer of the late nineteenth century, George Washington Sears, or "Nessmuk." Mather shrewdly guessed that "the mutton is probably from Farmer Dunning's flock; he has many heads roaming these hills."

> "Well, yes," said the old man (Nessmuk). "I met Alvah yesterday and he gave me quite a bit of a fore-quarter; in fact, all I would take, for he said he had more then he could keep fresh and was glad to find some one who wanted it and could keep his mouth shut. What made you think of Alvah Dunning?"
>
> "Merely this: I took dinner with the old man yesterday and he had a bit of 'mountain mutton' and I know, and so do all the other men in this region, that old Alvah lives in these woods the year round and believes that he has a right to kill a deer to supply his needs. I would not partake of venison out of season at any table in the woods except that of Alvah Dunning, and I would enter a complaint against any other man who had venison in June, if I knew it. But the old trapper does not kill for sport and firmly believes that these woods belong to him by virtue of a residence in them of over half a century."
>
> "That's my opinion," replied Nessmuk. "He will never exterminate the deer by taking an odd one out of season, and the people here know it, but the law cannot make a distinction between him and the so-called sportsman, who would come into the woods and kill 100 deer, to brag of, and leave them to rot."

Dunning was bitter about the stocking of black bass, saying Seth Green, head of the State Fish Commission, had done more to harm the woods than any man. Dunning remembered pulling 96 pounds of salmon trout out of Piseco Lake in 1833 in two hours, and also once catching one weighing 27 1/2 pounds.

After a lifetime in the woods Dunning could evidently judge the weight of fish. He once had some in a packbasket when, meeting a party who wanted fish he sold them some he estimated at eight pounds weight. "Ain't that a leetle hefty, Alvey?" asked one of the guides. "Maybe," he said, adding a fish.

He built a hunting and fishing cabin on Eighth Lake, in the Fulton Chain. Then, hounded by a sense of too many people there, he moved near the entrance to Brown's Tract Inlet. As fate would have it, this site was wanted for a station for the Raquette Lake Railroad, and he was bought off once again. The thought of tooting steamboats and screeching engines was too much, and at age 83 he headed west, to the Rockies. Donaldson was not overstating when he said, "Here was a rude king of the woods leaving his inherited domain -- a *Lear* of the forest being driven out into the night."

But within a year he was back, this time on Golden Beach, near the South Inlet of Raquette Lake. Near the end of his life he was cared for, more or less, by Charles Bennett, hotel keeper of The Antlers, on Raquette Lake, and J.H. Higby, of Big Moose Lake. Dunning began to leave the woods in the winters and spend them with friends and relatives, particularly a sister in Syracuse.

Donaldson's *History* picks up the tale:

"In March, 1902, he attended the Sportsmen's Show in New York. On his way home he stopped at Utica and put up for the night at the Dudley House -- a hotel where illuminating gas was still in use. The following morning he was found asphyxiated in bed -- the gas jet had been leaking all night. That the occurrence was an accident there seems no good reason to doubt. His death took place on March 10th, and the papers all over the country published lengthy obituaries of "The Last of the Great Adirondack Guides."

Dunning was described by Jack Sheppard, an outstanding guide in his own right, in these words:

"He was an honest and hospitable man of the old style, all of whom looked on game laws as infringements on the rights of men who live in the woods. He was the last of a type that is passed. He killed deer when he needed it, caught a trout out of season to bait his trap, firmly believed it a sin to kill wastefully, and destroyed less game than many who cried out against him."

An obituary writer at the *New York Sun*, perhaps looking out a grimy city window at the first faint hints of spring, waxed eloquent but true when he wrote:

"Dunning was a type of a fast vanishing class of men. They are to be found only in a new country and they disappear with the advance of civilization and modern development.

They are the men of the woods, the hunters and trappers, simple, hardy folk, who find contentment in the solitude of the forest. They are as tough as pine knots, with muscles like whipcords and of tremendous endurance. They can swing an axe mightily and know how to make a comfortable camp in the forest. Dunning was a pioneer of this class."

LYMAN EPPS, SR. guided in the High Peaks in the 1850's and 1860's. He cut the first trail into Indian Pass from the site where the present Uihlein potato farm is located. He was born in Colchester, Connecticut, on December 29, 1815, and was the founder of the North Elba library and the Baptist Church. Contrary to reports elsewhere, he was not an escaped slave; his father was a full-blooded Indian and his mother, Candice, part black. Epps married a free black woman, and was given land by the abolitionist Gerrit Smith for the North Elba colony of blacks. His last name is spelled, variously, Epps or Eppes; "Epps" is on his tombstone. He died in 1897 at 81.

LUTE EVANS was once guiding a nervous man who was worried about leaving something behind. In camp they had made a "bean hole" of coals to put the bean pot in. "This is said to be the best way to cook beans ever invented," said the man. Going to the new camp Lute said, "I did forget something!" "What?" the man asked in terror. "The bean hole!" said Evans.

ARTHUR FARMER guided in the St. Regis Falls area. He was born in Burke, or possibly Canada, in 1881. He worked four years as a teamster and watchman at William Rockefeller Park. In 1921 Farmer was fined ten dollars for "knowingly receiving and possessing the meat of a wild female deer without horns." His daughter Alice Freeman, age 77 in 1991, says there are two versions of the reason for the violation. The first is that the Game Protectors talked him into making 200 pounds of jerked venison and he shot a doe to do it. The second is that Farmer's hunting party wanted jerked venison, and paid the fine when he got caught. Farmer also worked as a chauffeur for the state, made maple syrup, and worked for the Brooklyn Cooperage saw mill. An undated newspaper clipping reports Farmer guided a party of 13 hunters who killed 13 deer in 12 days of hunting north of St. Regis Falls, including shooting five deer in one day. In 1944 Farmer was fined ten dollars for guiding without a license. He died in 1965.

JOHN FLEURY guided on Lake Champlain out of Westport, according to his daughter, Mrs. Lawrence, who was 73 in 1991. In the 1930's, he would row to Claire's Island in a Hayes boat, trolling from Westport Inn. He would row all day during the Depression for $25; later he used an outboard motor boat. The Inn would furnish his box lunches, including chicken salad and a pear, but Fleury would take potatoes, salt pork and frying pans: "He would catch pike, bass, and pickerel -- they're good if you get a big one. He'd land and cook these. The people said the hell with the box lunch." Mrs. Lawrence said her brother Roy Fleury was the youngest guide in the family, at fourteen. She herself likes to fish for perch in winter, and once caught one "so big he looked like Reverend Moon in the hole."

DANIEL J. FRAYNE (see interviews with his sons Daniel and William) lived in Lake Placid for 46 years, where he guided. He was born in Trench Park, Rosecommon, Ireland, on January 25, 1885, and died in 1956 at 71.

HARRY E. FREEMAN was born in Worcester, Massachusetts, September 30, 1860, the son of Mary Snow Freeman and Perez M. Freeman. He moved to Saranac Lake with his family as a child, and later to Coreys after his marriage to Lillian Duckett, in 1887. He guided Fritz Kreisler, the concert violinist, and Teddy Roosevelt. Most of his guiding was hunting and fishing; he also trapped. Freeman died November 30, 1950.

ROSS C. FREEMAN was born July 9, 1898, the son of Harry E. Freeman (see) and Lillian A. Duckett Freeman. (Lillian was the daughter of John Duckett and Nancy Graham, of Coreys.) Ross Freeman began hunting at an early age to supply meat to logging camps in this area, and trapped as well. He ran a lodge and cottages on the Indian Carry in Coreys, and guided for lake and speckled trout, and deer. Among his clients was the Remington of typewriter fame. He built Raquette River Lodge on Upper Saranac Lake. He died in February of 1980.

DUANE FULLER (1830-1903) was a native of Blue Mountain Lake. Fuller once shot a panther at night by aiming at the gleam of its eye. General Hiram Duryea, who had made over a million dollars in starch, bought the skin and had it mounted crouched on a limb. Fuller was also a boat builder, and lived almost opposite the present site of the Adirondack Museum. He is pictured and chronicled briefly in *Adirondack Portraits* (1986) by Noel-Reidinger-Johnson. (This book -- well-laden with Adirondack history -- is about the Adirondak-born poet Jeanne Robert Foster; Fuller was Foster's great-uncle.)

ROBERT GALLAGHER was a native of England who guided at Paul Smiths and at a camp on St. Regis Lake. He lived at Paul Smiths for 13 years and died at 44.

JOHN GALUSHA was a logger, guide, forest ranger or warden -- Vanderwhacker Mountain was one of his posts -- and farmer. He guided at the Tahawus Club, at the site of the Upper Works of the McIntyre Iron Co. One of his sayings recorded there was "colder than a step-mother's welcome." Galusha was born in Johnsburg in 1859 and lived most of his life in the Thurman and Minerva areas. Galusha had two brothers who served in the Civil War. One, Stillman, died at twenty from wounds and another saw 13 battles and was never wounded. Galusha said, "I knew a rebel colonel -- I guided him fishing. Every time I looked at him I thought of my brother lying on his bed, groaning...and I wanted to kill him. I didn't like him, but he was an all right fellow." The author Carl Carmer included Galusha in his book on the Hudson River.

One of the most surprising things about Galusha -- known as "Yankee John" and the "Adirondack Eagle" -- is that he was a folk musician of almost unparalled equal, especially for remembering lyrics of obscure songs. He knew dozens and dozens of folk songs dating back to the Revolution and before, some of which he'd heard only once or twice in childhood. Folklorist Marjorie Lansing Porter and musicologists Anne and Frank Warner interviewed and taped Galusha extensively, believing him "probably the most important single informant in the entire Northeast." It is almost as though there were two John Galusha's; I have found no mention of his music in the few accounts of him as a guide. He died in 1950.

ART GATES lived for fifty years on Durant Road in Blue Mountain Lake. He worked as a guide, "mostly hunting, because you could get away if you didn't like the company." He also worked as a carpenter and caretaker of the Hall Kirkham estate at Blue Mountain Lake. Gates died in 1989.

ARCHIE GIFFIN guided in the Stillwater area. (See "Sometimes Things Go Wrong.") In the fall of 1927 the artist Norman Rockwell signed The Guest Book (an ordinary notebook) in the North Branch Camp of the Stillwater Club with a rough pencil sketch of Archie. The club originated in the late 1880's in Clare, St. Lawrence County. During the early 1920's Giffin was a part-time guide, his eldest son Herb being a club warden and guide. In the late '20's Herb died and Archie took his place. After Archie's death, in 1956 at age 80, his son Kenneth replaced him.

JIM GOODWIN and his achievements are perhaps matched only by his modesty. In response to a request for biographical material he sent the following profile, written in the third person, but included a letter, almost a disclaimer, saying he felt he was "blowing my horn too loud, and not a real 'native,' having always been a citizen of Hartford or West Hartford, Conneticut." But he added, "Our family did, however, live year-round at times in Keene Valley and we witnessed among other 1920 activities the major lumbering operations riding down from the jobs on lumber sleds, etc., and we did attend a one room school house. I can claim to be 'part native.'"

Jim Goodwin was more a follower in the Adirondack tradition of Old Mountain Phelps than of the guides who specialized in leading hunting and fishing parties. Though at times he led successful fishing trips, his greatest love was mountain climbing. He has the distinction of having guided his first person up Mount Marcy at the age of 12 in 1922. His family spent summers in a cottage at Interbrook Lodge in Keene Valley where at an early age, Jim accompanied his parents and other guests up mountain trails which in those days were not serviced by the state with signs and markers because most of the land in the High Peaks area belonged to clubs or lumber companies. Hikers unfamiliar with the area needed leadership and when Melvin Luck, the lodge proprietor, was asked by new guests for trail information, he would suggest that they take Jim Goodman along as a guide. Starting with lesser walks and climbs, Jim was asked in 1922 to lead a school headmaster up Marcy on a day climb. He accepted the assignment, charging him $2.00 for the service, thus establishing himself as a professional guide. He was a registered guide for 30 years.

There were then no lean-tos in the Johns Brook valley and climbers use the natural rock lean-to, Slant Rock, at the foot of the mountain for over-night stays if they didn't relish the 20 mile day trip from Keene Valley. Jim slept his first party at Slant Rock in 1923 and continued to use it as a base for some years. He soon popularized a two or three day round trip for his patrons with climbs of Marcy and Skylight and a return through Panther Gorge which prior to the 1950 hurricane contained an open forest of large red spruce trees and with its cliffs and waterfalls off Marcy resembled a miniature Yosemite Valley.

In his college years, Jim confined his guiding largely to leading young people, sometimes as a camp counselor and at other times as a companion to children of families summering in Keene Valley. This involved leading his charges up most of the High Peaks as well as to out-of-the-way trout waters like the beaver ponds of Railroad Notch and the stillwaters of the Bouquet River's upper North Fork.

During this period, Jim came to know John Case, a veteran alpinist who taught him skills that allowed him soon - as a volunteer - to be leading his friends on ascents such as the cliffs of Wallface and the Marcy side of Panther Gorge. This interest led in later years to his organizing and heading two ADK rock climbing schools. He also became engaged in winter mountaineering including skiing ascents of Marcy as well as snow and ice climbs such as that of the Mount Colden trap dike and the now popular Bob's Knob, the face of Round Mountain south of Chapel Pond.

Starting a career of teaching in a private day school in West Hartford, Connecticut, Jim was free to spend parts of his summers in the Canadian Rockies where he learned climbing techniques from the Swiss guides brought there by the Canadian Pacific Railway. This enabled him to lead his students and friends on Alpine climbs in that region. With this background, he was able during World War II to win an assignment as a mountaineering instructor in the 10th Mountain Division before serving as a combat medic in Italy.

Though experienced in climbing in the higher ranges, Jim's great love has always been the Adirondacks. Following World War II, he and his wife, Jane, ran a boys' summer camp for a number of years followed by a summer program of climbing and canoe trips for young people living or spending summers in the Keene Valley-St. Huberts area. The most popular feature of this program which was joined by a number of adults involved his patrons climbing 4000 foot peaks and becoming Forty-Sixers. In the process of leading these groups, he made more than 30 trips over the Seward and Santanoni Ranges, wrote the ADK guide book description of trail-less climbing routes, and for a number of years maintained the registers on the trail-less summits.

During the late 1960's and 70's, Jim became involved for five seasons with leading inner city boys from Hartford in a two-week program of camping and climbing following their six-weeks of summer schooling at the school where he taught. On a flat area beside Johns Brook below the Goodwin cottage, 30 black and Puerto Rican boys camped in wall tents and were led on day and backpacking trips over mountains by their mostly white counselors, seniors from Jim's school. These counselors were trained for their assignments during a session the previous spring.

For most of his life, Jim has been involved with trail construction and maintenance. In his early teens, he cut the Mount Porter Trail from near the Garden Parking lot, later improved by the ATIS, and as a professional in 1951 constructed the Brothers-Big Slide trail followed by the Range Trail connector over Hedgehog, the Giant Ridge Trail and the Weld Trail up Gothics from the Lower Ausable Lake. During five years of his retirement he headed as a volunteer the trail maintenance progrma of the Forty Sixers and also maintained and supervised the trail system of the ATIS which he served as president for ten years.

All in all, his career as a professional as well as an amateur guide covered a period of 70 years and he hasn't quite finished yet. In 1992, he still managed to climb his beloved Mount Marcy.

DWIGHT GRANT built guide-boats in Boonville. He served in the Civil War and was captured by General Beauregard. He also worked as head guide for General Sherman and the North Woods Walton Club in the 1870's and he was a member of the New York State Assembly. He was hired as lodge manager at Little Moose on the Adirondack League Club property in 1897, and became Club Superintendent three years later. Grant is credited with being the main founder of the Brown's Tract Guides' Association (see.) His son LEWIS GRANT guided at the Adirondack League Club, and succeeded his father as Superintendent in 1906. Lewis was a bookkeeper at the club when the message came that informed Vice President Roosevelt that President McKinley had been shot. In 1916 he left the Adirondack League Club and went to Boonville to manage his father's guide-boat business. He died at age 82, on September 27, 1960, in Utica.

ALBERT LYMAN GRAVES, a.k.a. CLIFTON enlisted in the Civil War as a drummer boy, according to his grandson, Clifton West, of Hague. He was captured by the Rebels and served time in the Libby Prison in Richmond, Virginia. A hundred men, including Graves, tunnelled out beneath a road and escaped. He returned to his regiment, bought a new uniform, and went into battle again, where he was slightly wounded. When his lieutenant asked to buy his uniform, Graves handed it over, but the officer refused to pay for it. Graves 'beat him up' and went AWOL. He walked to Guilford, Vermont, swimming the Connecticut River and arriving at the home of his sister, Jane Gale, at night. To avoid authorities he was put in a wagon covered with hay and taken near Bennington, Vermont, where he changed his name to Clifton, the name of a friend in the service. He then went to Shoreham, and began guiding on Lake Champlain and fishing commercially. There he married Augusta Severance, and at one time operated the Larrab Point Ferry.

Early in the 1870's the family moved to Hague, where Clifton worked as a guide on Lake George and opened a hotel called the Island Harbor House in 1883. Clifton died in 1903 while sitting in a chair at the Trout House Hotel.

IRA GRAY guided for six years, beginning in 1910, at the Lake House, Harrisburg, N.Y. He once traced a client who left owing him money to Albany, and confronted him in his store, recovering the money -- to the delight of the clerks. Gray was born October 18, 1886, and lived to be well over 90. He lived most of his life in the Sacandaga Reservoir area. He wrote at least two small books, including *Follow My Moccasin Tracks* (1975), and *My Memories/1886 - 1 to 9 - 1977* (n.d.), each containing full and detailed accounts of his rural outdoor life.

FRANK GREY was known as the "guide recluse" of the Adirondacks; he guided for President Teddy Roosevelt. He was born August 4, 1878, and died February 12, 1909.

ELMER GRIMSHAW was born in Churubusco in 1861, and began living in Keene when he was 19. Grimshaw made two trips that were described in newspaper articles, one trip to Albany about 1913, and one to New York City about 1915. While in Albany he was quoted as saying, "he didn't see a fox or a deer...not a thing worth trailing down." In Albany he "blazed" his way around with chalk in various colors on the sides of buildings. On his trip to New York City he took marten, raccoon, and fox furs and sold them to furriers on West 42nd Street, but said that city was too big for a chalk trail. He saw quantities of money in the Sub-Treasury Building on Wall Street which could "fill every bog-hole in the mountain roads of Essex county," and wondered why the Brooklyn Bridge didn't sag and bust. He bought a hound in Philadelphia, with hopes of 'siccing' it on a fox in the Zoological Gardens to see if it had a good nose, but was dissuaded. He died in 1933 at Keene.

LeGRAND HALE was a lifelong resident of Keene. He was the son of guide DAVID HALE. It was said that with Horace Braman, LeGrande Hale had killed more deer by still hunting than any other two men in Essex County. LeGrande, a "protege" of guide Max Tredo, died at 75.

ASA B. HALL was born January 15, 1882, and died October 14, 1963. After the Civil War, his parents moved to Long Lake, where he remained a lifelong resident. Hall was caretaker of the Morton B. Havens camp on Long Lake, and a retired member of the fire department and member of the Mount Sabattis Lodge 1015, of the Masons of Long Lake.

FITZ GREENE HALLOCK guided the famous tuberculosis physician Dr. Edward Livingston Trudeau, of Saranac Lake. Starting about 1877, Hallock hunted with Trudeau, who was a crack shot. (An old guide named Hose Colbath arranged a shooting contest among "Adirondack" Murray, Mace Colburn, and Trudeau, a dark horse who won.) Near the end of Trudeau's life Hallock carried him in a specially constructed chair to the deer runways on Dr. Webb's preserve Nehasane; Hallock later became superintendent of the preserve. Hallock guided at Paul Smiths, and at Little Rapids, where he guided E.H. Harriman, a railroad magnate, and Dr. Walter James, a New York physician.

Hallock was born in Illinois, about 1835, but after the death of his mother moved to Peru, N.Y., with his six brothers and sisters. (A distant nephew, Richard W. Hallock, of Wilton, Conn., is married to a first cousin of this book's author.) Hallock, the first president of the Adirondack Guides Association in 1891, died in 1919.

HENRY HANMER was born in Black Brook and came to Lake Placid when he was five. His parents were Thomas and Elizabeth Hanmer. Henry Hanmer worked as a guide, boat builder, violin maker, and carpenter. He died at 73 in 1939, and was survived by his wife Bessie.

LES HATHAWAY still (1992) enjoys a legendary status in Saranac Lake, even though a typical comment applied to him is "you couldn't believe a word he said." Gill Slater, who owns Hathaway's .38-.40

carbine, an 1894 model, said, "He was inclined to hit the bottle and celebrate. He had a camp at the foot of MacKenzie Mountain up the Moose flow from the Saranac River -- when he was in his early nineties he killed a deer, tied it up behind Stack's hardware, he reached over to hold a horn up to show the Carson boys, and keeled right over dead." When Saranac Lake was written up by William Chapman White in the August 25, 1951, issue of "The Saturday Evening Post," Hathaway was described as "one of the old guides, a man who still gets his deer each season even if he is far beyond eighty," and quoted as saying, "The diff'rence between wet cold and dry cold is that the dry cold freezes you stiff without you feelin' it, while wet cold ain't so obligin'."

MELVIN HATHAWAY was a Keene Valley guide who guided on the Ausable Lakes. When that area became part of the Adirondack Mountain Reserve in 1887, new hunting and fishing regulations were instituted that Hathaway did not adhere to, and he was evicted. He became a squatter along Johns Brook Valley for 18 years, where the present Johns Brook Lodge of the Adirondack Mountain Club is located. Beginning in 1923, the Club began planning to develop their site for the Lodge. In 1925, however, the Club reported that,

> "At this time, the difficulty over making suitable arrangements with Melvin Hathaway, an old woodsman who had previously occupied the site, became apparent...it was determined the proper thing to do was build a cabin for Mr. Hathaway on the Club land at a suitable site...(he objected)...to the removal of his personal property from his old camp which had to be torn down to permit erection of the Lodge...because of his [Hathaway's] objections to plans to which he had agreed heretofore, Mr. Luck, the contractor, was reluctant to go ahead with the work. Therefore, on August 6, Mr. Myers of the Committee met Mr. Luck and Mr. Hathaway and made an arrangement with Mr. Hathaway to which the latter agreed, whereby he (Hathaway) relinquished any claim on the tract and agreed to move out."

Russell Carson, author of *Peaks and People of the Adirondacks* (1927), provided sympathetic description of Hathaway in a letter of 1952 in the files of the Adirondack Museum at Blue Mountain:

> "Mel Hathaway was a squatter on a plot of ground that was on the site where JBL (Johns Brook Lodge) was built. He had a vegetable garden he claimed to be the highest cultivated garden in the State of

New York...his garden was always very late. Our party was very friendly with Mel and he frequently gave us vegetables such as lettuce, radishes, onions, etc. We spent many an evening visiting with him in his shack and listening to his wild tales. I remember he stuck to it that wolves and panthers were still in the Adirondacks and their calls could be heard at night in the Johns Brook Valley. ...I think the ADK gave him a small sum to quit his place peacefully, even though he had no title to it. Bill Howard, Arthur Hopkins, Mrs. Meyers, and John P. Myers (Pres., Plattsburgh National Bank and Trust Co.) went up the brook and negotiated with him regarding moving out."

He died in 1932 at 84.

CHAUNCEY HATHORNE -- According to Ruth Timm, in *Raquette Lake*, Hathorne came to Blue Mountain Lake for the first time in 1855, and Eagle Lake in 1856 and 1857. He moved to Raquette Lake in 1877, on Golden Beach, and built "Chauncey Hathorne's Summer Camp," charging guests a dollar a day. The next year he built "Hathorne's Forest Cottages," which he ran until his death in 1891. A contemporary, Frank Carlin, described Hathorne, who suffered from tuberculosis, as well educated, but later a heavy drinker and recluse. "His only contact was his housekeeper, Elmira Rose."

On November 10, 1891, Hathorne was found between Echo Camp and Big Island dead in his guide-boat, one leg hooked inside. He may have had a heart attack; he is buried at Blue Mountain Lake.

More information on Hathorne is in Hochschild's *Township 34*. Hathorne was probably more of an innkeeper than a guide.

ARTHUR W. HAYES, the son of guide Ellsworth D. Hayes, was born in Black Brook and moved to Lake Placid as a small boy. He was a member of the village board and a charter member of the Lake Placid Skating Association. He was a contractor and builder and built many of the camps on Lake Placid. At the time of his death it was reported:

"When the Stevens House was first constructed Mr. Hayes helped mix the plaster that made the walls of that building, which was torn down only a few years ago. The hotel was one of the last landmarks of the old stagecoach days. When only a young man, Mr. Hayes worked as a bellboy at the Stevens House, one of his jobs being the filling of the lamps each morning in the lobby. Mr. Hayes first went to Florida in 1925 and stayed at St. Petersburg, but the winters following were at Orlando where his sister, Mrs. Edward

Brewster, had lived since 1917. For the past several years he has spent the entire year in Orlando. His wife died in December of 1947."

Hayes died at 79 in May of 1950.

CHARLIE HAYES lived most of his life at Saranac Lake. He was a contemporary of Mart Moody, and remembered obscure guides such as John Solomon, who camped on Third Pond in the Fulton Chain, Dan Bartlett, Peter Solomon, Charles Grenno, Rant and Reub Reynolds, and the not-so-obscure Tom Peacock (See). When Hayes came to Saranac Lake, the D&H railroad was being built, and horse-drawn coaches from Port Kent and Ausable Forks ran regularly, driven by Edson Harper, and McMannis and Fitch O'Brien. Horses were stabled at Tuff LaTour's livery. The first deer Hayes ever shot, when he was eleven, was a fawn that dressed exactly 28 pounds. Hayes once killed a swimming deer with a guide-boat neck yoke, but never killed a bear. He said, "I followed one two days and it was farther away than ever and I said t' hell with 'em."

ELLSWORTH D. HAYES came to Lake Placid in 1857 when he was nine. He learned woodsman's skills from his grandfather, Hiram A. Preston, who had come to the Adirondacks from England. Hayes had his first gun in 1860 when he was 12 years old, and in 1866 became a guide. According to his obituary, "He saw the disappearance of much of the game and he attributed it to man's disregard of the law of the woods that was laid down to him by his grandfather: 'Never kill anything that you do not need.'

Commenting on game conditions of long ago, Mr. Hayes recently said that the last moose was seen in 1860 at Mud Lake. Wolves disappeared at about the same time, and he believed that both went across the frozen St. Lawrence River to Canada. In 1875, there were great flocks of wild pigeons in this area, but Mr. Hayes said he had not seen one in 30 years. 'Wild life and society do not mix,' he declared. 'The Adirondacks are not much more than a flower garden to the old timers now. Everything is being done to entice visitors and more visitors. Now one can go over concrete roads in six hours, a trip that used to take three days in an Adirondack guide-boat.'" One of his sons was ARTHUR W. HAYES, also a guide. After the death of his wife he made his home with one of his children in Sayville, Long Island, later going to Syracuse, where he died at 88 in 1936.

ROSS HAYES, when he was eleven, sold muskrat skins at 25 cents each. He once had on a black rubber coat and saw what he thought was a hunter, so he jumped up so as not to be shot, and with a "whoosh" a bear ran away. He shot it, and recovered it the next day; it weighed 400 pounds. Hayes was a lumberman, and said he saw only one man killed in that work, and that was by lightning when they were sluicing logs through a small canal. He worked 15 years for the Rockefellers at Bay Pond near Paul Smiths, and guided Governor Lehman.

THOMAS T. HEALY worked as a guide for Virgil Bartlett in 1858. Bartlett ran a hotel, built in 1854, between Upper and Middle Saranac Lakes. During the Civil War Healy enlisted in the 16th Heavy Artillery.

BERT HINDS worked for Joseph Hinds and E.N. Kaplan, making a winter ascent of Marcy. By 1911, he had climbed Marcy 85 times.

FRANK HOLT was a trapper, butcher, taxidermist, and guide in the Keene Valley region. He built the Macintosh, Merle-Smith, and Taylor camps on Johns Brook.

HARVEY HOLT was born March 4, 1808, in the Keene Valley area, son of early settler Smith Holt, from Springfield, Vermont. While in his twenties, Harvey went to work for the McIntyre Mine at Tahawus. McIntyre recommended Holt to the manager, Andrew Porteous, in a letter that said Holt "is a very steady man through the year, yet in the winter, if a favorable season occurs, he always take a Moose Hunt. Overlook that, however." Holt was on the first ascent of Mt. Marcy, in 1837. He bought two farms in 1835, married in 1839, and bought two more farms in 1843, working all four farms. He attempted an iron business on the Ausable River, but a flood in 1856 washed it away. He died January 14, 1893.

MONROE HOLT was a contemporary of Orson Phelps in Keene Valley. The *Essex County Republican* for March 27, 1873 (when Holt was about twenty-six years old), reported that the year before Holt shot and wounded a swimming deer, which then upset his boat, and Holt "came up on the opposite side from the deer, (and) found instead of Monroe hunting for the deer, (the) deer was hunting Monroe."

After a terrific battle on land as well as in the water, Holt killed the deer with a clasp knife. The account continues:

> "What about rifle and boat? It will be remembered we left the boat capsized. Monroe swam about five or six rods for the boat, dove under water for his gun. Then how to get the deer into the boat was the question. He could not lift him, to do his best. After trying various experiments he finally settled on the plan of towing both out in deep water and filling the boat, and shoving it under the deer and then bailing out the water with his hat. It was said to be the largest and fattest deer ever killed in these parts."

FRED HOOD guided in the Saranac Lake area in the 1940's. In 1993, he was remembered by Jay Vandenburgh, Jr., for his humor. When Hood was out in a boat with a guided party that included a woman and he needed to go to the bathroom he would announce, "I lost a canoe on this island, I heard it was here, and I'm going to look for it." His women clients learned to ask, "Did you lose a canoe?" when they had the need for a bathroom.

When the fish were biting and his clients were still playing Canasta, Hood would say, "Don't be afraid to hurry!"

ED ISHAM guided 1905-1907 with Pete Lamb at the Ausable Lakes. In 1905 with Lamb, Ed Phelps, and Charlie Beede, he helped cut the Range Trail. He also cut a trail up Ore Bed Brook to connect with the Range Trail. Two brothers, Fred and George Godley, were regular clients.

WILL ISHAM started guiding in 1900 with Frank Holt (although Isham reportedly didn't come to Keene Valley until 1905), charging $3.00 a day and board. He reported that women hikers, once they were in the woods, took off their skirts and hiked in their bloomers. He dug the grave for Orson Phelps.

GEORGE JENKINS was a Raquette Lake guide circa 1900. A memorial poem in the Adirondack Museum library says, "In the pools where the trout always lie will his presence renew and so long as they do, the spirit of George will not die."

FORDINAND JENNSEN was a native of Denmark whose guiding career began in the 1850's. He lived as a recluse for over 50 years in the Tupper Lake area, and died at 87.

ERNEST H. JOHNSON, a grandson of Saranac Lake pioneer settler Jacob Moody, was popular as a singer, violin player and story teller. Johnson worked for Dr. Alfred L. Loomis, Little Tupper Lake, and then Johnson guided William C. Whitney, of the 97,000 acre Whitney estate at Sabattis, between Tupper Lake and Long Lake. From this association he became superintendent of that preserve for 40 years, at the time of his death working for Harry Payne Whitney. Johnson maintained a home in Utica where his children were educated, and managed the Metropolitan Hotel with his sons. Under Governor Hughes' administration, he was assistant superintendent of the State Foresters. Johnson's son, Ernest Johnson, Jr., died three months before his father in a drowning accident on Raquette Lake. When Johnson, Sr., died it was noted he "had been receiving treatment for a mental breakdown," possibly related to his son's death. Johnson was born in Saranac Lake, and died in Utica in December, 1919.

JAMES KELLY was born in Boston in 1852, and guided in the Lake Placid area. He was caretaker for 33 years for the camp of Edward Bartlett, later purchased by C.W. McCutchen. He often made hunting trips alone; thus, in 1922 he was not missed for two weeks when he left the end of Averyville Road alone for Moose Pond and the camp of Harvey Alford. His body was found about a mile beyond the end of the road. He had been shot once through the heart. Earlier, when he was still alive, passers-by had seen him cleaning his rifle at the spot. The exact circumstances of his death remain unknown.

EDWIN W. KENNEDY was, at the time of his death, reported

"born in Wilmington on December 25, 1847, the son of James and Eliza Parrish Kennedy. For a number of years he worked in Lake Placid before making it his permanent home. In 1870, his parents moved here and occupied the Parkhurst Farm near the Ware bridge. This property is now owned by the Lake Placid Club. Mr. Kennedy was a carpenter by trade; he was also an expert guide whose services were in constant demand. Later he became outside manager for the Lake Placid Club and remained in that position for several years.

His first business venture was a partnership with the late George Chellis under the firm name of Kennedy and Chellis, contractors and builders. Upon the death of Mr. Chellis, Mr. Kennedy took over the business. Many of the fine cottages and camps in and around Lake Placid are a credit to his excellent workmanship and ability as a designer. Later he engaged in the hardware business. He retired from active participation in the business of Edwin Kennedy & Sons in 1915, but always maintained a watchful interest in the affairs of the firm, and was always ready to give the active partners the benefit of his advice and experience. Mr. Kennedy was an ardent Democrat and maintained a constant and active interest in politics. He served as justice of the peace for a number of years before the village of Lake Placid was incorporated. On December 25, 1877, he married Emma R. Summers of Keene. Following their marriage, Mr. and Mrs. Kennedy lived at what was known as Seven Gables at the Lake Placid Club where all their children were born. When the young couple first occupied the house, what is now the extensive Club property was largely given over to farming."

He died on January 17, 1926, at 78 in Orlando, Florida, where he spent the last three winters of his life.

MELVIN KENNEDY was born in Wilmington, N.Y. in 1854, the son of James and Eliza Parrish Kennedy. The family came to Lake Placid in 1870 and lived on the old Parkhurst farm near the current location of the Olympic ski jumps. Melvin became a carpenter and guide, eventually moving to Indianapolis, Indiana.

MILES KENNEDY was born in Wilmington, N.Y. in 1853, the son of Alec and Jane Kennedy. There is no indication that he was related to Melvin and Edwin. In the 1880's he came to Lake Placid, where he worked as a carpenter and guide. He married Jennie Lawrence of Upper Jay; they had two daughters, Mrs. Frank Grisdale and Miss Mildred Kennedy. He died at Lake Placid in 1934.

GERALD KENWELL was born at Indian Lake on February 3, 1887. He lived most of his life in the Sixth Lake area or at his camp on the South Branch of the Moose, 12 miles south of Sixth Lake. His father, WELLINGTON KENWELL, who died in 1942 at 84, also guided. The elder Kenwell ran the Raquette Lake House at Tioga Point. It was the first hotel at Raquette Lake and was built by Isaac Kenwell, Gerald's uncle. Wellington established a hunting camp on Moose River in 1891, which he sold in 1901 to Lt. Governor Timothy Woodruff, and purchased the Wood Hotel on Fourth Lake from Fred Hess, a pioneer builder and woodsman of the Inlet area. It was at the Wood Hotel that Gerald first met Alvah Dunning (see).

Gerald said, "I once heard some hunters ask my dad what was the most horrible sound he had ever heard in the forest, the cry of a panther, or the howl of a wolf? 'Neither,' my father replied, 'The worst sound I ever heard is the cup scraping the bottom of the flour barrel. That means I have to go 55 miles over that damn road to North Creek to get more flour.'"

Gerald guided his first party in the Moose River area in 1896 at nine years of age. In the party were C.T. Chapin, president of American Car Wheel Works of Rochester, Mert Lewis, attorney general of New York State, and George Aldrick, the political head of the Republican Party in Rochester. In 1898 and 1899, with his father, he guided Governor Frank Black.

NOAH LaCASSE was born in Canada in 1864, and came to the Adirondacks at eighteen. He guided for 38 years. He was also fire warden in charge of the Cornell Hill fire tower at Saratoga Lake. LaCasse is most remembered for guiding Vice President Teddy Roosevelt at the time President McKinley was assassinated. Roosevelt had reached the Tahawus Club near Newcomb on September 11, 1901. Recounted LaCasse: "The next day he wanted to take the trail to Lake Colden and asked me to guide him. We set out early and camped at Lake Colden. In the morning Roosevelt wanted to climb Marcy." Roosevelt wanted to try carrying a packbasket, and carried LaCasse's up Marcy. They had left a party at Lake Tear, climbed Marcy, and returned to Lake Tear for lunch. A guide named Hall ran up with a message about McKinley's turn for the worse. "Complicated, complicated, complicated," Roosevelt said. They set out immediately for the Tahawus Club. From there Roosevelt set out on a wild horse-drawn ride to North Creek and the railroad. Later Roosevelt gave LaCasse a frying pan into which a clock had been constructed.

JAMES LaMONT was born in Jefferson County, near Watertown, in 1850. At age eight he left home after a dispute with his father and lived with neighbors named Hardy. At thirteen he tried to enlist in the Union Army during the Civil War, but was refused. He worked 22 years off and on at the Graves mill in Watertown and 2 years at a mill in San Francisco. With a man named Henry Miller he spent some winters deer hunting and selling venison in Harrisville and Natural Bridge. In 1892 he married Ella Gordon, of Lowville. In 1884 LaMont took over a hunting camp on Smith's Lake built by Chris Wagner and Bord Edwards, and made it into a hotel. Four tons of provisions and a cow were packed or floated there. The charge for boarders was $7 per week. In the winters his wife (Ella Gordon) and children stayed in her hometown of Lowville while LaMont remained to work on the hotel. "Many a night I have camped out in the snow, rather than go back to that lonesome house by myself," he said. LaMont ran the hotel 15 years, but felt the charm was lost when the Mohawk and Malone Railroad was built nearby. His small tract was then surrounded by land owned by Dr. W. Seward Webb. About 1909 LaMont operated a hotel at Brantingham Lake, then later at Onekio, below Thendara. He then became a resident of Old Forge and worked 19 years as a caretaker for the Dr. Herman M. Briggs estate at the Little Moose Club. He died in 1934.

CASSIUS LAMOY was born in Wilmington and came to Lake Placid about 1894. He worked as a carpenter and guide, and built a house on the Wilmington road. In 1944 the house was called the Crowley cottage. For the last seventeen years of his life he lived with his daughter Mrs. Rudolph Hanna of Elizabethtown. He died at 86 in June 1944.

JOSEPH B. LAMOY was a lifelong resident of Essex County and a guide in the Saranac Lake area for over 50 years. He fought in the Civil War in Company C, 118th Infantry. He was born in Moriah, and lived briefly in Wilmington. He died at 83.

MARSHALL LAMOY was born in 1847, parents and birthplace unknown. He was a Civil War veteran, serving in Co. E and in the 96th Infantry of the Adirondack Regiment. He came to Lake Placid in the late 1870's and built a large house on Main Street in 1880, which he and his wife operated as a boarding house for summer people. Lamoy guided people on the side. The building, much enlarged, is now the oldest on Main Street and is occupied by The Warehouse. He died July 1, 1921. He had one son, Harold, and two daughters, Effie and Frances.

ORRIN LANPHEAR was born in 1889 at Lake George and moved to Raquette Lake in 1911. "Ott" worked as a carpenter and guide, employed by Dr. Evans on Tioga Point. Lanphear died in 1964.

BEECHER LaPRARIE was descended from the LaPrarie's from LaPrarie, Quebec, who settled at North River. He guided for many years at Blue Mountain Lake, and with his father at Tirrell Pond. He was one of the last firemen on the steamboat "Tuscarora" on Blue Mountain Lake and others on Raquette Lake. In the winters of 1913 and 1914 he carried the mail on snowshoes from Blue Mountain Lake to Raquette Lake. He died at 66.

WILLIAM LeBEAU lived in Saranac Lake. He was born in 1865 in Black Brook and died at 79 in 1945.

FRANK LUCAS lived at Hopkinton and Joe Indian Lake, and guided from the 1850's for about fifty years. With his wife he operated a hotel on Joe Indian Lake. He died at 87.

CHARLES MARTIN lived in Lake Placid for more than 56 years, where he guided. He was born in Bloomingdale on December 2, 1869, and was 78 when he died in 1948.

DOUGLAS MARTIN guided in the Paul Smiths and St. Regis Lakes areas. He was born in Franklin Falls and died at 80, having suffered a severe shoulder injury shortly before his death. He was guide and caretaker for Mrs. Godfrey, of New York City. Martin's sister was the wife of Paul Smith.

HENRY MARTIN died at 75. He had been the superintendent of the Japanese camp of Frederick Vanderbilt on Upper St. Regis Lake. At a gathering of the Union League Club in New York City one sportsman boasted he knew an Adirondack guide -- Martin -- who could ride a log across the East River. Martin took a log to New York City intending to perform the feat, but the ride never took place, the sportsmen agreeing he could have done it. Martin may have been Teddy Roosevelt's first guide when Roosevelt was a lad. Martin was a brother of Mrs. Paul Smith.

FRED "MOSSIE" MAXAM was born in 1856 in Bakers Mills. Maxam, a mason, guided at Raquette Lake for Morgan at Camp Uncas, and at Kill Kare for Lt. Governor Woodruff (who Henry Tyler refused to guide, because he didn't like him.) Married a second time at 66 in 1920, Maxam fathered a son, and twin girls, Molly and Kate, whom he called "Kate and Duplicate." Maxam died in 1930.

ALBERT McKENZIE guided for Dr. Edward Livingston Trudeau in the 1870's in Saranac Lake. McKenzie later went West and bought a ranch where he contracted tic douloureux, a nervous affliction so severe that sufferers often commit suicide. Trudeau arranged for McKenzie to come East and asked the famous Johns Hopkins Hospital surgeon Dr. Harvey Cushing to operate on McKenzie, which he did for free. McKenzie was cured and returned to Colorado.

SANFORD P. McKENZIE was born in Keene, N.Y., in 1845 to Mordecai and Mary McKenzie. The McKenzies were a pioneer family in Keene and Keene Valley. Sanford had a watchmaker and jewelry store at Keene in the 1880's, and then moved his business to Lake Placid, probably in the 1890's, where he guided on the side. In his old age he moved to Vermont and is probably buried there. An anonymous article in the *Elizabethtown Post* for July 5, 1906, insinuates the weight of a bear McKenzie trapped might have been exaggerated because only the head and skin were in evidence:

> "Sanford P. McKenzie, veteran soldier and tinkerer of watches...recently appeared in the village of Lake Placid with the head and skin of a 700 lb. black bear which he had caught in a trap near Cold Brook...notwithstanding that the bear was hitched to a heavy clog the bear went a long way, about two miles.

'UNCLE BILL' McLAUGHLIN died at Tupper Lake at age 95, around the year 1905. He guided Grover Cleveland.

JOHN McLAUGHLIN guided at Paul Smith's Hotel from 1858-1887.

JONATHAN MEEKER guided, as well as owned and operated the first steamboat on the Fulton Chain in the late 1800's, according to his great-granddaughter Shirley Daily, of Rome, N.Y. The steamboat, called the "Hunter," carried mail and passengers. Meeker and his daughter often had to hide from inebriated Indians when traveling from Boonville to Fourth Lake on mules.

LOYAL A. MERRILL, along with Robert Scott Blinn, guided the author Alfred Street up Mt. Marcy and through Indian Pass (Street wrote *The Indian Pass* in 1868). JACOB WOOD, Blinn's nephew, was also a guide.

REUBEN MICK was born in 1878 in the Town of Denmark, Lewis County. He was a caretaker at the Hasbrouck Camp on Raquette Lake for 50 years, outliving the family of owners; the camp went into the Forest Preserve. He was a Justice of the Peace and an election inspector. In 1958, at age 80, Mick said he was still a guide -- "for men who can't go too far or walk too fast." Mick died at 99 in 1977.

MOODY -- JACOB, HARVEY, SMITH, CORTEZ, DANIEL, MARTIN, ETC. The Moody clan included numerous guides. Jacob S. Moody was the progenitor; he was born in 1787 in Unity, New Hampshire, and moved to Saranac Lake in 1819. He had nine, and possibly ten, children, including six sons, five of whom -- Harvey, Smith, Cortez, Daniel, and Martin -- became well-known hunters, trappers, and guides. Some of their sons were also guides, such as Harvey's sons Phineas and William. The Moodys are often mentioned in Adirondack literature. Harvey, Cortez, and Martin received the bulk of the veneration; Smith and Daniel (who was also a blacksmith) were quiet and not flamboyant story tellers like the others. According to Daniel's grandson Alfred Moody, Daniel did not drink and frowned on smoking, and "in fact had a habit of breaking pipes he saw lying about so they could no longer be used."

Phineas, son of Harvey, enlisted in the Civil War as a substitute for his brother Alonzo in 1863, and died in the same year, apparently from illness, in New York City. Harvey's son William also served in the Civil War for three years, in the 96th Regiment. Daniel's sons Cleveland and Alaric were also guides. Jacob Moody's daughter Eliza was the mother of ERNEST H. JOHNSON, a Tupper Lake guide. (See.)

Vital dates for some of Jacob Moody's children are: Harvey 1808-1890, Smith 1813-1891, Cortez 1822-1902, Daniel 1826-1892, Martin 1833-1910, Eliza 1837-1900. (The Moody family history has been considerably revised from what is found in Donaldson's *History of the Adirondacks*.)

Harvey Moody found himself an unwitting participant in a legal imbroglio in about 1879. A man named Benton Turner had cut off 1000 logs on land the State said it owned. Turner said the land was his because

> "the title to the premises in the State was void for the reasons that the tax sale under which the deed to the State was given was illegal by reason of irregularities in levying the taxes from which the sales were made and that the land in question or some part of it was occupied when the time of redemption from the 1877 tax sale expired and notice of redemption was not served on the occupant."

Turner's claim that the land was "occupied" and could thus be claimed rested on the fact that for years, starting around 1860, Moody had cut grass in August or September for fodder from a natural meadow on the property, which Moody didn't own. He would stack the fodder, and then wait until January or February when the marshy ground was frozen, to haul it away. On two occassions Moody scattered seed, "herds grass," and "red top," and burned over the dry brush and stubble -- the area came to be known as "Moody Meadows." The legal tangle included whether Moody was "in occupancy," or the land under "cultivation" -- the decision was there was no "actual possession," and Turner lost.

CLEVELAND EUGENE MOODY, the son of Daniel Moody, is described in a Moody family history by Cleveland's son, Alfred Moody, as a guide in the summer and a caretaker in the winter for Dr. Edward Livingston Trudeau of Saranac Lake. Cleveland married Christine Summerville, from Scotland, in 1866, and together they kept cure patients at 60 Lake Flower Avenue. (The family history describes Christine as governess for young Charlotte and Edward Trudeau "four years preceding her marriage." But the Trudeau's didn't get married until 1871, or settle in Saranac Lake until 1876.)

MART MOODY was born in Saranac Lake on June 27, 1833, the son of pioneer settler Jacob Moody. In January, 1861, he married Minerva Reid of Bloomingdale. Mart moved to what is now the settlement of Moody in 1868, and built the Tupper Lake House, afterwards the Mount Morris House. He guided the authors William H.H. Murray and Alfred Street, as well as the naturalist Louis Agassiz, Grover Cleveland, and Lady Amelia Murray, maid of honor to Queen Victoria. During President Arthur's administration, Moody, who had guided him, was appointed postmaster. He was also highway commissioner, assessor, and justice of the peace, and at one time Moody had studied in a law office in Elizabethtown.

Moody was an inveterate teller of tall tales, such as, "I tried to grow cucumbers but the vines grew so fast they wore out the cucumbers dragging them over the stones." Once when rowing President Arthur, the President shot numerous times at a swimming deer and missed each time. Moody bet him he could kill the deer with one shot, rowed up to it, grabbed it by the ear, shoved his pistol in and shot it with a .22. The President paid up, but under protest. Another time, President Cleveland shot a deer and his friends Daniel S. Lamont and Samuel J. Ward disputed the weight. Moody rigged up a kind of balance scale with a rope, put the meat on one side and stones on the other. "297 pounds," Moody said. "How do you know?" he was asked. "I guessed the weight of the stones," he said. Moody once said he had to kill an aged cat, and cut off her head and threw the head and body in the lake and soon the cat returned home with her head in her mouth.

Moody died at 77, in 1910.

WILFRED MORRISON guided in the Oswegatchie and Cranberry Lake area and he was active around the turn of the century. In addition to guiding, he worked for a time at the Wanakena Ranger School. He is remembered best in the book *Man of the Woods*, by Herbert Keith. Morrison was in his fifties when Keith, a young boy living in Wanakena, first knew him. Morrison believed his birthday fell on Thanksgiving each year, and could not be dissuaded from that. Scotch-Irish by birth, Morrison was brought up by French-Canadian relatives in Quebec when he was orphaned. As a young boy he came to the Cranberry Lake area and began working as a chore boy at the Inlet Hotel, where he soon learned guiding from his Uncle Steve Ward. Morrison, in turn, taught Keith his woodsman's skills. Two stories from a newsletter from the Wanakena Ranger School agree with the person described by Keith: One time Wilfred was with Mr. and Mrs. Jessup at a side camp from the Indian Mountain Club. In the night Mrs. Jessup went to the outhouse and sat on a porcupine. The other guides later got wind of it, and asked Wilfred what he did about it. "We have pull out de quills wid de plier." "Who pulled them out?" "Mr. Jessup he have pull dem out!" "What would you have done if Mr. Jessup hadn't been there?" "My lan', I do not know!"

One morning out in the woods Wilfred and his client wondered whether to have fish or illegal meat for breakfast. Looking around, Wilfred saw the color and amount of smoke from a down river fire change, indicating water was being poured on the fire. Says Wilfred, "We will have fish for breakfast." Soon the game warden showed up and searched the camp to Wilfred's taunt of "Why don't you look under the fish?" After the game warden left, Wilfred said, "De damn fool, did he think I would hide de buck on de same side of de river wid de camp?"

In 1933 Morrison was arrested and charged with illegal possession of game, specifically venison. A game protector named Cone searched the camp Morrison was in and found some meat in a pack basket, which he had taken and then showed to the jury. The foreman of the jury told the judge it wasn't proven the meat was venison or the pack basket was Morrison's -- and even if the basket was his, anybody coming by had access to it. Wilfred was tried and acquitted -- twice. Protector Cone also tried to keep Morrison's blood-stained coat and breeches to send to a lab in Albany to prove the blood was that of a deer, saying he'd get a conviction or know why; they were returned, however.

WALLACE MURRAY came to Saranac Lake in 1865 at age 16. He was born in Brookfield, Vermont; his parents moved to Keene when "Wal" was six. He became a lumberjack and guide, then owner of the Riverside Inn in 1886; five years later he introduced electric lights to Saranac Lake. He built a small power plant that supplied current for illumination of the hotel and a few stores, and later for a considerable part of the village until the year 1905. Murray held a ball at the Riverside Inn in honor of Governor Roswell Flower in 1894, when the lake was given the name Lake Flower. Murray was the third village president, in 1896, serving two terms.

GEORGE W. MUSSEN was born in Keeseville in 1847 and at 14 joined a cavalry unit in the Civil War. He worked for 37 years for the Augusta Polhemus camp on Spitfire Lake. He died at age 76, in 1924, at 246 Broadway in Saranac Lake, while playing cards.

MARSHALL EUGENE MUSSEN died in 1946 at 75. For over 45 years he guided and served as caretaker at the Polhemus Camp on Spitfire Lake, retiring in 1932.

BILL NYE's guiding career started inauspiciously for a guide who one prominent Adirondack historian -- Mary Mackenzie of Lake Placid -- ranks among the six most famous from the period 1850-1900.

Nye was born in Berlin, Vermont, in 1816 -- in the east the "year without a summer," with frost or snow every month. At nineteen, disappointed in love, or bored with the monotony of farm life, or perhaps both -- accounts differ -- he shipped out on a whaling vessel bound for the Indian Ocean. (It was an experience that paralleled that of a nineteenth-century writer on the Adirondacks, George Washington Sears, "Nessmuk," who also signed on a whaling ship at sixteen, and later wrote, "The dog's life of a sailor sickened me forever of a life before the mast.")

One whaling trip was evidently enough sailing, at least for the time being. After a respite farming, Nye next went to Charleston, South Carolina, and for a year operated two sailing vessels of 40 or 50 tons each, manned by slaves, on the Ashley River and in

Charleston harbor. He then shipped out again on the seas as first mate on a brig for three and a half years.

After another period of farming, Nye decided in 1848 to join Colonel Fremont in the West, but got "fever and ague" on the way to St. Louis and returned home.

In 1851 Nye settled in North Elba. A year later on the west branch of the Ausable River he built a saw mill, which he sold in 1855. For the next almost thirty years he remained a bachelor and spent his time hunting, fishing, and guiding. His hunting experience included hearing, he said, "the unearthly screams of a panther that started my hat up some, but it did not fall off."

At his own expense Nye cut the first trail up Whiteface, the first trail from Adirondack Lodge up Mount Marcy, and made the first recorded ascent of Gray Peak on September 16, 1872, with surveyor Verplanck Colvin. On the same trip they apparently discovered the Hudson River's ultimate source, Lake Tear of the Clouds. That their "discovery" on the shoulder of Mount Marcy, thirty-five years after Marcy was first climbed should take so long seems unlikely. According to the 1891 Forest Commission Report, "It (Lake Tear) was always known to the guides as Summit Lake, or Summit Water; but Mr. Colvin, while in charge of the State survey, renamed it "'Tear of the Clouds.'" It was also called Perkins Pond.

But it is the story of "Hitch Up!, Matilda!" that has secured Nye a place in Adirondack history for all time. One of the best accounts appeared in Seneca Ray Stoddard's *The Adirondacks Illustrated*, in 1874; the quotations that follow are mostly from that.

In 1868 Nye was guiding a hiking party of three who came from downstate on the Hudson -- Mr. and Mrs. Fielding, and their niece Dolly. Dolly, seventeen, was in Nye's words "a splendid girl, handsome as a picture," and made Nye wonder if he had made a mistake staying a bachelor. Mr. Fielding he described as a "quick motioned, impulsive sort," and his wife as "taller and heavier."

Their hiking route was from Nash's on Mirror Lake, run by J.V. Nash -- himself a guide and founder of Lake Placid Village -- through Indian Pass to the Tahawus Iron Works, on to Mt. Marcy, and home by way of Avalanche Pass. They followed their route to the iron works, then camped two nights at Lake Colden with a climb of Marcy in between. The last day they started through Avalanche Pass to North Elba. The Pass is flanked on both sides by high sheer rock holding Avalanche Lake. Nye related: "...along one side is a shelf from two to four feet wide and as many under water, and when we got there they wondered how we were to get past. I said I could carry them, or I could build a raft, but to build a raft would take too much time while I could carry them past in a few minutes."

The Fieldings tossed the matter back and forth and opted to be carried. Mrs. Fielding -- Matilda -- agreed to go first, on Nye's shoulders. At first, out of modesty, she attempted to mount him sidesaddle, both feet on one side. Rearranged with her legs on either side of Nye's neck, they started along the underwater ledge, Nye holding her legs with one hand and steadying himself against the wall with his other.

Mrs. Fielding began to slip downward. "Hitch up, Matilda! hitch up, Matilda! why don't you hitch up?" screamed Mr. Fielding. Nye hunched forward and completed transferring Matilda safe and dry, then went back and got the others.

Nye described himself as a bashful man and said he appreciated that after the tale leaked out no women ever alluded to it in his presence.

Before the Civil War Nye became acquainted with John Brown the abolitionist, who lived in North Elba. After Brown was hanged for treason his body was sent home. Mrs. Brown asked Nye to have the body carried upstairs in the Brown house, and for it to be made suitable for public viewing. For this, as well as assisting in the grave site preparation and other courtesies, Mrs. Brown gave Nye the collar taken from Brown's neck before he was hanged.

In 1890 Nye moved back to Vermont and reported he had given the collar to his sister for safekeeping, but, he said, "she has laid it away so carefully that she has not been able to find it."

Alas, on February 12, 1893, when Nye was 77, his habit of using a candle in his bedroom rather than a kerosene lamp evidently caused a house fire that consumed both him and the historic collar.

Nye is commemorated by a mountain bearing his name. At 4,160 feet, it is one of the Adirondack's 46 peaks over 4000 feet. He is also remembered by a substantial and well-used catwalk along Avalanche Pass at the spot known as "Hitch up, Matilda."

HUBERT NYE was born in St. Huberts, May 28, 1912, and lived there most of his life. He worked as a construction worker and then a full-time guide on the Upper Ausable Lake. He retired in 1982.

JOHN O'CONNOR was born in Ausable Forks and became a guide and caretaker of the Kirkwood camp on Osgood Pond. He had a stroke or heart attack and died at 57.

JIM O'MALLEY was born in Colton, and died at 87 at Loon Lake, guiding from the late 1850's. Among his clients was John D. Rockefeller.

ALBERT OTIS was a guide and state fire observer from Paul Smiths. He lived from 1855 to 1928, and was found dead of a heart attack in his cabin at St. Regis Mountain.

ALFRED H. OTIS was born at Harrietstown in 1850, one of 19 children. With his father, Joshua Otis, he cleared the land for a farm that was later occupied by part of the Paul Smiths' golf course. Guiding, lumbering, and farming were Alfred Otis' chief vocations, but he delighted in singing the ballads his father had brought to the Adirondacks from Vermont. "Such was his repertoire of these old-time tunes that he could divert a gathering for an entire evening without repeating a melody," according to his obituary. He guided for 50 years. Among his clients was President McKinley. Otis died unexpectedly in bed July, 1931, at 81. The summer before he had pitched two tons of hay.

ARTHUR L. OTIS lived and guided at Paul Smiths and died at 63.

HARRY G. OTIS lived at Paul Smiths and died in 1945 at 74.

MILLARD OTIS lived at Lake Clear, and died at 89 in 1948. His grandfather had come to the Adirondacks after the Revolution; his father, Horatio, and mother were born in Vermont; they owned much of the land at Lake Clear. Otis cooked at the Saranac Inn when it began, and once picked some spruce gum for President Cleveland's wife.

OREN OTIS lived in Bloomingdale. After giving up guiding he became a caretaker of summer homes. He died suddenly in February 1914:

> "After the evening meal he and his wife went to the sitting room, where his wife began to read the current news from a daily paper. She had been reading for some time when Mr. Otis said to her, 'You are skipping some of the words -- why don't you read it all?' Mrs. Otis responded that she was reading the news as it appeared in the paper, and hardly had she responded, when looking at her husband she saw him slipping down in his chair. She hastened to his side, but by the time she reached him the spark of life had flown. A

physician was summoned and when he arrived and made an examination of the body he stated that death was due to the bursting of a blood vessel."

SIDNEY EDWIN OTIS died at Lake Clear, age 75, on December 22, 1921, following a long illness from a stroke. He was born in Harrietstown in 1845, and was a Civil War veteran who served three years in the 18th New York Cavalry. In addition to guiding, he farmed and ran a boarding house.

SYLVESTER OTIS was stricken and died on a street in Saranac Lake at age 84. He was born in Harrietstown, and served three years in the 118th New York Volunteers during the Civil War.

JAMES OWENS, a Keene Valley guide, received two letters from officers of the Adirondack Mountain Reserve in June, 1893, cancelling him as an authorized guide and banning him from the Reserve for a fishing violation in May.

HENRY PACKARD was born in Milton, Vermont, in 1852. He married Emma Bull; they had no children. Packard came to Lake Placid in 1883 and worked as a carpenter and guide. He died in 1923.

ANSELM PARSONS was born in Becket, Massachusetts, on June 5, 1855. At 19 he contracted tuberculosis and moved to the Adirondacks. In 1887 he married Ellen Nichols, granddaughter of early settler Jesse Corey. Parsons died July 13, 1943, at 88, and his wife died at the same age April 15, 1954.

THOMAS PEACOCK was the son of William and Louisa Peacock, who came to North Elba from England in 1847. He was born March 5, 1853, in North Elba. The Peacock family and the family of John Brown the Abolitionist were neighbors. When Peacock was 13, he shot his first deer with a flintlock musket owned by Henry Thompson, John Brown's son-in-law. When he was 18 he blazed the first trail from Middle Saranac, or Round Lake, to the top of Ampersand Mountain. As a young man he moved to Saranac Lake and married a Stearns girl. He guided President-to-be Grover Cleveland in 1878 and 1879 at Prospect House, Saranac Inn, and hired out under Verplanck Colvin.

According to W.H. Burger, in an article in the Winter, 1953, issue of *North Country Life*:

"He (Peacock) recalls W.H.H. (Adirondack) Murray as being very strong. Once while Murray and his friends were lolling around, someone egged Murray and Peacock into a wager about 'hefting' a huge packbasket filled with stones from a sitting position on the ground. Murray tried, but only half-heartedly, Peacock said. Peacock did it by rolling against a log and grasping a protruding stub...(Peacock) was sitting in the Guide Room at Martin's on Lower Saranac Lake one evening when old man Martin came in and asked if anyone wanted to take a telegraph message up to Big Tupper. Nobody answered, and as Tom said, he didn't answer either. But finally, when silence was getting strained, Tom said, 'I'll take it,' although he didn't like going through the Seven Pole Rapids at night. The dam had raised the water in the Raquette River 15 feet in places and thousands of acres were flooded. The trip was arduous but uneventful. The lights were on at Bartlett's as he made the carry. He carried over Sweeney's, cut across the Oxbow, and rowed into Big Tupper just as it was coming daylight. Forty-three and a half miles in one night -- not bad for one man and a guide-boat. Unlike most Adirondack guides, Peacock travelled widely and guided in other regions than our North Woods. He hunted moose in Canada for fifty years and made several trips 'out west.' During one of these he visited the Theodore Roosevelt ranch in North Dakota. One winter he kept a railroad construction gang in Colorado supplied with elk and deer meat. He worked at the Hotel Breslin in Lake Hopatcong in New Jersey for ten summers and lived in New York for many years.

And there in Tom's own words is his valedictory -- the Ike tale.

'Back in 1903 and 1904 I had a camp in the Narrows on Long Pond. We had just arrived at my house in Saranac Lake when a boy came in. He was badly scared. He had just come from camp and said he had seen the "awfullest" animal there. We went right up on the train. When we arrived at camp, we found a moose walking around. I went up to him. He reached out his nose and I patted it. He stayed around all summer. He seemed to be very tame. I called him "Ike" after our game protector. He would always come when I called him even if he was way up in the woods. But he didn't like women. His eyes would turn green if he saw one and he'd start for her. One time some boys saw him on a ridge on Slang Pond. He started for them. They ran to their boat and he swam after them. They carried their boat across the carry into Long, but he came right after them even to camp and followed them up onto the porch of a cabin into which they ran. Then he looked in at them through windows and the glass door. Finally I was down at my house in Saranac Lake. Old Mr. and Mrs. Turner were in camp. The boys came down and told me the moose had nosed up the swing,

146 Guides of the Adirondacks

which was hung on 1 1/2 inch rope. His horns got caught and hung up in the rope as he struggled to get loose. Gilbert Turner tried to cut the rope. He lunged at Turner, his horns broke, and he went wild. So old man Turner shot him. That was the end of Ike.'"

In later life Peacock was sought out for his recollections of John Brown. He said his father William was working shares on John Brown's farm when Brown was planning his raid on Harper's Ferry. Thomas Peacock said he remembered a meeting of the neighbors being called, surrounded by great secrecy:

"I can still see him riding up to the farmhouse on a huge brown mare. He took part in the meeting of the neighbors in the living room of the house. While going home that night, my father cautioned me to say nothing to anyone about what I saw that afternoon.
Several days later my father and I attended the farewell to Brown. He kissed us all goodbye and rode off to Plattsburgh. We heard of the raid on Harpers Ferry and that John Brown had been hanged. My father was greatly upset and didn't eat or sleep for several weeks. While this was going on he again cautioned me to say nothing of what I had seen on that afternoon at the farm."

According to North Elba Historian Mary MacKenzie, these memories must be weighed very carefully: "He was only six when John Brown was hung, and therefore could not have had a clear memory of John Brown's years in North Elba from 1849 through 1859, especially since John Brown was seldom here the last few years of his life...his John Brown stories...are completely contrary to historical fact and should NOT be repeated, in the interests of historical authenticity. However, it would certainly be correct to say that the Brown and Peacock families were well acquainted." Thus, I have, indeed, repeated the spurious stories; Peacock died in June, 1942, at 89.

DONALD "RED" PERKINS was born in 1896 in Old Forge. He worked as a guide at the Adirondack League Club. In 1914 he delivered a new Parsons guide-boat about 20 miles on foot, from Little Moose Lake to the president of General Electric at Honnedaga Lake.

EZEKIEL "ZEKE" PERKINS guided in Duane and Lake Meacham. He worked for fifty years for Colonel William Skinner, of Hartford, Conn., first at Lake Meacham, and later at Camp Florence in Duane.

Perkins moved to North Bangor in the last years of his life, and died there at 81 in 1941, following "paralytic shock."

ENOS PERRY died in 1908 at Plumadore when he and another occupant of his boat, a Mr. Benway, attempted to change seats. "When Mr. Benway got to shore, a corpse clung to the other end of the boat. His hat was still on his head, and his head had not been under water. It was supposed that death was due to shock and cold water. He leaves a wife and 12 children, 6 sons and 6 daughters." He was a resident of Lyon Mountain.

SANFORD PERRY, the proprietor of the Forge House, drowned November 1872, after falling out of a guide-boat on Limekiln Lake.

ED PHELPS (1850-1934) lived in the shadow of his famous father, Orson "Old Mountain" Phelps, but at least one influential writer, Russell Carson, thought Ed was not only a better guide than his father, but possibly the best of all time. Ed Phelps was born in Keene Valley. In 1866, he and his father cut the first trail to the summit of Giant Mountain, over Hopkins and Greene Mountains. In 1871, with Seth Dibble, Ed cut a (third) trail up Mt. Marcy and, in 1874, he was on the first ascent of the mountain named for Mills Blake, Colvin's assistant. In November of 1879, while with Blake, Ed fell through thin ice three times on Lower Ausable Lake -- he was saved by having a fallen cedar tree pushed to him. Ed made seven first ascents, besides Blake, including Armstrong, Dial, Lower and Upper Wolf Jaws, Porter, and Redfield -- only the first 46'ers, the Marshall's and their guide Herb Clark, have more first ascents to their credit: eight.

Ed stayed with Colvin through the approximately 25 years of his topological survey work. Supposedly it was Ed who gave William Murray the nickname "Adirondack." He is buried in Keene Valley.

ORSON PHELPS -- "When city strangers broke into the region, he (Phelps) monopolized the appreciation of these delights and wonders of nature." -- Charles Dudley Warner.

Orson "Old Mountain" Phelps is the most famous guide in Adirondack history, probably because he got the most widely-read literary attention. First described by a parade of admiring writers, he began to gradually embellish their romantic characterizations, and create and live out his own role. Eventually he became, in the opinion of historian Mary Mackenzie, "something of a humbug as a guide -- lazy and inefficient, more entertainer than woodsman -- whose flamboyant personality cancelled out his sins of omission."

But on the road to humbuggery -- if that, indeed, is where he ended up -- Phelps distinguished himself not only outdoors in the mountains, but in a variety of other ways. He was poet, sawyer, journalist, botanist, and lender of his name to an epoch, what Russell Carson, author of *Peaks and People of the Adirondacks*, called "The Phelps Period," from 1849-1869. As he grew older the man with the "soul of a philosopher and poet," as both Carson and Charles Dudley Warner described him, distanced himself from the physical exertions of his early days. In many ways he was a mountain renaissance man. In Charles Dudley Warner's sketch "A Character Study," he says, "The vulgar estimate of his contemporaries, that reckoned Old Phelps 'lazy,' was simply a failure to comprehend his conditions of being."

Orson Schofield Phelps was born in Wethersfield, Vermont, on May 6, 1816. ('The year without a summer' -- see also biographies of Bill Nye and Alvah Dunning, both born the same year. Phelp's birth year, 1816, is given in "Genealogy of Orson Schofield Phelps," by Aimee Angus Barber. This date conflicts with the usually cited one of 1817.) He came to the Schroon Lake area with his father, a surveyor, about 1830. He worked for a time at the Adirondack Iron Works at Tahawus, then moved to Keene Valley, married Lorinda Lamb, and built a house near Prospect Hill. He died in Keene Valley on April 14, 1905, nearly 88 years old. In the interim he became a legend.

Phelps' quaintness and laziness have been stressed to the detriment of his quality of expression, and his accomplishments. He could be quaint -- "Soap is a thing that I hain't no kinder use for," he said. "I don't believe in this eternal sozzlin'." His clothes were described as "put on him once for all, like the bark of a tree." A bush whack was a "random scoot" that could escalate into a "reg'lar random scoot of a rigamarole." His favorite camping spot on the Upper Ausable Lake was on the north side, which necessitated rowing out on the lake to see the magnificent view of Gothics. Phelps took in the grandeur of Gothics in small doses because Gothics "ain't the kinder scenery you want ter hog down!"

But in gentler moments he would whisper, "So, little brook, do I meet you once more?" And on seeing an exquisite flower high in a lonely crevice say, "It seems as if the Creator had kept something just to look at himself," and, another time, "...any righteous thing that has life and spirit in it is food for me."

Phelps established postal service in Keene Valley in 1865. He carried the mail at no cost for six months until the government officially took over. He wrote articles for the *Essex County Republican* from 1870-1875. When the Thomas and Armstrong Lumber Company agreed to let guides build camps on the Ausable Lakes property, it was Phelps who helped negotiate the agreement.

Charles Dudley Warner wrote an essay in the *Atlantic*, in 1878, that both captured and furthered Phelps' fame. Warner thought Phelps unsophisticated until he became a disciple of Horace Greeley's *New York Tribune*, an influential weekly in the hinterlands, and until the advent of strangers into Phelps' life, who brought in literature and various other 'disturbing influences.'

But Phelps was drawn to these strangers, and told Warner, "To have had hours such as I have had in these mountains, and with such men as Dr. Bushnell and Dr. Shaw and Mr. Twichell, and others I could name, is worth all the money the world could give."

Warner wrote, "I think he prized most that (the friendship) of Dr. Bushnell. The doctor enjoyed the quaint and first-hand observations of the old woodsman, and Phelps found new worlds open to him in the wide ranges of the doctor's mind. They talked by the hour upon all sorts of themes -- the growth of the tree, the habits of wild animals, the migration of seeds, the succession of oak and pine, not to mention theology, and the mysteries of the supernatural." (Horace Bushnell -- for whom Bushnell Falls is named -- lived from 1802 to 1876, and has been called the father of American religious liberation. He was a major figure in the country's intellectual history. He must have been very liberal -- in 1852 Bushnell's North Congregational Church in Hartford, Conn., withdrew from the local consociation in order to preclude an ecclesiastical heresy trial by conservatives. Farfetched as it may be, some allowance must be made for the possibility Phelps influenced Bushnell, thus giving Phelps a role in the development of the country's intellectual history.)

But it was in the mountains that Phelps earned his fame and his nickname. He climbed Mt. Marcy for the first time in 1849 from Elk Lake. He could see Marcy from the Blue Ridge area where he worked lumbering in 1847 and 1848. In 1858, he guided the first two women, Mary Cook and Fanny Newton, up Marcy over a trailless route (this date is sometimes erroneously given as 1850.) Phelps was one of the first guides to build a camp on the Upper Ausable Lake; he cut the first trail from there over Bartlett Ridge to Mt. Marcy in 1861. In 1873, he cut the present route out of Panther Gorge to Mt. Marcy. The same year, with surveyor Verplanck

Colvin, he made a first ascent of Skylight and the mountain later named Colvin. He cut a trail to Skylight's summit two years later.

Phelps and his son Ed cut a trail to Giant in 1866. Phelps named, or helped name, Skylight, Haystack, Basin, Saddleback, and possibly Gothics. He also entered into controversies over the names of Nipple Top, Colvin, and Dial. With Uncle Dave Heald and Smith Beede, Phelps was at the core of the formation of the Keene Valley Guides Association in 1887. (See "Private Preserves and the Commercial Hunting Camps.")

Phelps met Mark Twain and "Adirondack" Murray. He was able, because of his celebrity status, to supplement his income selling his own trail maps, Stoddard photos, a Phelps-model fishing pole, and guidebooks.

In 1902, Harry Radford, "Adirondack" Murray's biographer, wrote that Phelps was undoubtedly the greatest mountaineer this region has produced, and had earned the name of "Old Mountain" for his natural ability "to seek out the easiest and most accesible routes to most lofty and rugged summits in the State." (Evidently the greatest mountain guides shared such a trait. Bob Marshall, who with his brother George and guide HERB CLARK (see), were the first to climb all the Adirondack peaks over 4,000 feet, made a similar comment about Clark.)

Warner's assertion that Phelps was the "ideal guide" with his *New York Tribune* and other "disturbing influences", flew in the face of the conventional notion of the ideal guide, an unsophisticated person removed from urban influences. However, he said Phelps not only knew as much woodcraft as any other guide, but in addition he brought his clients "to a test of their naturalness and sincerity, tried by contact with the verities of the woods."

Warner drew a comparison between Phelps and Socrates, the canny old philosopher who would draw you along in a dialogue until he had you against the ropes in terms of what you'd previously believed. Phelps took people to his mountains. When they went home they had a greater appreciation of their experience than merely the view they'd seen. He was teacher, philosopher, and the most famous Adirondack guide.

SETH PIERCE was born in 1828. A guide and carpenter in the Raquette Lake area, Pierce lived at Joseph Bryere's Inn, Brightside.

JEREMIAH PLUMLEY was the brother of "Honest John" Plumley (sometimes 'Plumbley'), "Adirondack" Murray's famous guide.

According to his grandson John Plumley in a recent interview, Jeremiah was "more proficient and diligent than John" as a guide. Jeremiah lost part of a hand in a Civil War battle at Fairfax, Virginia. After that he walked from Albany to Long Lake, learnd his wife had died two years earlier, and walked back and re-enlisted. He worked as a caretaker at Brandreth for 33 years, leaving "in a huff" in 1906 when they started lumbering. He then moved to Holland Patent.

JOHN E. PLUMLEY was William "Adirondack" Murray's guide, better known as "Honest John." He was born in Shrewsbury, Vermont, in 1828. When he was nine his father moved to Long Lake, becoming one of the first residents of the town. John began guiding at 21 and continued until he was 70, three years before he died. In 1850 he married Zobeda Hough. Plumley died in May 1900. On hearing of his death Murray wrote: "They tell me that he is dead. It is a foolish fashion of speech and not true. Not until the woods are destoyed to the last tree, the mountains crumbled to their bases, the lakes and streams dried up to their parched beds and the woods and wood life forgotten will the saying become fact. For John Plumley was so much of the woods, the mountains and the streams that he personified them. He was a type that is deathless."

WILLIAM POHL died at age 60 in January 1948. He drowned in two feet of water at Aldrich Pond near Oswegatchie when he fell into a spring that had been boxed in.

WILLIAM D. POND was born at West Pierrepont on November 2, 1861. He worked for a few years at the Melba Iron Works in Oriskany, but in the early 1880's went to Childwold. There he worked as a carpenter, helping to erect Addison Child's Childwold Park Hotel. A half-century later he helped tear down the hotel, and salvaged enough lumber to build a home in Childwold, only to see it destroyed by fire in 1953. Pond worked for the State Conservation Department most of his life, helping erect fire observation towers and serving as observer on Moosehead Mountain, in the Childwold area, and on Bald Mountain, near Old Forge. In 1953 the Genesee Conservation League honored him as the "oldest active hunter" in New York; he shot a buck the last fall before he died in 1958 at 94.

WILLIAM "UNCLE BILL" RING guided Dr. Edward Livingston Trudeau. Ring was a charter member of the Adirondack Guides Association, and died in 1925 in Saranac Lake.

BEECHER ROBLEE was born at North Creek in 1881. He was a caretaker and guide in 1916 for J.H. Ladew on Osprey Island. He died in 1934.

FRED RORK guided in the Paul Smiths area. He was a contractor and carpenter and was living in Frederick, Maryland, at the time of his death at age 53 in 1918.

JED ROSSMAN was born April 6, 1866, in Morrisonville, N.Y. He moved to the Lake Placid area in 1907 and lived on the farm of Harvey Alford, of Averyville. He worked 16 years as guide and caretaker at the Adirondack Lodge on Heart Lake. There he told a camper who was about to sleep in a lean-to his first time that nearby he found "two bears in one trap and 8 sitting on their haunches waiting patiently go get into the trap," thus assuring the camper a sleepless night. An article in the *Lake Placid News* in 1975 by Hal Burton contains the following:

> "Jed Rossman, the caretaker at Adirondack Loj before it got to be civilized, fell into a roaring quarrel with his wife. 'You go to hell,' he said, and proceeded to the Loj for a poker party with some old friends. An hour or two later the door swung open, framing Mrs. Rossman. 'What the hell you doin' here, woman?' demanded Jed. 'Well, said Mrs. Rossman, 'You told me to go to hell, so here I am.'"

MITCHELL SABATTIS: During his lifetime Mitchell Sabattis was challenged the first time he went to vote at Long Lake in 1862 because he was "an Indian and the Legislature (did not have the) power to make him a voter," and credited with being the inventor of the Adirondack guide-boat. In between he reversed the course of his path toward alcoholism, became a respected preacher, fathered eight children who grew to adulthood -- three sons became guides -- and became a commissioner of highways. He was not the inventor of the guide-boat, but he was a skilled and reknowned guide with a lasting place in Adirondack history.

He was a pure-blooded Abenaki, born in Parishville, St. Lawrence County, in 1824. The traditional lands of the Abenaki were in what is now Maine and Canada; how and why his ancestors reached St. Lawrence County is not recorded. Sabattis' birth date has been recorded as early as 1801, but he himself gave it as September 29, 1824. He was the son of Captain Peter Sabattis, born about 1750, who fought in both the Revolutionary War and the War of 1812.

Peter Sabattis is reported in Donaldson's *History of the Adirondacks* to have been a pure blooded Huron, a tribe whose traditional lands were north of Lake Ontario, but he was most likely an Abenaki. (Oddly, within three pages Donaldson calls Peter Sabattis a pure-blooded Huron and his son Mitchell a pure-blooded Abenaki.) In Carson's *Peaks and People*, Mitchell and his father are called St. Francis Indians who gave names to "many natural features of the Adirondacks. Mount Marcy, in the language of the St. Francis Tribe, was known as Wah-um-de-neg, meaning 'it is always white.'" The matter of tribal ancestry in Carson's account is not necessarily in conflict with Mitchell Sabattis' alleged heritage, as the St. Francis Indians are said by William Beauchamp, in *A History of the New York Iroquois*, to be comprised of the Mohicans, and Saco Indians belonging to the Abenakis. St. Francis is more of a term of geographical location than tribal affiliation. Other sources refer to the "Abenaki Tribe of Hurons of eastern Canada."

Mitchell Sabattis recalled his first visit to Long Lake as a lad when, with a Mohawk boy named Thompson, they were left overlong by their parents and ran out of provisions. They had an old flintlock musket and some wet powder, but no bullets. They dried the powder, gathered pebbles, loaded the musket and shot a deer from a canoe.

If 1824 is correct for Sabattis' birth year, he was only nineteen when he inadvertently was hired to guide John MacMullen, a teacher, and his friend, whose name is given only as Jim R., on the Raquette River. MacMullen and Jim had bought a yawl, a type of sailing craft, on Long Lake, and abandoned it in the face of the Raquette's rapids. They attempted to proceed on an improvised raft, which proved unsuitable.

Sabattis was part of a party of Indians totalling three men, two women, and a baby. All, apparently, were travelling in one boat, a birch bark canoe. The addition of the two white men to the canoe loaded it to a dangerous level, so Sabattis and the other Indian men built another canoe of spruce bark, somewhere along the Raquette. The canoe was sewn with spruce roots, and cedar was cut for gunwales.

At one point MacMullen was astonished to see Sabattis "kissing" the canoe when it was overturned on land. Wondering about this sentimentality, he asked him what he was doing. "Suckin' for holes," he was told. Sabattis had, indeed, located some holes in this manner. Using small pieces of rag and heated spruce gum, Sabattis repaired the holes. When he ran out of rag stock, Jim volunteered a torn cuff from his shirt. Sabattis requested more and more cloth until all that remained of Jim's sleeve was "an irregular fringe just on his shoulder."

The party canoed all the way to what is now Colton, where they were told MacMullen and Jim were the first white men that ever came down the Raquette River.

By 1849 Sabattis was reported in the *Spirit of the Times* to be using a "skiff" that was a "very lightly, but well built boat (constructed by himself), and weighing between 50 and 60 pounds. He requested me to go down and assist him in 'pitching' his boat. We put it in good order (for, though almost a new boat, it leaked somewhat from having been kept in a dry place for some time), and found it would float perfectly dry."

The author wished to hunt and fish, and writes,

"As we had no bait, Mitchell remarked that we must shoot some bird or squirrel, with the meat of which to catch minnows, pieces of which latter are used in that part of the country, perhaps more exclusively than any other, as a bait for trout. Before we reached the shore, Mitchell espied, and called my attention to, what he called a stake-driver (Ardea Sentiginosa) [Note: probably a great blue heron], at which I shot. The bird fell in the rushes, but we could not find him. Mitchell then went into the woods, and ere long procured a nuthatch, which parts of which we soon took a number of bait fish...

Although it was then almost too dark to aim correctly, and but a small part of the doe was to be seen -- and at that time she must have been over a hundred yards distant, yet, notwithstanding all these disadvantages, the unerring aim of my experienced guide had proved fatal...(later) Mitchell went down to the boat to dress the deer and brought a piece of one of the leg bones..., the marrow of which, after warming it by the fire, he greased my rifle -- by the way, a very common mode, among hunters, of greasing their guns."

About ten years later, Sabattis met and guided Lucious Chittendon (1824-1900), a Vermont lawyer, legislator, and Treasury official in Lincoln's administration. Chittendon devoted a great deal of attention to Sabattis in his *Personal Reminiscences 1840-1890*, which came out in 1893. Chittendon went hunting with Sabattis on a rainy, foggy night. Chittendon heard a deer, but couldn't see it. Estimating its location, he shot, and the deer bounded away. The following is Chittendon's account of that encounter:

"Well! we have lost him," I said, in a tone of disappointment. "I am sorry, for he was a noble buck. I got one glance of his antlers."

"How can we lose what we never had?" was Mitchell's pertinent inquiry. "But we will have him yet before daylight. He is hard hit and will not run very far."

"Why do you say that?" I asked. "He bounded away in a very lively manner as if he was uninjured."

"For two reasons," he answered. "He did not snort or whistle as an unwounded deer always does when suddenly startled. The one of his fore-legs appeared, by the sound, to be crippled."

He pushed the boat rapidly across the marsh to the hard ground, and with the light in his hand soon found where the deer had passed through the thick weeds and grasses. "It is all right," he said. "Here is where he went out, and it's as bloody as a butcher's shop."

I came near where he stood. "Show me the blood," I said.

"Why there! and there! and there! all over! Don't you see it?" he exclaimed.

"I see nothing but wet leaves and bushes," I replied. "Now stop and show me what you call blood."

He plucked a leaf with incurved edges, on the wet surface of which there was a discoloration which he said was blood. "It is a plain as can be," he said; "you would not expect a wounded buck in a hurry to stop and paint a United States flag for our benefit. I am going for him," he continued. "You stay in the boat until you hear a shot, which may mean that I have found him or that I have given up. Then you fire a pistol, which will give me my bearings and save time."

With the lantern in one hand and my gun in the other, he disappeared in the foggy night. How long I lay stiffening in the boat or stamped along the shore in an effort to keep my blood in circulation, I do not know. But after what seemed hours of weary waiting, away up on the side of the mountain I heard the faint report of a gun. I fired the revolver in answer and waited again until I heard something threshing down the hill.

"Is that you, Mitchell?" I shouted.

"Yes," he answered. "I have got him. He is a splendid buck; not too old and in prime condition. He will provision the camp for a week."

He now appeared, dragging the deer after him.

"How did you find him?" I asked.

"I followed his track over the wet leaves," he answered. "Where he stopped the spot was marked by a pool of blood. These were nearer together as we went up the hill. Finally I overtook him. He was standing with his head down and I saw he had been hard hit. I held the jack in one hand and shot him with the gun held in the other."

Mark, now, what this Indian had done. His ear had detected an injury to one of the animal's forelegs. In the dark and rainy night, by the light of the "jack," he had found his path out of the marsh, had followed it over fallen trees, through the thick brushwood, a mile or more up the steep hillside, until he had overtaken the wounded deer, and holding the light in one hand and the gun in the other had given him the fatal shot. Such a story seems incredible. Had I not seen the results I think I would not myself believe it."

Sabattis was living in Newcomb then, and was in danger of losing his home by default on the mortgage. Sabattis told Chittendon he would "give his life" if Chittendon would buy the mortgage so Sabattis' wife Bessie (Dornburgh) and her children would have a place to live. Chittendon made Sabattis promise not to drink liquor for a year, and, with Alonzo Wetherby, to meet him at Bartlett's between Upper and Middle Saranac Lakes, the following August.

In February Sabattis traveled a hundred and fifty miles to Chittendon's home in Burlington, Vermont, with a horse-drawn sled. Sabattis said since his promise not to drink, and the relief from his worries about the mortgage, fortune had smiled on him. He had steady work as a guide, he had never killed so many deer nor got such good prices for venison. He had paid his smaller debts and saved one hundred dollars, which his wife thought he ought to take to Chittendon. He brought as well, as a present, a sled-load of game.

"A refusal of his gift was not to be thought of. The next morning I took my butcher to his little load of game. There were the saddles or hind quarters of twenty-five fat deer in their skins, two carcasses of black bear dressed and returned to their skins, the skin of a magnificient catamount, with the skull and claws attached, which he had heard me say I would like to have, a half-dozen skins of the beautiful fur of the pine marten or the American sable, more than one hundred pounds of brook trout, ten dozen of ruffled grouse all dressed and braided into bunches of a half-dozen, and some smaller game, with some specimen skins of the mink and fox. There was more game than my family could have consumed in a year.

I selected a liberal supply of the game and took the skins intended for myself and family. For the balance my butcher paid him liberally, and this money with his savings would have more than paid his mortgage. But I would not so soon lose my hold upon him. He had told me that if he could build an addition to his house his wife could keep four boarders while he was guiding in the summer. I induced him to save money enough for this addition, and to purchase the furniture then and there. He paid the interest and costs and a part of the principal of his mortgage, and went home loaded with presents for Bessie and the children -- a very happy man.

On the 2nd of August, this time with two <u>gentlemen</u> and their wives, all safe companions in roughing it, as we approached the landing at Bartlett's Mitchell and Alonzo were waiting for us. There was no need to ask Mitchell if he had kept his promise. His eye was as clear and keen as that of a goshawk. The muscles visible in their action under his transparent dark skin, his voice, ringing with cheerfulness, all told of a healthy body and a sound mind. His wife, he said, had her house filled with boarders, his oldest son had been employed as a guide for the entire season, and prosperity shone upon the Sabattis household."

Sabattis maintained a camp on Crane Point on the east side of Long Lake. In 1865, he was deeded a quarter of an acre of land for $25 for a meeting house site for the Wesleyan Methodist Church of Long Lake.

Sabattis had guided well-known ministers from Boston, Pittsfield, New York and Philadelphia. He set out to visit these clergymen, who included Rev. William Walker of Philadelphia, Rev. Thaddeus Norris of Philadelphia Trinity Church, and Rev. John Todd of Pittsfield. (Todd had organized a Congregational Church in Long Lake about twenty years before.) Pleading his case before the various congregations, Sabattis returned with $2000 for the new church.

Sabattis and his wife kept boarders and sportsmen until 1878. In 1886, Sabattis had a stroke, which mostly curtailed his guiding. He died at Long Lake on April 16, 1906. He is remembered by a recreational park in Long Lake named after him and a settlement once called Long Lake West, along the railroad, named Sabattis.

PETER SABATTIS was the father of Mitchell Sabattis (see.) In his youth, at about age 16, Peter, an Indian, is alleged to have been along with Benedict Arnold on the expedition to Quebec, serving as cook. During the War of 1812 Sabattis blazed trails for roadmakers from Lake George to Lake Ontario, and was made a Captain in the U.S. Army. He boasted that he never slept in a white man's bed, preferring to sleep outside, or inside by the stove. He died in 1861.

MOSES SAWYER was born in 1849 in Canada and lived for 77 years at Paul Smiths. As a child he was tutored along with Phelps

Smith, son of Paul. He guided Dr. Edward Livingston Trudeau. Sawyer died at Paul Smiths at 92 in 1941.

FRANK SEARS began guiding in the 1860's. He was born in Morrisonville, but moved to Lake Placid. He died at 81.

LOUIS "FRENCH LOUIE" SEYMOUR, who probably didn't know his age, came to America from France, or possibly Ottawa at about 17 years of age. He worked on the Black River Canal, but after a mix-up with some canalers went to Speculator and worked as a lumberjack. He then moved into the Canada Lakes region to hermit, trap, and guide. He lived first near Pillsbury Lake, then West Canada Lake, where he stayed more than 50 years. In 1906, he dragged a 150-pound boat with 200 pounds of unwanted ice in it about 25 miles, from West Canada Lake to Lime Kiln, saying, "It takes too much time to thaw him out so I take ice and all."

Louis raised hens to keep bugs out of his garden. He boiled their eggs, mixed them with venison and potatoes, and fed that to the hens. Seymoure kept outpost trapping camps about 6 or 8 miles apart. He once trapped a fisher live and kept it until the pelt became prime and he once kept a beef paunch in his cabin until it got ripe enough to use for fox bait. On supply trips to Speculator, he engaged in his legendary binges, bartering furs for drinks. "Adirondack French Louie" died in 1915, age about 80.

NAT SHEPARD lived from 1865 to 1922. He was a lumberman and guide in the Town of Wilmurt.

EDWIN "JACK" SHEPPARD came to the Adirondacks' Fulton Chain from Michigan about 1855 in search of health. In 1862 he enlisted in the 117th New York Volunteers and served until the end of the war. He was studious, and acquired a private library. His nickname "Jack" came from Jack Sheppard, the English bandit, who was hanged in London in 1724; a novel called *Jack Sheppard* came out in 1839 which glorified the bandit. The Adirondacks' Sheppard owned and operated the first locally built steamer to ply the Fulton Chain. He also assisted Colvin, and was reported to have shot the last panther in the Adirondacks. Discouraged by the advent of the railroad, Sheppard left the Adirondacks in 1893. He moved first to Oregon, then Idaho, where he died in 1921; at his death a newspaper caption said, "He elevated the position of guide."

JAMES SHORT was a guide from the Town of Minerva, Essex County. He was born about 1823, and owned a 200-acre tract on what is now the North Woods Club. Short stayed at the home of the innkeeper Otis Arnold in Thendara in September of 1868, with a party of sportsmen he had guided from the eastern part of the Adirondacks. While there he bought a hunting dog from Otis, and a collar and chain from another member of the family, unbeknownst to Otis, who thought Short had stolen them. An argument ensued, and Otis shot Short, who died soon after. Otis then took his own life in remorse.

ELIJAH SIMONDS, who was born in Elizabethtown in 1821, was called by George Brown, long-time editor of the *Elizabethtown Post and Gazette*, and author of *Pleasant Valley, a History of Elizabethtown*, the "greatest hunter and trapper the Adirondacks ever produced." This assessment was agreed to, in the 1920's, by "a gathering of veteran Adirondack guides and trappers in the Saranac region," according to an article in the *Chateaugay Record* and reprinted in the *Essex County Republican*. While Simonds accompanied Verplanck Colvin on his ascent of Mt. Hurricane in 1873, and undoubtedly did other guiding, his fame rests on his hunting and trapping prowess. Simonds claimed to have been the first to traverse Hunter's Pass, between Nippletop and Dix. He set the summit of Nippletop on fire so he could descend and see the effect.

Simonds made a number of trips west trapping, in Michigan, Iowa, and Wisconsin. He once shot six deer without moving from his spot, being downwind of a herd, and was alleged to have totalled "3,000 foxes, 2,000 deer, 150 bear, 12 wolves, and 7 panthers, besides more mink, otter, and martin than any other man who ever lived in the Adirondacks." He died in 1900.

EDWARD G. SLAVEN lived in Brighton and guided in the Paul Smiths area for about 25 years. He died at 43.

CHARLES H. SMITH, of Petrie's Corners, was honored by the Brown's Tract Guides' Association for guiding King Edward VII in 1857.

LESLIE SMITH was born in 1829 and lived in Saranac Lake. He began guiding at 14, and was employed by Grover Cleveland and Charles Steinmetz.

PETER SMITH died at the end of 1936 or early 1937, just short of 76 years of age. He was a native of Wilmington, came to Lake Placid at 21, and worked in stone masonry, forestry, and guiding.

WARREN H. SPRAGUE was born in Peru, N.Y., lived in Brighton, and guided at Paul Smiths for 40 years. He worked for many years at the camp of Louis F. Slade, of New York, on Upper St. Regis Lake. Sprague died at 70 of a heart attack.

PERLY J. SQUIRES was born in Vermont in 1862. He lived most of his childhood in Plattsburgh, then moved to Saranac Lake where he worked as a house painter. According to his great-great neice, Elizabeth Squires Botten, Squires had a 99-year lease on land near Sabattis where he kept a camp on Grass Pond. "There were wealthy people on both sides of him that tried to get that land in any way even to breaking the lease. I believe they weren't able to," says Mrs. Botten.

MOSES ST. GERMAIN died at 70 in St. Cloud, Florida, October 30, 1915. He had lived in Hollywood, St. Lawrence County, and Paul Smiths. He was a veteran of the Civil War.

JAMES H. STANTON, a guide, was born in 1859 and died in 1948.

JOHN H. STELL was born in 1850, and guided at the Adirondack League Club for 50 years. He guided President Cleveland, who he said 'chickened out' of shooting a deer, and also guided Vice-President Sherman.

HYLAND STEVES (sometimes listed as Stevens) drowned in Raquette Lake in South Bay while rafting logs near Diameter Mountain in 1924 at age 65. His brother Warren (see) also guided. They guided for 10 years from "Under the Hemlocks" at Raquette Lake, which was owned by Ed Bennett.

WARREN STEVES was born in 1851 and died in 1933 in Oneida, N.Y. He was one of the first to establish a permanent camp at Raquette Lake, with a summer home on Strawberry Island and winter quarters at South Bay. Steves guided Andrew Carnegie for 15 years, J.H. Ladew for 12 years, and J.P. Morgan, Cornelius Vanderbuilt, and ex-Governor P.C. Lounsbury of Massachusetts; he also led a party for General U.S. Grant.

DAVID W. STICKNEY was born in Duane, September 1868. He was a guide at the Meacham Lake Hotel, and became caretaker of that property when it was sold to lumbering interests.

M.R. SUTTON was a guide on part of an important nineteenth-century survey called *Report on a Survey of the Waters of the Upper Hudson and Raquette Rivers, 1874.* Included in that account is the report of Frederick F. Judd, as follows:

> "About the first of June last I accepted the position offered to me by you, as assistant on the surveys...our party consisted, beside myself, of Messrs. William B. Benedict, Theo. F. Judd, with M.R. Sutton as guide and boatman, especially fitted for this service by long experience in wood-life, and in surveying and locating lands...I will only mention, in closing, as an index to the extent of our wanderings, that we traveled by boat over these beautiful lakes and streams, more than 360 miles, and that our guide, boat on back, made about fifty miles over the intervening carries."

A later mention of a Sutton, guide, is by Charles Loring Brace (1826-1890), a reformer and pioneer social welfare worker who founded the Children's Aid Society of New York City. His biography includes a letter to a Doctor Howard datelined Little Tupper Lake, July 31, 1889: "My dear George: Here we are in our old tracks. Just met Sutton, a hale old man, our guide on our first trip on Long Lake (wife says thirty-four years ago!)...the desolater, the lumber-man, has not reached here, but next year he will come, and all will be ruin." Whether the Sutton mentioned in both accounts is the same one is uncertain; the evidence suggests it certainly might be. Using the details above, therefore, Sutton's active guiding span would have been at least twenty years.

MITCHELL SWINYER guided in the Vermontville area. He died in 1924 at 72.

ANN TELFER guided in the Speculator area. She was born January 1, 1896, and named Anna Christiana Klein. Her parents, Theresa and Emil Klein, were German immigrants who farmed in West Nyack, New York, in Rockland County. Ann married Andrew Telfer, and they moved to Speculator with their two daughters around 1922. Telfer learned hunting from her father, who hunted rabbits, partridge, pheasant, fox, deer and bear.

With her husband she built and assisted in the heavy work of a large garage in Speculator called the Mammoth Garage. She bought a two-story log camp at Perkins Clearing, off the Speculator-Indian Lake road, that necessitated a three mile walk in. The camp, on land leased from the International Paper Company, was near the Pillsbury Mountain fire tower. The area was known as Blue Ridge, and Telfer called her camp Blue Ridge Camp. Here she began taking in hunting parties during big game season. They included businessmen, doctors, restaurant owners and a sheriff.

One tradition in Telfer's hunting camp was that any hunter who missed a shot at a buck had a piece of his shirt tail cut off. These were sewn together into a small quilt-like piece.   According to her daughters, Carol Rogers and Muriel Benson, who jointly prepared a biography for inclusion here, her daily routine in camp went like this:

"Every morning before daylight she got up and started a fire in the wood stove in the kitchen and also the wood stove in the main room of the camp. Then she started cooking breakfast. The hunters were well fed - - pancakes, eggs, oatmeal, sausage, bacon and johnny cakes. She then made sandwiches for every hunter as the whole day was spent in the woods, up and down mountains. At lunch time a fire was built in the woods were they happened to be and they warmed themselves and also the sandwiches and whatever there was to drink. They would return just before dark. Then our mother had to get supper ready for the hungry hunters. Sometimes she had a woman in to help her. I guess it was all according to how big the hunting party was. Sometimes she also needed help with the hunting and would hire another guide that knew the woods well. His name was Artliss Slack and he lived in Speculator. He would put out the drivers and she would put out the watchers because she knew just where the deer would go when driven. She loved the woods and hunting there and the hunters never went home without game. She knew those woods like the back of her hand. Anytime anyone killed a deer she was the one to have to dress it out. The hunters did not seem to know all that had to be done when a deer was killed. Some of the men couldn't stand to watch this process. Our mother shot 13 bear during her life, and I don't believe any men around this part of the country can say they did that. She loved to hunt bear. She could carry a deer or a bear on her shoulders as well as a man. It is a whole bear, dressed out. She loved to hunt and climb those mountains and a lot of the men couldn't keep up with her. She was a strong person and could also chop wood when needed. She had a favorite rifle which was a 303 Savage. She loved to fish and would fish beaver dams up beyond her camp and the Miami River that flowed near her camp. She had favorite spots to fish and never told anyone where they were including us.

Another thing she liked to do was to trap and it was another way you could make a living. She had a trap line in around Jessup River and other places as well. The trap line was 3 and 4 miles long and she tended these traps every day. Beavers are quite heavy and if you got three beaver in one day you had to carry them in a pack basket. You always had a pack basket anyway to carry shovels, pick ax and extra traps. When she returned home she had to skin the beaver and that was no easy job as a beaver is hard to skin, not like a deer. She then pulls the skin and nails it to a flat board and then sold them to fur buyers that would come along. She would get as much as a dollar an inch, so that's why she had to stretch them. Every inch counted. When the skins dried they were very stiff. She also trapped foxes and sold the fur. She had a beautiful fox jacket made for herself. Also in later years she trapped enough beaver to make coats for herself and us girls. We had beaver hats and muffs also.

When she sold the garage she bought some land in Lake Pleasant that had a house and barn on it. She was in her thirties then, we believe. She built a motel and cabins on this land and that helped to make a living also. A lot of the carpenter work she could do herself.

When she was 75 to 79 years old she still went to her camp and hunted, mostly alone and hunted all day long. At that time you were allowed to drive a Jeep in. You had to have a camp in on the road to do this. International Paper Company put a chain across the road with a lock on it. You had to have a key from them to drive in, otherwise you had to walk from Perkins Clearing. At her age we would worry about her, but she would go anyway. She had favorite spots to watch for deer and they all had names that she called them. When she was 77 years old we got her to go to Florida for the winters, but not until after the deer season.

You would think that someone who loved hunting, walking up and down mountains and fished in ponds and brooks in the woods would have a homely, unpolished, rugged appearance. This is not true, when it comes to our mother. She always looked pleasant and refreshing and well dressed."

In later years Telfer married Dr. R. Leo Dewhirst, a dentist; they lived in Lake Pleasant. She died in Florida on April 17, 1975, at 79.

HENRY THOMPSON (see Thomas Peacock) married the oldest daughter, Ruth, of John Brown the Abolitionist. On September 1, 1858, Ruth wrote a letter to her brother, saying, "Henry has gone to Mt. Marcy with some gentry from Middlebury College. He has been two trips as guide this summer and made $13.00 in that way. There never was so many visitors here before as there has been this summer. A gentleman and lady came all the way from Boston on horseback, just for the scenery, I suppose."

JOHN H. TITUS, JR. was a nephew of Paul Smith. He was a guide and worked for Benjamin Muncil, contractor. Titus was born in Bloomingdale and lived in Keese Mills. He drowned at 34 on Upper St. Regis Lake during construction of the Alice Huntington camp. His death was an accident believed the result of an overloaded barge.

WILLIAM H. TITUS was born in Duane in 1867 and died in 1940 at 73. He was a nephew of Paul Smith. In 1937 he said "it ain't like the old days when you brought along a side of salt pork, some flour for hot cakes and you stayed in the woods from the opening of hunting season until every one in the party got a buck. Nowadays people hire a guide for a day or two, learn the spots he knows, and then they say they don't want him anymore."

LUCIAN (LUTE) TRIMM guided in the Meacham Lake area. He guided Governor Lounsburg, of Connecticut, for 38 years, first at Meacham, then at Raquette Lake. Trimm was a supervisor of the Town of Duane and long-time vice-president of the Malone Fish and Game Club. He died at 72 on October 29, 1929.

MELVIN TRUMBULL was born in Elizabethtown and joined the Union Navy at fourteen by lying about his age. The accounts of his service differ, perhaps from the faulty memories of his listeners. One account states he served on the "Kearsarge," that sunk the Confederate cruiser "Alabama" off the coast of Great Britain. Another says he served on Admiral Farragut's ship "Hartford" in the Battle of Mobile Bay and with Admiral Porter in the Battle of New Orleans. After the war he moved to Keene Valley and became a guide; his clients included Charles Dudley Warner, Reverends Joseph Twitchell and Horace Bushnell, landscape painter Alexander Wyant, and Yale president Noah Porter.

When the land around the Ausable Lakes was purchased by the Adirondack Mountain Reserve in 1887, the guides who already had camps there were allowed to keep them for their lifetimes if they obeyed A.M.R. regulations (which included not shooting deer.) By 1921, all the guides in this group were dead or had other livings; Trumbull had the last guides' camp on the Upper Lake.

He regularly attended the Keene Valley Congregational Church. He died in 1927, and the church bell installed in the early 1930's was named for Trumbull.

LOTTIE E. TUTTLE was one of the first, or possibly the first, women Adirondack guides. She moved to Old Forge in 1906 with her husband Orley and two young daughters when the Barge Canal took over their farm at New London, N.Y., near Vernon. Orley built the Bay View Hotel on the south shore of lower Fourth Lake, catering to fishermen in the spring, hunters in the fall, and 'endured the summer tourists,' according to Edith Morcy, one of the Tuttles' daughters. Lottie and Orley guided together, Lottie becoming a guide about 1912. In addition to guiding, Lottie entertained guests evenings with poetry and piano playing, and painted ads for sporting magazines, including pictures of the 'Devil Bug' fishing lures Orley invented in 1919.

JAMES UMBER died in December, 1940, age 86, in Glens Falls, where he spent his last five years with his daughter, Mrs. Hartwell Fisk. He was a former resident of Jay, and had guided in the Saranac Inn area.

GARRY VANDENBURGH was born in Keene. His family, with three other families from Keene, settled in Saranac Lake where they established Keene Street, according to his grandson JAY VANDENBURGH, JR. (see.) Garry Vandenburgh guided out of Paul Smiths and Saranac Inn as well as the Ampersand and Algonquin hotels. He was captain of the local guides' rifle team. His clientele included Irvin S. Cobb, the humorist, journalist, and short-story writer. Vandenburgh died at 75 in 1943.

JAY "ZEKE" VANDENBURGH, JR. (whose father was not a guide) was born in Tupper Lake in 1923 and began guiding out of Crescent Bay in Saranac Lake. His clientele included Eisenhower's Chief of Staff George C. Marshall, and General Biddle Smith, Eisenhower's liason to Stalin. As a youth he skipped school two weeks at Easter time to trap muskrats, beaver and mink. He served as state campsite caretaker on the Lower Saranac Lake chain in 1944 and 1945. Vandenburgh remembers selling a Martin guide-boat for $125 in the early 1950's.

JAMES EDGAR WEAVER was born at West Hill, Town of Wells, July 22, 1882, and died December 6, 1966. Known as Edgar, he guided near the "Shaker Place", an abandoned Shaker settlement on the Arietta road near Piseco Lake, and at Abe Lawrence's hunting camp at the "Whitehouse," at the end of West Hill road. He also had his own camp on 'the long level,' on Weaver Brook, about one mile above Elm Lake, northeast of Speculator.

RAYMOND E. WEAVER (1907-1988) was the only son of JAMES EDGAR WEAVER, with whom he guided.

AUGUSTUS WERNER had his 85th birthday in 1948. He was a farmer, guide, postmaster, butcher, game warden, logger, and violinist. In 1948 he was the proprietor of Camp Oma Cash (which supposedly means "bound in buck") near Stillwater. His parents, John and Lois Werner, came from Germany; Augustus -- known later as "Uncle Gus" -- was born in New Bremen. Supposedly the author Gertrude Atherton used Werner as a model for one of the characters in her *The Aristocrats*. A cryptic comment about him in a newspaper article is that "Werner impressed John Norton, who wrote *The Keg*, about contests in Saranac Lake in 1881." The author Norton and the title are unknown; it might have meant something along the order of "he impressed the author W.H.H. Murray enough that his *Stories the Keg Told Me*, and/or Murray's character John Norton, were based partially on Werner." At 28 Werner married Louise Hilmilger.

When Werner was lumbering he floated logs over Eagle Falls to Castorland, getting $3 for 1000 board feet of hemlock. Spruce was more -- $5 per 1000 board feet. In those days it cost $300 for 100 acres of timberland. After two saw mill fires Werner went to work as caretaker on G-lake for the Black, Salmon, and Wright families. He built a camp on Big Burnt Lake and leased land from the state at $20 per year.

JAMES E. WHITE was born June 3, 1880, in Plattsburgh. He moved to Saranac Lake, where he was caretaker at Pinehurst Camp on Lower Saranac Lake, owned by William Haase, for 33 years. He died at 66 in 1946.

PETER WHITE was an Adirondack League Club guide for more than 20 years. He died at 81 in New Hartford, in March 1966.

THEODORE WHITE, while a guide, was most noted for being the owner of the first steam boat in Lake Placid. The "Lake Lily," a wood burner, was built in the 1880's to carry passengers to the camps on the lake. Supposedly the local guides, who viewed ferrying passengers, in guide-boats, as their province, burned the boat. According to his daughter, Leila Wells (who was born in 1880 in the John Brown farmhouse), her father bought another steam boat, which sank at the dock and wasn't worth salvaging. Other reports say it was the "Water Lily," not "Lake Lily," that burned, and the boat that sank was the "Mattie," and that it was raised and repaired and in use in 1881, but might have burned later. To further complicate matters, still other accounts claim the "Water Lily" was brought to Lake Placid by George Billings, not Theodore White, and that "her previous owner in Saranac Lake had similar trouble with guides."

Leila Wells remembers, in her book *Once Upon a Time*:

"My father was an Adirondack guide and told us some interesting experiences of his life in the woods. He told about taking a party of college boys up Mount Marcy once on July 7th and they found a large drift of snow and had a snowball fight. Years later, he picked up a hitchhiker and the man told him about the snowball fight he had once had on Mount Marcy in July with some of his college mates. He was surprised when Dad said that he remembered the occasion."

Theodore White died in 1934 at age 81, and is buried in Lewis.

CALVIN WILBUR lived in Speculator in Hamilton County and had a camp in the Kunjamuk area that could accommodate parties of 25 to 30; he also worked as a carpenter. He used a 351 Winchester automatic. His wife Amelia did the cooking at their camp, which was in an area called Oregon or Big Clearing. The Game Warden at the time was George Howland, who would give warning of his arrival at "the bars," a cattle gate, allowing Amelia time to get any venison off the stove and replace it with ham or a pot of beans. Wilbur also fished for lake trout on Owl Pond over a baited anchor, fishing 30-40 feet deep in a continual jerking motion, using suckers for bait. Wilbur died in 1940; his son Harry continued the camp until 1950. His grandson Paul is the Hamilton County historian.

HARRY WILLIAMS guided in the Blue Mountain area; he lived to be 111. He was born in Cardiff, Wales, in 1825. As a youth he stowed away on a windjammer bound for America. Cholera broke out aboard ship, many of the crew died, and Williams was pressed into service. He worked first in a mill at Ossining owned by Dr. Benjamin Brandreth, an acquaintanceship that brought him to the Adirondacks. When Dr. Brandreth purchased all of Township 39, he hired Williams as a gamekeeper. He met and married Viola Hough, of Long Lake, who died at 45. Williams died in 1937.

CHARLES WOOD was born at Lake Placid June 27, 1872, to Jacob and Amelia Mooney Wood. Jacob was a pioneer of North Elba and had a large farm on Adirondack Lodge Road. The house is still standing as of this writing. Charles guided Professor Charles E. Peck, State Botanist, during his 1893 survey of North Elba and Adirondack plants. The two were the first to make a recorded ascent of Wright Peak, in 1893. Wood also guided for Henry Van Hoevenberg, builder of the original Adirondack Lodge, and took Van Hoevenberg's guests to nearby destinations in 1894. Wood worked for 45 years for the J&J Rogers Co., as forester, timber cruiser and outside superintendent of their lumbering operations. He made the first known ascent of Mount Phelps while surveying timber for Rogers in 1904. He eventually owned large tracts of land in North Elba. He married Gertrude Mooney in 1897; they had five children. One son was the famous Craig Wood, one of the nation's top golfers, for whom the Lake Placid municipal golf course is named. Charles Wood died in July, 1947, and is buried in the North Elba Cemetery.

EDWARD YOUNG was born in Chillicothe, Missouri, on September 21, 1872. He was the son of William and Florella Hanmer Young. A resident of Lake Placid most of his life, he moved to Whallonsburg in 1947. He worked as a carpenter, cabinet maker, and guide. He died January 18, 1967 in Ticonderoga at 94.

FRANCIS YOUNG was a former school teacher who built the second camp on Twitchell Lake. He once rowed his guide-boat up to the dock by his cabin, but was too drunk to get out of the boat. He rolled out of the boat into the water and pulled himself ashore by grabbing bushes. He and his neighbor LOW HAMILTON were friends who feuded constantly, Hamilton once chasing Young with an axe. Young, Hamilton, and REUBEN BROWNELL (see) used to have fly casting contests in the winter, casting to holes in the ice. When guiding hunters, Young would put them on watches and leave to drive the deer, supposedly. Then he would go back to his cabin for a few hours. Young had a run-in with a bear in a trap -- he had no gun and attempted to club the bear, but the bear knocked the club away, ripped out the seat of Young's pants, including the drop seat of his long underwear. Young had a small farm at Petrie's Corners, and may have died there. (The above information from William Marleau's *Big Moose Station*.)

WILLIAM B. YOUNG was born at Black Brook in 1880 and guided for 21 years, working with "Old" Sam Barton (see) for many years, and also with Henry Van Hoevenberg. He made 99 ascents to the summit of Whiteface Mountain. In 1915, he moved to the state of Washington, where he owned Young's Inn at Silver Creek until 1945, when he retired. He was descended from Brigham Young and died December 7, 1946, in Lacoma, Washington.

Artist Winslow Homer sometimes used guide Rufus Wallace (center) as a model.

A guide-boat is carried on the shoulders, resting on a wooden yoke.

"Spring Trout Fishing in the Adirondacks—An Odious Comparison of Weights" is the wry title of Frederic Remington's painting done in 1890.

In 1886 "Forest and Stream" magazine came out against hounding in this illustration, "Hounding an Adirondack Deer," wryly subtitling it "To Make it 'Shy,' so that the Still-hunters will not get it." By 1897, both hounding and jacklighting were outlawed.

Alvah Cole and Tommie Sommerville, guides with their boats, are shown with young sports in this photo by J.F. Holley, taken about 1884.

The mundane chores of camp life about 1910 included doing laundry.

d Arnold was a guide on the Fulton
'hain. He was born in 1829 and had
n insatiable appetite for fish, as well
s prodigious snoring power.

E.A. McAlpin, the owner of McAlpin Camp at Brandreth Lake, watches as guide Reuben Cary dresses a deer, about 1890.

A guide at Blue Mountain Lake was the subject of this artotype by photographer Edward Bierstadt, about 1884.

"Lunchtime in the Woods" is the title of this photo of guides taken by Alonzo Mix c. 1890.

Mel Hathaway (l.) age 83, guided in the Keene Valley region and lived along Johns Brook. Jed Rossman (r.) age 58, guide and caretaker at the Adirondack Lodge near Lake Placid. Photo taken about 1920.

Guide Bert Chase is poised under a guide-boat at Upper Saranac Lake about 1905. Note lapstrake skiff on ramp, different in many ways from a guide-boat.

Dogs were legally used to drive deer in the Adirondacks until 1897. Photo by J.F. Holley, c. 1890.

Guides at Raquette Lake, about 1890.

Guide Herb Clark of Saranac Lake stands between Robert and George Marshall on the top of Mt. Marcy, about 1920. The three were the first to climb the forty-six mountains over 4,000 feet high in the Adirondacks.

Guides John Jones and John Baer, from the Blue Mountain and Raquette Lake areas, with deer hunting dog. Photo by Alonzo Mix, c. 1880.

A bark hunting camp at Newcomb Lake in 1884.

Guide Mitchell Sabattis at Long Lake, c. 1888.

Guide John H. Champney also made rustic furniture. Photo c. 1890.

Unknown guide and sport, c. 1890.

Guide Charles Fenton at Number Four, Lewis County, c. 1904.

Guide Alvah Dunning at age 84 on Sagamore Lake near Raquette Lake.

Guides Will Kelley, Seth Pierce, and Ed Gilmore at Raquette Lake in 1910.

Guide Ferdinand Cortez Moody of Saranac Lake, in 1889. He lived from 1822 to 1902.

Guide Chauncey Hathorn, of Raquette Lake, c. 1870. He ran a tourist camp on Golden Beach.

Guide Gary Riggs, of Inlet, c. 1895.

Hand-drawn carts, such as shown in this picture, and horse-drawn wagons sometimes replaced guides to carry boats between lakes.

ST. REGIS CANOE OUTFITTERS

GUIDE/INSTRUCTOR REGISTRY

NAME_____
ADDRESS_____
TOWN_____STATE_____ZIP_____
TELEPHONE: DAY_____EVE_____

1. CERTIFICATES - Please attach photocopies of all releven
   licenses and certificates, Driver's license, Red Cross,
   ACA, etc.

2. Do you have a valid NYS Guide's License?_____ Please
attach photocopy.

3. Do you carry liability insurance for your guiding
services? Yes____ No____ If yes, attach copy of
certificate.

4. What geographical areas(bodies of water) do you feel
comfortable on or would prefer to guide in?_____
_____
_____

5. What activities?

       Trails&Canoe Routes_____   Map & Compass Use_____
       Canoeing Technique_____   Animal Lore_____
     White Water Paddling_____   Natural History_____
          Bird Watching_____ Plant Indentifcation_____
          Edible Plants_____   Outdoor Cooking_____
      Adirondack History_____   Fishing_____
      Low Impact Camping_____   Fly Fishing_____
             Geology_____   Astronomy_____
Other:_____

6. Boats and Paddling - Check Areas of Experience.

   Flatwater_____Moving Water_____White Water Canoe_____
   Solo Flatwater_____   White Water Kayaks_____
   Touring Kayaks_____ Special Children's Paddling_____

7. What type of group are you most comfortable with?

   Clinics_____ Women's Groups_____ Men's Groups_____
   Mixed Families_____ Children_____ Teens_____
   Special Needs_____Other_____

8. Length of Trip:One Day_____2-3 Days_____4-6 Days_____

9. Days of Week you are available. SUN M T W TH F S

10. Your comments are welcomed. Please use back of sheet

The Cilleys, St. Regis Canoe Outfitters, sometimes subcontract guiding services.

Every Body Knows

That we build the Finest and Greatest Variety of

Pleasure Boats and Cano

and keep in stock the finest assortment of Oars, Paddles,
cks, Masts, Spars, Sails, Cleats, Blocks and everything nece
a first-class outfit.
   Send stamp for 60-page illustrated Catalogue, and if in the
o not fail to call at 178 Broadway. It costs nothing to lo
em.

J. H. RUSHTON,
Canton, N. Y.

J. H. Rushton of Canton, N.Y. built many boats in the nineteenth century. He called his version of an Adirondack guide-boat the Saranac Laker.

Guide Garry Vandenburgh (r.) in a hunting camp with college boys.

The Adirondack Guides Association staged an exhibit in New York City at the Hippodrome c. 1920. Guide Garry Vandenburgh is seated at left.

Guide Garry Vandenburgh in stern of guide-boat near a boathouse on Upper Saranac Lake.

Guide Garry Vandenburgh could still handle the oars in his later years.

Guide Sam Dunning, (center), tends the pot while D. Dunning (l.) and a man named Russell, all of them probably members of Colvin's survey party, look on.

Guide Guilford D. Puffer

Joe LaPrairie (l.) and his brother William were both guides for Verplanck Colvin's survey party c. 1890. Notice Joe's double-bitted axe.

PART THREE:
Nine Interviews and a Diary

Much of the research for this book was slow dredging, but the interviews were immediate and exciting. A few were done by mailed questionnaires. For most of the others I used a little portable microcassette recorder I worried and fussed with. There were problems with tapes and batteries; once I tried to hold the thing up to the phone to record a conversation, with disastrous results. I progressed as an interviewer from totally naive in my questioning to less so as I went along; the order of the interviews here may not follow this progression. But it is disheartening to read where I fumbled the thread of the conversation or asked somebody a foolish, repetitive, or mostly unanswerable question. Everybody was cheerful in the face of this, enthusiastic about the topic. I think they got to tell their essential information.

The interviews served as a check on what I was learning about twentieth century guiding. My own most frequent response was "I'll be darned". I would be especially darned if my recorder and I could be transported back to 1830; as long as I was going anyway, I'd take my fishing rod.

Brian McDonnell

"Sometimes I can't believe people are actually paying me. Other times no amount of money would be enough."

Early in the preparation of this book I decided to prepare a questionnaire and send it to all the Adirondack guides listed in the then-current (1991) "Guide to the Licensed Guides of New York State," put out by NYSOGA (New York State Outdoor Guides Association.) This lists licensed guides actively seeking clients. I drew up a questionnaire and as a trial gave copies to about a half-dozen guides of my acquaintance, mostly in my area of Saranac Lake. I asked them not only to complete the questionnaire, but critique it. I got only two replies, which caused me to shelve that little project. Brian McDonnell was one of those who replied. The questionnaire format probably restricted the range of his answers somewhat.

Brian is as big as a professional football lineman and can put a heavy Coleman canoe on the top of a canoe rack quicker than I could start looking around for someone to help me if I were doing it.

He believes strongly in the profession, and promotes it well. He has served two terms as president of the New York State Outdoor Guides Association. One bit of promotion he organized was a "home-and-away" cooperative venture we did with some Montreal Canadians. About a half-dozen Adirondack guides went to Montreal, and the Laurentian Mountains north of there, to meet and hike with a like number of Canadian guides. At our dinner in Montreal Brian delivered the toast -- "Bonjour! Bonjour! Bonjour!" -- the extent of his French. Subsequently he began French lessons.

What follows are the questions on the questionnaire, and Brian's answers.

1. Age? Male or female?
   A: 33, male.
2. Are you full-time, or part-time? What times of year do you guide?
   A: Full-time.
3. Where do you guide (place names)?
   A: Mostly Tri-Lakes area; Hamilton and Franklin Counties.
4. What do you do when you guide?
   A: Camp, canoe, fish.

5. What types of people do you guide? Where are they from, what do they do?

   A: Friends, families, and business people, high school kids, college kids, all male, coed, all female, corporate groups -- part of business meetings or "executive retreats." Clients come from all over, Montreal, Germany, France, Spain, New Zealand, England, Japan, Holland, Colorado, Florida, Texas, Ohio, New Jersey, Metro New York, Pennsylvania, New England.

6. What do your clients say they are seeking, and what do you believe they are seeking?

   A: Relaxing outdoor adventure; change of pace, stress free environment, minimal decisions or pressure, relaxation, fun.

7. What background information do you request of your clients before they arrive? What background info do you ask your clients after you meet them? Do you ask them what they do for a living?

   A: See form enclosed (Form requests name, address, phone, age, sex, SS#, person to notify in case of emergency, previous outdoor related background, and medical information re: any physical conditions, allergies, medications, or recent medical history, and mentions guides are trained in First Aid.)

8. Do you get people with attitudes, good or bad, which they hope their trip will help change or reaffirm? What kinds of attitudes? Do you see changes in clients' attitudes as trips progress?

   A: Yes. Most are looking to cleanse their mind, body and "soul" in some way. Most find the woods soothing -- become less inhibited -- especially on camping trips there is a period of mellowing, of introspection and calm. I could count the negative client experiences I have had on one hand and not use all my fingers -- presentation, identifying client needs and attention to those verbalized anticipations of the journey. Often people have no idea of the vastness of the woods, the balance of nature, and the concept of minimum impact. Most are willing to learn and anxious to absorb knowledge.

   Fairly typical urbanite 5-day trip: First day pace is fast, rush, rush -- always checking watch, need to know itinerary, pretty rigid, stressed. Second day -- begin to relax, take off watch. Third day -- soothed, calm, feeling of never wanting to leave. Fourth day -- planning a business in the Adirondacks -- "If I had it to do over." Fifth day -- reality oozes its way back, watches are back on, stress about job, family, flight connections, pets, etc., start making their way back to the surface -- wish they could stay.

9. Do you feel you teach as you guide? How and what?

A: Yes, in a low-key informational way -- camping and woods skills, survival, minimum impact camping, flora and fauna identification, diet, energy conservation, skills -- canoes, hike, ski, etc.

10. Regardless of what you actually do, what do you feel your actual role should be?

A: Facilitator for improved interpersonal skills, either individual or group. Build self-esteem, assist others to find inner peace, develop cooperative group sense, "team building," enhance attitudes of "healthy competition" -- not cut-throat -- steward of the woods -- educate clients subtly about the need for areas like the Adirondacks, teach skills to enjoy a safe adventure -- provide quality equipment to make clients comfortable.

11. What equipment do you use?

A: Eureka tents, Coleman and Camptrails backpacks, Coleman Peak 1 stoves, Wenonah and Coleman canoes, Savage paddles, Vasque and Merrill boots, Trak and Kartle skis, Tubbs and Iverson snowshoes.

12. What problems are there that interfere with your guiding?

A: "?"

13. How does the State help or hinder you?

A: (positive) Stock fish in the rivers and ponds, promote use of the Adirondacks to neophytes, developing a licensing program. (negative) Lack of personnel to enforce DEC rules and regulations, hassle over group size -- no definite policy, inept "management" of Saranac Lake Chain regarding motorboats, should be size limits, enforcement of speed, Middle Saranac should be small boats and canoes only. What ever happened to Unit Management Plans?

14. Do you like guiding?

A: Yes. I can't think of anything I would rather do.

15. Do you think there should be more or less canoe-only areas? Whether you say yes or no, where could they be created?

A: Definitely more. Middle Saranac Lake, Raquette River above Axton Landing to Long Lake, new lands acquired by the State. Whitney, Lake Marion -- even one motor boat can ruin your whole day!

16. Regarding guiding, if you were King or Queen, what would you change?

A: "?"

17. What is the importance of guiding in the grand scheme of things?

A: As the world becomes more and more urban and as humans become less and less acclimated to the woods, skilled woodspeople are necessary to provide the skills, expertise and equipment for a brief submersion into the natural environment. To truly enjoy the woods for what they are, a guide can remove many of the associated hassles an inexperienced woods traveler would have with faulty equipment, unfavorable weather, overfriendly animals, or a rain soaked map.

18. What do you charge?

A: Varies on type of trip, but basic guide wage is $125 per day.

19. Do you get tipped, how often, and how much? Do you expect a tip? If you do, how do you feel when you don't get it?

A: Yes, often, 10-50% no hard and fast rules. I don't expect a tip most of the time.

20. What problems have you had with getting paid?

A: None -- paid in advance or no trip!

21. Do you feel you get paid the right amount for what you do?

A: Does anyone? Sometimes I can't believe people are actually paying me. Other times no amount of money would be enough.

22. Have you guided for other related businesses, such as outfitters or other guides? How has this relationship worked out?

A: Yes. It was a good place to start to identify strengths and weaknesses, but I just wasn't designed to work for someone else.

23. Do you have your own guiding business?

A: Yes.

24. What do you do in addition to guiding?

A: Anything that will make me money! Location work for businesses, municipal projects.

25. How much of your income do you report?

A: All of it.

26. Your additional comments on any matter.

A: --

27. Highest formal education you have obtained?

A: Bachelor of Science in Labor and Human Resources.

28. Do you have any ancestors or other relatives who were or are guides? What were/are their names? What do you know about them?

A: No, they wouldn't adopt me.

Clarence Petty

"To look out on the lake in the late afternoon and not see him coming down was like looking out and not seeing an island there, because for fifty-six years he worked at that one camp."

Clarence Petty's accomplishments are probably too numerous to list but include guide, Conservation Department employee, Navy pilot, Forest Preserve Specialist on the staff of the Temporary Study Commission on the Future of the Adirondacks, and much more. His vigorous physical constitution, acute mental faculties and self-effacing manner well into his eighties have been the envy of many a younger person. Clarence grew up on Upper Saranac Lake and Coreys, about mid-way between Saranac Lake and Tupper Lake. He lives in Canton, but still owns the house he grew up in at Coreys where he was interviewed.

CB: What did some people in Coreys do for a living when you were a child?

CP: Will Schryers, he was a guide up here; just about everybody here, you know, just guided - that's all they did up here. My father bought our place in 1910 and we moved here in 1911, and Will Schryers had a party up in Shadow Clearing, I think it was about 1914 or 1915, I can't remember the exact date, and he was shot by a member of the party that he was guiding. It was along late in the afternoon and Will Simons was the other guide, him and Will Schryers and they had this group from Rochester and Will Simons and Will Schryers were coming in from the river with their guns over their shoulders like that and this fellow from Rochester had seen these big deer tracks and he was all excited, as people are, and he saw what looked like horns and he pulled up and shot and got Will Schryers right in the stomach. It was late in the afternoon and Will Simons went out to Long Lake and it's quite a ways from Shadow Clearing to Long Lake, and was able to get a team of horses and there was an old log road that used to go along Long Lake into Shadow Clearing and by the time they got Will out, it was the next day, and of course, he had died enroute.

Will Simons had the reputation of killing deer for the market, long after I guess it was declared illegal to do it, but years ago I remember people used to tell me that down in Tupper Lake he would hang up the deer down there in a locker and he would kill probably 100 deer or more in a year and sell them. He used to hound them.

Now up above here Will Duquette was also a guide and they used hounds back in the 1800's of course, and Mrs. Comfort, who had a camp over here, she actually was one of the first ones to contact him as a guide here and she used to tell about going out on the Raquette River when they watched for deer, they'd watch along the water. They'd send the dogs out and then they'd just hope the deer would run to the water, which they usually did. The dogs would go after the deer and they'd all take to the water, and so they chased a lot of deer that they never got because the people weren't where they thought the deer were going to come out. But that's the way they used to hunt them - they didn't bother going in and really hunt very much except at night.

Back in about, I think it was 1895, my father was guiding a lieutenant governor; his name was Worthheim and he used to take him up on the river jacking deer and they had these lights they rigged on the caps and on the front of the guide boat, and when the deer would look up, his eyes would shine, and then, of course, they'd shoot the deer. He killed several deer on the river and I think it was the second year that he came up, my father liked the gun so much, and he remarked about it. It was a Model 95, a taper barrel 30-30, and he gave it to my father and I used it for years. I killed a number of deer with it, and then I gave it to my son, who happens to be out in California right now. Kind of an antique, but that deer rifle has killed quite a few deer on the Raquette River during the days of jacking, which is, of course, long gone now. Even back in the late 1800's, my father said that there were times when the deer were pretty darn scarce in the fall of the year. As the lumbermen got in and they cleared off a lot of the land and got a lot of sprout growth for them to eat, it stimulated them, as long as they had a good winter, but it was the winters that killed off the deer when they have good deer population in the Adirondacks. A lot of people think it's the hunters that do, but it's the winters that do the business when it comes to controlling them. And you'll notice we've had now three or four pretty good years and there's lots of deer around, but if you get one of those winters like we once in a while will get, when you've got deep snow and it comes early, and it lasts late in the spring, then you lose all your yearlings, certainly, and the fawns of that year, and then you've got a big shortage.

CB: Who was at Coreys, on the Indian Carry?

CP: Here on the Carry there was Will Duquette, Will Simons, Bob Canning, my father, and Freeman up here, Harry Freeman. Those were the guides here at that time when we were here. And of course, they're far different than the guiding today. No such thing as a license. My brother and I, we've guided parties for years, long before they had such a thing as a guide's license. People would call up and we'd take them out in the fall, even when we were going to school. Pretty near every weekend of hunting season, we'd have parties we'd take up hunting. And it was fun. It was a lot of work, too, but it gave us the money and when my father was guiding and we lived over there on the lake, the fee was two dollars a day. When Bill and I started to guide, we got four dollars a day, and boy that was a lot of money.

That was back in 1917, 1918, and even in the 20's and 30's, we had parties out, and even when we were going to school, they'd ask us if they could come up and spend a week. Well, we couldn't take the time off from school to go, so we'd tell them the weekend come, why, we would guide them. But we had people coming from New York and Rochester and Buffalo and all over the place. Because when a party got deer, we never advertised or anything, they just called us up and asked us to go out. Most of these people up here that were guides, they were pretty busy all fall, and in the hunting season, and during the spring, in the fishing season, too.

When it come winter time, guiding was over, so what they would do, the guides would work for these people that had camps around and of course, camps were always closed, but they had ice houses. They'd fill ice houses, they had the wood to cut, and that's what kept them going during the winter. Well, just as soon as the spring come, people would come to fish, and so the guide season would go through until the end of the hunting season in the fall. But then in the winter, believe me, it was pretty scarce business, and so they would pick up what money they could on trapping. All of them were trappers, you know. And that's why you probably saw lines of fur here in these pictures.

It was around 1915 or '16 that these camps up here began to hire more people and then they'd hire caretakers. At first my father was a caretaker from the time people would come in, in the spring, or usually it was around July or first of June, July, and then they would leave around Labor Day, and then he'd be on his own again. He worked for these people up there so long that they would hire him on a full-time basis, I think it was along about 1920 or somewhere along, 1919, 1920. And he was then the full-time caretaker there. So he didn't have to depend on people calling him for guiding. And that's what most all of those fellows did up there, that were guiding.

Mart Moody was a guide in the area. He was a great storyteller, of course. He was so good at it that the sportsman's club down in New York would actually get him to go down there, pay his way, and go down and he'd put on one of these story telling deals for the sportsmen. He'd tell stories that were factual to start with, and then he would begin to stretch them and pretty soon I think my father says he thought he believed them himself. One of them, he'd say, "Now, I was hunting over there at the foot of Mount Morris, and there was a little knoll there," and he shot a couple of grouse and he was coming around the field, and all of a sudden, he said he saw a deer there and he said, "God, I'm tempted to get that one." But he didn't have any shot there and he says there was a bunch of pin cherries right near him. He said, "I swooped those things off and sucked off the food off of them, and put those pits right down into the barrel," and he says, "I pulled up and shot like that and the deer ran." He says, "I missed him. But a year later I saw a tree moving right along the ridge just like that," and he says, "By God, there was cherry trees growing right off his back."

When I think of it now, paying a guy $70 for a guide boat to see the amount of work they put in it, it gives you some proportion of what the value of a dollar was then compared to what it is now. It's just amazing. I often tell people I'm living in the past. I go into a store and see stuff that, you know, I used to get a pair of shoelaces for a nickel, you know. You go in now and pay almost a dollar for the same thing. Boy, it's amazing, isn't it?

...My father was very friendly with Jake Vosburgh, who was the game warden up here. He worked this whole area over here for years back in the early part - about 1900. At least he was the game warden that come over in 1908 and told my father that we would have to move from state land because he said there was a lot of squatters up around Long Lake and they were cutting trees and everything else on state land. And he says we're going to have to move them off, he says because we can't have that. So, that's why we moved out of there. Guides all around the lake, they build their camps wherever it was convenient for them, and nobody cared. There was a lot of land, few people, and entirely different now.

CB: Getting back to guide boats for just a minute, this may be a foolish question. But, if you paid by the pound, what incentive was there for the builder to keep the boat light?

CP: Well, there wasn't any incentive. I say it was a dollar a pound. They didn't actually weigh the boat and you paid that, but that was the going price of guide boats at that time. I mean they didn't just weigh it and say well, if it weighed 60 pounds, it's 60 dollars. No, but everybody knew that less than 100 dollars always was the normal price of a guide boat. It was 1939, the Walters Camp here on Upper Saranac changed hands. They were going out. They had six or seven guide boats up there. And, so, they were for sale. My mother heard about it, and she says, "I'll buy one of those," she says, "they're selling them for 40 dollars." So I went up and got one there. Forty dollars apiece is what was paid for those guide boats. So, it gives you some idea of what happened from 1939 even until now. So, when they were new, 60 or 70 dollars was the going price for them. And then they had church boats, what they called church boats. They had a few of those around, and my father had one up there on the lake. His party had one. Of course, they'd take people over to Church Island, to church on Sundays. And they carried about twice the size of a normal guide boat, I think about five people, six people, something like that, in addition to the guide.

CB: Wasn't there something they called a freight boat? Was that different?

CP: Well, those things were ones that they carried trunks and stuff like that in. For instance, it was 1908 when they had the big fire. The fires that went across Floodwood and burned out the trestles on the railroad tracks in that area there. My father was working out of the Wawbeek Hotel. They got scared that they were going to get burned up in there, and so, they hired all the guides around the lake to take them down to the train in Saranac Inn, because they wanted to escape out of there. My father worked all that day. He made two trips down and back that day, and it's from Wawbeek down to Saranac Inn, six, five miles, 20 miles, carrying trunks and people down there. The second trip, after he got down there, he found out that the trestles had burned out between Tupper, and so they were down in Saranac Inn and some of them went out on the lake because the smoke was so thick. They went out on the lake, they were afraid the fire was going to come through and burn them up. Actually, it didn't get close enough to Saranac Inn, although that area around Fish Creek all burned out, you know. The whole thing burned up there. And all the guides had a job just hauling people from Briarwood's and the Wawbeek down to Saranac Inn because they wanted to get out of there.

In 1903 and 1908 there were two big fires. The wind was from the north most of the time because my mother said that in New York City, they had the gas lights on all day because it was so dark, the smoke from the Adirondacks was coming down from the north. They had one of those high pressure areas from the north. That was the time when Long Lake West burned up and the trains burned up there. Byron Cameron, who was a game protector in Saranac Lake, told me. He said the wind blew so hard that it actually blew the fire out along between Saranac and Lake Placid. There was a channel there almost like a venturi.

CB: I'll be darned. What year were you born?

CP: 1905.

CB: So you would have been around when the first cars started coming, the Model T's or whatever they were?

CP: They weren't Model T's. They hadn't built any of those. The first cars I can't remember because I didn't pay any attention to them. They sat way high and they had a brass radiator on the thing, and they had a chain driver. I remember seeing the bicycle chain, which activated the rear wheels. One of the funny things that happened, I was looking out through the woods and watching them dig the things out and we got a little bit less timid, and we'd get a little closer and a little closer. Finally, they got stuck down in the road, and about that time we heard a lumber wagon coming from up here. Fred Woods used to have a team there. Of course they worked in the woods, and he was going down to Bartlett's apparently at the time, and here this car was in the road. It's the first one that we ever saw and knew that had come up here, and I think it was 1909 or 1910, I can't remember which year it was. But anyway, we knew Fred, so we came down from the road and these people asked him if they would unhitch his horse and pull them out, because they were right down in the sand. Well, he took his wagon. He drove it out there and unhitched the horses and hooked on to the old car and pulled it out. And they turned around and went back toward Bartlett because they owned Douglas Point. They were going back there,

I guess to leave it. And after they had gone, I remember, oh, Fred Woods hooked up his wagon again, lit up his pipe, and he looked down at Bill and I and he says, "Them things will never amount to anything."

CB: Do you think that the car had anything to do with affecting the use of guides in that era?

CP: Yeah, I think that the transportation and the improvement of roads really changed the whole thing because pretty near all the travel was the guide boats. For instance, when we were kids and were there on Upper Saranac, when we wanted to get our teeth fixed, we would get into the guide boat in the spring, and we'd go to Bartlett's. My father would carry the boat over to the Saranac River. We'd get into the guide boat, go down to Saranac, get our teeth fixed. Incidentally, the dentist had a drill that he worked with his foot, just like those old sewing machines. He'd pump it like that and the drill, that's what he'd drill into your teeth with. And I can remember that so well because it hurt like hell.

I remember going down to Saranac on the river and then coming back. It was at night. And it was so dark, my father would have to keep throwing his head up to look at the trees. You know how the Saranac winds, well, he'd throw his head up like that, and we'd get back, and oh boy, I'd be tired, you know sitting in that boat coming up the river. Because it's a long haul down there and back in a day's time.

...There's no place where you can really shed the problems that you have better than going back into the wilderness. That's one of the things Bill and I had the advantage of years ago. We'd go up into Cold River, sometimes alone, and we'd stay there for two or three weeks when school was out. And when you would come out, when you walked out, not having heard anybody talk or anything, at that time there was no airplanes flying over and you heard no internal combustion engine. And I remember coming down here at the Carry and hearing somebody talk and it was kind of strange. We used to go back in there, you know, and we'd hunt, fish with Rondeau. I remember my father one time saying to him, "Well, suppose you cut yourself bad here with an ax?" and Rondeau says, "You have no business cutting yourself."

...I remember Carlos Whitney coming in one time and he says, "I'm not going to kill another deer." He was, I'd say maybe at the time he was in his 60's. He was a big, husky guy. He could pick up a 200 pound deer and walk off with it. He was one of those guys you think of carrying a bull moose under each hand. Great big husky guy! And he shot this deer up on the side of the mountain over here and he said it was a nice buck. He shot it and he walked up there and just as he got up to it he says, "The deer come up and looked me right in the eyes," just like that, he says, "as if to say what did you do that for?" It just struck him so, he says, "I'm not going to kill another deer." And he'd killed a lot of them. It just shows you how people change, too. I see this happening in people as they get older. I think they have maybe a greater respect for life than the young people.

CB: Did you hunt when you were younger?

CP: ... Bill and I used to hunt for the market before they had a law against selling stuff. We would hunt, we got 40 or 50 cents apiece for snowshoe rabbits, well, snowshoe hares is the correct name for them. On our way to Saranac on our snow shoes, we had our guns with us, and we'd kill rabbits on the way down, and the next morning we'd take them in to give them to market and sell them for 50 cents to the people. They used to have them hanging out right along the sidewalk there in Saranac Lake. And then when we were here, when we weren't on a trap line somewhere, we'd actually drive for them, just like you do for deer. You could take these swamps around here, well, one would set right there, and the other guy would go up in the end of the swamp and he'd just zig zag back and forth, and the rabbits would come out there and they'd shoot them on the way down, and take them down in Saranac. Another way we would hunt them, when it was snowing. You could start a rabbit and you knew that if you kept on his track, it would be only a few minutes that he would be right back there again, at that same spot. They had a run, you know. So, we'd go out when it was snowing, and you could pick up their fresh track right away so it wouldn't get confused with all the rest of them around these swamps. We'd go out together and just walk the swamp and one would start, the guy would stand right there and the other would just walk around within 15 to 20 minutes, if you walked right along, you'd be right back there, bang, and you shot him. So we'd hunt rabbits.

... Hell, my father worked as a caretaker for years and years for 60 dollars a month, and I think that even in the '20's and '30's I don't think he was getting much over, certainly the '20's, not so much over 100 dollars a month. That's all he'd get. You needed to make a living.

This fellow who was a guide, several of them that used to stay there at the Rustic Lodge, guides that is, Henry Jones, and there was one guide that had killed a number of deer way late in the season. The season was almost Christmastime, and old Pete McCormick had a team that he kept right there at the lodge, the barn right there. And he was going to Saranac Lake. This fellow said he wanted to take the venison down to Saranac Lake. So, he put it in a great big chest and put in on the sled and just about the time they got the thing all set up and the blanket over it, along comes Jake Vosburgh, who is the game warden. And Jake says, "You're not going to Saranac are ya?" and he says, "Yeah." "Can I get a ride?" "Yeah." So Jake rides to Saranac and they both sit on this box with the venison in it and this guy said that he said he was scared all the way that Jake would want to know what the hell was in that box. They were never asked a thing. And some of them, I'm sure because they were friendly with the guides, that they weren't too tough on them. It's pretty hard for a person that you know for years, and you camp with them and all that kind of stuff, and they're friendly, to come along and knowing that they've done something. It's pretty damn hard for a game protector to say we've got to fine you for doing it, or catch you for it. So, you know darn well that some of these people just overlooked it.

CB: You were telling me about your father.

CP: The Regional Supervisor was here at the time, and of course, when he heard that my father hadn't come home that evening, why he alerted the Forest Ranger and they come out looking for him, and my mother called me and said that he hadn't showed up and by this time it was about eight o'clock at night, and so I drove up from Parishville. They were looking for his boat along the lake, it was raining and blowing. There was a big storm going on. I met Bill here and I said, "Well, we better start going out looking for him, anyway." So, we got a guide-boat up at the Wawbeek. They had another guide-boat there. And while Bill stood in the back with a flashlight, I decided to just go to the camp where he worked and I knew the wind was blowing pretty much towards the east. The waves were rolling. I said, "We'll follow the shore because if something happened to him, he'd be floating against one of those shores over there."

So it was about midnight before we got really going off of Wawbeek. It was still raining and blowing like the devil. We followed the shore all the way down in back of the island, Birch Island in there, and we got down near Douglas Point, and all of a sudden, and he was showing the flashlight along the shore, and we saw a shine against the boat on the shore, and we drifted in there, one oar was still in the oar lock, the other one was gone, and the boat was floating up against the shore about half full of water, and he was lying in the boat back like that, just kind of looking up at the sky, and he was dead.

We put him in our boat, and took the other boat, pulled it up where we could get it, and dumped the water out, and towed it back, and the next day, my brother went over and found the other oar. It was floating up against the shore. He had been coming down headed in the wind, and apparently, he collapsed out in the middle of the lake somewhere, and just floated. It was about two o'clock in the morning when we found him. I said, "Boy, we were lucky that he didn't go into the lake." People would call Mother here sometimes and they'd say, "We saw him out on the lake in that awful storm, and he disappeared behind the waves." The waves were so bad, and what was he doing out there? Well, he'd insist on going up and back and forth anyway, regardless of what the wind was going. He used to say, "Well, that boat will take care of you, if you just lay right down in the bottom of it."

I think what happened was, he probably, when he got that awful pain in his chest, and he had about two days before that, he'd told my mother that when he opened that door over there, there's a door that you pull up. He said, "I got a muscle pain." Then coming down rowing you know, against the wind, why, his heart just gave out, and so he was floating up against the shore. That ended that. To look out on the lake in the late afternoon and not see him coming down was like looking out and not seeing an island there, because he worked at that one camp, the White camp, for fifty-six years.

He'd walk over here, a mile and a quarter to the lake, get in his guide-boat, go three miles up the lake to Deer Island, come back in the afternoon. He was actually rowing six miles and walking two and a half everyday just to get back and forth to work. He was raking the leaves, and putting in ice and doing all that kind of stuff up there and it was just as much a part of him. You know, he thought more of taking care of that camp up there than he did this place here. He was just a part of it. I used to say, "Why don't you quit?" Give it up. No, he couldn't do that. He was going to work.

Carl Hathaway

"A caretaker's in trouble when you hear him say 'my camp.'"

Carl Hathaway -- guide, caretaker, guide-boat builder -- and teacher. For a number of years North Country Community College in Saranac Lake offered an evening course in guide-boat construction under Carl's tutelage. The course ran the gamut from digging up spruce roots (for the next class) to a finished boat in which every student had a hand. Perhaps the satisfaction for Carl came in seeing the sense of achievement the students gained. He remembers seeing tears of happiness in the eyes of one student when the members of the class took turns rowing their completed boat.

His former students are scattered in the area and beyond, many making and repairing guide-boats. Their anecdotes about Carl are legion (which he might not know), but the common thread is always the same -- "He knows what he's doing, and he was able to teach me."

The printed page can't convey the wonderful inflections and cadences of Carl's speech. With his pipe, slim -- almost gangly -- frame, the easy-going manner of a born teacher, and his storyteller's gift, Carl might have just stepped out of a guide-boat a hundred years ago -- a notion that would, I believe, appeal to him.

CB: You just said when you became a guide.

CH: That was in '48, 1948.

CB: Right here in Saranac Lake?

CH: Yeah. Basically the guiding we did was for hunting. We hunted with Ross Freeman, Gene Freeman. They were guiding for the Remington's out on Deer Island on Upper Saranac. They were hired guides and I'd work for them, and then I worked with the Lemoy's, Ken and Braynard out of Tupper, and guided up around Big Tupper for hunting in the fall. Most of the time, in summer, I never got into fishing or canoeing because I worked with my father as far as caretaker and I got the job over where I am now.

CB: How long have you been there?

CH: I've been there 37 years, and it got into a different facet of guiding. I think there are a lot of misconceptions as far as guides being ignorant, rough, coarse and so on. There was also a difference in, well, your economy. The people you had in here were very wealthy people that you were guiding, the guide was here trying to make a living, and in turn, he had their whole life in his hand. There was a lot of things that go on in these camps that you'd never go ahead and document, but it was a good education, and you could see the types of life and character that these people had. Some of them good, some of them pains in the butt, and so on, but overall, a guide had his duties to do and they did them, and I think that to me they should be, their image hasn't been put out to the extent that I'd like to see it put out.

The men that I worked with like the Lemoy's and so on, they knew how to handle the people. They knew how to handle boats. If they got in a storm, they knew what to do. If you wanted to protect them, they could put up some kind of a shelter or get a fire going, so the people wouldn't suffer. They'd cook for them, depending on what kind of a job you had as guiding. Just like Dave Cilley up here, and a lot of the Frenettes and so on. A lot of them are darn good guides.

But there was a few that had a pretty rough reputation. I know at the time when I was guiding with the Lemoys there, there was somebody that was up there I think at Sunmount, he was hiring out as a guide. He'd put up the people's lunches and take them up off the highway up there near Corey's, put them back in the woods. "Now, I'm going to be hunting all around trying to get you a deer, but I'll be back about a quarter to five," and he says, "I'll pick you up. Now, you stay right here and keep your eyes open because I'm going to be going around and make sure you stay," and he'd get them on their post with their bag lunch. He'd go back and drive into Sunmount, go to work, and when he got done from work, he'd go out and pick them up, and he'd have a story as far as, "Well, didn't you see that? I had a big buck and I know it was right there almost to you," or "You moved and I see where he ran back."

You mentioned Clarence Petty, Dick Emperor, to me, you just can't beat those people. They're down to earth. They aren't spilling their guts, they aren't bragging about what they've done. I'd say 15 years back, I give up my license because for a while if you were a caretaker and went out and took people out on a picnic you had to buy a guide's license because as a technicality, you were working for hire guiding these people. Finally it got to me where it was just ridiculous. If you're going out taking them on trips, camping with them, or taking them in the woods hunting, yes, that's guiding.

CB: The Lemoys and some of these older fellows that you mentioned, how did they get business?

CH: Mainly reputation. Word of mouth, and a lot of them would take and have, well, they'd leave word in the hardware stores and the sporting good stores. At that time there was a guide roster, I guess state-wide, but their main money came from word of mouth and from your sporting stores. I did some guiding on my own. I'd get another man to help me because initially, any of the sports you brought in, they stayed on the run-ways where the deer would be driven to them. You had on an average of one guide to three, possibly four men for hunting. So, you had a fairly large party. About the minimum you could do as far as hunting deer, you had to have three guides. Because you had to have one man to put the sports out on the run-ways, the men that you were guiding for, and then you had to have somebody to drive, so it'd take at least two men.

Then it got where the economy was, they were starting to cut down. It got to where a group of say, eight or ten men, wanted to hire one guide. And there was men that would hire out. And to me, when they hired out with one man, as far as a guide goes for a hunting party, it was ridiculous, because you figure by the time he went around and put all the watchers out, and he went around and tried to make a drive, especially on bare ground, it's a waste of the people's money, and you just couldn't do it. One intermittent stage, there, was they would hire two guides. One fellow would take care of the guiding and the other fellow would put the watchers on the run-ways and they'd switch off, but they were using, say a couple of the young men out of a party, to go with the fellow to make the drive.

CB: Now, on the drive, I've heard from some of the old-timers they did everything from bark like a dog to I don't know what. What would you actually do when you made the drive?

CH: Well, as far as legal guiding, you'd either bark like a dog, or another thing, they would take a split stick and knock it against the trees because it would be a sharp noise and a lot of the guides professed that was the best way. Just to hit it, because it'd crack, and as you know, if somebody just shoots or cracks a stick like that, and you're out in the woods, you can't locate it with just one crack, and then all at once it's over here and over there, and pretty soon, to me, it was a good way to move deer. Then some of them would hunt through, but as far as the time I was guiding, it was illegal for a guide to carry a rifle. You had to carry a hand gun. There were some that would go right ahead and hunt through, with rifles, and if they got a shot, okay, it went with the party when they left. They may be barking, but hell, you could be barking right along and a deer could get up within 20 feet of you, and let you walk right by because they know exactly where you are. You'll hear a deer jump and you look and you walked within 20 feet of that thing, barking like hell. And other times some of the guides that carried rifles, they used them mainly to finish wounded deer, or like that. There's so many variables, some of them pro and some of them con, that it was hard to draw a line.

CB: What was the average guide wage when you started?

CH: About six, seven dollars a day. Something like that.

CB: Who furnished lunch and stuff like that?

CH: Most of it when you were guiding for a party like Lemoy's or Remington's up there, they furnished the food and then you'd prepare it. What it was, they'd reach into cupboards and it was kind of unique because they'd reach in the cupboard, say take out eight cans of soup, that's what it was -- eight cans of soup. It might be chicken noodle, might be pea soup, tomato soup, and it all went in the bucket, and a lot of times, they would prepare the sandwiches and so on, and you'd always have 12-quart pails, brewed up a pot of coffee, and that was what you usually had for lunch. If they were like some of the ones that we hunted with up there to Lemoy's, wherever they were staying, they would take their bag lunch and you'd carry whatever you wanted for yourself. Braynard always had his pot of coffee and a 12-quart pail. He was a real gentleman and comical as hell. He'd start in and no matter what party it was, he'd put a 12-quart pail of water hanging over the fire and he'd start measuring out from the pound can of coffee. Right from the start, you knew damn well that whole pound was going into that 12-quart pail. Well, he'd take it off the fire, take a cup of cold water, pour all over the top and settle the grounds. He made it pretty good, had real character.

CB: What were your clients like?

CH: We ran into different situations, hunting and the different sports. Some of them were game hounds, they wanted everything they could get. I got into one experience. I was carrying a .22 and this fellow, one of the sports, he shot, hit a deer, and he wasn't hit that hard, and we tried, killing a deer with a .22, it's quite a chore, wounded. So I asked him, "Can I borrow your rifle? I'm not allowed to carry one, or come with me. You finish your own deer." "Well, that's what we hired you fellows for." I said, "Well, can I borrow your rifle?" "I don't loan my rifles to anybody." So, to make a long story short, a box of .22 shells later, he got his deer and he came back, oh, three or four weeks later, and stopped in to see Bernie Lemoy, and he said, "I got a complaint to make. You know that buck that I shot, that guide finished?" he said, "I didn't get a pound of meat that didn't have a bullet hole through it." Old Bernard says, "Next time you're hunting with somebody and they want to borrow your rifle, there's a reason for it. They know hunting, and if you don't want to kill your own deer, to finish it, my suggestion is let him take that rifle," he says, "You'll have a deer with some good meat in it." And so, I mean that's one of those cases, guide story.

Up to about five, six years ago, what I've seen as far as licensed guides go, didn't impress me too good. It seemed as if they could just go out and pay their money, and they'd get a guide's license. I'm awful glad to see the qualifications and the testing that is being done now because these people that were just trying to draw guide's money on weekends and so on to pick up some extra money, they weren't qualified. Somebody's going to get hurt, because they didn't know how to take care of their people. A lot of them weren't actually woodsmen as far as fishing goes, they had a boat and a motor or a canoe or a guide-boat or whatever, and that was about it, and as far as handling people in heavy weather and so on, they weren't qualified. Now with first-aid classes and so on, CPR, and everything else, I like what I see because to my estimation, before when you were recommended by a couple guides to get a license back when I was getting it, you could pretty well bank on what that guide said, or else he wouldn't sign his name to it, and also at that time, I don't know how it is now, but you were supposed to report any game violations, you were just like a special game protector. I don't know that many of them did, but that was supposed to be part of a licensed guide in the state of New York.

CB: Can we talk about guide-boats for a minute? You took over from Willard Hamner, is that right? When was that?

CH: Twenty-seven years ago -- '63, '64.

CB: Were guides still using guide-boats in the '40's?

CH: Very seldom. They were getting into your outboard motors. The old Lightning 10-horse Mercury was coming into play there. Your guide-boats started declining with the advent of the gasoline engine. Then the launches come in, then all at once you had your in-line inboards and your small outboards started up and gradually they started taking over as far as fishing because you could cover a lake a lot quicker. Dad had bought me an old 18-footer. Well, somebody had put a disappearing motor in it, one of those disappearing propeller jobs. And there was just a rough hatch on the bottom. That was my boat to play with, and because I was the only child up there and you didn't get acquainted too much with anybody else, even on the north end of the lakes, so if I wanted to go out on the lake, I took that old 18-footer. Dad knew I could've walked right around on the gunwales and it wouldn't tip over.

I wasn't allowed to use the camp boats because I was a caretaker's son and I had my own guide-boat and it was an old clunker and it leaked some and so on and so forth, but if I wanted to go someplace, that's what I had because at that time there was an extreme class distinction between the people that owned the camp and the caretaker.

I still like the situation that I've been in. We've been there 37 years with these people and it's "Yes, ma'am and yes, sir." If they want to sit down and visit, fine. They'll say, "Carl, can we see you a moment?" or something like that. Otherwise, I go about my chores, making sure the boats are all set. If they want to go out in the boat, "Carl, we'd like to have you take us up to Saranac Inn," or something like that. Fine. But, we've held the distinction, separation there and it's, to me, it's been ideal. I like it. Some of the children, they'll say, "Well, after all, Carl, you've been here so long, you're one of the family." I don't want to be one of their family, and that was what went on right from the start, and that's the way I was brought up. Now, I know my daughter and son-in-law, they wouldn't think of calling their boss "Yes ma'am." And if they did, she'd be insulted because she would know it was a polite insult they were using. It'd be kind of derogatory.

The biggest thing is almost a joke - that is, that a caretaker's in trouble when you hear him say, "My camp," because mentally he is in trouble. You've got to treat it like your own for twelve months out of the year. They just use it, say, for three or four months out of the year, but regardless I don't own that camp and as far as that goes, the house we live in, it's my home, but it's their house, and at times it's a hard distinction to keep, but if you don't, some way or other you're going to come up against it, because they're going to have to let you know they're still boss, whether it's to tear down a building or no matter what, even if it's against the grade. If she said something about she wanted that main house tore down, I'd say, "How quick do you want it down?" I'd get Trudeau up there, and if she wanted it cut in half, I'd go up and sharpen up the chain saw and mark on the side and start cutting because I haven't got a cent in it. To me, we've had a good life. I can't complain a bit. If I had it to do over, I'd do the same thing.

CB: For a long time when you had the shop, you were obviously caretaker also, so you had to back off on boat work in the summer?

CH: All the boat work stopped until I was able to hire, oh, I've had three or four good men in there, I'd hire them and as far as I was concerned, they ran the shop. The first of May was usually when I had to start getting the camp ready, 'til after they left in September, because that was the eating money. The shop was an insurance policy. And if something'd happened up there, I had no qualifications. I graduated from high school, that was it. No degrees, no nothing. It was a way that if I get fired up there and you're working for one person and if they get up on the wrong side of the bed some morning and you get up on the wrong side of the bed some morning, that afternoon you'll be going down the road, and there isn't any severance pay that's guaranteed by the unions or anything else. And so that's basically why I bought the shop in the first place. I enjoyed wood working and I worked around boats quite a lot, brought up with them up there on the Upper Lake.

CB: Did you work with Willard for a while?

CH: About two years. That year he died, we were talking about me taking over the shop, but it never jelled out, he died and that was it. I would've loved to had a couple more years, it'd been a hell of a help to me because a lot of things, he showed me an awful lot, and I learned an awful lot from him, but there was still a lot of the boat builder's secrets or tricks of the trade and so on, that it would've been a big advantage to me to have him looking over my shoulder, kind of pointing me the right way.

But there's one thing with guide-boats, I don't know just how to put it. To me, I've seen two poorly built boats since I had the shop for 26 years. The rest of the time, there's a lot of what we call bastard boats, because there's no name on them. Anybody with any expertise at all, or patience basically, can take a guide-boat that somebody else built, and make an exact copy and when that copy's done, painted, varnished, you give that 8 - 10 years, there's no way that if you copied a Hamner boat, there's no way that you can say that that boat is a Hamner, and it can be an exact replica. We've had the same thing, like for instance the college boats we've built over the years, they've been the same boat that I've been building and the only difference is that the decks are a little different, and also we burned into the bottom of the deck that it was built by the college, you know, the students from the college.

CB: As far as quality goes, did you know of any correlation between guides and guide-boat builders in the sense that any of them were one and the same?

CH: I would say yes, definitely. Willard Hamner, he was a guide before he started building boats, and some of these guides that went into these hotels or wanted to start guiding themselves, they would after all, during the winter, unless you were a lumberjack, after hunting season in the fall, there was nothing there, only trapping. What money you made during the summer, that's what you lived on until spring time, and there was damn little year-round work, as far as industry, until you got into logging or something like that. If you were a logger, you certainly weren't going to be guiding because you were going to be working basically year-round with the exception of the spring break up and then there was no time to guide there or anything to guide for. I feel that a lot of the guides and a lot of the what we call bastard boats were built by guides and because during the winter, they had all winter long to build one. If a board didn't fit, they kept working at it until it did. So they might have taken all winter to build a boat and they'd either build it for their own use for the following year, or maybe they'd build a couple over the years and they would sell it. About the first I can remember of boats, they were selling for about, Willard was selling them for about $350.

CB: About when would that have been?

CH: It'd be in the '40's, early '40's, along in that era.

CB: And when you started building them, in the beginning...?

CH: I think it was around $600 or $700 and then it just gradually went up and it got so you had to watch yourself because the next thing you knew you weren't charging enough to survive on.

CB: When you began building them, what type of people were your customers?

CH: I would say at first, there was a few middle class or working people, but when it went above three dollars and a half an hour, like as far as boat repair, the working man couldn't afford to have me work on their boats, because it takes time, and that's about what they could afford and the other factor is that, like when we had that mini-recession there, what, was it ten years ago? Something like that. I lost nine boat-orders. People that would order boats, normally I would just send them a contract and I'd get it back, but I sent out a couple contracts and received nothing, so then I went ahead and got where I would call and that one year, we lost nine orders and because it's going from a necessity to a recreation or status symbol, the Adirondack guide-boat was. The minute a recession hits, recreation's the first thing that's cut off.

CB: Were you doing a lot of either building or repairs for some of the nicer camps, for their boats?

CH: It was right up 'til the last five or six years, that there was better money, as far as the hourly wage goes on repairs than there was in building. Then finally when it took a drastic jump from say, $3,000 to $6,000 in that period of time, people still wanted and they had the money to pay it, so Ralph Morrow and myself started figuring out and we kept track of how many hours we'd put in a boat, and it was roughly 300 hours of labor. Then we went at it and figured out what the materials were worth and cost to us, or cost on the open market would be, for quarter-sawn lumber and so on, and we took the standard wage that had been increasing, and was still building a boat for say $4,000, we sat right down and figured it out exactly roughly $300 at $15 an hour plus say $800 for materials, that's what the price of the boat was, plus tax, and that's the only logical way we could, and I hated to see the price go up because it got where it was up there where it was hard for a common man, and a lot of people to come look at a 16 foot boat, and see it's $7,000 for that boat, and it takes quite a wealthy man to be able to justify that kind of expense. A common man can't. So it cut the town and market right out, and so there's been quite a transition.

As for repair on wooden boats, I know when I took over the shop, my financial advisors told us that's foolish because wooden boats were going out and fiberglass, steel, plywood, and aluminum and so on were coming in. I don't know where they were coming from, but you look up at Spencer's Boatworks, they're busy, Charlie Keough's busy on restoration, Ralph Morrow is doing quite a lot; he's, well, since he went on his own, he's made his livelihood out of restoration and building. I know that one year we had that rough year, I had two men working for me, and I told them, "We've got to go into a different situation. I can't guarantee you a two week notice." I says, "If you're willing to stick with me on it, that's the way it's got to be." Because we didn't have enough work Labor Day to last us 'til Thanksgiving, and so, but all winter long, we'd be just about within two or three days of getting caught up, it might be colder than hell, or a snowstorm or something like that, and I'd see a car drive back down the driveway and there'd be a boat on it or a trailer behind it.

Thank God, we lucked out. It was good luck instead of good management because the economy wasn't there, but we were able to get by, well, like on oar orders, people would order three or four pair of oars, couple pair of oars, like Ausable Club and so on, like that. That gave us another week to build them up, and so we'd see green grass all right, but it wasn't a comfortable business situation by no means.

CB: I'd always want to ask if it's not too airy of a question, what's the essence of a guide-boat?

CH: Practicality. I know that's an awful short answer, but basically, to me the essence of an Adirondack guide-boat is practicality and necessity are the two things that develop the Adirondack guide-boat. They had to have something that was light, that they could carry between down the rivers and so on over the carries, they had to be able to be handled by one man, and the uniqueness of it was one man could take one of these big church boats, 20-foot church boat, you could load it right to the gunwales, put it right down.

CB: What's a church boat?

CH: A church boat is hard to define. I would say anything over three seats would be some people would consider it a church boat. A freighter was basically a heavy planked and a heavy ribbed boat, an economy model, they were built with white pine. Some of them were built with iron screws and so on, so they were a cheaper model, but they were built extra heavy. You'd put trunks in them. The ribs weren't so fragile. To me a freighter is a heavy built guide-boat. The planking might be 5/16 instead of 3/8 or 1/4 inch. The ribs are damn near an inch wide by damn near 1/2 inch thick. They were built heavy, they weren't made to carry just people, they were made to slip off, slip like in Saranac Inn boat-house and go down the lake and bring material back and because the only other thing they had was scows and you start figuring, well, they didn't even have scows the time guide-boats were in heyday because all they had was hand power so anything that went into these camps that are on islands and so on, went in during the winter, on the ice or in these freight boats. Lumber had to be taken in and so on, fine. They might throw six or eight bags of cement in the boat to take it over. They'd use a work boat or what they call a freighter.

A lot of the big camps had boats that were light, made out of cedar. They're the ones they put on the train and sent to Old Forge with a group to come down through the river. They were a good, light guide-boat. But that's all they were used for. The rest of the time, in some of these big camps, those were put aside because they were carry boats and they were used to go over the carries and so on, but the normal use for like guiding on the lake or to go up and get the mail and so on was a heavier boat, more sturdier, take more abuse and so on.

CB: This business about painted boats and varnished boats, did they overlap for the most part or was it a break between a painted boat?

CH: Basically, a varnished boat was a Sunday-go-to-meeting boat, because a lot of your guides said they were too bright for fishing and at that time, they could jack and they didn't want a shiny varnish boat, they'd use blue or green, well it looks black, but it's Prussian blue mixed with varnish.

CB: On the outside?

CH: On the outside. Their green, I can't remember the name of it, but it was a coloring they put in their varnish. It wasn't a paint. But not only that but as far as I was concerned, your people that were using the boats heavy in the time when they were being used, I would say the majority of them were painted boats. They're easier to maintain, if they were scratched up, naturally through use, they were going to be scratched up even more, you'd put another coat of paint on. I'd say your varnished boats were Sunday-go-to-meeting boats, special occasions, or if you were just going out with the boss and he was in and he had his own boat, well, that's the one they used. The guide wouldn't take and use that to go across the lake to go jacking with.

CB: So when might the varnished boats have come in?

CH: I don't know. I can't even guess how far back, but I would say, no doubt, with the appreciation of the craftsmanship and so on, I wouldn't be surprised if they started shortly when they started to build guide-boats. I know there was some boats that we would run into that would be shellacked and it was a son of a gun because you'd try to take it of, and it turned to almost glue and it was hard to get off. They used shellac on some of the old, old timers because I know we've had some problems stripping them. But, I've seen I would say damn near as many old varnished boats as I have old painted boats. But the old painted boats always were in rougher condition because they'd been used more. I wouldn't want to go on record as far as the absolute authority on that, but just from my own opinions. And the rest of your guide-boats are varnished because people want something of beauty and as far as that goes, I know I said when I was in the business, that I would never paint a guide-boat. I'd varnish it and build up the finish full because to me the value of a varnished boat compared to a painted boat, there was an awful difference, but if anybody wanted it painted after, okay, you'd paint it, but I'd make sure that way there was very little problem with remover, somebody could have a varnished boat back.

CB: So you never made a painted boat?

CH: I never built a painted boat. A lot of people have come in and wanted us to take a painted boat and finish it in varnish which is just about impossible. We have stripped some that I know have started out as varnished boats. Probably when they got so badly stained up and passed down from buyer to buyer somebody said, "Well, wouldn't that look nice as far as being nice and blue on the outside and green on the inside?" So, they went ahead and slapped a coat of paint on it. Some of them we have saved and brought back as far as varnishable. And by using a light stain, it wouldn't cover, but it would blend the staining, weather staining, in the wood.

CB: When you see a boat with a front deck with a hole in it, and it appears to be an old boat, can you assume that that was for a jack light or was there other reasons they might have drilled a hole in it?

CH: A lot of them had a flag. Especially your large 18-footers, you'd see a metal grommet in the deck and they had the camp flag on that boat. They might have had the flag on to let them know the boss was coming down the lake, I don't know. It always used to be up on the lake when the flag was up at camp, the party was in. When the party left, even if the caretaker was there, the flag came down.

CB: So it's not safe to assume a hole in the deck was for a jack light in every case?

CH: A large wooden boat, you'd probably be 75 percent right. Some people like to restore, they want to go beyond restoring of the original boat. It isn't above some people's ideals to take a boat and restore it and if there was no jack staff in there, a hole, they'd put one in. Because I've even seen one fellow here in town bought a boat. He brought it in and he said, "Boy, did I get a jewel," and I said, "What is it?" and he brought it in. "There's a Hamner boat." I took one look at it. It was one of the two that was a Forest-built boat. It never had the shaft. I said, "That isn't a Hamner." Tags were right on the front deck. "Well," I said, "Ok, do you want to make a side bet?" and I said, "It isn't a Hamner." "What do you mean? The plate's right there." I said, "I'm betting under that plate the paint is just as old under that plate as it is the rest of the deck and the same color." Because I looked and you look at the screws close, there's little burrs. I took a small screwdriver and took it off, somebody's got a plate, one of Willard's plates, they put on the deck, and sold it to him for a Hamner boat.

CB: I'll be darned.

CH: It isn't a rule, but it's an exception rather, that there is some people around that have pulled this stuff. You could take just a guide-boat and if Hamner's boats were running high, put a Hamner deck in it. I'm not taking anything away from Hamner at all because he was the top craftsman and I hold him in the highest esteem, but what I am saying is there's an awful lot of good boats in these lakes up here, where the craftsmanship was just as good and they were built by some of the known builders, Vassar, and Martin, and so on. Some of them were built by people, one man might have built just one boat or a couple boats and not a professional boat builder because I've already seen it.

I've seen some of the students we had from the college. By the time they got done, they made every part of the boat. Each one had made a piece of planking, each one had put in a rib and so on. Bill Michelfelder down there in Keene, he's doing some beautiful work. Right off the bat, I would've said he wasn't a professional boat builder, but he was one hell of a good craftsman, and it was coming along and I don't know where the turn would be from a craftsman or a teacher into a professional boat builder, I'm not sure, but he is a damn good man. He's doing some beautiful work and not only that, his presentation of the boats in exhibiting them and so on to me, has been darn good because it isn't an "I, I, I" situation all the time, but collectively he is continuing the reputation of an Adirondack guide-boat, and he's doing it nicely. They aren't fiberglass, he did laminate some ribs there, I don't know if he has yet or not, but I know in the last write-up he was talking about using spruce.

So when they took the class, I said, "We're all human. It took a human being to make them. All we have to do is learn how." So it went well, the class. Great big guy works for the state? Anyhow he took her, Tony. He came in. I like Tony. The first night was just more or less orientation, we went to the shop, looking a boat over, "Carl," he says, "There's no way I'll ever build that boat - a boat like that." "Well, Tony," I says, "There's no reason why you can't, but I want one thing understood. If you sincerely feel that you are not going to build a guide-boat, don't waste my time." I says, "As far as I'm concerned, when you get out of here, you will be able to build a boat with no question." He said, "I never can." I said, "Well, it's up to you. When you come back to the next class, don't come back with the attitude you'll never build one or that you can't build one because there'll be no reason why you can't. Whether you do or not that's depending on your job, your time that you can afford, and so on." He had one pretty well built during the summer.

Dan and Bill Frayne

"I fished with Alice, and questions...all kinds of questions. Alice said to me one time, 'Bill, you know everything, don't you?' I said 'Yeah.' She said, 'If I ask you a question and you don't know the answer, you make up one?' I said, 'That's right.'"

Dan and Bill Frayne found what many guides today seek -- a special and secure niche. Sons of Lake Placid guide Dan Frayne, Sr., they worked for many years for wealthy Lake Placid summer residents, some connected with the Lake Placid Club. Most of their guiding was fishing; Dan, Jr., had his fill through the years, and doesn't fish anymore. For the interview we met at Dan's house on Johnson Avenue in Lake Placid. Dan was dressed in olive khaki and looked like a retired Forest Ranger. Bill, who lives nearby, looked like he was getting ready to go fishing, or had just been. Bill's stock of funny stories is endless; I left feeling I could have stayed for days and the tales would not run out. Contrary to the heading above, the stories rang true, with just the right quixotic attention to detail to give credibility.

CB: Both you men guided a great deal, is that right?

BF: Oh yeah, back when it was good, fifty years. Yeah. What knocked the hell out of it for the people who were guiding was the Lake Placid Club, Placid Manor, Whiteface Inn, those were all the places we got calls from. They closed down.

CB: Were you born here in North Elba?

BF: Yes.

CB: When was that?

BF: 1916, November 9, 1916.

CB: And then how did you get involved in guiding in the beginning?

BF: My father was a guide and I was in the woods with him all the time.

CB: So you learned the ropes?

BF: Yes. My father fished with Mrs. Heimerdinger, and when her brother's wife started coming, they talked me into getting a guide's license.

CB: Did they have a camp on...?
BF: On the East Shore. She died in 1985, so there was no, I was out in the cold anyway. Gotta have one good one anyway. One good client. I was with Martin Ervin for fifty years.

CB: Dan, when were you born?
DF: January 23, 1914. I was two years old when Bill was born.

CB: And in that time when you had that long, steady employment, did you guide for other people?
DF: Oh, yes.

CB: How would you get work? How did people know about you?
DF: We had, I guess our father's name. It went way back.

CB: What was your father's name?
DF: Dan. He was the number one guide in this area for years.

CB: Who did he guide or what type of people?
DF: Let's see, way back, Dad started in with a guy called George Griswold. That was his name, George Griswold. He was a veteran of New York Telephone Corporation, he stayed at the Lake Placid Club.

CB: So, his business came from the Lake Placid Club members, pretty much?
DF: Oh yes, my father went with Mrs. Heimer. He guided Mr. and Mrs. Heimerdinger since 1941, but how long before that I don't know. They bought that first boat for them, remember, tell them about it.

CB: Guide-boat?
BF: It's listed as a square-backed canoe, a 16-footer. Takes a 6-horse engine, outboard motor. The first motor I had was a 3-horse Johnson with the gas tank on top, in 1934, and I was guiding them. I was in the Army three and one-half years. When I come back it was more or less, Mrs. Benwolf and her

sister, I was with them pretty steady. But today, if a young fella goes into it today, he's gotta have one good one to fall back on or forget it. Now they're guiding for canoe trips, rock climbing, mountain climbing, camping. Young fella goes into it today, he could make a deal, trail work mostly, back into beaver dams, and brooks that are back in. Speckled trout is getting to be a thing of the past. You got a place where you get brook trout, you keep it to yourself. When I was 14 or 15 years old, caddying, my father had a rubber boat I used to use, I remember Galinger. I used to take them into the mountains for some time fishing, for $5 a day.

CB: Was that in the '30s, Dan?
DF: Oh, yes, back in the early '30s.

CB: Did you have a guide-boat, Dan, or an outboard?

DF: That was when I was only 14 or 15 years old, just by going into the ponds, usually it was Winch Pond down on the Wilmington Road.

CB: Was that a good brook trout pond?
DF: It was then, you could catch one or two good ones every time you went there. Thirteen inch brook trout.

CB: Oh my. Did you get a guide-boat, Dan, after a bit?
DF: Not until 1950, I bought...when Mrs. Heindinger's brother and wife, that was too many for my father, so I got a guide's license and fished with her brother and his wife, and also back in those days, you'd get dozens of calls, everybody wanted to fish, but it has more or less faded away.

CB: When did it start to fade?
DF: You can't guess that really. If you had one good steady one, like Judge Proskaver, I had for years. Back in those days, fishing in Lake Placid was very, very good. You'd get a good catch of fish each time. One day we left Placid Manor, we'd go in for lunch at one o'clock, I'd pick them up at two. And we'd be gone just an hour at the head of the lake. We couldn't let our lines out the fish were biting so good. And

we were back to Placid Manor with eight clean rainbow in just one hour.

CB: Other clients?

DF: I started guiding Jack Adams in 1967 and when I retired I was still with him. He guides me now. When my father died in 1956, May 2, Mrs. Heimerdinger wrote me a letter, asking if I'd guide her, which I did, and I was with her about 32 years. Like I said, she died in 1985. Wonderful woman, wasn't she, Bill? I worked seven days a week for years with Frank Backman, Harry Goldsmith and the Judge.

BF: But they all wanted, God, I look back on those pictures, they all wanted their pictures taken with the fish. Lake Placid was good for lake trout. As good as it was around here. I got a two-week extension on Lake Placid, on Mirror Lake. The season is over on September 30, but you could fish for two weeks. I was working downstate of here. That's gone on for 9 years now. Lake Trout. Bill Shackett, if I had to name the number one lake trout fisherman around this area it would be Bill Shackett. And he quit. He got skunked three times in a row and he put his stuff away. There's a guy who could go out and catch three lake trout whenever he wanted. We used to be able to do that, about a year ago. We'd catch 15-18 lake trout and just keep the best size. We're allowed 3.

CB: Do either of you, are you guiding now?

BF: No.

CB: When did your father start guiding, would you say, approximately?

BF: Mr. and Mrs. Heimerdinger in 1941. Before that, I don't know. It had to be back in the '30s. Because there's one guide here in Lake Placid, at the Majestic Restaurant who started picking on me because my father was getting $10 a day for guiding and he was only getting $6. And he got thrown out from there, the bartender threw him out.

CB: He was jealous?

BF: He was a drinker. He picked on me because my father was getting $10 and he was only getting $6.

CB: Would you say that your father...let me put it another way. I keep hearing about the old time guide, and I have a notion of what that is, but I'm thinking people have a different idea of what an old time guide is. How would you describe an old time guide?

BF: In what way?

CB: Well, maybe you're one, maybe your dad was, maybe there was before your dad...how many years would you say since you had a call for a guide?

BF: Oh, I still get them.

CB: Still get them?

BF: Yes. I just tell them that it's all over. When I first started it, I was getting $20 a day, and towards the end, I wouldn't take my boat out of the boat-house for less than $125. That was back in the early '80s. And if our wages had gone up like everything else, you wouldn't be able to afford it, we'd have to charge $200. And instead of an 8-hour day, we went out for a 6-hour day. You can't catch any business in 6 hours. Nobody out there.

CB: Did you guide hunting also?

BF: Yes.

CB: Where'd you go for that?

BF: Not very much in that. Topridge farm section. Charlie and his crew got two deer there in that area. Remember when you and I got lost up there and Dad found us? When you got lost in the woods, and you were right-handed, you had a tendency to bear right. If you were left-handed, you had a tendency to bear left. It was pretty near dark when Dad found us, we were going around in circles. Mom was with us. We were up there. Remember you and Charlie Bryant one time? You stayed in all night. We stayed overnight in Warren, just downhill. There were search parties out for us, but they were right beside the river. We could hear them but they couldn't hear us, with the noise. We went in in the morning with pants like this and came out in the morning we had shorts on.

CB: Now if you guided pretty much full-time in the summer, did you have work other time?

DF: No, we went all out for two months, maybe had two months maybe two and a half months. You had to make enough to get through the winter. I worked in a ski shop for 20 some odd years, it was my winter job. In the Marcy Hotel for George Bestler. But I had the experience for fishing for myself and fall for hunting in between the two jobs. The old timers right back with dad, there was Rufus Perks, Herm Sibley and a man you should have met before, Loren Wrisley...he used to visit us, and say, "Hi Jane, Hi Joe, any luck?" So I'd show him the same fish four times, and he said to Bill, "Let's go." He said, "Did you see the four rainbows that son of a bitch had?" But he had his arms out like that. Remember the time with the white fish? You tell that one...

BF: The judge and I were trolling, and as I was reeling in I had this stripe coming in, it was a whitefish, pretty near 4 pounds, and I got it right up close, and netted it, and they didn't even know I had one on. And I said, "There, I'll take it down to the village, it's worth $4 a pound." You can imagine what the Judge said. Whitefish is terrific eating. Nobody fishes them. We caught them trolling for rainbow. Everyone caught one one time, six pounds, and halfway in he says, "Bill, this fish's stronger than I am." We caught them on -- What's the one shaped like a fish?

DF: Sidewinder. Dad used to call it a Sidehillwinder.

BF: Sidewinder. I caught, in my boat, maybe caught eight. Scrapper, too. We used to take our lunch with us and eat out on Lake Placid. And Bob Agnew, you know Bob Agnew? Standard Tire, Bob has, in Saranac, on Broadway, upper Broadway. Anyway, we used to have about one o'clock on Bob's porch, on his camp on Lake Placid, north end there, and have our lunch. And Mrs. Heimerdinger says, "What the hell time is the feeding period today?" and I'd say, "Twenty minutes of two." "Let's get the hell out of there." By the time we got out there, I'd put my line out, and bang, lake trout. Another one, bang, lake trout. "Jesus Christ, you're hotter than a pistol today, Frank." Anyway we both started to catch them. We caught thirteen and kept the six, three apiece limit.

CB: The folks that you guided regularly, year after year, you had to be some good friends with them. Did you confide in one another? What was the relationship with them?

BF: You had to handle each one differently. They were all...the Judge, when he was catching fish you wouldn't want better company, but when he wasn't you'd wish he was in somebody else's boat. The last eight years I guided, the Judge had a hell of a time. Didn't want a day that he wasn't going out. He didn't fish Sundays. He took Sundays off. A day that I wasn't with Proskaver, I was with George McNeeley. And now the last eight years, the Judge didn't pay me. I got a check from his office. $250 per week. And that was good. That was good.

CB: What was a typical day like? What time did you start?

BF: About usually nine o'clock. They didn't get up early. The old group, nine o'clock until four, four thirty. Mrs. Heimerdinger was always nine o'clock. For years, for Bachman and Proskaver, I begin the day then, and you had the best fishing, and I'd go by myself. It was nothing to go across into West Lake, Whiteface Inn, McCutcheon, the whole West Shore line. It was nothing to go over there and catch three, four or five big rainbows. Usually, we used any kind of streamer. You troll that with about a hundred, hundred twenty-five feet of line, troll real slow. And if they were rising, you didn't have to troll. But that's gone. It'll never be like that. I told them the other day over there. You know Leo Demong? I fished a lot with Leo. He was the boss over at Ross Park. He's in EnCon now and he has charge of all the brook trout. I fished a lot with Leo and Bruce. I think the reason the speckled trout has gone down, speckled trout need a lot more care than the rainbow or brown trout. Brown trout are hard to fish, they live in water that brook trout would die in, temperature-wise. I told them the other day over there, I said, the way you handle Lake Placid, it couldn't be worse the way you've handled it down over the years, and three years from now you're going to have the best perch lake in the north country, and they will.

Perch are in there. Perch are a hell of a good eating fish. They aren't that hard a sport fish to catch.

CB: When you were out -- some of the old timers used to tell stories and they were wide ones -- were people looking for stories from guides, or didn't they care?

BF: Oh yes, they were always asking questions...Rosenthal, Rosenthal has thoroughbred horses, and I fished with Alice, and questions...all kinds of questions. Alice said one time, "Bill, you know everything, don't you?" I said, "Yeah." She said, "If I ask you a question and you don't know the answer, you make up one?" I said, "That's right." And she caught a lot of fish. I took her fishing one time, and it was supposed to be cold, she had all her winter clothes on, a jacket, oh, everything. Her own seat and sat down in the bottom of the boat. She had a jar with whiskey in it mixed with water, 'cause it was supposed to be cold out. So she drank the booze and she fell asleep.

The first time I took out George McNeely he had a bottle. He drank a lot and so when we got back into the landing, he'd say, "So Bill, when are we going back out again." I said, "We aren't." He'd say, "What do you mean we aren't?" I said, "When you hired me and we started fishing, I told you no company, I wanted one in my boat." He says, "Yeah, there was one in your boat." I said, "No, there was two. You leave Johnny Barleycorn behind and you can fish with me." And he never took a bottle again, and he never missed a cocktail party on the lake ever.

BF: What was the convention we picked, you and Dad and myself, General Motors?

DF: Yes, General Motors.

BF: And they had in my boat a case of scotch. I don't know if they had a case of beer or what. Remember what Dad hollered, I'm gonna swear, you can erase that... I have to tell him what Dad said. Guy was standing up in the boat and Dad said, "Sit down in the boat, you big son of a bitch." We went out the first day, and we each had two in our boat, and Dad quit right there, said, "Nope, no more, I don't want them." I said, "Dad, these guys are up here on vacation, they're having a good time just like when you go on vacation you want a good time." So I had a little talk with them.

"There's no drinking in our boats." He guided, Fisher, Vern Fisher, he was a big wheel in General Motors. We set Dad right aside for him. I went over one night and had a talk with him. He said, "You know, Billy, I caught bass all over the country, all over the state. I caught bass weighed a pound and a quarter, pound and a half, and before I got through and got back here, those bass weighed two and half pounds. Remember we told the guys we'll take them back to the club and we'll catch some fish for them. So we took them back to the club and got rid of them and went out and caught the limit. Then went over to one of the club cottages, remember, they were sitting there sleeping and you slapped one of them with a fish. Anyway we had the limit for them. They said, "Now here's ten bucks apiece, you guys get the hell out of here" -- They wanted to say they caught them...

Out across from my boat-house, there's a little boat-house over across from the island, the lake trout always collected there in the springtime. You cast the shoreline, and if they don't hit, you'd anchor fifteen, twenty feet offshore, and cast the lure deep and retrieve it. Went across there, and we caught six. He caught five and I caught one. Remember the time you walked in there with the big lake trout? This lake trout weighed seven and a half pounds. Who was it? He had invited seven other people from different countries to have dinner with him with this seven and a half pound lake trout. I remember one day I took a young fellow from Portugal out with us and fishing and spinning was good. The guy wanted to buy the outfit.

CB: Did these people tip pretty good?

BF: No, they didn't. Well, my deal with Mrs. Heimerdinger was I got paid whether she fished or not, from the middle of June until the middle of September, I was on her payroll. My father, like I say, he fished with her, died in 1956. In 1954, 1955, once in a while if he wasn't able to go, he'd have me go and take Mrs. Heimerdinger. I remember one time he was laid up, he used to have trouble with his back. I went out with Mr. and Mrs. Heimerdinger, he was a nice man. He had cancer, Fred Heimerdinger, and he lived for ten years with it. Anyway, I went out with him that day, 'cause dad wasn't up to it, and at the end of the day, he said, "Well, Bill, how much do I owe you?" I said, "You don't owe me anything, I did it for my father." He never quite got over it.

Wayne Failing

"Sitting on a beach, by a fire, watching the stars while the warm wind gently blows a faint hint of balsam by your nose. It's good for the soul, it's good for the spirit. A good guide can take you there and back again."

Wayne Failing is one of the best-known guides in the Adirondacks today. When a major magazine or newspaper wants to do an article on an Adirondack guide, Failing is likely to be the one they call. His Middle Earth Expeditions is named after author J.R.R. Tolkien's realm where people grow in character, gain insights, and learn to cope with the challenges of life on their return to ordinary living. Wayne works year-round at guiding, and is certified in all phases of it, from whitewater rafting in the spring straight through the usual summer activities, fall hunting season, and into winter skiing and mountaineering. His multi-fold activities are at the same time both the source of his satisfaction, and his main frustration -- "My only problem (with guiding) seems to be lack of time. There's a little <u>too much office work</u> for my liking. Mail, calls, advertising, brochures, insurance, marketing, reading. It all cuts down on my time in the field by half, but it's the nature of being self-employed, I guess." Wayne is aware of the irony of paying this kind of price for seeking the peace of the wilderness.

He guides anywhere in the Adirondacks, but mostly in Essex, Franklin, Herkimer, and Hamilton counties. He replied to my questions:

CB: What do you do when you guide?

WF: The first thing is to try and help the customer figure out what they want and need. Then I go about providing the experience as safely and competently as I can. Specifically, after the initial conversation and booking, I: plan the itinerary, plan the menu, send both to the customer with a suggested packing list for them (being prepared doesn't happen by chance), teach the skills they want to learn, take them where they want to go, or catch fish and hunt deer. I also cook the meals, wash the dishes, tend the fire, dig the latrine, and set up and take down the tents. But most importantly beyond these obvious things, I am their friend and companion for the length of their stay, and sometimes beyond. Around the campfire we can solve the problems of the world, or personal issues haunting the person at home can be resolved with a friendly ear and peaceful evening. In short -- butler, cook, teacher, counselor, and protector.

I have guided juvenile delinquents and millionaires, and everything in between -- some real characters, but mostly genuinely nice people. They are from the cities and are mostly professionals (guides aren't cheap.)

CB: What are your clients seeking?

WF: It varies -- for example, those who book a hunting or fishing trip usually have been trying on their own for a while with little to no success. So they are, predictably looking for success in catching fish or hunting deer. My whitewater rafters are seeking, and get a dose of, excitement and adventure in their lives. Those seeking canoe and hiking trips are mostly seeking peace and solitude from a world pressing hard on them. They are all seeking _fun_ and a good time.

(Wayne uses a one-page application form that asks for occupation, person to call in an emergency, height and weight, date of last physical, special medical considerations, dietary preferences, relevant interests or aptitudes, and past outdoor experience. It also has a 'release and assumption of risk' clause. His medical information form asks about problems with vision or hearing, teeth (such as denture or bridge), dizzy spells, fainting, convulsions, motion sickness, and persistent headaches.)

CB: What are peoples' attitudes when they come?

WF: If you've done your pre-trip cheerleading well, most people come with a positive attitude, expecting a great time, and I try not to disappoint them. People's attitudes do change as the trip progresses. They are usually tense and stressed out when they get here from the rat race and the packing, etc., etc., but leave feeling refreshed, rejuvenated from the slower pace, no phones, moon rises and loons calling from misty lakes, and the magic of a campfire.

I feel I teach my clients about life best. Putting things in perspective, not being afraid of following your dreams, and a sense that anything is possible. There's so much time in the canoe and around camp life that talking about and developing a philosophy of life just comes naturally. Of course, depending upon their goals, I also teach them the skills they want to learn, i.e., to paddle a canoe straight, or tie a knot, or build a fire, or what to eat if you're lost. In addition, I teach and demonstrate minimum impact camping skills, so if they go off on their own next time they will treat the wilderness areas with care and respect. What I actually do is what I feel my ideal role should be, or I would change what I do to be in alignment with my values. My roles are <u>protector</u> (keeping the client physically safe), <u>teacher</u> (everything from skills, to values, to ethics), and <u>philosopher</u> (developing a long-lost spiritual connection between them and the earth.) The best way to teach any of the above is by example.

I use the best equipment I can find. Tools of the trade. Having the best equipment is usually safer, more efficient, it lasts longer, and is one of the first ways your client forms an opinion of you as a guide. To operate year-round with all my specialty areas I have about $30,000 in equipment inventory in three rooms. From rafts and wet-suits, to canoes, tents, stoves, lanterns, life jackets, etc.

The state helps me in many ways. The 'I love New York' advertising, building lean-to's, maintaining public land with access sites, hiking and canoeing trails, stocking fish, maintaining and protecting wildlife, and printing information and educational material. They really don't hinder me yet, unless they pass this funding package on the Draft Open Space Plan -- a fire building tax, a fee to use backcountry trails and a fee for State parking lots <u>and</u> boat launch sites, and a tax for registering canoes and rafts. On top of all my other State taxes and licenses these new fees and taxes would ruin my and my client's sense of freedom and wilderness. Time to move on to a wilder place...guiding is a labor of love. There should be more canoe-only areas -- the Whitney estate if they are ever willing sellers or give conservation easements. Also, Lake Lila to Nehasane to Stillwater Reservoir.

CB: If you were King or Queen, what would you change?

WF: I would pay off all my loans and hire an office manager so I could spend more time in the woods, both with and without clients. The significance of guiding is to remind us how insignificant we and all our problems are in the grand scheme of things. A good guide can help raise a client's consciousness. Coming from the city to the wilderness allows the average urban person to come in contact with their roots again. A closeness to nature you can't get from the inside of an office window or in a car at rush hour. Sitting on a beach, by a fire, watching the stars while the warm wind gently blows a faint hint of balsam by your nose. It's good for the soul, it's good for the spirit. A good guide can take you there and back again.

CB: Do you expect tips?

WF: I usually get tipped for fishing and hunting trips, at least fifty percent of the time in these areas. Tips range from $10 - $200. I usually get tips for exceptional service or exceptional success. I don't really expect it, so I'm not disappointed if I don't get one. They have already paid fairly for the service I provide.

CB: Any problems getting paid?

WF: I have no problems getting paid. I require a 50% deposit and the balance before we leave. No pay, no trip. When I guide I'm promoting me and my business. It's an important part of marketing. It's hard not to promote yourself when working for others, so I usually don't put myself in that position. When I do it is usually a professional courtesy to help out a fellow guide. When I don't have a trip of my own I spend the time trying to get my own business going. I would rather be independent and self-employed than work for others.

CB: When not guiding, Wayne helps with the maintenance, renovation, and financial management of the Mt. Van Hoevenburg Bed and Breakfast, which is next to Middle Earth Expeditions. His other interests include music, photography, writing, travel, and reading.

       He reports all of his income, because "since I need banks to support my growth, they need to know I have a profit making, financially viable enterprise."

       Failing has a bachelors degree in education, and believes "the half-dozen major expeditions I've been on and my two years running adaptive 28-day outward bound courses with delinquents helped give me the structure and organization skills, together with my experience, to make a first class guide service."

Dick Emperor

"A guy that never got lost never went in the woods very far."

In his interview Dick seemed to see his work first as a guide, and later as an employee of the Conservation Department, as one continuous experience; the anecdotes blended together. One he told on himself was stopping a car and asking what was in the trunk. "Game Protectors," he was told. Annoyed, Emperor, then Game Protector, looked in the trunk to discover three bushels of horse manure. Ed Betters, of Saranac Lake, who guided during the latter part of Dick's era, called him "the best Game Protector we ever had in this country." This sentiment was repeated in other interviews. Dick and his wife live in a tidy home on Jenkins Street in Saranac Lake. He keeps his guide's badge -- one of the first issued by the state -- in his jewelry box in his bedroom; he was polite but firm that it be photographed at his house and not taken away.

The following are his comments on the Cold River Country and Noah John Rondeau, the hermit:

DE: Rondeau was up in there. Him and Game Protector Savard didn't get along so good. They always said Rondeau shot a hole in Vosburgh's hat. He was the Game Protector before Savard. Vosburgh. He didn't like Vosburgh. Vosburgh would have killed him if he'd ever shot through his hat. I know damn well he would have, because he was short-fused, too! We were coming out, you know where the big hill is, the CC's (Civilian Conservation Corps, referred to by those who remember it not as "CCC's," but "CC's"), they fixed that road up there, there's a gravel pit. Rondeau was in there somewhere, it's pouring, we weren't supposed to give anybody a ride, and I said, 'Christ, give Rondeau a ride.' We stopped, Rondeau didn't see Clarence, he didn't like Clarence, I stuck my head out, "You want a ride out?" He looked, it wasn't anybody he knew, he saw me, "Yeah," he said. "I'll ride." He had, I think, a Model 80, I used to have one, I called it a crow bar, a .35 caliber rifle, an automatic, two barrels. He had his gun, and he's got the barrel pointing down in the thing there, and it's pouring, we went about a mile, and Clarence says, "Is that gun loaded?" "Yeah, I think it is." Clarence stopped the car. "You better unload it." He stepped out of the car, never unloaded it or nothing. I says, "Aren't you going to unload it and get in?" "No," he says, "I'll walk." Stubborner than hell. And he walked all the way out, he was madder than hell!

CB: How did guiding work here in Saranac Lake?

DE: You'd start from the hotel, take 'em up if you had a car, or they'd take you up in a taxi, and you'd get a boat, let 'em pay for a boat.

CB: How did you get a license?

DE: The Game Protector had to go around--let's say you go up and you want to be a guide, they take your name, address, telephone number, everything, then I call on you. You send this paper in, what your qualifications are, if you've been a hunter, different stuff. Then you've got to be recommended by another guide, I asked you all these questions, then -- personally you knew a lot of them -- if the Davises came up and wanted a license, you know they know something about hunting...some of the guys couldn't swim, now you have to do all that stuff. A lot of guys only wanted to take people fishing, well, what the heck, give 'em a guide's license. But when you came to hunting and stuff they were a little more particular because you could lose 'em. They had this little magazine, all the guides were listed. They're all dead. The first ones were put out by Remington, that goes way back from the Paul Smith's bunch.

CB: You worked for five dollars a day?

DE: Today they probably get seventy-five or a hundred dollars a day, and they've got all the trails made for 'em, and they put their canoes in and they bring all their stuff. Christ, we used to make a lean-to for the guys, do their cooking, and carry the guide boat and the pack basket. You come up from Albany or New York you hire a guide, you gotta pay him a hundred dollars, that's the last time they're going to hire the guides. They got signs on all the trails where you want to go, so why hire a guide? You really don't need a guide, all you need is a good compass and a hatchet or a jackknife and a .22.

     I took 'em all over. You must have had twenty-five, thirty, forty guides right here in Saranac Lake, right in town, way back, in the horse and wagon days. So I've got a big party, we go up on the lake, you're going to have a guy left right there to do the cooking when you come back, all you done is row the boat and show 'em where to go.

CB: When did you start?

DE: In the '20's, I was 16 years old. I've got an old badge; when I went to work for the Conservation Department as a Game Protector, I had to turn my guide badge in, that one was sort of hectagon, like this (indicates), brass, but I'll show you this old one from way back, it's got a little lean-to.

CB: How did you get into guiding?

DE: I had to make some money and I liked it. I was tending bar in the Hotel Saranac, I opened the bar in 1933. Liquor'd come back in '33. Scopes sent me to New York to learn how to tend bar. I had a lot in my favor, when I came back they didn't know what in the hell they were getting anyway. We worked with the regular bottles but they were watered, the only real thing we had was beer. I run the bar for ten, eleven years. I was getting $25 a week and my board. I used to give one of the waiters -- we were getting seven to ten dollars guiding, they'd buy the groceries -- when it was ten dollars, I'd give one of the waiters five dollars and I made five dollars, they wanted the extra money, too, and I was out having a good time. The waiter could tend bar.

CB: How did you get business?

DE: I went in with Ed Lamy and Fred Bailey and some of the old timers, I went hunting with them. The first guy I ever fished with was old Matt Otis in Lake Clear, we fished Little Clear then, and you could catch lake trout on almost a bare hook. We'd use these jigs, in the '20's, '30's ...

CB: Did the state put out a list of guides?

DE: There was a book. The guy that was the head of the Association at the end there was a Fuller, not related to the other Fuller's that used to be up on Broadway. I think his name was Harold Fuller, I think he was from Tupper Lake. On the -- it was one of them paperbacks -- all the guides from different hotels and stuff was in there and your numbers, some guides were listed for fishing, some for hunting, some for camping. I had the whole works on mine, and a lot of 'em like that. I think we paid two dollars and a half for the guide's badge ... the only meeting I ever went to, I was working as a Conservation Officer then, they talked about how much to charge ...

CB: Where did clients come from?
DE: You'd get these calls, I took guys from Chicago, New York, all over different places. I had my own guide boat, I paid fifty dollars for it, brand new. It was a Vassar boat, made in Bloomingdale. This guy died in Lake Clear, he was a sick guy, he'd used it only 2 or 3 times. Natural wood, all inlaid, I had all the seats. Willard Hamner used to kid me, he'd say, "When are you going to get rid of that wreck and I'll make you a brand new one?"

CB: How much did you charge?
DE: I charged $5 to guide, before that I'd get a couple of dollars from some of the guys to help make the drives. Let's say there's a deer runaway [sic] here, you'd either put the watchers out on a runaway, or you'd go ahead and make the drive with some of the guys, all depended on how big the party was. Some of them were so cheap they wouldn't hire another guy.

CB: This is a magazine article on your Conservation Department days?
DE: This guy was taking the pictures, everything was described as "forty miles back." I says, Christ, you can't go forty miles, you're coming out of the woods. You go forty miles straight here you come out twice.

CB: Don't people give Game Protectors problems?
DE: I got along with 'em, pirates and all. The one's that were shooting deer illegal, we used to call 'em pirates ... You were Game Wardens, and then you plug for another raise, then you were Game Protectors, then you were Conservation Officers. Now it's Environmental Conservation Officers and they got 'em doing everything but what they should be doing. They should be doing just fish and game, and the APA (Adirondack Park Agency), whatever it is out there, have got

'em doing all their stuff, any new outfit comes up the Game Warden or the Game Protector has to enforce the law....

CB: Where'd you get boats?

DE: You'd hire 'em from Duso's or Emmon's, at the foot of the hill up there, Alvord's, that boat-house ain't there anymore, and Devarney was an old one, and Moody's down here, that marina off Duprey Street, the old one was Milo Moody's ... a couple dollars for a good boat, when gasoline first started it'd be $5 for the day, $3, it depended. They never used 'em much, it just got 'em there if they was hunting and they stayed there 'til they came back.

       I've carried that guide-boat five miles into St. Regis Pond, then we carried into the Duck Hole, which was about eight or nine miles. They didn't have all them lean-to's up there in the first part, and there was no trails in there way back ....

       ...You could put two people and all the equipment in that guide-boat, it was only fourteen feet, that far from the water, if you had a big load that guy in the back had to paddle, we used a long paddle.

CB: Did the boat ever need repairs?

DE: Willard put me on -- they were spruce, the gunwales -- and he put me on two cherry ones on the side and when I went up there and he put them on he took two pieces, measured the guide-boat, and he just cut them two goddamn pieces off, he figured the bend and everything, brought 'em over, he didn't even use a ruler, all he had to do was sand 'em a little bit and fit. That was in the '30's. I had canoes. I paid fifty dollars -- no, fifty-five -- for the guide-boat. Before that I had some boats I only paid ten dollars for second-hand.

CB: What did the clients use for guns?

DE: They had their own guns, they used .44's when I was first hunting and .38-.55's, big long shells. I even hunted with a muzzle loader...

CB: Where did you get pack baskets?

DE: The Indians used to make 'em from St. Regis Falls, you go down there and you'd get 'em for a dollar and a half. Stark's used to go down there and buy a big truckload of those packbaskets in St. Regis -- not St. Regis Falls, St. Regis -- what the hell is it where the Indians are up past Massena? Right off the reservation. They'd make those packbaskets for him for a dollar and a half, two dollars, he'd take 'em -- I think five dollars was the most he ever paid -- he's ship a big carload down to Abercrombie and Fitch down there, Christ, they'd get ten, fifteen dollars for 'em. You buy the name, you know. They sold cheap -- you could buy a Browning shotgun there for fifty dollars, thirty-five dollars, automatic -- .30-.30 you could buy for twenty-five dollars -- new.

CB: Were the Game Protectors involved in fishing?
DE: We use to do all the work the biologists are doing ... I wanted some trout for St. Regis Pond, I went to the hatchery, first thing the biologist says is "Any perch in there?" "Perch? Loaded with perch. But there's trout in there, too, and lake trout." "Can't have 'em, that's out, nope. You can't put those trout in there with the perch in these small ponds." I said, "Do you know how big St. Regis Pond is?" "Haven't seen it." I went over and pulled down that great big map, I was madder than hell, showed St. Regis about that big, he says, "It is a large pond, isn't it?" He was talking, he didn't even know what the hell he was talking about. And Lydia Pond, we used to catch perch like that in it and they were better eating than the trout ... Big Fish empties into Little Fish, you stand there in them little rapids there if you've got hip boots on, you'd catch a pack basket of fish ... they were pretty near all natural in there.

Dick is nostalgic for an earlier, simpler time when issues were clear-cut, the fishing was better, and bureaucracy less -- all of these are sentiments that have been around almost since the start of guiding.

Sandy and Fred Fountain

"They'd sit down, their whole butts were covered with leaves and black dirt.   But to them that was roughing."

Sandy and Fred Fountain are both native Adirondackers -- Sandy to Keese Mill, near Paul Smiths, and Fred to Lake Placid. Neither came from rich families; their accounts today of 'making do' in their childhoods are told with a certain nostalgia -- they believe a sense of community has been lost. Both are well aware of the sociological gaps between summer rich and local poor. They describe the contrast with humorous but telling accuracy. Sandy remembers Marjorie Merriweather Post having her chauffeur stop so she could pat Sandy on the head, saying, "I DO love these native children!" Fred guided and worked as a caretaker for the same family for twenty-three years on Upper St. Regis Lake near Paul Smiths. He stressed the family shuns publicity, and asked their name not be included. Sandy is the switchboard operator at North Country Community College. She enjoys a popular and legendary status, even among strangers who call the college, for her ever-cheery, "G-O-O-D morning, North COUN-try!" Fred is also a professional wood carver. They live in Bloomingdale, near Saranac Lake.

CB: What's it like guiding on Upper St. Regis Lake?
FF: When you worked for any of those people up on the lake, that type of person, you come to work in the morning, you don't know which hat to put on. You can be friend and go in town and take somebody shopping or do this and that, or you can be a baby sitter for the kids and take them fishing down on the dock all day, you could be the caretaker and get an order of things to do this long, and a reprimand for not getting some of them done. You can be the bosom buddy of your boss or you can be his whipping boy, and you never knew until you get there in the morning. My father was a guide in the off-season and in the summertime he was completely at the disposal of the family that he worked for, Rose, Alfred Rose, and he did a little guiding in the winter, hunting. He usually went to hunting camp and he'd do the cooking and stuff like that, and two or three or four guides would get together and they'd establish a hunting camp, and bring parties in; like my father would do the cooking and the

other guys would take them out hunting. Caretaker and guide, I put them the same.

CB: Did he have any other line of work that he would do in the winter?

FF: They still had to go up and check on camp at least once a week, for snowfall, and for ice damage, and for vandals, and all that sort of thing. He had to maintain that, but he worked on the snowplow, that's when they plowed the streets in Lake Placid with a horse and plow. It would have been late 1920's to late 1930's.

CB: Was your father a good outdoorsman, hunting and fishing?

FF: Yeah, my father was an Indian. That doesn't say it all, but he was very good. Very good. A Mohawk from Akwasasne. He knew every little track and every little tree and how to identify it and some in the winter; I mean, that was the T.V. to the little kids like when I was young. My father would entertain us just by giving us a stick and tell us to find out what kind of wood it is. How do you identify it, you know, maple trees are like this, and birch trees are like this...The guides would tell stories. Some of them were just a little off-color.

I'll tell you a short one. There was this Irish fellow and his wife came over here from Ireland. They arrived here before the end of the fall season, so they got into this little farm that they had bought. They got into the house and it snowed and they were just about locked in for the winter, but they made it through the winter and early in the spring, he decided he would go into the town and get some of the things they hadn't had all winter, because they had a little bit of money, and he had to get some seed and stuff. He went into town and it was about a six hour trip, so when he got back he came in the house and he hollered to Minny and told her to come, that he really had a surprise for her.

So, she said, "Now, what would it be that you're giving for me that would be surprising?" He says "Well, do you remember my Uncle Louie?" and she said "Oh, I just adored him," he says "I don't know how it came about, but I know you adore my Uncle Louie, but I went into this shop in town and low and behold, I turned around and there's a picture of him, a beautiful picture of Uncle Louie," he says, "and I just bought it and had it put into a sack and I brought it home to you." And she says, "I've got to see it. How much money did you spend on it?" and he says, "More than I should have," so he told her and she said yes, it was more than he should have spent; but anyways, she just had to see it, and he said, "Well, it's right here; you close your eyes, and I'll take the paper off it, and then you just look at it."

So she closed her eyes and he pulled the paper off and he says, "There, look at that, Minny" and she says, "You lying son of a Protestant whatever", and she says, "that's no Uncle Louie, that's some old whore you met in town and had a way with her." So it turned out to be a mirror. But I cut that way down, because a good story teller would really drag it out. My father was a furniture maker. He made this Adirondack furniture that's so desirable now, out of yellow birch and white birch. He just went in there and made all the porch furniture and all their good furniture for their rooms and chairs and tables and whatever, and it was something he was sort of expected to do, but they were lucky he could do it.

CB: Now, would he bother with getting a guide's license or didn't he?

FF: Your Game Protectors were your Conservation Department, and if you knew them ... There's an old fellow that used to own the Arena Grill or what's now the Arena Grill in Lake Placid. His name is Clark Hayes. He was an old Game Protector. Probably one of the worst outlaws in the North Country; but he was on good standing with all these guides, you know, and it was no big thing. My father had set lines out, you know illegal. They would always stop at Clark Hayes' and drop him off a lake trout like this, and they'd get a couple of beers, and they'd shake hands and go home. He knew them and they knew him, and that's all there was to it. We had a man in Lake Placid who was a big teddy bear, but he made a life of being very stern, but he was a wonderful man. His name was Reg Wolfe. He was an institution in Lake Placid. He came in right after this Clark Hayes.

So everybody, if you wanted a pistol permit, you had to have a character reference from him. If you wanted a guide's license, you had to have a character reference, and he made no bones about it. He just said, "Ok. I've known you.

I've known you since you were a little kid. So take the damn test, bring your papers back tomorrow filled in, I don't care where you get the information, but if you don't know something, I want you to look it up and have the right answer on the paper." That's the way he was. He didn't want to give you a test and then fail you. He wanted you to pass so he said, "Look up the answer, or call somebody and find out. If you have to, as a last resort, call me and I'll tell you."

The Game Protectors were your best friends. If he knew that you had trapped illegally or something like that and he said to me, "I know you're using illegal traps, now don't make me do something I don't want to do. Take care of that situation." "Yes, Mr. Wolfe." and then after he'd leave "I'm going to get him out in the woods, I'm going to put a bullet through his dog." That kind of guide story always got back to Reg because he had more friends than people knew. Everyone was his friend except these individual guides, and he really had it in for them, because he figured that those guides were hurting all his friends, which they were. But the game protector was God Almighty.

CB: Years ago you worked at the Majorie Merriwether Post camp. What was that like?

FF: Every Thursday at the Post camp they took people through the seven carries on guide-boats, so there were about six of us there working that had experience enough to carry a guide-boat and put people in and out of it, and take them and give them a good time for the day. I was assigned this man and his wife, and he came down in sneakers and shorts in a t-shirt and so on. And he came over and introduced himself and then his wife came down along behind him. She had a nice dress on and high heels and silk stockings and her hair was all made up nice, and I said to them, I said, "Fine, you're going on this outing today?" He says, "Oh, yes, we're really looking forward to it." And I said, "Well, let me acquaint you with what you're going to get into." I said, "You're going to wish you had some long pants on. And that t-shirt will never do. I said, you should wear a hat because you're bald-headed. We're going to be out on the lake."

Well he couldn't understand that and I said, "Well, it's up to you." And he said, "Well, I'll take your word for it." So then I turned to his wife and said, "You're very pretty, but I'm going to have to ask you to take off those high heeled shoes. You can't wear them in the boat." "I will not." I said, "That's fine, you can swim." She said, "Do you have a right to tell me things like that?" I said, "I'm looking for your comfort. Put on an old sweatsuit and some sneakers or something. You're going today to enjoy yourself. You're going to be sitting on the ground." "On the ground!" I said, "Yeah, you're going to be eating fish and pancakes and whatever out of a paper plate and you're going to be sitting on the ground, probably even beans and you might spill something." "Oh." And they started talking, they were all standing on the dock. They didn't know if they wanted to go on this trip or not. So anyway, believe it or not they did go up and change. Then they came back down.

Some of the other guides didn't have the gall to tell their people that they really should change because they weren't going to enjoy the day if they didn't. Anyway, they put all the guide-boats, about eight of them, on a big scow, and we went down to the carry into the Bear, Green Ponds and in that way. They brought them down in the big Chris Crafts. They didn't want to be out on the lake that long.

But anyway, we got all ready for them. Then the fella said, "You want me to help you carry that boat?" I said, "No, no, this isn't heavy." He said, "It must weigh a hundred and fifty pounds." I said, "No, this happens to be an eighty pound boat. This is one of the light ones, it's a good kind though." He said, "You're going to carry that by yourself?" I said, "Certainly, you can walk behind me or ahead of me, but give me room. Give me six feet." So we all got the people going. A group of guides, four guides, had gone ahead and taken all the provisions in. They had gone down in one of the other boats and tied it up and filled up a hundred, hundred and fifty pound pack and they took it in -- it was all the food and everything.

So we got going across through the slough there into what's the first little pond, Bog Pond, and of course, the mosquitos, they like to carry you off. Some of these people, women, you know, had short sleeved dresses and nothing on their legs, and said, "Oh, the mosquitos are killing me."

Boats weren't going to be back there to pick them up until 4:00 in the afternoon. So the people that I had were sort of green, and the guy said, "Well, thanks to you, I think we're going to enjoy the day." Because I had brought some alcohol pads that had some stuff on them and they could just wipe on their face and their arms and that kept the mosquitos off.

But we got going across this one, what was it? Green Pond, it was so crystal clear you could just see the bottom. Nothing in it, no vegetation. Yeah. And it was just so beautiful and this woman says, "Oh, this water looks so good, so clear, so nice, I think I'm...Do you have something I can get a drink? So I had a fold-up cup that I handed to her, and her husband grabbed it and says, "You can't drink this water, this is out in the wilderness. This water is polluted. Birds drop their stuff in it and everything. It's polluted. You can't drink this stuff." This is back in the middle 70's. Then the water was just as crystal clear. So I didn't pay any attention to them. I just pulled up the cup and drank, people were surprised, and poured the rest on my head and put my hat back on. They couldn't figure out that anyway. But he wouldn't let her drink that water.

But when we got down to mixing drinks for them, we'd just go down to the dock and get water. They had a ball, a lot of them, even the ones that got all chewed up really had a ball, because we cooked for them. You should have seen them come back to camp. They've arrived, you know. They maybe would have gotten into the ashes and scratched themselves and there'd be charcoal on their faces. They had their high heels in their pockets or in their purses. The men were a mess. They'd sit down, their whole butts were covered with leaves and black dirt.

But to them that was roughing. Roughing, I guess it was. It was rough. They got everything served to them. And they really enjoyed it. And they drank more than you could possibly think. There were four trees on this little island on Long Pond, as you go in on the left, place where we always used to camp. There were four trees there, hollow to their roots. And they would send probably two hundred dollars worth of liquor for this group. And we'd always take it, some of it, and hide it in the roots of the tree. And the guides, the six of us that went, always knew it was there, so any time that we would go that way, we would stop and check, and maybe have a drink while we were there. I always used to check it, I never drank any of it. But Bob Rottner would go all the way in there on his snow machine just to get a couple of bottles...

My dad would go out, times were tough along toward spring you know. All the tomatoes and stuff that my mother had canned, and elbow macaroni she had saved up was running mighty thin. But Dad would go out in the evening, I'd never think a second thing about it, he'd come back with four or five snowshoe rabbits. Big rabbits. And he would have a place down in the cellar where he would tie the hind legs and he would clean them and quarter them all out. And then set the stuff outside in a bag or something so it would freeze. Then he would take the meat and all that sort of stuff upstairs and wash it and clean it all up nice and mother would keep two of them and cook them for the family and the other two he would take with him when he went to work. And I always wondered, but every once in a while we'd get a big chunk of salt pork, maybe a half a chicken or half a turkey, or some potatoes.

What he was doing is, he had a snare line set around the edges of the village and he'd go out and check his snares, and he would catch three or four rabbits, sometimes a night. That's when rabbits were plentiful, I mean we had rabbits, the great big snowshoe hare. You'd clean two of them and we'd have them to eat. The other two, he would, of course there were no phones, telephones in those days, that sounds old, but we didn't have telephones. But he would get in touch with this buddy, or that buddy or somebody else, and they would swap. He'd swap them a rabbit for a chicken or a peck of potatoes, or just something to vary the meal at home. And you never wondered where rabbits came from and later when I got big enough I used to go with him. But I never thought anything about it. We were poor and he was providing for the family.

SF: When my father died in '57, winter was coming, little did we know how awful it was going to be. But the focus of the neighborhood became how the hell those Betters women were going to survive. Gould Hoyt, who was supposed to be one of those hoity-toity college professors, got a bunch of his students together and they dragged lumber from the old mill.

Dragged it down, put up a skirt all around, they banked the house. The first year we ever had running water the entire year. In the spring, four or five of the men from the community decided that that damn tin roof was dangerous. So they came in and put on a new roof. People stopped to see if you needed anything, 'cause my mother didn't drive and my sister wasn't old enough to drive. And I was no good for nothing, 'cause I was too young.

FF: I used to follow my father, I adored him. I used to follow him and go to work with him on weekends. And when they would stand around, the things they would talk about, it was fascinating.

Dave Cilley

"Some of the best guides in the Adirondacks have sort of drifted our way in the course of years."

Dave Cilley and his wife Kathy run St. Regis Canoe Outfitters, on Floodwood Road near Lake Clear. In addition to outfitting, they offer instruction, canoe and camping gear rentals, shuttle service, guided trips in both the Adirondacks and Everglades National Park, and sell equipment. Promotion of their business includes a 24-page brochure with maps, route suggestions, information on Forest Rangers, weather, fishing, checklists, and more. Among guides in the area the Cilleys have a reputation for attention to detail: "If Dave says you're getting 50 noodles, it's 50 -- not 49 or 51," as one guide put it. Dave admits he has memorized every scratch on every rental canoe -- and woe to the client who brings back a new one.

CB: How would you describe yourself as a guide?
DC: I'm 41 and I guess I would best describe myself right now as a part-time guide although I'm available full-time, there's times of the year when I really do not have time to guide. I really don't have time myself in the summer time to guide simply because of our canoe outfitting business, but in that time period of course, I talk to a lot of other people guiding. I guess the start of my guiding probably really went back to about '66 when I was 16 years old, I started working in the Scout camp in north central New Hampshire, in Center Sandwich. It was kind of a unique situation that we had. It was a 13 acre chunk of land that the Boy Scouts leased from the National Forest, and it was right in the middle of the National Forest and they ran trips out from there. We ran pack burro trips, we had a Conservation Week, a Survival Week, and we ran groups by patrol, we had a 50 mile week, where people would hike from the Center Sandwich area up to Mount Washington. That's where I got a lot of my experience in terms of helping other people outdoors. My outdoor experience goes back a lot more. My father was a County 4-H Club agent in Jefferson and Lewis Counties in New York State, ran Camp Wabasso, a 4-H camp, from the time before I was born. Until I was 21, I spent every summer in summer camp. My mother was water-front director and my father was camp director, so I kind of grew

up in that kind of a situation. But during the early Boy Scout years, really the '60's, was the time period that I really was getting the basics.

My college degree is in botany. I got a BS in Botany from the University of New Hampshire. During a lot of the time that I was in school, I spent a lot of time in the mountains, you know, in the White Mountains, and after school I started to work for Eastern Mountain Sports and I started working as a guide in their climbing school and I got involved in rock climbing. It was a very exciting time to get into that kind of business because it was in a period when rock climbing was first becoming popular. You know, there was kind of a big surge in the '70's in rock climbing and then there's been a recent surge now, too. But that time period was really neat because that's when a lot of new routes were being done and it attracted people from all over the country, which was fantastic. People like Shenako, Henry Barber, John Bragg, Rick Wilcox and people like that. Everything kind of fell together. What actually brought me to the Adirondacks was opening the EMS store in Lake Placid in '74. We started the store there and managed it from '74 through '81.

CB: Did you do any guiding then?

DC: That was a time period when I really didn't guide. You know, it was an occasional thing, people would come up, I'd meet them in the store, and I'd arrange a day off and take them out, but it wasn't as though I was actively guiding. But it was a time period when I did do a fair bit of rock climbing here in the Adirondacks and did some hiking and so forth. In '82, that summer, we took the summer off, and spent that summer in Northern Saskatchewan and there was a canoe outfitting business for sale up there which kind of got us, stirred our interest a little bit. On the way back, we stopped in Minnesota and took a look at the canoe outfitting businesses there and realized what there is in Minnesota in terms of outfitting businesses. So we came back here for the outfitting business that we put together, which was in the spring of '84.

Most of my "guiding" is more instructional in nature now than anything else. This summer is the first summer that I can honestly say I really have not been out to guide at all during the summer. Other summers I've been able to sneak away here and there. I'd say one of the most frustrating parts of trying to run a business like what I do in the Adirondacks is trying to find people to do the subcontract kinds of work, and I'm thinking not just about guides in particular but also inns and lodges and things like that. It's the constant battle to get people, and I'm saying this in general terms, to get people to do what they're hired to do, whether it's a lodge that's trying to provide a type of atmosphere that you're looking for, or trying to provide the quality food that you want, or the type of experience that our clients are looking for.

I think our clients are essentially looking for an Adirondacky kind of experience. They're looking for something that, you know, when they look in the picture books, they say, "Ah-hah, that's the Adirondacks," and they picture a log building, that kind of thing. We have found probably some of the best guides in the Adirondacks. They have sort of drifted our way over the course of years, and we are extremely lucky. We pack the food really well, we do everything else really well, but it's the other people that we have to hire to hold up part of the trip.

On the other hand, the guides are probably the easier part in the sense that we've been very lucky. We've found really great people. There's been times when we just couldn't find guides and had to turn people away, but the most frustrating thing I think in terms of guides is to find good fishing guides -- fishing guides who really know the area that they're talking about and can consistently catch fish. We get people who say they're very good guides and they've had a lot of experience and they go out and either have a lot of trouble catching fish or they don't know the particular pond, we have people who they're ready to come with their fish finders and all their high-tech stuff, but they aren't willing to sleep on the ground. It's hard to find a real guide, a person who is familiar with a wide range of natural history kinds of things, maybe has a specialty, like fly fishing, for example, and can go out in the wilderness for five days and take care of himself and catch fish for people and come back and have the people be comfortable the whole time, through any kind of weather and so forth. That's the kind of person that we need and that kind of person when you start filing through the guide lists is relatively rare.

CB: Now, what about just the fishing business? Do you feel the fishing is good enough that they ought to be able to catch fish anytime they take somebody out if they're good? You hear a lot of complaints about the fish.

DC: I think if a guide comes and is hired to be a fishing guide, I think it would be good for him to catch fish first of all. I think in general, that's possible. I think a guide should have some aces in his pocket if he knows that the trout fishing is really going to be bad, then that should be communicated ahead of time, and say, "Look, the first week of August isn't going to be your best time to brook trout fish. Maybe we should spend time in this pond brook trout fishing, and then we can switch over to this pond here." You kind of have to weigh out, weigh out what the guide's real purpose is. If the client has kids, the thing with kids brings up a whole different thing with guiding. Yeah, I think in general if he's hired to catch fish the guide should be able to do what the customer expects. And some customers expect that. I think the more experienced people who are hiring a fishing guide realize that that's not always going to be the case. I really can't think of any time when people have been completely skunked on fishing. If they've had a fishing guide, generally, they've caught fish, and I think that that should be the way it is.

CB: What happens when someone says they want a guide?

DC: Usually there's a couple of contacts with the people before they come. There's a list of things like natural history, fishing, fly fishing, astronomy, so they can check the things that might be of interest to them, or put them in priority listing and then there's a few questions like, "How old are you? Do you want a male guide/female guide? Smoker/non-smoker?" you know, this kind of thing, so we run through that so we try to match up the guide. We get a brief idea has the person ever been guided before, what are the age and sex of the members of this party, what the primary purpose of their trip is, things like that, so that we can try to match a guide to what he wants. Sort of along that line, I make a couple of contacts to the people that I personally want to guide ahead of time and try to make sure that I'm the right person for them, to try make sure that I am confident that I can do what they want, and I do the same things when I've got other people coming to do this, but for myself I do that ahead of time.

Then when the people get here, obviously greet them. I usually go through their gear, check that out, and then if we need to drive, we'll drive to where we're going. Actual guiding depends totally on what the people want. A lot of times I've found that most people who are hiring a guide, a modern guide, are hiring a guide specifically to get instructional information from the guide. Either instructional type stuff on canoeing, camping techniques, so they're hiring a guide, I think number one because they need information. They hire a guide because they might want a companion or simply to help with the physical work. A person might also hire a guide because they want to spend more time with their family. You get somebody that's in their '30's, they've got two kids. His wife and his children may have never paddled. So, here they are in two canoes, and you've got a situation where either the husband or the wife doesn't have the necessary experience to be a solo person in the canoe, yet they've got a small kid in the bow so they really need the help of an additional person. So there's a weakness in the party somewhere that they need to offset by the services of a third adult, or they simply want it so that they can have the guide do some of the work and they can spend more time with their family. I think as young professionals spend more and more time with their work, the time they do spend with their families becomes more and more important, and so when they're out, they like to be able to spend the time essentially playing.

A lot of times we'll try to get into camp fairly early when we're paddling, I like to get in at least an hour or an hour and a half to two hours before dinner and give the people plenty of time to catch fish. People have probably as many different reasons for hiring a guide as there are people out there. I try, and I think our guides for the most part really try, to bring to light anything that's in the outdoors that would be, could be of interest to the people, again depending on their interest, whether it's a particular place that's good to fish, or for example, if you're passing a bog, showing them some of the flowers you might see.

   We will try to point out some of those kinds of things to people regardless of what their interest is, because if they're out there canoeing, they like to know what's going on around them. I think the guide has quite a bit of responsibility in terms of in some parties, basically, as an entertainer, a person who can be a bridge, if you will, between the person whose life is centered around the city, and the area that he is in.

CB: What kind of people want to guide for you?
DC: We have a lot of different experience levels of people coming to us that want to guide. We have a lot of people who come to us, and I'm not belittling at all any of the type of educational systems that they have in the outdoors now for training guides, but we have a lot of people that come to us and the only experience guiding that they've had is guiding other college-age group kids or youth groups. I mean most people guiding for a living are probably going to be ending up guiding some adults sometime and it's pretty hard to go from a youth group guiding situation to an adult and family guiding situation if that's been your only background.

   The people that are hiring a guide are people that are relatively well to do, they've done a lot of traveling in a lot of different areas, and they like a person who is say, a specialist in the Adirondacks, but is also worldly in a sense, has some experience of other places. We've found that the people we've had guide for us are in the 30, 40, 50 age ranges, basically because I prefer to have older people who have had a sense of what the world is all about. I think one of the primary considerations is personality and knowledge of the outdoors, worldliness, they need to know if a great blue heron flies over or an ostrich flies over.

   Natalie, who did some stuff for us, I feel very confident now that when she goes out with a group of people, you know what's going to happen. She has spent a lot of time with us out in the woods. It's hard for me to just pick a guide off the street and know what that guide's going to do. Because when I think of a guide I guess I kind of expect a little bit of the old time kind of guide. I think that in order to make a go at guiding you've got to be adaptable enough to do what the people want.

CB: Do you get people with attitudes good or bad, who hope their trip will help change or reaffirm and what kind of attitudes?

DC: I can tell a little story here. Kathy and I were guiding a trip party. We had a fellow come on the trip and he had a lot of trouble holding on to a canoe paddle. He literally could not hold on to the canoe paddle. He had some kind of physical problem holding the paddle and it was obvious that there was some kind of problem getting his hands to do what he wanted them to do, and we were very patient with him and we went through our trip with him, being very patient, and we were fortunate that we had a relatively small group and two of us, because one of us could pretty much work with him. In any case, at the end of the trip, he didn't say anything about this, he thanked us quite a bit, he wrote us a letter from the Hotel Saranac explaining what had happened. Apparently he was in some kind of car accident or something like that, and was in a coma for quite a while, like over a month, and he came out of this coma but he was paralyzed on his right side and he was trying to overcome this, and the letter he wrote was so heartwrenching, it was incredible. He couldn't thank us enough for spending the time with him.

A pretty good number of the people that you get, they've got some major change in their life, husband left them, or wife left them or something like that. They've got some kind of major change in their life and they're trying to accomplish something new. I think that this kind of thing is good for them because they get totally out of their whole surroundings and they're able to re-think attitudes and life and so forth.

CB: Does that put the guide into the role of counselor to some extent?

DC: Oh, yes, I would say so. A guide is definitely a counselor.

CB: Would you require anything else of a guide uniformly across the board?

DC: I feel very frustrated by the whole New York State outdoor guide's situation in terms of what's required by law. I think all guides should know how to handle emergencies, first aid emergencies. I think part of first aid emergencies include water sports. Even if the guide is a specialist in deserts, if his van goes off the road and into the lake on the way across the only river in the desert, he should be able to help take care of that situation. So I think water-type things are really critical and certainly being in the Adirondacks where water is so prevalent.

I also think that the system for doing it in New York State is really poor. I've got a Maine guide's license and it's interesting the system there. They have a panel that you go in and you talk to a panel of five people and they can ask any questions that they want and they ask questions on your cooking experience and they ask you questions on your fishing and hunting experiences and they ask you questions on water sports. They ask you what kind of equipment you use, why you're running these trips, why you're doing this and so forth and the panel is really interesting. It would be equivalent in New York State to having somebody look at a DEC person, having maybe another guide or another outfitter on the panel that could ask you any questions, maybe somebody from a retail shop, like maybe the manager of EMS or Sam Grimone [sports shop owner] or somebody in the Chamber of Commerce or different people from different walks of life, but people that are all affected by the tourist trade are there and can ask you questions, a DEC person would be there, probably an APA person would be there. So you have a panel of people that you go before. I was very frustrated by that whole guide's law process here in New York and what happened.

CB: Was it, in your own opinion, an improvement or not over what was before?

DC: I think there's no question that it's an improvement, but it hasn't solved the problems. You still have guides who are incompetent. You still have guides who don't have the knowledge. You still have guides that don't have basically the First Aid experience or the water sports experience that they need to do what they're doing. For example, I can guide a whole children's camp and all I have to have is my adult CPR for my guide's license. I don't even have to get in the water. I can guide them on a week-long canoe trip, you know, without having any experience with children before, without having child CPR or any experience actually in the water.

CB: Except for your Basic Water Safety?

DC: Yeah, to be honest with you, I don't know. Do you have to get in the water for that?

CB: Yeah, I did. It was in a pool, but it was in the winter.

DC: Yeah. I don't know exactly what you have to do for Basic Water Safety, but ...

CB: How did you get your license if you didn't take it?

DC: Well, in order to get a guide's license, you have to have either Basic Water Safety, or you could have taken it 50 years ago, there's no time limit on Basic Water Safety. If you took it ten years ago, that's all you had to do. You only took it once. That lasts for life.

CB: If you'd taken it before the licensing regs. went into effect, you could grandfather that in to your license?

DC: You can use any kind of water sports activity that you've ever done. You can use it in place of Basic Water Safety. For instance, if you've had a basic swimming course you can use that in place of Basic Water Safety. That's my understanding.

CB: I wish I knew that, because I used to teach lifesaving, but when I went for my guide's license, I took Basic Water Safety.

DC: You didn't need it.

CB: I'll be darned.

DC: No, you didn't need to. I think the guide's law was probably not strong enough when it was first proposed, and then it got watered down from there. I think the thing, the biggest measure of a person's guiding and guiding performance is whether he's able to get repeat business. You can't get repeat business if you haven't ever guided and you can't guide without a guide's license.

So you're going to have a certain percentage of people that have their guide's licenses who don't really have much experience. Most of the people that are in guiding in

New York State are people working for non-profit organizations and they don't need a guide's license. I think it should be that everybody needs a license. Non-profit organizations should maybe get a free license, the individual should.

CB: Do you think there are more people with licenses than there is work for them? Do you get more people asking to guide for you than you could use, assuming they're qualified?

DC: Yeah, I would say so, definitely.

CB: I mean that's what gives you the pick of the field to some extent, if there's competition for those guiding jobs, you can pick the best guides.

DC: Because there's too many people in the guiding business who are doing it part-time. They aren't relying on it for income. The reason they aren't relying on it for income is because they can't because they don't charge enough. You know it's a vicious circle. They look at it as getting paid for something you like to do. That's the only work we do. We don't do any other work the entire year.

CB: Can anything be done about that?

DC: Probably a stronger guide's association could help something like that.

CB: Does the state help or hinder you?

DC: One thing that I recommended to the state is if they do go this next year to a maximum of ten people in a group, to have an over-flow area, a group site area, that may not be on the shore of a pond, like St. Regis or Long Pond. I had suggested a group camping area that was away from the edge of the pond. If you have the occasional group of 15 you could come and camp, but maybe not necessarily on the shore of the pond, but they could go through and use that canoe route. They wouldn't have to avoid the whole area simply because they couldn't camp there, but it would be nice for that kind of group to have a place that was designated as say, 15, 20 group site. There are hundreds of places like this even in the canoe area where you could have a fairly nice campsite in places where people could be pretty much by themselves without bothering other groups. All the

262 Guides of the Adirondacks

little swamps and little rises and knolls around Long Pond would be good examples of this, but they would be back 150 feet away from the shore of the pond.

CB: Do you like guiding?

DC: I can't say as I've ever met a client that I've guided that I wouldn't want to go out with again. I've just had a great time. Just fantastic people, by and large. Do I think that there should be more or less canoe areas? Canoe-only areas? That one's obvious. Let's see. Where could they be created? Well, I think that there's not only places where there could be more canoe-only areas, I think there could be some motor restrictions on certain ponds. Right where we are, for example, I think a motor restriction on Floodwood Pond would be ideal. That's really a good place. The people that are there, you don't need a motor for them, 10 horse power, to fish on that pond. Other places that are similar that could use either motor restrictions or no motors areas could include all of that Fish Creek Pond area or there could be motor restrictions on Fish Creek Pond itself for the campground. Other canoe-only areas, I think even certain bays or certain areas of places like Weller Pond would be a good example of a place that would be no motors area.

Reginald Whitney

"You've got to like your solitude. I love the woods, and that's the thing. I can't walk that much anymore. I'm always the one who likes to see what's over the next hill, even though I've been there a hundred times before. I expect you know what I'm talking about. There's always something new there. You get your favorite places and you like to go back to them."

Reg's son called me enthusiastically when he heard I was looking for information on guides -- I had to talk to his father, he said. When I called Reg he was a little embarrassed by that -- "I'm not an old-time guide." But he was a <u>bona fide</u> guide, with his own story to tell about working on the Upper Ausable Lake. Reg lives in an old frame house high on the hill above Keene on the old road behind Pitchoff Mountain to Lake Placid. He's bothered lately by arthritis that has kept him housebound.

CB: Were you down to the Ausable Club?
RW: Uh-huh.

CB: And when would that have been?
RW: Since 1966 to 1976. I was up there before working on jobs. When this other guy got done, I took over his job. Roger Bailey.

CB: Who did he work for?
RW: Welds'. David Welds'. On the Upper Ausable Lake.

CB: What would that involve in terms of what you had to do?
RW: Well, you had to maintain the camp, get all the wood in in the winter, take gas up, which you had to get in later years, because they didn't cut ice anymore. You used to have to bring the ice down from an ice house to keep the food in an old ice box. But they gradually switched over to gas refrigerators, gas stoves, because the wood was getting depleted, because they didn't want you to cut any near the lake shore because they didn't want the camps to be shown.

CB: With the gas, what was the procedure there?

RW: Well, I took the bottles up in the wintertime, Paul Lewis, the honcho up to the club, there, would haul them in for us, truck them up to the Lower Lake? They'd take them to the Lower Lake and we'd take them from there up on our snow machines, sleds.

CB: And then in the winter what? How often would you go up to camp in the winter?

RW: Oh, it would take you two-three weeks and then you'd have to go up and shovel the roofs off, and I have took people in in the winter, which was a pain.

CB: I'll bet.

RW: You have to chop a hole in the ice to get water and carry it up, but that didn't happen too often.

CB: Did they just want to come up, you mean in the winter?

RW: Yeah. They'd stay overnight up there and freeze and think it was great but ... You might know the Governor of Massachusetts, William Welds, have you ever heard of him? Well, that's the people I guided for. He was a young man in college when I worked there, someday he'll be President, you see, or he'll run for it.

CB: I'll be darned. I'll watch for that. He a good man, is he?

RW: Yeah, they seem to like him up there.

CB: Good.

RW: I had a brother died right in his bunk up there, 10 years ago. He was a guide for years. He loved it. My other brother worked for them as a guide, too.

CB: What were their names?

RW: Jess Whitney and Donald Whitney. I worked 10 years for the Welds' and then I developed this form of arthritis and I had to give it up.

CB: You guided in addition to these duties we've just been describing?

RW: Yeah. You would row them around the lake in a boat, and they'd fish, but that's all you did up there; you couldn't hunt up there. You could hunt up near there. I didn't, but the boys had a hunting camp on the stillwater up there. They'd let us go up through there and hunt. I did it one year, but it's pretty rugged in there.

CB: About when would the family come up in the summertime?

RW: Oh, God. Mr. Weld always like to come up early, Memorial Day, that's the one right?

CB: Yeah.

RW: He'd always make it that one, then he might come up one more time, then his brother's wife whose name was Webb and still is, actually, but married Alfred Weld, would come up and stay ten days -- two weeks all summer and her daughter would stay. It was on-going all the time from Memorial right through Labor Day.

CB: Now, were you living here then? Would you go up each day or would you stay up?

RW: No, we stayed up.

CB: How'd that work as far as quarters went? Did you have a separate camp?

RW: Separate camp, back a little bit. Sometimes I'd have a helper, I'd take one of my kids up, or a boy around that wanted a little work.

CB: A typical day in the summer when they were in camp, what would that involve for you?

RW: Well, I'd get up about 6:00, go down and start the fires in the kitchen, cook bacon and whatever they wanted, eggs, oatmeal for the kids, coffee. An they'd eat on the porch there, and they had a fireplace on the porch which you'd light, then you'd do their dishes and some would want to go hiking, you would have to make lunches for them, and or else go fishing, or sometimes they'd go up to Stillwater, you'd have to pack a lunch and go up there. Each family has their own boats, like I had three on the Lower Lake, you go up 3 1/2 miles, you rowed guide-boats, there was no motors allowed on the lake, except Paul Lewis had one in case of emergency and you can use it on a scow in the spring and fall to do the work. When I was younger I worked up there with Charlie Gillen, he was the one who preceded Roger Bailey. He worked there for 28 years. I worked with Charlie and I went and got married and went down to Albany for a while and in the meantime Charlie died, and then Roger took the job over. He worked seven years and anyway, he got done, and then Charlie's wife, Arlene, wanted to know if I'd like it, and I thought about it, and I said, "Well, I'll try it," then I went to work for him.

CB: In the winter, were you working at anything else?

RW: Well, I worked for Harvey Branch, a contractor, you know, carpenter work, plumbing, mason, whatever they needed, because they didn't pay, you know, you had to supplement it.

CB: The summer people, you mean?

RW: Yeah, I guess they pay better now, I don't know.

CB: Now as far as that pay goes, whatever you're comfortable talking about, but was it pretty uniform in the Ausable Club what they paid the caretakers and the guides?

RW: Now the club was altogether different. You could guide for the club, and people would hire you for so much a day. When you worked like I did, you got a salary, so much a month. Which I started out at $275 a month, year-round, but I got up to $500 toward the end there, which wasn't a hell of a lot to feed a family of my size, which I had to work other than that.

CB: What was the going rate do you figure?

RW: I don't really know because everybody got different wages. I think some of the other ones got more money, I'm not sure.

CB: Did they pay any benefits or anything?

RW: No.

CB: How were they to work for?

RW: Oh, they were nice, they were good, you know. They weren't slave drivers, is that what you mean?

CB: Yeah. Considerate?

RW: No, they were good.

CB: Would you get some time off in the summer or would you stay up?

RW: Oh, yeah, in between families there. Then I worked for Mrs. Webb up here and she kept me busy in between times, which I got extra money for that. She still lives here.

CB: Was it necessary that you have a guide's license?

RW: At first you did. I used to have the real old metal ones, then they come out with those tin things.

CB: Now, the metal ones, what year was that?

RW: Oh, gosh, 50's and 60's, well, they had them before the 60's backwards. Then they come out with those things that looked like fishing licenses. We had to turn them in and I just never went after it again.

CB: Did you have a guide's license before you started guiding for the Welds?

RW: Uh-huh.

CB: And what was the purpose of that?

RW: Well, I thought I might want to start a little guiding business. I did a couple of times. I didn't really like it because the people were crazy with guns, you know, it was more hunting. These guys from the city would come up here and I didn't quite trust them. I said I don't think I want to do that. That'd have been in the 50's.

CB: How did you solicit business for that?

RW: Well, my father had a restaurant between Keene and Keene Valley where the bridge is there, the old log cabin, and he got to know them in there, and they wanted somebody to guide them, and so I went and got a guide license and started that, and I said to hell with that.

CB: You hear too many stories.

RW: Yeah.

CB: Did you have any close calls with those city guys?

RW: Just once. Down off the mountain, here, and a buck run right out like that and them guys shooting tops out of the tree and everything and I was right in front of them and I said

"We're going back to camp" and that was the end of that. We were walking out of the hunt, actually.

CB: I'll be darned. Where was your camp?

RW: Right up here on Davis Ridge. We still have it actually, but we keep it more for the family now. I can remember the first time I went up the lake there with Charlie. I used to work for him, you know, and as I said before, Roger. He was a great fellow, he used to like to take a dip now and then, but the man wasn't well anyway. That's another story. I was rowing and he was setting in the back, and he was telling me about the rocks. He said you don't have to worry about any of the rocks in here, he said "I know where every one of them are" and about that time, I hit one and he said "There's one now". I'll always remember that. But it gave me a lot of exercise, I'll tell you.

CB: Did you have to work on the boats?

RW: Yeah, you'd paint them and make sure they were ... I never had to soak mine, I don't know why, but a lot of guides would go up there and sink theirs in the spring before it started, you know, make them swell and tighten up.

CB: If one of the boats had needed a major repair, would you have done that?

RW: No.

CB: What would you have done?

RW: Got in touch with Carl Hathaway.

CB: Ok.

RW: We would take them over to him and he'd fix them and either he'd bring them back or tell us they were ready, and we'd bring them back home.

CB: Now the boats that you used -- were they painted or varnished?

RW: Mine were painted. The canoes were canvas, painted. We had one aluminum one, I guess.

CB: As far as working for people on the club there, I'm trying to get a feel for how the clubs and the preserves may have been different, if they were, like the Adirondack League Club down at Old Forge and Ausable Club, as opposed to say being in a similar position on Upper Saranac Lake. Can you think of anything that made the Ausable Club people any different as far as your job, your work went? Was there anything about the regulations on the Club?

RW: Well, you had to be a member to be up there; it wasn't an open club.

CB: So this family went back how far?

RW: Oh, God. Years.

CB: Even before Charlie?

RW: Yeah, I called his son up the other day and asked him. The original, that was the first camp, where I worked was built in 1907. Homer Brown used to be the caretaker there.

CB: Then there was somebody between him and Charlie, or Charlie takes over there?

RW: Yeah, must have been I think, because Charlie took over in 1938 or '39, he couldn't remember. That would be quite a span there, wouldn't it?

CB: When you were helping Charlie, would you go up and get ice out and stuff like that?

RW: You'd have to hose it down, and haul it down to the cook house, there.

CB: Would you layer it with sawdust and like that?

RW: Right, but then they all rotted out and they went to gas. Like everything else in the old days -- gone. I'd much rather live back in them days. Of course, not with what I've got today. Because you've got to be physically fit to do that stuff.

CB: I'll bet. Do they have somebody else working up there now, to the camp?

RW: Brett. Brett Lawrence. I was trying to think how many private camps are up there. I think there's eight. I was on this, what would that be? My two brothers were on the other side of the lake. Don worked for Notman, and Jess worked for Lefferts.

CB: So, eight camps on the Upper Lake?

RW: Yeah, I can't remember that next one. Smith's got a big one up there. Harold Heald worked there. He worked there for a long time. Bobby Hickey worked there. Do you know Bobby?

CB: No, I don't.

RW: He used to bob sled.

CB: Oh, that name's familiar.

RW: Yeah, his brother there was big in it. Billy Hickey, Jimmy Hickey. They worked for Lefferts, not Lefferts -- Van Sinderen. Somehow them people are all related...the guy that took my job over kind of fancies himself as -- he's got a beard like yours -- he's small and short, just like "Old Mountain" Phelps was. He wears them little glasses with not plastic like mine, but with metal around it. He's good for them...I don't talk to the boys too much. I used to talk to them, but then my brother died up there. He was only 61. He was in and didn't come out when he was supposed to, and they sent somebody over to look for him, and they couldn't get into the camp, you know, he locked the door, and then actually, it was his grandson who was working for somebody and they went and called somebody and broke in and he was dead. He died from an aneurysm, near his heart or something. My other brother died from an aneurysm.

CB: I guess we'd all like to go quick, but not until we've been around awhile.

RW: Well, I was 59 in October. I'd like to be 109, but ... You've got to like your solitude, I think. You know, I love the woods, and that's the thing -- I can't walk that much anymore. I'm always the one who likes to see what's over the next hill, even though you've been there 100 times before. I expect you know what I'm talking about. There's always something new there. You get your favorite places and you like to get back to them. I've never been much of a person to fish, although all my kids do, God, they can set out on a lake all day in a boat; that drives me crazy...

You'd have to be a jack of all trades and a master of none. You know, you had to know every aspect, like plumbing. Of course, you didn't have electricity, but you had to be a carpenter, or a mason, boat fixer-upper, no major thing, you'd have to take it out, of course. We'd build docks, you do just about a little of everything, but not a whole lot of anything...usually there was somebody on the lake that would know how to fix it or had a piece of board, or, then you'd just go around until you found it or you'd just ask somebody, you know. There was a lot of camaraderie then amongst the guides that were there, they called us guides, but like I told you, we were no more than glorified caretakers. To be a guide, is the one that goes out and takes a party into the woods and makes a camp, campfire and cooks there and has a lean-to to sleep in. The Upper Lakes, you set down to a dinner table with dishes and silverware and water glasses and their cocktail hour before. To me that's not a real guide...when the guide passes on or retires, the second one in command usually takes over. It falls down like that. I built a couple of camps up there, re-did them...If I had a lot of work to do, like cut wood and that, I'd hire Don, my brother. That would give him a little extra income. You have to cut way back and then you'd cut it, split it, stack it and in the winter, you'd take your snow machine with your sled and haul the damn stuff in. You know, you can't get that much out of a sled. So it takes a good week or two to do that. You cut on the club property, preferably trees that were down, for the lean-to. Most of your young ones slept in the lean-to, when the older folks wanted their camps, they slept in their beds.

CB: Would you do it again?
RW: If I was able, sure I would. I'd make a little different arrangements maybe, but I loved it up there actually. It's hard when you've got a young family, you know. You're away a week or two at a time and you leave them home with mother, but Michael he used to go up with me a lot. He's the one that called you. He kind of likes that. That's what he thinks his father is, a guide.

Frank M. Wardner Diary

"It has snowed and blowed beastly ever since."

In 1886, when he was twenty-three years old, Frank Wardner of
Rainbow Lake kept a diary for the year, making entries every day.
Frank was the son of James and Delia Wardner, early settlers at
Rainbow Lake, who married in 1858 and built the Rainbow House
(sometimes listed as Rainbow Inn) there as a resort for sportsmen.
While not expressly stated in the diary, Frank was evidently living at
home and on the premises in 1886.

Rainbow House was about seven miles equidistant from Paul
Smiths and Bloomingdale. Wallace's 1887 "Guide to the
Adirondacks" stated "Mr. (James) Wardner's great experience in
forest life, renders him a most suitable conductor of such an
establishment. Nor should we omit to call attention to Mrs.
Wardner's talent as a taxidermist, a most important matter to those
desiring to have the trophies of their skill properly dressed and
mounted." Stoddard's guide, "The Adirondacks," for 1889, stated of
the area near Rainbow House, "This is noted fishing ground and
claims the proud distinction of yielding the largest trout on record,
one with a weight of 52 pounds, and waters have been stocked with
500,000 trout in the past five years, and affords rare sport and
sometimes astonishing results to even the unpracticed fisherman."

Frank Wardner's diary, now in the Feinberg Library at S.U.N.Y.
Plattsburgh (and reproduced with permission), is a quintessential --
although typically laconic -- Adirondack diary for the time, full of
fishing, bears, deer, guide-boats and guides. Most of the entries
dealing with guiding are excerpted below, as well as some that detail
his daily life and work as they were geared to the seasons. In 1886
Frank Wardner, according to an account summary in the back of his
diary, earned $2.50 a day plus board in guide wages in May, June,
and July, and $3.00 a day in August. His total cash transactions for
the year, all conducted between May and December, included
$113.25 received and $27.77 paid.

The Uncle Seth referred to is James Wardner's brother, who
guided for the well-known artist Arthur Fitzwilliam Tait, beginning
in about 1858. Uncle Seth, who is listed in Stoddard's guide for
1903 as the manager of the Sunset Rock Cottage, "who although new
to his house has had 20 years' experience in hotel life..." died in
1898 at age 75. Frank Wardner went on to take guests in his own
boarding house, according to the 1904 Stoddard's guide; 1904 was

the year James Wardner died at 73. Frank Wardner died in 1925. Minor changes to standard punctuation have been made, but spellings are unchanged.

1886

March 17	Will Betters drove the team drawing logs and he got drunk and corked one of the horses and left the sleds somewhere on the road and he came home and went to bed and Henry and I took care of the horses and bandaged up the one he hurt, etc. Nice day.
March 18	Henry and I helped Will get the sleighs out of the brush where he left them last night...
April 2	Jack came tonight. He had his crooked finger taken off the other day and it is doing nicely. I have got a fearful cold am most sick.
April 3	I cut stumps up the inlet this forenoon and went hunting and shot a partridge and a rabbit and a squirrell. My cold is not any better.
April 5	I cut wood in the woods. Jack went to Lilypad fishing. He got two little trout. Nice day.
April 6	It began to snow at noon and it has snowed and blowed beastly every since. It is a wild night.
April 8	Jack and I went to the Jones to hunt for an otter, did not see him. Saw two wild geese.
April 9	Went to the Jones and tried to shoot two wild geese, did not get them.
April 14	We put out the bees today. There are six good swarms, only one swarm died all winter.
April 15	I done chores and painted my boat on the outside and helped draw a load of hay from the horse barn into the middle barn, etc. Nice day.
April 16	I painted my boat on the inside today. Pa went bee hunting, did not find any.
April 17	I helped run off a barrel of lime and finished painting my boat ... I went to Bloomingdale and I bought me a pair of boots. Paid $4.00 for them.
April 21	Pa will be here tonight with the young trout from the forks.
May 4	I worked repairing boats today.
May 5	I fixed boats, etc. Jack and I went up to the inlet and set a bear trap this afternoon.

May 10	Charlie Stearns and Will Kirby came to the shanty tonight. They are picking gum. [Spruce pitch for chewing gum.]
May 13	Uncle Seth and I started for home. We carried our packs over to Round Lake. It is a five mile carry, and then took our boat and came down to Bloomingdale. We are staying at Seth's and we are tired. You bet.
May 14	I went up and looked at the bear trap. It was not disturbed.
May 18	I went to Round Pond ... caught a trout that weighed 2 3/4 lb. on my way back.
May 20	I put sawdust on the ice and fixed boats and made a trap to try and catch bullpouts in.
May 26	I worked making a pair of oars. It snowed last night and most all the forenoon and then turned to rain.
May 27	I guided the Needhams. Went up the north branch fishing. It rained and drove us home. Got 7 nice trout. I bought me a pair of shirts, paid $4.50.
May 28	I guided the Needhams. Went to Round Pond trolling, got one laker weighed 3 lbs. and some speckled trout.
May 29	...got a good mess. One weighed 1 3/4 lbs. We saw a deer.
June 4	I guided the Needhams. Went to North Branch and Sandy Hook and fished all day and only got 6 small trout.
June 5	I guided the Needhams. We fished our buoy in Rainbow Lake this forenoon and went up the inlet this afternoon.
June 13	Went over to the Jones fishing and got 28 nice trout.
June 15	I painted a boat and made a pair of oars.
June 18	I am twenty-three years old today. I went up to the other house and ate strawberry shortcake for supper.
July 6	I cleaned out the boat house and worked in the garden and mended harness.
July 19	I heard two bears and shot an owl.
July 22	This afternoon I went to my bear trap and I had a bear in it and I shot him and brought him to the house. It is a yearling. It is the first bear I ever shot or caught in a trap either.
July 23	I skinned my bear and raked hay.

July 24	Pa and I went up the inlet and set my bear trap and bated it new.
July 25	Caught 20 1/2 lbs. of trout. 175 by count.
August 1	I went to my bear traps and I shot a crane.
August 5	Mr. Slicer made me a present of a beautiful revolver. It is as nice as there is made. It shoots .38 cal. center fire and it is heavy enough to shoot straight. It is a daisy and I appreciate it as a present. [Note: unsure if this means Daisy brand or "highly esteemed."]
August 6	I guided Mr. Slicer. We went fishing to North Branch, got a basket full.
August 7	I went and cut some fish poles this forenoon and I guided Mr. Slicer this afternoon. Went up the inlet, got a good mess of trout.
August 9	I done chores, run after the cows and froze the ice cream. I went to my bear trap.
August 11	Mr. Slicer and I heard a catamount yell up the inlet tonight.
August 12	I broke my watch today.
August 17	I guided Mr. Thompson. Went up North Branch got a good mess, three of these weighed three pounds, averaging a lb. a piece.
August 20	I worked in the field binding grain this forenoon and guided Mr. Thompson this afternoon, went to North Branch fishing. We got 4 trout, the 4 weighed 4 lbs. Mr. Fuller came tonight. My watch came back tonight, so they fixed it. The hair spring got kinked and that was all that was the matter with it.
August 24	I raked and set up buckwheat this forenoon and I guided Mr. Slicer this afternoon. Went to North Branch and Sand Hook, got 7 nice trout.
August 25	I guided Mr. Slicer this forenoon and Mr. Thompson this afternoon. Went up the inlet.
September 2	I guided Mr. Lines. Went up North Branch, did not get any fish. Pa and I went up the inlet after I got back with Mr. Lines and caught a trout that weighed 3 lbs. and one that weighed 1 lb. There was a frost last night.
September 4	I raked buckwheat this morning and then went and took the Lineses out to Ray Brook House. I took dinner with President Cleveland there.

September 6	I worked in the field all day. Pa killed a deer in front of the house today.
September 9	I guided Mr. Goodridge and another gentleman. Went up the inlet, got 5 trout.
September 10	I mowed oats this forenoon and guided Mr. Goodridge this afternoon.
September 13	I sorted onions and done chores, dug potatoes, etc. Went 6 miles after the cows tonight.
September 23	I worked in the garden and drew in grain, etc. Uncle Seth killed two deer today. I put out dogs. Drove two. Uncle Seth killed one. There has been nine deer killed between Paul Smiths and Loon Lake today.
October 4	I guided Dr. McGay and Mr. Bullhouse. Went fishing pickerel to Bloomingdale. Got two. The threshing machine came today.
October 5	I worked around the threshing machine. We threshed 210 bu. of oats today. Nice day.
October (?)	Pa and Henry and Jack and I went cranberrying down the Osgood River. Got 13 pints.
October 13	I dug potatoes and I traded watch chains with Henry for his fly pole and accordion to boot and I traded knives with Jack and paid 50 cents to boot.
October 17	I ran two deer on Blue Hill. It snowed some today. The inlet froze over last night.
October 18	I shot a nice deer today with my revolver.
October 19	I picked stones. We saw a deer run through the field. We tried to shoot him but failed. He broke ice near the house.
October 24	(Sunday) I rested and shot a partridge. Paid $1.00 for a pair of pants.
October 29	Uncle Seth paid me 25 dollars that he owed me today. He now has 25 dollars and 75 cents of my money on interest.
October 30	Henry and I started for Cold Brook to fix up a shanty. We will stay all night.
November 2	Election day. I went up with Pa and voted this afternoon. Picked stones this forenoon.
November 3	I went up on Clear Pond Hill. We killed two today. Henry got one on Square Pond and Pa got one in Clear Pond.

November 5   Henry and I worked fixing the water for winter today. I shot a duck this morning with my rifle.

November 8   I went still hunting on Blue Hill. I followed 3 deer til half past noon. I did not start them. I am tired.

November 19   We killed a beef and a pig. It is snowing and blowing fearfully now.

December 31   Alfred and I chopped wood, Henry drew one load here and skidded some and went to Bloomingdale with a load. Mr. Fuller came today. Mr. Bradford and Eunice went back to Dannemora today. It snows and blows. Good bye old year -- welcome the new.

PART FOUR:
Two Trips to Hamilton County

Note: This account, subtitled "Rough Notes Stolen From the Journal of an Angler," appeared for the first -- and apparently only -- time in *"The Spirit of the Times"* in the issues of March 4 and March 11, 1854. "Two Trips" is the narrative of a mid-nineteenth century Adirondack outing, complete with guides. Some spellings, such as "Couch" and "Cooch," vary within the text.

Written for the New York *Spirit of the Times*.
Dear P. -- I believe it was Horace who used the words, "Nil ego contulerim jucundo sanus amico," or, in plain English, the greatest blessing is a pleasant friend. The truth and force of this adage is never more fully appreciated, than in the happy solitude of forest life.

For some years past, it has been my custom to pay an annual visit to the fishings grounds and wild retreats of the northern parts of this State. The selection of a companion of the right "mental and bodily material" has always been my first "look-out," and thus far, I have had the good fortune to hit the right man. Last May I secured the companionship of my friend James S. Pe-r-e of this City, an ardent lover of legitimate angling schooled on Scottish lochs and streams, and now, memory returns with satisfaction and pleasure to the joyous fortnight passed with him in the wilds of Hamilton County.

Our journey to Lake Pleasant was cheered by the society of Mrs. P. and two daughters, and would that I dare with delicacy and propriety, speak of the "incidents of, travel!" from the city to the Lake. When round the hospitable board of friend "P." those incidents have oft and oft been recounted, and three ominous looking black books, that might have been used as a diary by some astrologer in the dark ages, as often opened to settle some disputed point. Well, good "Spirit," I have run the risk of getting into P.'s "black books" -- I stole them -- I did -- those three black books of angling and sporting, and here are the contents: --

Thursday, June 3d, 1852 -- I am sitting on a rock by the edge of "Round Lake," and while my guide is tinkering up the oars of his skiff, I commence my journal, hitherto neglected.

Stock had been taken, the semi-annual account made up, and rendered, and the necessary remittances made, when feeling, like a boy let out from school, with mind "buoyant and free," I drove down to the steamer Oregon, for Albany, at last, on my long thought-of excursion to Hamilton County. We had a lovely evening, and I did not "turn in" until after 10 o'clock; the quivering motion of the boat prevented sound sleep. At 3 1/2 A.M., we reached the warf, when I got up, dressed, and went to the Delaware House, breakfasted, and took the train West, leaving at 6 1/2 o'clock passing through Schenectady, stopt at Amsterdam in about an hour and a half after leaving Albany. Three other gentlemen got out here also, bound for Lake Pleasant -- Messrs. B., K., and W., and we there met another person, Mr. A., a lawyer from Greenfield, Mass., also going North. The last had expected to meet my friend Mr. M. here, and we both regret he cannot come. As we should have been together by previous arrangement, we have agreed to be come "compagnons du voyage," and as he is experienced, I mean, in all things, to yield in deference to his judgment. About 11 A.M. the mail arrives, and then we start in a comfortable four-horse stage, which goes on a plank road as far as Northville; our route is through an undulating country, and the names of the villages through which we pass, show that my fellow countrymen had been the original settlers; first came Perth, then Broad Albin. As we go North it becomes more mountainous. We pass the "fish house" on our way, so called from its being a sporting retreat of Sir William Johnson's in the olden times. It is on the banks of the Sacondaga river. There are few trout here now, and the deer have gone long ago.

About 5 P.M. we reach Northville, where we must stay all night and take the mail stage at 7 next morning. A quiet country village always seems very stupid and insipid to me, and the tavern usually an infliction, although here I found comfortable quarters, and a good bedroom.

Wednesday, 2d. -- We started about 7 A.M., a pleasant party full of laugh and joke, and soon we got into the woods and among the mountains.

The driver, Mr. Brundage, is proprietor of the stage, an old man, and something of a character. The valley through which we pass, reminds me somewhat of that of the Esopus about Shandaken, in Delaware County. The road is very bad, and Mr. A., and I walked more than half of it. At last a quick turn brought us in view of Lake Pleasant. It is a beautiful sheet of water, about 4 miles long and probably a mile and a half wide, partial clearings and houses here and there. Parallel with the shore and on the Southern side is a splendid range of lofty and wood-covered mountains; near the Western end or head of the lake, stands our hotel.

What an excitement the arrival of the mail produces! -- every one on the stoop to see who's come, and hear the news, for the mail is a weekly one. It was about 3 P.M. when we got there. Mr. Holmes, the landlord, is a hardy healthy looking man, with a countenance radiant with good-humor, and he holds in high esteem. The house is full of gentlemen. Some fishing here, but the sport, they say, is very indifferent, for the lakes in the vicinity are fished out. But look at your sixteen pounder, which is just brought in -- what a noble, finely shaped fish, caught in Lake Pleasant by Mr. Penniman of New York. It is the largest that has been taken this season, in this region.

The bar-room is a curiosity. The walls are covered by deer's antlers, stuffed animals, and birds, like a museum. Yonder stands the savage panther, here a mouse, and there a wild cat, with lots of martins, weasels, and smaller fry. Sketches of notable fish, drawn in pencil on the white-washed walls with a brief description, make you feel as if you would like to have been the lucky captor.

A fine dish of broiled trout was duly dispatched, and some chopped moose meat, which had been cured, dried, and smoked, was a relish, so new and delicious, that it will even cling to my recollections. Mr. K., and I took a flyrod, and strolled down to Lake Pleasant, but we could not make a cast, for the lake shores appear to be all densely wooded. I see Mr. A. has his gun with him, and he tells me such stories about his deer shooting at Louis Lake, &c., that I very much regret not bringing one.

I have arranged for my guide -- Mr. Couch, a very respectable looking little man, some forty years of age, and I think I shall like him. As he is a Justice of Peace, I must be careful how I behave myself before "his honor."

Thursday the 3d. -- Breakfast early -- keen to go at it -- and to Round Lake we go, which is near the house. I troll with my bass-rod, and the suggestion of some one put in the short tip, though I didn't like it, for it makes the rod too stiff -- not spring enough.

All the others go to Lake Pleasant; the big fish of yesterday attracts them there. By the way, I am glad here to meet my friend Mr. McIntyre, of Philadelphia -- and a most cordial shake of the hand we have had. Now for Round Lake. I sit in a cranky little skiff, face towards the stern, and rod in hand.

The train of hooks is about four inches long from the tip hooks to the tail ones. To a gut leader of two yards long this train of hooks (or gang as the guides call it) is attached, and two large gaudy flies put on, one perhaps eighteen inches below where the line and gut are looped together -- the other half way between that, and the hooks. Well, away we started, trolling with about sixty yards of line out, for it was rather still, and the fish lay in deep water, and a buckshot is on the gut for a sinker. Round we row, talking about deer, moose, trout, and game generally, and the conversation, to me very interesting, beguiles the time which would otherwise have hung heavily on my hands, for no trout comes at my bail -- at last we hook, and got a little brook trout, not over half a pound, and that is all, during forenoon.

Once a heavy fish struck my minnow -- but I jerked too hard, and probably tore out -- my rod being too stiff.

The middle of the day is usually an unfavorable time for fishing, so, after dinner, I lounged about the Hotel, until between three and four, when, having put in the longer and more slender tip of my rod, and taking down with me to Round Lake my fly rod also, we resumed our fishing -- using a rod and line from each of the skiffs.

I was more fortunate than during the forenoon, for we caught three lake trout and three speckled ones -- the largest three pounds -- the smallest half a pound. The stronger rod, carrying a sinker on the line, caught all the lakers, while the other without any weight took the brook trout.

I tried "Buel's patent Spoon," on my fly rod, and took one fish with it, but the other two were caught on the flies. On examining this spoon in the evening, I found gut on which it twirls, already so much chafed as not to be trusted, so I must rig it anew, and this is a radical objection to the thing, that half a day's trolling frays the gut so, that it must be renewed.

Friday, 4th -- This day was entirely devoted to making arrangements by Mr. A. and I, in view of going into the woods, and on consultation with our guides, we have determined to visit a small and secluded Lake, in the so called Canada region, that is, out of which the West Canada Creek forms its head. 'Tis said this have never been fished, except in winter, through the ice, when some straggling hunter in pursuit of moose, in that secluded region, may have desired to provide himself with a meal.

Saturday, 5th -- Packed our traps last night for the woods, rejecting every thing of weight or bulk, not indispensable. Our guides are, first, Mr. Couch, my immediate mentor, then Silas Call, who is attached to Mr. Alvord, and we take a third young man, Frank Courtney, to aid in carrying the extra baggage, and necessaries. Each carries his rifle, Mr. Alvord his gun, and I have borrowed one from Mr. Holmes, a goodstout piece of No. 14 gauge.

We take a couple of boots with us, the one smaller than the other, so that it can be put inside -- then both are placed on a long bodied wagon, drawn by a couple of horses; with this team we shall proceed some ten miles, where we yesterday sent forward a pair of oxen; thence the horses will be sent back, for they are useless, where there are no roads. Couch and Call take their hounds. Among our necessaries are:

18 loaves of bread,
16 pounds of butter,
22 pounds of pork,
 6 bottles of brandy,
 3 1/2 pounds of tea,
15 pounds of sugar,
 7 pounds of candles,

besides cigars, tobacco, pipes, salt, pepper, matches, &c.

I had made for me in the city a stout canvas bag, rigged with a couple of leather shoulder straps, so that it might be carried on the back like a knapsack, and this the guides highly approved of; the candles we take are not to luxuriate with in our abode in the forest, but to be used in deer hunting at night on the lakes.

We have fine weather, and we start in good spirits, full of jokes; the poor dogs seem to understand that they are soon to be active participators in the sports, and look as happy as the rest of us. They are chained under the wagon. The road for the first four miles is along Lake Pleasant, and the same by which we had come from New York; then, however, we struck due North, and here the travelling was so miserable, that we all got to walking. The lumbering wagon proceeds but slowly, rolling about, and sometimes with the wheels up to the hub in mud. About a mile north, we pass the cabin of "old Sturge," who is a noted character, and I had a few minutes' chat with him -- a hale powerful looking man, about forth-five years of age. He was originally from Vermont, and a shoemaker by trade, was very much afflicted with asthma, and came to this region by the advice of his physician, to take up the occupation of trapper and hunter -- he has a family of fifteen children, the oldest, "Burr Sturges," is a chip of the old block, and one of the best guides in the country. There was a swarm of boys of all ages around the house, and a ragged but hardy looking set they were. Many a joke is told of "old Sturge" when he was green and first came out here, how he blundered into trouble with moose, bear, and panther, until he become au fait at a woodsman' life.

Well, on we tramp, and somehow Silas and I had got into some discussion about shooting, when I expressed some want of belief in that certainty of aim which many claim. "Well look here now," says he, "it is no great matter, I know, to hit a quiet object, but do you see that little cedar bird out on the bush there?" pointing to one some sixty yards off. "Now I'll shoot that." And sure enough, up went his rifle, carelessly as I thought, off it went, and down fell the bird, which I picked up a confused mass of flesh and feathers.

About 11 A.M. we reached Jessup's River, a beautiful stream, and said to be full of fine trout; this we crossed by a rude bridge.

A mile further on, we came to a spot of some hundred acres without any trees on it; this is called Wilcox's Clearing. The land is apparently very fertile, and was covered by a luxuriant crop of natural grass -- but no one lives there now. Two or three families at different times have tried it, but it is too solitary. A man may get along at such a place, but the woman must have her neighbor to assist in time of trouble, or sickness, and perhaps to gossip with occasionally too.

Here we find our oxen waiting us. Now the road or path becomes so very rough and abstructed, as to scarcely discoverable.

Now the order of our march is somewhat changed--first goes Silas a quarter of a mile before the team, with an axe, to clear any abstruction from the track, such as a fallen tree. Then Courtney, with another axe, for the same purpose, A. and I, as it suited our fancies to be, next to the wagon with John Gilman the teamster and his "Gee whoa" to the oxen. Behind, Couch to see that nothing was lost by being jolted out. Crossing the Maumes river, a small stream, flowing east, and like Jessup's, one of the head waters of the Hudson, we eat dinner, and rest awhile, first making a smudge fire--this is with just as much green wet stuff in it, as will burn, and throw out a first-rate smoke, for by this time I have made acquaintance with the dreaded "black fly," of which I had heard so much. This small insect very much resembles the common house fly, but it is only one quarter its size; its bite is very poisonous, but more so to some than to others; it is only seen during the months of June and July, and then during the day. They are sound sleepers, and never stir at night. On a still day, they are most troublesome to keep them off. I had a green gauze veil sewed together at the sides like a bag, but open below; this put over my bread-rimmed felt hat, kept the blood-suckers at a respectable distance, but this veil is sadly in my way, and with it on, you cannot of course smoke a cigar; besides, it has a smothering feeling on a hot day.

Having rested, and dined on a woodmen's fare, again we make a start. The trees are so thick and high that I can tell little about the scenery, or "lay of the land," most of the time, but I find ourselves long and steadily ascending, and am told we are crossing by the notch of the Blue Mountains, a lofty and conspicuous ridge, and which seemed blue and misty looking in the distance, when they were pointed out to me at Lake Pleasant. At last the summit is reached; the now weary oxen progress but slowly, and Alvord and I are ahead of all. Understanding that we are to camp that night at Cedar River, in the next hollow, we descend the mountain and refresh ourselves by the pure cold stream. Here we wait till almost dark, for the team, and wonder why it don't come. At last we see Courtney alone, who comes to say that the oxen had given out, and they had camped about two miles behind. To take the back track, and that up a steep mountain, was anything by pleasant -- but there was no help for it.

On reaching the chosen spot for the night's rest, I see it is like a clearing, and area of about 200 acres, and this the guides call "a fly," caused by some severe hurricane of wind, which had levelled all the trees. The oxen here browsing on the luxuriant natural grass, and the smoke of a large and cheering fire, over which the kettle was now boiling, pointed out the place of our bivouac. Already some small trees have been felled and used for the frame of a temporary shanty. The boughs laid on the ground were to be our bed. The smell from the frying pan was really very inviting, and never was a meal more relished by me than on this occasion; although bread and butter, with fried pork and tea, made all the variety. A rousing fire of great logs was within three yards of our feet, and necessary it was, for the air was chilly, and we were at a very considerable altitude--with my knapsack for a pillow, and plaidy drawn over me, I lay down beside the rest, who soon fell fast asleep; but I could not, for although very tired, my mind was all in a flutter and excitement. I could see the stars above and hear the rustling of the wind among the forest trees; then a villainous owl, commenced chanting his song "too-whoo, too-whoo," which sounded most dismal. I thought of bears and panthers, and many things besides, all equally ridiculous. My feet felt roasting, which my back was cold; then my clothes being on annoyed me, and my feet seemed to swell inside my boots, so I kicked these off--all would not do; hardily did I ever dose, so, with the first peep of dawn on.

Sunday, the 6th, I jumped up, left the camp with its still drowsy inmates, found the clear cold spring, where, with a copious draught, and a good wash, I feel more comfortable.

The dogs were still chained up, and had been fed on bread, but soon now we hope to get them some food more congenial to their tastes from a deer's carcase. Breakfast dispatched, it is decided that we shall now descend to the Cedar Lakes, lying about two miles from our camp to the Northwest. So our two most experienced guides take their axes to reconnoitre and explore for the best route to go down; deciding on which, they notch the trees every 15 yards or so, on the adopted tracks to the lakes. Mr. A. and I find our way down, and gaze with interest on this interesting sheet of water, so beautiful, yet so still and wild. The only living things we see, are two or three gulls, who scream resenting our intrusion, and a "loon," or the great northern diver. These birds come here to raise their young. Long we stay and anxiously look for the men, and it was 2 P.M. before they got down with the teams, for they had to fell many a tree to make a path for the wagon. A suitable place being selected near the Lake shore for a camp, near a good spring, the boats are launched, and the dogs tied up; Frank and John Gilman remain to build a shanty, while Couch and I, in one skiff, and Mr. A. and Silas in the other, start off to catch some trout for dinner.

We soon found a few small fish for bait, and with these we troll, as in Round Lake. In less than an hour we had at least 30, and these were soon in the frying pan, and thence transferred to our now hungry stomachs. Oh! how fine a pipe of good tobacco goes after such a meal! Imagine me sitting under a shady hemlock, with my back to a log, puffing out the smoke, and listening to the detail of some moose hunt by Silas in this very region. It might have been 5 o'clock when it was decided to turn out the dogs, and run some deer into the lake--so we again got into the boats as before dinner, while the two other men each take a hound and lead them forth up the mountain to turn them out; hardly had they let them loose when each strikes the scent; and away they go; there is something solemnly impressive in listening to the tongue of a good hound on the mountain's side; Couch and I ran west to a narrow sort of strait, dividing the Lake or rather chain of Lakes, and here drawing the skiff in close to the bank, and under the dropping branches of a mighty spruce, we look up and down intently for our prey, at the same time keeping ourselves as well contented as possible, consistent with the keeping a good look out. A. and Silas Call, in the other boat, are watching near our camp. We listen to the deep bay of the dogs, now near, now farther off, and one of them "old Hector," has made almost a circuit of the Lake, and his loud yells especially, show the deep interest he feels in the business; half an hour elapses, when Cooch discerns a deer in the water, trying to swim across, and about half way between our station and the other boat; we got into our skiff in a hurry, and little Cooch strains his hardest at the oars--the skiff seems to fly--we must cut off the deer from either bank; and then A.

and Silas have seen it too, and are making the water fly, trying who will have the first shot; we see Cooch's dog now swimming in. In our hurry my man runs his boat right on the top of a rock, some inch or so only under the surface, and there stick. "Confound the skiff," ejaculates Cooch, springing out and meaning to get on the rock and pull us off; but instead of that he jumps into the water up to his neck, and almost upsets the whole concern. So you see, here we realized the truth of the old proverb, "the more haste less speed." In the meantime the other boat was rapidly approaching the deer, and the poor animal seeing it, had turned, and was swimming down the lake straight for us. Away we spin again, and now we are within three yards; the head only is above water, although I can see the hair on the ridge of the back now above the surface, now a little below. Cooch stops the boat, steadies, and I fire--the poor deer turns on its side, and I have put a buckshot through its brains; we drag it in, and I turn away as Cooch almost severs its head from its body with his knife; poor thing, I feel sorry for you, and had it not been for the excitement of the circumstances, I certainly could not have had the heart to kill you. Again we hear both hounds in full cry, but we have got all we need, and return to camp; our deer is dressed, the saddle hung on the limb of a tree, the balance thrown on the ground to feed the dogs.

We had fine venison steaks for supper, and some delicious trout split up and tacked on a board, and then roasted before the fire. It was dusk by the time we had smoked our pipes, and Cooch's dog had come in, and taken his supper too, but we saw nothing of old Hector, and Call was getting anxious for his safety. How soundly I slept this night, and the rest had been stirring for an hour before I woke up.

Monday, 7th--It was raining gently when I turned out, and the leaden hue of the skies showed that there was more in store for us; we concluded to send back the oxen, from where we now are, but Silas Call, and John the teamster start to reconnoitre and decide on the best course for us to pursue in reaching the Canada Lakes; while they are about this, Alvord and Frank in one boat, and Cooch, and I again go fishing.

These Cedar Lakes are composed of three, as it were, connecting lengthwise by narrow straights, and a fourth lies on the North, joining the middle one of the chain--here in the last, we catch a very great number of splendid trout; they bit so fast, that before I could have my bait worked out ten yards, I would hook a fish; fine large, speckled beauties, so fast did we take them, that a dozen at least would be jumping about alive in the bottom of the boat at once. At one time the spare rod which I was using, but which was rigged up with a cast of flies, was lying along the boat, and somehow the line and flies had fallen overboard, when a large trout leaped at a fly and hooked himself; he was secured by Cooch, for my hands were then full with another.

By this time the rain was pouring down in torrents; from this I was protected by an India rubber coat, but poor Cooch was drenched to the skin, and begged of me to return to camp, which we did. In the morning the guides used the precaution of peeling the bark from some large spruce trees, and with these covered the roof of our shanty, so that it was perfectly water tight and dry underneath. Thus we had a very cozy house to come to. Soon after our return, "the boys" who had been off exploring, returned; they had forgotten to take a compass with them; the dark rainy day bewildered them as to their direction--they had not found what they wanted--got lost, and were very lucky to find the camp as easily as they did.

After dinner Cooch and Frank start to see what they can find out, and take a compass with them. Still no sign of Call's hound, and the poor fellow was very unhappy in consequence; he thought the wolves, or bear, or panther had made him their victim. About dusk Cooch and Courtney return--they had found a small stream running west, and were sure it connected with the Canada Lakes, and had caught a few small trout and brought them with them.

The rain still pours, but we don't mind it, for our shanty is perfectly water proof; and again a sound and refreshing sleep places us into

Tuesday, 8th--There was not quite so much rain this morning I may as well mention the bait I have found to answer the best here, it is the golden minnow, the same beautiful little fellow, who sports in our Scottish streams, and under the angler's care attracts to destruction the noble trout; we tried shiners and small chubs, but the minnow was the thing.

John Gilman has started with his oxen and wagon for home, and takes with him about 130 pounds weight of trout, while we collect all our traps, and getting into the boats with our now only hound, and row up to the head of the lake, which goes off laterally from the chain, and towards the north--passing over the place where we yesterday had such successful fishing; we pulled out the boats into those dark gloomy roads. The timber here was almost exclusively of spruce; the ground was all trod up with the moose, and here we saw a space where a lot of them must have "yarded" last winter--great quantities of their dung was scattered around. It is about the size of a pigeon's egg, and resembles the same in shape. The portage across from the Cedar Lake to the Canada Lake stream was not more than two miles, but there was a steep ridge to climb, very rocky and uneven, with a great deal of underbrush. This being wet, made the walk exceedingly uncomfortable. The boat had to be carried across, and this was done by fastening poles to them with stout cords, these poles resting on the shoulders of the men. What with the oars and other articles to be carried, we only got one of the skiffs across this afternoon, then a bark--covered shanty had to be made, for the rain came down as "hale water."

It was a miserably comfortless day, but we all slept soundly from sheer fatigue.

Wednesday, 9th -- The wind howled dismally through the night, for it blew a gale, and as daylight broke it shifted to the northwest, when, as the guide said, we had "a fresh hand to the bellows." The creaking sounds of falling trees in various directions was rather exciting to the nerves; but the other boat was got safely across by about 10 o'clock, when we immediately embarked. The small stream swollen with the rain was rushing down with fearful speed; no need to row then; on the contrary, each boat had a guide seated in the stern with a long stout stick, or pole out behind to steer with, and to jam down on the bed of the stream to check our speed. It was ticklish navigating, sometimes rushing through dense groves of alders -- and chin-scrapers they were; then again floating gently over a deep pool, by some precipitous crag. Fallen trees frequently obstructed our course, and occasionally large rafts, or accumulations of drift stuff. Repeatedly we were within an inch of being upset. The axe was very useful in cutting away impediments. Sometimes again we would all get out, and lift the boats across the barricades.

About 1 P.M. we reach a beautiful lake -- immense mountains around it, covered with trees to their very summits. I never saw a more attractive spot. This is one of the Canada Lakes, but not the one we want; we go ashore here and lunch; the guides do not recognise it, and we call it "Lake Alvord." How impressive is the solemn silence of such a spot. Again in the boats, our course still westward, row across Lake Alvord, passing through its outlet, where we find a large body of water running out; the descent is frequently uneven and very rapid. Here Cooch's hound caught sight of a deer, and although I caught him by the leg, he got out of the skiff, swam ashore, and we heard the forest ring with his deeptoned notes. It was useless waiting for the dog, so on we went; we had descended some three or four miles, when the guides, on consultation, decided that we were on the wrong track, and were in fact, from some places they recognized, going down the West Canada Creek. So we must return, but to do so against the swift current seems to me impossible. It must be tried, however, so Alvord and I get ashore, carrying as much stuff as we could, and the men get into the water and drag the boats after them. It was hard and laborious work; at one time, Call, who, being the strongest, had hold of one, in trying to get it over a small fall, and by the side of the creek, was swept, skiff and all, over the ledge into the deep pool below. The boat was half filled with water; and Call soused over head and ears. Bread, cigars, powder, &c., soaked and ruined; fortunately my pack was on my back, containing my smokeables, ammunition, &c., while my gun was in my hand.

This was a bad business; Call's watch and compass too were spoiled.

We bail out the skiff, and still ascend, reaching Lake Alvord after sundown, and camp on the west shore; no time to make a shanty, but we kindle a roaring fire, cook our supper, and never did mortal men enjoy it more, for we were both cold and hungry. It was cold during the night, and rained somewhat; when we woke on the morning of

Thursday, 10th -- We had observed a large inlet discharging a great quantity of water into Lake Alvord from the southeast, and expecting this would lead to the lake we were in search of, we determined to go up that; so with the break of day we at once made for it with the boats. The current was very strong and the brook narrow; oars could not be used, so we pushed up against the stream with the poles from the stern. In this way we had proceeded some mile and a half, but still no lake was visible, so we hauled into the bank and went ashore. Silas and Frank determined to walk forward and explore, which Cooch staid by Mr. Alvord and I to cook us some breakfast. In hewing down some trees to make a fire, one in falling got jammed against another one which was standing; it hung against this for some minutes, when giving way one of its limbs struck poor Cooch in the face, inflicting a fearful gash on his chin, and laying open the flesh to the bone; I had fortunately some sticking plaster with me, so I acted as surgeon, bringing the gaping wound, or rather flesh, together, and putting strips of the plaster across; taking my pocket handerkerchief, I wound that round his face, and left nature to do the rest. We got the kettle to boil at last, and had our meal, although it was rather a comfortless one. By this time the other two guides had returned, and had seen no lake; stupidly they had left their rifles with us, which they sorely repented, for half a mile from us they came across a large buck and two does, who stood and looked at them for several minutes, within ten steps of the boys, who stared at them like a pair of fools, and then the deer slowly trotted away.

Breakfast discussed, we descend the stream, and go back to where we slept last night, and here determine to build a bark-covered shanty, so that we may have something like a home, at least, and protection from rain. While occupied at this, we hear a pack of wolves in full cry, doubtless chasing a deer, about half way up the mountain right behind our camp; instantly seizing each our gun or rifle, we scatter along the verge of the Lake, and crouch among the brush, expecting to see the poor deer leap into the water, with the wolves at his heels, and then woe to Master wolf; but the chase wound round the hill, and at last the sounds of the herd die away in the distance.

The shanty ready, we take comfortable possession, arrange our traps, and two of the boys start out again to reconnoitre, and ere long return with the joyful intelligence that they had found the long sought-for lake in a quiet, secluded spot, its inlet falling into Lake Alvord, amidst a clump of tamaracks (the Scotch Larch fir); so while two men go round by the inlet Cooch conducts Alvord and I by land across. Again the rain is pouring. A good bark shanty is now constructed for we feel that here at least we were to remain for several days. We tried to catch some trout for supper, but only succeeded in getting one of about a pound weight. It was very cold, and at such a time a dram is a perfect godsend. All our baggage was wet, yet in spite of thunder, lightning, rain, and hail, we all slept soundly.

Friday, 11th -- It has cleared off cold, wind W.N.W., blowing fresh, and cold enough for March. After breakfast, we trolled in the Lake, but with very small success. We saw a number of deer, but they were too far off for a shot, and now unfortunately we are without any dog to run them in, for Cooch's hound never appeared since we lost him at the West Canada Creek; for from our being so much about in boats we, of course, left no scent for him to trace us out.

This Lake is very deep, with dark and gloomy forests all round, and we have named it Lake Petrie, as we are certainly the first white men who have ever fished here, excepting an occasional hunter through the winter. As the sun ascended it became warmer, and the trout bit better, and what we catch are large and very fine; short, chunky, full fed fellows, their flesh redder than a salmon, and spots bright as vermillion; we are somewhat troubled to find small bait fish, and the air is too cold for flies.

I write this whole morning in our shanty; the black flies have bitten my hands very much, and I dislike to wear my gloves as well as veil, for the last seems to be a smothering affair.

Find I have taken with me an insufficient supply of brandy, tea, and sugar, but, thanks to Mr. Alvord's experience, he has provided for my want of knowledge.

How the mind reverts to that day of plenty by the Cedar Lakes, and how we long for some of that venison, which we left there for the wolves to devour; wish we were back there now, where the speckled trout were in such abundance.

How indispensable pork seems to be in the woods; and this reminds me of John Cheney, the celebrated hunter of the Adirondacks. The last question he asks of his companions, when starting on a hunting excursion, is -- "Got your pork? Got your matches? All right! Let's go!" My segars are fortunately uninjured by wet, while Alvord's were soaked, and are now strewed all around the shanty, and stuck under the rafters to be dried out. He growls about his gun-wads more than all, which have been reduced to perfect mush. After all, for these woods give me a pipe and tobacco, and how soothing their influence, while the fragrant exhalation keeps mister black fly at a respectable distance. It seems singular that with so much exposure to we don't catch cold; the guides say men never do out in the forest, and that those roasting fires at the feet are the great prevention.

By the way, I have not shaved since leaving New York, and it feels very nasty -- for I am continually passing my fingers and thumb across my jaws and chin; still there is no doubt but the stubble keeps the black fly from biting.

I washed thoroughly in the Lake this morning, and put on a clean shirt. What a luxury! This is the great hunting ground for moose, and the least unfrequented in the county.

I have just presented to Silas my compass, for his was ruined by his immersion yesterday into the creek; Cooch has a very good one.

Saturday, 12th -- A delightful day; weather softening -- warm in the sun -- and the trout bite tolerably; we caught a number of very fine ones last evening -- all brook trout -- no lakers; they remind me of those taken in Lock Arklet, in Scotland -- not even the saucy and greedy "Cardinal;" I can only account for it by the fact that the water is very deep, and they cannot see a small object on the surface; or, what is still more probable, the insects and flies of this County are of far greater magnitude than those in the "Land o' Cakes."

The sun and wind have at length dried out our clothes thoroughly, and we begin to feel ourselves perfectly at home, "and comfortable, at that." This is a most extraordinary country to get hungry -- the appetite seems no sooner appeased than it comes on again.

One o'clock, P.M. -- Silas has just returned from another scouting expedition, and reports that we are on the wrong lake yet, and that he has discovered the "El Dorado" at last, and no mistake. So we eat dinner, again pack our "plunder," and abandon our shanty for a new home, less than two miles off; in fact, across the ridge in the next valley to the north. Mr. Alvord, Silas, and I, cross through the woods, while the other men with the boats must go round by the outlet; we meet them on our way -- that is, by the outlet of our newly-discovered Lake; this is much obstructed with rocks and falls, over which the boats had to be carried. We see fresh moose tracks in abundance, and Silas wishes me to join him, and follow them up, feeling certain that he may get a shot; but as the afternoon is wearing away, and it takes a good deal of time to get round, and a new shanty has to be made before dark, we conclude to let the moose go, very much against my decided wish.

But an object now attracts my attention, worth coming out here to see, and this was an old beaver dam; of course, there are none of the intelligent animals here now, and this very ruin before me may have been constructed a century ago. We still see the spiles as they have been driven in across the brook, although burst out about the centre; how they manage it is a mystery; they all appear to project about the same distance above the surface, and as close to each other as the posts in a stockade. Now we are at our new lake, and to avoid the flies I get on the top of a rock, with the water around me, book on my knee, to scribble this. The black flies are in myriads in the woods, but the fresh breeze along the Lake keeps these pests at a distance.

The men are now engaged in getting round the boats. The woods are still, spruce, balsam, hemlock, yellow-birch, and maple, and occasionally tamaracks in the swamps; the brush is mostly young balsams, mountain ash, and many flowering shrubs, including currants and raspberries, only yet in blossom. This is not to be wondered at, for we have frequently seen ice and snow in our journey. This, then, the guides say is the wildest part of the State of New York, never now entered by man except in winter, when a few hunters on snow-shoes here pursue the moose.

This is a magnificent sheet of water -- splendid mountains all around, on the north side especially, where they are very precipitous and wild. The Lake is twice the size of the one we have left -- the water is clear as crystal. It is strange that Silas Call should not have piloted us here before, but he says that now in its summer garb everything looks different from what he has hitherto seen it; but we are certainly right now, for we see the old shanty used by Silas last winter, and yonder is where he says he shot a moose; Peter Esty was with him then, the "guide preacher."

What a change for us city men; the weary cares of business are forgotten; and with all its hardships and exposure I enjoy this life exceedingly. We are totally dependant, though, on these guides, and it is but little we can do to help with much of the work which must be done. It is a pleasure to see these men swinging their axes, and equally wonderful what they can do with them. How indispensable an axe is in these woods.

I notice that the tops of almost all the young balsams, even seven feet high, are broken off, and am told the young green shoots are the favorite food of the moose. It spoils the beautiful symmetry of this very handsome tree, which, growing up like a perfect cone, seems as if it were a large boxwood, carefully cut into shape, from the hands of a gardener. Here a good light pocket telescope would be an acquisition, for spying out the deer around the lakes; this County seems full of them.

Strange what one often thinks about; I have just been comparing myself to "the man all tattered and torn," but here is no "maiden all forlorn;" forlorn indeed would be a woman in such a wilderness, and yet the time must come when settlements must exist even here, when these magnificent falls will be made available as water power to drive factories, and railroads will convey their thousands in an hour over the space which has taken us days to accomplish.

Yet such a contemplation is perfectly painful to me, and may the time be far off when this interesting region will be exposed to the contaminations of so called civilization. Well, our baggage is stowed into the skiffs, and taken to the place where we are to shanty. It was 6 P.M. when we started in the boats to fish; there is a fine trolling breeze, and in a few minutes I strike a good sized fish; it took me full twenty minutes to use him up, and before he could be gafted; this trout was a laker and weighed only 5 1/2 pounds; from his game I had expected greater size. We immediately rowed ashore, and our fish cleaned, and splitting him up the back like a shad, nailed it on a board, and roasted it before the fire; it was exceedingly fine, and in splendid condition; I never eat, and so we all agreed, a finer fish. Mr. Alvord had taken some excellent speckled trout, which were also served up at the same time, but these we considered far inferior to the laker.

I am much pleased with this wild Lake -- the water is so pure we can see the bottom at a great depth. There are two small but picturesque islands in it, covered with trees and shrubs, and I observe a very considerable number of gulls and wild ducks flying about, apparently in great trepidation at our encroachment on their nursery.

Sunday, 13th -- Silas caught a lake of three pounds before breakfast, which we needed for our morning meal. It has died away almost calm, and although we fish from breakfast time until 1 P.M. we had poor success, each boat only catching two, barely averaging a pound and a half a piece. The fact is, it is too still. I cannot look enough to satisfy me at the scenery around this Lake, and it is so very grand and wild, especially that rugged mountain to the north. See you little brook, which comes down the ravine, tumbling and frothing; we go ashore there, and in the small pool under the last fall we see the bottom covered black with innumerable suckers, working up, the boys say, to deposit their spawn; they must like cool quarters, for the water is so cold it chills one to drink it. Up this dark hollow we scramble a little way, and I see to my gun, for I almost expect to find bear or panther in such a spot; such, however, was not out luck.

We feel certain that there is a great abundance of trout here, but we are too late for lakers, they always bite the bait immediately that the ice disappears, and this is generally about the middle of May, and then you must have a good breeze, for with the water so transparent they can see a boat a long way off. There are many shoals of small fish about, which the guides call "white fish," and on examining the stomachs of the lakers we have caught, we find the trout feed on them; now we don't catch these little fellows, they won't take any bait, and we have no suitable net to capture them. We rowed alongside of some rocks today, on which were the nests of several gulls; they were composed of a few small sticks and a little coarse grass; most had eggs in them; some had young, and the little rascals hissed at us like so many snakes.

The banks of this Lake are very steep and rocky, and not at all suitable for deer coming in; they like a gradual descent, with a sandy or muddy bottom, where they can wade in for some distance, feed on the leaves of the water lily, and get away from the flies and mosquitoes. We tried for deer round the Lake tonight, with the jack lighted -- that is, after dark, but saw no sign of any.

Monday, 14th -- Very warm morning -- still and close; rose at daybreak, while all the rest were asleep, and went out trolling for an hour and a half alone on the Lake, only catching one laker.

The Lake is smooth as a mirror, not a breath of air stirring and I suggest to Mr. Alvord that after breakfast we make a move homewards, to which he assents with reluctance. We have a long journey before us, on foot, as we must leave the boats here.

It was about 10 o'clock when we left Lake "Peter Alvord," as the boys call it, and take a course nearly due south. A most weary and fatiguing tramp through the woods and swamps brought us to an old shanty at Spruce Lake about half-past eight o'clock P.M.; all hands very tired; for my part, I was completely exhausted. The day had been intensely hot, and no breeze stirring.

Tuesday, 15th -- I felt stiff and tired even this morning when I woke up, and felt a strong disinclination to stir, but we made a second start about 8 A.M., first ascending a steep mountain, then directing our course for Lake Piseco.

In the course of the forenoon I fairly gave in, and lay down on the ground completely prostrated. Cooch brought me some water from a spring, which soon brought me right, and then relieving me of my knapsack and fishing basket, I got along famously, and having then only the gun to carry. Soon after Mr. Alvord broke down; and afterwards Frank Courtney, but we made out to get to Piseco about 3 P.M. Call, as strong as a horse, had preceded the rest of us, and by the time we got there dinner was in a state of forwardness; as we were very hungry, I perhaps never enjoyed a meal more than in this humble tavern. We had stewed venison, ham and eggs, boiled potatoes, coffee and cream. Ye Gods! what a feast, and how all disappeared. Trout are fine for a day or two, but "toujours trinte" is quite as bad as "toujours perdrix," even though varied somewhat by pork and bread, and venison we had not eaten for the last week. At 8 P.M. reached Lake Pleasant, and had a good substantial supper, with steaks from a fresh killed moose.

It appears that on Monday, the 7th, two men, who reside at Lake Pleasant, had gone back into the woods, some seven or eight miles, to fish in a small lake, where they had a boat; while fishing they observed a young bull moose leap in from the bank, and attempt to swim across. They succeeded in heading him off, and finally shot him, as they had their rifles; before they had secured him, Call's dog, "old Hector," had swam off alongside their skiff -- so it was he who had chased it in. He doubtless drove this animal from the neighborhood of the Cedar Lakes to where he was killed. The dog knew these men, and went home with them, they being neighbors of Call's. The moose weighed six hundred weight.

Wednesday, 16th -- When I retired to my room last night I could hardly keep my eyes open, and I had for several days been looking forward to the glorious sleep I should have on the first night at Holmes' hotel; but I was very much disappointed; for sleep I could not, the bed was too soft, and it seemed as if I should smother in the confined air of the bedroom. The fact is, the change was too sudden from the pure, untainted atmosphere of the woods. As a last expedient, I pulled a few of the bedclothes on the floor, laid a pillow down, opened the door and windows, and then, about two o'clock in the morning, had an unrefreshing doze.

It was late when I breakfasted, for I took my time for my ablutions, and had a two week's crop of beard to remove, and then, with an entire change of raiment, felt once more like a gentleman.

I was still tired, and had had enough of fishing, so, this being Court week for Hamilton County, and the county buildings being opposite the hotel, I stepped over to hear and see what was going on. They were trying some silly assault and battery case, which I cared nothing about. The judge was a very intelligent looking man, and is a great favorite with the people; in fact, Judge Peck is the most popular man in the county. "Tis said, that at Raquette Lake, where there are three families settled, that when they have a poll or election day these people seldom see a newspaper, and consequently don't know who are the candidates for office! So they put down Judge Peck's name for each office, that they may make sure of supporting him in whatever post he may be running for. I see Mr. Brundage, (our stage-driver to Northville,) in Court; he is the Sheriff, and J. C. Holmes, our happy looking host, is the County Clerk. All the men in the settlement seem to hold some office or another. Silas Call is Register, and Cooch a Justice of the Peace.

Near the Court House stand the ruins of the jail. It was burned down about a year ago, and they say it is quite as serviceable now as before, for it never could have held in a prisoner desirous of escaping.

Speaking of the jail reminds me of a story: A few years ago, big Coles, the guide, who is one of the most experienced woodsmen, and best hunter in the county, held the appointment of jailor. Now he always looked upon the office as a sinecure, pocketing a salary of some $25 a year, and expecting to do nothing for it. But it so happened that a rogue was at last detected in the community, convicted of horse-stealing, and sentenced to be shut up in the jail.

Now this bothered Coles exceedingly, and worst of all, when winter came, and he wanted to go some way off for hunting. The only thing to be done he did; he started off and took his prisoner with him -- gave him a rifle and ammunition, and away the two went, on snowshoes, to the region somewhere about the Cedar Lakes, after Moose. They succeeded in shooting three; the meat was partly packed on small sleds, which they dragged into the settlements by hand. Now this being rather hard work the prisoner rebelled, and when Coles wanted to start a second time the thief insisted on remaining in jail, and so Coles had to stay home to attend him.

Cooch, my late guide, suggested, that as there was a good prospect of a still warm night we might probably get a shot at a deer in the water after dark, so I agreed to go. We left the hotel about an hour before sunset, ran across Round Lake, and approached the mouth of an inlet or brook called the "Mud Lake Stream." Here the candles in the Jack are lighted and we paddle slowly and noiselessly up the stream.

By the way, this jack is something like a lantern, put on a pole in the bow of the boat, with a board behind so that the light is only thrown out in front and partially at each side, while all behind is in the dark. The light penetrates some thirty yards ahead, showing all that comes within its reach with perfect distinctness.

It was necessary to sit very still, and I tried my best, but I felt like a martyr, for the mosquitoes were in myriads; there was a constant hum from them in my ears. Still I sat as quiet as possible on a seat immediately behind the jack, in the bow -- gun loaded with buck-shot, already cocked and resting on my knees. We glide along as if by magic, peering into every nook and corner; soon we hear a slight splash in the water ahead! On we go, steadily, and the full figure of a fine buck, with his side towards me, is faintly discerned in the water -- near the left bank. Quickly, I raise my gun, take steady, cool aim, behind the fore shoulder, and fire! The smoke prevented my seeing the effect for a moment or two, but from the commotion in the water I knew we had made sure of him. There he lays on his side, already quite dead, and the shot has taken effect exactly where I intended.

Now I am pleased and satisfied with myself -- for I kept perfectly cool, and there was no buck-fever about me. We paddled still farther up the stream -- heard one moose deer snort and clear himself -- he saw us, but we did not see him.

Returned to the hotel and got to bed about midnight. I should like to have taken the antlers of my buck home with me as a trophy, but at present they are "in the velvet" -- that state of half flesh half bone in which they grow out each spring before they become perfectly hard, so I had to leave them. The weather too, was very warm, and I could not take any of the venison.

Thursday, 17th -- I had a very refreshing sleep, and was aroused from it my Mr. Holmes, who told me the stage was ready and waiting for me at the door; so I dress and breakfast in a hurry, shake hands with Mr. Alvord -- and off we go on the road home! I am happy to return, for often, in the dark woods, I thought of its happy attractions, and longed to be there. In the stage I find a gentleman from Lake Piseco, also going home, (Mr. James A. Stevens, of Hoboken,) an enthusiastic fisherman, who has been in Hamilton county for a month. Comparing notes we found that he had gone as far "in" as the West Canada Creek.

Reached Northville about four P.M., and staid there all night.

Friday 18th -- By stage, as before, to Amsterdam -- thence, by rail, to Albany and New York; getting home at 9 P.M. -- happy to be there, and still more so to find all my family well.

GENERAL REMARKS

Lake Pleasant is at an elevation of 1650 feet above the level of tide water, and I estimate the lake's back where we fished to be about 2250 feet.

Winter lasts long in that region, and they had five months sleighing there last winter.

Hence the probable reason that there are no poisonous snakes in Hamilton county; and this is a very comfortable reflection when one is travelling in, or camping out in the woods.

This year the ice did not leave the lakes until the 11th of May.

For lake trout fishing, they invariably bite the best so soon as the ice disappears, and the largest are usually caught first. As the season advances you seem to catch small ones, and fewer of them. The reason may be that such small fish as they feed on are scarce in the lakes, until about the first of June, after which they abound.

For brook trout, the greatest number are taken in the month of June, the guides say also in September. There are no small brooks near Lake Pleasant, where one can stroll and cast the flies for trout, for the brush and woods are very dense and give you no chance.

After the larger trout have worked up from deep water in the lakes below, there is occasionally fine fishing in Jessup's river; but here one must get into the stream and wade, and it is wide enough in most places to throw a fly without difficulty. In July the trout collect in large quantities about the spring holes in the river, and I have heard of very great quantities being taken from one pool where the cold spring water was running in.

In making up your pack for an excursion in the woods, it is necessary to be very discriminating. Take as little as possible; be sure you have a suit of strong coarse clothes, and boots large enough in the legs to admit your trowsers inside; a blanket or woolen plaid is indispensable; and I found great comfort and protection from having an India rubber coat. Let your hat be of soft felt, with a wide brim.

Don't forget a good strong knife, and a compass; and there are times when a "drop of gude brandy will do you na harm" -- after the fatigues of the day. As most gentlemen are not in the habit of using a rifle they should carry a gun, and that of either No. 11 or 14 gauge, as the former chambers four ordinary sized buckshot, the latter three.

A steady day's trolling, seated in a small cranky skiff, is rather trying to the comfort of one's "t'otherend," which might be relieved by taking with you an India rubber cushion, which can be inflated when you wish to use it. Be sure that your stockings are of thick wool. I prefer a pipe to cigars, as the former may be taken apart and carried safely in your pocket -- such as a Meerschaum, with a flexible tube. Have a water-proof knapsack, but not of India rubber -- which is apt to melt in the sun and smell bad. I was recommended not to shave, and am satisfied that the stubble beard keeps the black fly from biting where it grows.

The black fly, mosquitoe, and punkey, (small gnat), are all troublesome. The first are only met with in June and July, and never trouble you after dark. To prevent them biting, you might rub on the skin a combination of oil of pennyroyal and sweet oil, in equal quantities; a 4 oz. vial full would be enough. The smell of it, however, is to me perfectly nauseating.

In travelling in the woods, caution your guides not to walk too fast -- for they "go it" at a round pace -- and be sure you follow their steps closely, as they, from experience, know and avoid all the bad places. If a log lays in your way step over, don't jump on and off, which would fatigue you more than walking fifty yards.

Always have your gun loaded, and in readiness -- with balls in one barrel, at least; you may have occasion to use it when you least expect it -- and your game may vary from a partridge to a panther.

For a guide, I would prefer a stout young hunter, from 22 to 25 years old, to one more advanced in years; old men are apt to be opinionated and morose; the young are enthusiastic and accommodating. Burr Sturges and Silas Call are model guides.

It is best to write on to Mr. Holmes, at Lake Pleasant, a couple of weeks in advance of your going there, and request him to engage your guides, naming such as you prefer. And I would recommend only one city friend with yourself as a companion. Two will mostly act in concert, while more are likely to differ. You require each a guide, besides an extra man to cook, or carry necessary burdens.

Don't omit a piece of sticking plaster, in case of a cut, and a bottle of tincture of arnica, as a lotion for a bruise.

Your tea and sugar had best be taken with you from New York; and a good ham would be a luxury. Guides generally gaff their fish, but never carry a landing net themselves; so you had best take one. October is the best month for hunting; the deer and moose being then in very fine condition.

I would recommend you to take three rods, two for trolling; one of them 12 or 14 feet long, the other 10; and then your fly rod. Your trolling tackle must be of the BEST single gut, and a complete assortment can be had at Conroy's. The leader two yards long, and that which has the train of hooks on about a yard more.

Take some trolling hooks of various sizes, and swivels, as well as gut, and if you run short of tackle, "the boys" will soon rig you up a set -- not so neatly made, perhaps, as Conroy's, but certainly far more reliable.

LOUIS LAKE, 1 P.M., JUNE 1, 1853

It was on Friday afternoon, May 27th, that we left New York by the Hudson River Railroad -- sultry and crowded in the cars, and with no water wherewith to quench the thirsty soul; slept at Albany, and left it at 6:30 A.M. 28th, by the cars, for Amsterdam. Here I found I had left my stout boots behind, so purchased a pair from an old Irishman -- a curious joker -- told us how he had lost $800, when he had to "step out to" Illinois, on account of voting before he was a citizen. Having asked him whether there were many Scotch about there, he told us "they were as thick as fiddlers in h--l." B. laughed and I joined in, for we had never learned that the regions below were remarkable for mirth and music. Starting with a good team, reach Willstown about dusk and stay there all night. Thence went to Lake Pleasant next morning -- took us 4 1/2 hours, although the distance is only twelve miles, but the roads are execrable and constantly tending up hill. Mr. Holmes received us kindly, and Mrs. P. and my daughters have got over the journey with less fatigue than I expected.

Monday, 30th -- Took a troll on Round Lake, but the wind was high an blustering. We only caught two small lakers. During the afternoon it poured rain as it can only do in a mountain region.

Tuesday, 31st -- Mr. B. and I started for Louis Lake, he with Burr Sturges for a guide and I with Silas Call. Wm. Randall, a third man, accompanies us throughout. We picked up a couple of the boys of "old Sturge" as we passed his cabin, to help carry in the traps, of which we had considerable bulk. It was cool and pleasant; still, the walk from Wilcox's Clearing to the lake was sufficiently fatiguing, for the boys, packs and all, go it at a round pace. At the lake found a very comfortable shanty. We had time to fish a little before supper, and I caught eight or ten smallish brook trout at the falls by the outlet.

Wednesday, June 1st -- Slept very indiffently, from the novelty of our situation, and hardness of our bed; for there were not boughs enough for a substitute to a hair mattress. Mr. B. shot a yearling buck last night; I did not try, thinking the weather too cold to find them by the lake. This morning was cold too -- not a trout to be seen rising; but we trolled and caught some few, but these run small. Unfortunately broke my trolling rod, but as B. had two he kindly tendered me one of his. After dinner took a stroll in the woods, but saw nothing to shoot. We had partridge for supper, pigeons and partridge for dinner -- in addition to our fish, pork, and bread -- and fine venison steaks for breakfast. Think of that, ye poor miserable devils boarding at Lake Pleasant, where fish for breakfast, fish for dinner, and fish for supper, are perfectly nauseating. We are perfect epicures here. Now I am in the woods, seated on a knoll by a babbling brook -- gun lying at my side, and jotting down these memoranda, while "the boys" take their siesta and B. has gone off in search of worms. Ye Gods, overlook his fault! What! B. deign to use the angle-worm! -- but "to what base uses do we come at last." Last evening I found the flies no go at the falls, and B. is going there this evening, and should the feathers not prove sufficiently enticing, they must suffer through the worms. Confound the flies! they are in clouds. I write with book on knee inside my veil, and it is indispensable. These miseries are bad enough while you are in motion, but if you seat yourself they collect in myriads. I hear a gun not far off. Oh the bungler I am, thinks I, they have got a partridge nearer the shanty! Descending, meet Call; my absence had made all hands uneasy, thinking I was lost, and Call had come in search -- the shot was a signal. B.'s reproof for my rashness, as he called it, was sharp, but from the heart -- there I treasure it, and may no foul demon of discord disturb its grave! Poor fishing here at Louis Lake, but it a glorious place for getting hungry -- and we have a bountiful supply of even delicacies to satisfy that. As twilight approached, I drew the small shot from my gun, substituting the pills for deer hunting, and soon we start -- Silas shoving and paddling along the lake shore; light the candles, whose dim light, thrown on the edge of the forest, creates a mysterious influence. I peer into every nook and corner till my eyes almost ache with straining them. Imagination too is busy; as we recede from the bank the indistinctness of vision raises fanciful illusions before me. I see palaces, domes, and arches -- ruins contained in a drapery of moss -- a bridge, and the spirits of the waters, with the gnome king; but all are silent as death, save "you screeching owl" across the lake. Still no deer -- nor sign of one, and having almost gone round old Louis, we return to the shanty. My bones ache, and I am stiff with sitting in a cramped up, immovable position, and can hardly use my limbs, but ere long I stretch myself on the balsam bed and sleep in perfect unconsciousness.

Thursday, 2nd -- How fresh I feel this morning! -- eat a hearty breakfast, and the elasticity and buoyancy of mind prove that I am in tip-top condition. Our traps are packed and placed in the boats, and we start on an excursion to Indian River. B. casts a fly at the falls, but a small trout only rewards his pains.

It's very hot, and the river is very winding, and current slow. It was rather monotonous, and uninteresting -- much of the timber along the stream is dead, from a dam constructed at the foot of Indian Lake, which backs up the water for many miles. It was about 3:30 P.M. when we got to Porter's Clearing; what a wild place for man to select to live and bring up a family in! I wish he had kept away, for the stumps and log-buildings were an eye-sore, and a detraction from what would have otherwise been magnificent scenery. Still, the wild, rugged mountains are all around, and many a peak may be seen almost fading blue in the distance.

At Porter's we deposit all our plunder, then fish for an hour or two, and obtain a number of speckled beauties. To bed at 9 o'clock; very tired, and B. and I have to pig in together -- our couch about narrow enough for one, and feathers at that. My great coat serves for a pillow, and in a moment I am in the arms of Morpheus.

Friday, 3rd -- Rainy and cloudy, Silas and I went to the lower end of the lake and fished under the dam, and on the rips below; but the trout were very small, and we threw back all we caught. Returning thence we went ashore to visit "old Cibeele" the Indian, at his cabin. We found him at work preparing ground to plant potatoes, hale and hearty, though wrinkled and grey. He was glad to see us, as he always expects some little presents from strangers. A stiff horn of brandy set his tongue a running, but I could not fully comprehend what he said, speaking as he did, in broken English. He told me his father was officer (chief) of a tribe in Canada, and supplied the British army, under General Wolfe, with provisions. Cibeele himself was twelve years old when the battle between the Revolutionary war commenced, his sympathies were with the Americans, whom his tribe opposed, and he had "to run away" to the States. In Canada he lived near St. Francoisville.

He prated a great deal about a silver and gold mine he had discovered ten days' journey hence, and says he means soon to visit it, and promised to take Silas Call with him; said they could go all the way by water except a quarter of a mile; gave me some details about his discovering it -- which was at night, when he discovered a brilliant reflection among the rocks; cut two forked sticks, placed them in the ground, and then, laying another straight stick along these, pointing exactly in the direction of his mine, had no difficulty in finding it next day.

His son Lige lives with him but was absent, and the centenarian did not like it; he frequently spoke of Lige: "D--n Lidge; he earn money -- get drunk; d--n fool!" Said he had had no provisions for two days but potatoes, of which we had over one hundred bushels on hand. We gave him a pound trout, and with a present also of a gold dollar, we returned to the lake.

I was rather disappointed in his personal appearance; he is shourt, and his nose, having been flattened by the kick of a horse, injured his looks. His house is built of square logs, with a hole in the roof to let out the smoke. I asked him if he was not afraid to live alone; he said no -- he had a gun and could shoot the bears or panthers. "Me not poor," said he, "work hard -- can see well -- can shoot deer so far," pointing to a young colt 40 rods off. "Indians' stomach good -- good as gentleman's -- legs getting weak." Poor old fellow! This lake takes its name from his settling here; and there is another of his tribe here, too, whose shanty is on t'other side of the lake, named John Camp.

Cibeele has two grand-daughters, both married to white men. He loves drink like all his race, and considers it himself a great medicine. My time was much broken up by this visit, (which I would not have missed for a great deal,) and B. had in the meantime beaten me all to sticks in catching trout, but in the afternoon we both struck steadily to fishing, and then my pile was quite as large as his. We have selected about forty pounds of the finest, and George Sturge, a boy 15 or 16 years, is to carry them to Lake Pleasant to-morrow, on his back! Verily, he is a curiosity, too -- a perfect chip of the old block; told me he had shot at least 100 deer last winter -- the young varmint and exterminator! Well, our day's fishing has been a glorious one; but the black flies have almost eaten me up.

It is almost Saturday night with candle tallow candle, (the end of the wick,) so I must to bed; and my lullaby will be the peal of the thunder, and its rolling and echoing grumbling among the mountains near.

Saturday, 4th. -- The thunder-storm of last evening has gone, and this morning we have the wind fresh; nor'west, and cold, of course. The fishing is poor, comparatively, but it improved towards afternoon and evening, as the wind abated. What a blot and eye-sore are these clearings in such a place as this -- and I am tired of our staying at Porter's house. I don't object so much to the poor man's dwelling, but the house, and bed, and bad cooking, &c., destroy the illusion I like to feel, of living out here according to first principles -- "Life in the woods for me!" There are no deer around here -- that is, they don't come in of their own accord to the lake.

Sunday, 5th. -- It is stiller, even here, on the Sabbath day -- for the commandment which enjoins that on the seventh day "thou shalt do no work, neither thy ox," &c., is strictly respected. We breakfasted very late -- say 8 o'clock, and B. and I, with the boys, went again to see "old Cibeele." He was in his log-house, squatting on the hearth, about lighting his pipe, which he laid aside, gladly accepting a cigar. The house was very dirty; the floor had apparently not been washed for many a month. In one corner was a bedstead with a very dirty blanket on it, in another lay some deer-skins on the floor; against the beams, under the roof, were some three or four rifles and a shot-gun. A lazy looking young man of the tawny race lounged in a chair as we entered, but got up and threw himself on the bed -- this was John Camp, Cibeele's grandson. Little of the conversation which passed was worth noting.

Indian John showed us a small pond in the woods near by, which is much frequented by deer, but there were none in it when we got there. As we returned to our boats the young Indian came down to his canoe, followed by his dog, and carrying a rifle; carefully stepping in he quickly paddled up the stream. As Silas remarked, now you see the Indian at home. We rode to the lower end of the lake, sat on the dam, fought off the black flies for a little while, and returned to Porter's for dinner. Had some nice croalers for dessert. Now Annie tell me -- Why were these croalers no croalers? Because they were some pumpkins!

The clearing here is two miles from Cibeele's cabin and across the lake. While B. is sitting on a log writing up his notes, I lounge on the grass at his feet, smoking my meerschaum and enjoying the "doice far nieute." We see a canoe crossing the water, and at first suppose it is George Sturges coming back, but a nearer view shows it is the old man Indian. He paddles swiftly -- and we go down to the landing to meet him. He tells me he walked to the shore opposite me, two miles through the woods, then "hook canoe," and come over to see Porter and his squaw. He walks up the hill very much bent, and leaning on a staff; but there is a hale expression in his face which seems good for ten years to come.

Monday, Sept. 6th. -- Left Indian Lake soon after breakfast, fishing along as we rowed up the river -- catching a few trout; B. took twice as many as I. At the forks where Jessup's River and the outlet of Louis Lake join, they take the name of Indian River. There is a fine pool here, where many trout are usually caught. Here we went ashore and dined. The outlet of Louis runs some three miles before joining Jessup's River. As we rowed up this, B. being ahead, shot a deer about fourteen rods off, and tumbled him over; he jumped up, however, and made off. The guides followed and tracked him by the blood for some distance, but did not find him. It's a hard job to carry the boats round the falls, some quarter of a mile. It was six P.M. when we got to Louis. Propped up on a log, found a piece of bark, right in our path, on which was written a message to us that a letter and supply of bread, had been deposited for us at Sturges' new house across the lake.

Having supped, Silas and I started to look up a deer; after going half round the lake I shot one. It jumped into the bushes. We went ashore, taking a candle from the jack, but could not find it, although we saw a great deal of blood thickly scattered on the leaves. It was between 10 and 11 before we returned to the shanty. William had made a roaring fire -- grateful at first, but eventually a great nuisance, as it made our bedroom too hot, and I could not sleep until far into the small hours of the morning.

Tuesday, 7th. -- "See how brightly breaks the morning," and a lovely one it was. Burr and Silas leave the shanty at daylight to find the deer I shot, and soon fetch it in. Poor doe! had I thought you were a buck, I should have been sorry to pull the fatal trigger; we cannot eat this animal, for she was with young, and I perpetrated a double murder. It is a rare thing to find the does down on the lake shore at this season -- for they are almost all up on the ridges with their fawns, and these are now generally some six weeks or so old. We had tolerably good fishing to-day, and it is delightful to stay here. I may as well note that all the tackle we have had from Conroy's is most unreliable; the hooks miserably secured and the leaders of irregularly sized gut. My bass pole is too stiff for trolling -- something of a style between that and my Scotch fly-rod, would be the thing, and twelve feet long.

The gut leaders should be two yards long. The train and gut on it, three strands, or nearly a yard more -- which makes quite gut enough.

Hereafter, should I ever visit Hamilton County, will bring good salmon gut, double hooks of all sizes, and swivels, and the guides will tie me up trains every way suitable, and to be depended on. We have found the drag on our reels a great convenience, and so far unobjectionable. The pace for trolling is to row at from a mile and a half to two miles an hour -- and about 35 yards of line out. If rough, less will do; if smooth, 50 or 60 yards may be necessary. A breeze from the north-west prevented us from going out deer hunting this night, so we stretched ourselves on our balsam bed soon after dusk, and a sleep as profound as mortal man could wish, was the happy fate of all -- have some indistinct impressions of William's getting up more than once to fix the fire, but the half raised eyelid soon again fell, and I slept far into the morning. It was delightful this morning to receive a letter from Catherine, and to learn that she was on the trail of that seventeen pounder; and I sincerely "wish she may get it" -- and Cice was teaching school too; well, I dare say she thinks it very nice fun, and better to teach than to be taught.

Wednesday, 8th. -- Another fine day; it's a perfect blessing for us this glorious weather. We fish and fish again, and a couple of the Sturges boys arrive in from Lake Pleasant, but bring no news beyond the welcome intelligence that all were well; that Burr's cow had not yet calved; and Silas' dog had tore up his deer skins. I might have mentioned that on Monday, while coming up the outlet of Louis Lake, which stream flows through a flat bottom or marsh, we saw a very great number of wild ducks -- mostly black duck, and not less than fifty; frequently one would fly out from the small brush bordering the stream, and close by our boat, alighting a very short distance off, and seeming to wish to draw our attention to her, and her young brood, which was doubtless in the marsh. Of course we did not shoot at any under such circumstances.

Now I write this while our boat is drifting on the lake, and Silas is tying me up a gang of trolling hooks, or I have not a set left, and were Mr. Conroy here and heard the expletives ejected under the circumstances, he would doubtless profit by the <u>gentle</u> hints.

Beautiful Louis Lake! -- gem of Hamilton County, let me describe your wild loveliness. The sheet of water is two miles long, and barely one wide; the dense unbroken forest is all around; back are gentle sloping hills -- covered with all hues of green; there are many trees of the brighter hues, mostly maple, beech and birch, interspersed with pine, balsam, spruce and hemlock; farther off to the north the Blue Mountain range in the distance terminates the view; here are rugged peaks and precipitous crags. On the south, a beautiful range lies between us and Jessup's River. At the west end is the inlet, infusing its cool waters through banks fringed with alders and tamarack. After supper, started after deer, Mr. B. with Burr Sturges going down the lake, while Silas and I paddle by its head. Near the inlet we hear a rustling among the alders, and ere long a stately buck stalks out from the brush and commences cropping the lily pads. The boat is slowly and noiselessly paddled up to within three rods, and then I take aim and fire. A splashing is heard, but I could see nothing for the smoke of my gun. The gentleman managed to scramble out, but we soon found him, and after a sharp tussel with Silas, our deer soon became venison. B. was less fortunate, not getting a shot. Turned in a 11 P.M.

Thursday, 9th. -- The fishing here is poor, and we trolled all the forenoon, catching but very few. The glory of Louis has parted for the season, and we mean soon to change our quarters. That was fine buck we got last night, and our morning meal and dinner from his carcase were eaten with "gusto." B. tells me there are six shot holes in his skin, so he was tolerably peppered.

It is very hot, and the southerly wind comes in puffs only across the lake. I cannot help sympathising for the miserable New Yorkers, who are probably now half stewed, fried and wasted, blinded with dust and dirt, and breathing an atmosphere impregnated with the fumes of a putrifying garbage. We sent out one of the Sturges boys this morning with a pack load of trout to Lake Pleasant, that they may be put on the ice. B. and I have had a discussion on the very important question whether in putting on our baits the trolling hooks should be inserted in the back of the shiner or its belly. He gives for the belly, I the back -- the guides agree with me, but B. in fishing matters is generally "au fait," hard to beat, and perhaps more difficult to convince, where opinions conflict. Within the past few days I have used an application for the skin to prevent the black flies biting, and it does very well, until it evaporates, or is rubbed off. This was composed of a pint of Olive oil, in which two ounces of Crude Camphor had been dissolved. We both took a turn round the lake for deer after dark, but saw none.

Friday, 10th. -- After breakfast again on the move, starting with our "plunder" in the boats across the lake. "A--a--dieu, old Lou--!--is Lake!" sung out B. with a tense and gesture from which Tamburini might have copied, and shouldering the packs, up the mountains we start. We are bound for Jessup's River, near the Indian Clearing, and on the rips there we hope to catch a good many trout, by strict and legitimate fly fishing. Half way up the hill we fell in with a hen partridge and her young brood. The little ones scattered, hiding under the leaves -- the poor old bird kept within a few feet of us, and whined like a young dog. Poor bird! she would not desert her little ones, and her maternal solicitude would have done honor to the most tender hearted lady in the land. Long life to all our party for their sympathy. We had some four miles to tramp, and on our way, Silas discovered a young fawn. We judged it to be but a few days old. The poor little thing was not afraid of us, but looked piteously in our faces, with its large and lustrous eyes. They told me it might have been easily tamed, and we spoke of taking home with us, but the distance we had to go, and the trouble in carrying it in, laden as we were with baggage, induced us to leave it behind.

So setting it on its legs, William barked like a hound, when off it started, and soon disappeared in the bushes. It was a pretty little animal and beautifully spotted. Doubtless its mother was near bye and watching us, although we did not see her. On reaching the river we commenced fishing, but with miserable success; the trout was small, and it is evident the large fish have not yet worked so far up stream. We shantied near the river, and suffered great torture from the swarms of black flies and mosquitoes. There is no way of fishing the stream here, except by getting in and wading, for the trees and brush are very dense up to the water's edge. I observed many beautiful flowers to-day as we tramped along. They were literally the "flowers of the forest," born to blush unseen, and waste their fragrance on the sesert air.

Saturday, 11th. -- What between too much fire and myriads of mosquitoes, I never spent a more comfortless night. Twice I left the shanty and endeavored to sleep among the bushes, but the villainous "long bills" were even more annoying than within doors. At last, about two A.M., wrapping myself in my blanket, and putting on my veil, I threw myself on the ground outside, regardless of the hum of the blood-suckers, and dozed for a couple of hours. We rose very early, and started on our tramp out for Lake Pleasant. After a walk of five miles we find a team waiting us at the State road, and thence ride to the house of Mr. Holmes, where I am delighted to hear that the young girls are well and so also Mrs. P., who has caught during our absence, a lake trout larger than either B. or I. Have you ever been in the woods two weeks, without shaving, a thorough wash, and your clothes torn and saturated with perspiration? If so, I need not tell you the glorious and soothing comfort of a thorough change of raiment, perfect ablution and a clean shave.

Monday, 13th. -- Left Albany at 3:15 P.M. by Hudson River Railroad, returning to New York about 8:30 P.M.

NOTE -- General Wolfe fell at Quebec, on September 13th, 1759, thus making Cibeele 106 years old.

We took into the woods with us 3 1/4 lbs. of tea, 13 lbs. of sugar, 6 bottles brandy, 175 cigars, besides smoking tobacco; of all we had enough exactly, without scrimping, and about 1/4 lb. left -- sugar perhaps a little short. The men were all fond of tea, and took of it at every meal.

Thus ends this journal of a good fellow, a good sportsman and a good friend. I can add nothing to his truthful picture; but "once more ye woods adiew;" and when I visit ye again, may I be accompanied by the same Scotch matron and two "Scottish Lassies," who, I doubt not, will long remember their first trip to Hamilton County.

B.

Appendix A: A List of Guides from Eleven Selected Lists 1874-1992

The following alphabetical list of Adirondack guides is an integrated compilation of eleven separate lists from the years 1874-1992. The "area code," where it appears, indicates the locale from which the guide worked, and was initially derived from the groupings in the 1893 Forest Commission Report; a list of areas and their codes follows. All current guides are licensed state-wide; in most cases their place of residence is listed. In an effort to consolidate what was originally a list of over 3,300 names, many of which were duplicates, all the source listings for one individual were combined where it was thought possible. That is, "Orrin Otis...FCR,S74,S81,S95." However, discrepancies among the lists as to spellings or completeness -- i.e., Oren Otis, Orin Otis, O. Otis -- may cause inaccuracies. Consulting the original sources may help in some cases. From left to right the columns are guide's first name, last name, general area where he guides or guided, historical source(s) of information, and place of residence. Also, see additional list of guides on pages 362 and 363.

The individual lists included, with their abbreviations as to source, are as follows:

S74   The Adirondacks Illustrated (1874) S.R. Stoddard
W   Descriptive Guide to the Adirondacks (1876) E.R. Wallace
S81   The Adirondacks Illustrated (1881) S.R. Stoddard
FCR   New York State Forest Commission Report (1893)
S95   The Adirondacks Illustrated (1895) S.R. Stoddard
BTG   Brown's Tract Guides' Association Membership List (1911)
RG20   Registered Guides in New York State (1920)
RG27   Registered Guides in New York State (1927)
RG42   Registered Guides in New York State (1942)
AL   "Guides at the Ausable Lakes," from Up the Lake Road, by Edith Pilcher, 1987.
LG92   Guides living in or near the Adirondack Park, selected from "New York State Licensed Guides," N.Y. Dept. of Environmental Conservation, current as of 10/15/92.

ADIRONDACK GUIDES -- AREA CODES

Area Code	Areas Covered	Post Office, Communities	Counties
AKL	Adirondack Lodge	North Elba	Essex
ALA	Aiden Lair	Minerva	Essex
BEL	Belmont	Mountain View	Franklin
BGM	Big Moose	Big Moose	Herkimer
BLM	Bloomingdale	Bloomingdale	Essex
BMT	Blue Mountain	Blue Mtn. Lake	Hamilton
BVR	Beaver River	North Four	Lewis
CED	Cedar River	Indian Lake	Hamilton
CHA	Chateaugay	Chateaugay Lake	Clinton
CHZ	Chazy	Dannemora	Clinton
CLC	Clinton County		Clinton
CRA	Cranberry Lake	Harewood	St. Lawrence
DIC	St. Regis River	Dickinson Center	Franklin
DUA	Duane (Ladd's)	Duane	Franklin
ESC	Essex County		Essex
ELZ	Elizabethtown	Elizabethtown	Essex
FRC	Franklin County		Franklin
FUL	Fulton Chain	Old Forge	Herkimer
GRS	Grasse River	Gale	St. Lawrence
HAC	Hamilton County		Hamilton
HEC	Herkimer County		Herkimer
IND	Indian Lake	Indian Lake	Hamilton
KVL	Keene Valley	Keene Valley	Essex
LEC	Lewis County		Lewis
LEW	Lewey Lake	Indian Lake	Hamilton
LGL	Long Lake	Long Lake	Hamilton
LKP	Lake Pleasant	Sageville	Hamilton
LNL	Loon Lake	Loon Lake	Essex
LOS	Lower Saranac	Saranac Lake	Franklin
LUZ	Luzerne	Luzerne	Essex
MCC	McCollum's	Paul Smith's	Franklin
MEA	Meacham	Duane	Franklin
MER	Hunter's Home	Merrillsville	Franklin
MOO	Moose River (Kenwill's)	Indian Lake	Hamilton
MOR	Morehouse	Morehouseville	Hamilton
NEW	Newcomb	Newcomb	Essex
NOH	North Hudson	North Hudson	Essex
NOR	North River	North River	Warren
ONC	Oneida County		Oneida
OSW	Oswegatchie	Harrisville	Lewis
OTT	Otter Lake	Glendale	Lewis
PLD	Lake Placid	Lake Placid	Essex
POT	Raquette	Potsdam, Colton	St. Lawrence
RAW	Rainbow	Rainbow	Franklin
RAB	Ray Brook	Ray Brook	Essex
RAQ	Raquette	Raquette	Hamilton
SAC	Santa Clara	Santa Clara	Franklin
SCH	Schroon	Schroon Lake	Essex
SLC	St. Lawrence County		St. Lawrence

STR	St. Regis	Paul Smith's	Franklin
TUP	Tupper	Moody	Franklin
UPS	Upper Saranac	Saranac Inn	Franklin
WAC	Warren County		Warren
WOD	Woodhull	White Lake Corners	Oneida

Number of Guides Licenses Issued by Year 1924-1963

1924	1154	1944	457
1925	1034	1945	452
1926	1045	1946	522
1927	962	1947	569
1928	935	1948	541
1929	906	1949	586
1930	837	1950	524
1931	736	1951	494
1932	605	1952	491
1933	612	1953	496
1934	636	1954	510
1935	620	1955	(unavailable)
1936	615	1956	496
1937	626	1957	468
1938	657	1958	554
1939	648	1959	510
1940	549	1960	536
1941	715	1961	571
1942	357	1962	548
1943	(unavailable)	1963	516

The cost of a guide's license during the years shown above was $2. The badge issued to the guides at the time of voluntary licensing in 1919 is thought by many to be the most beautiful of all, picturing an Adirondack lean-to and the state seal. At the time of mandatory licensing in 1924, a button (yellow) was issued. An octagonal metal badge was issued from 1941-1962, then the buttons returned. An oval metal badge began to be issued at the time of the most recent licensing requirements. (I am indebted to David Hunt for permission to use his list above.)

First Name	Last Name	Area	Source	Residence
Louis	Abare	FRC	RG27	Paul Smiths
James	Abbot		LG92	Wells
H. L.	Abbott	BLM	FCR	(appears twice in 1893 report)
Henry	Abbott	LNL	FCR	
Benjamin	Abel	POT	S81	Raquette River
Benjamin F.	Ables	POT	W	
David	Abrams	LKP	FCR	
Floyd	Abrams	LKP	FCR	
Randy	Acey		LG92	Old Forge
Irving	Ackerman	OSW	FCR	
Zina J.	Adams		RG42	Madrid
William	Agne	HAC	RG42	Newport
D. R.	Ainsworth	BTG	RG20,RG27	Big Moose
Richard O.	Ainsworth	HAC	RG42	Big Moose
Rodney R.	Ainsworth	HEC	RG27	Big Moose
Paul	Akey	SLC	RG27	Wanakena
Peter	Akey	SLC	RG20	Wanakena
Willie	Alden	NEW	S74	Newcomb
Henry	Alders	NOR	S81	North River
William M.	Aldin	NEW	S74,S81,W	Newcomb
Peter	Aldridge	PLD	S74,W	North Elba
Hendry	Aldrus	IND	FCR	
George	Alford	PLD	S95,FCR	Lake Placid
Harvey	Alford	PLD	FCR	
Rufus	Alford	PLD	FCR	
Carlos M.	Alger	BVR	W	
Frank W.	Alger	HAC	RG27	Blue Mountain Lake
Eugene	Allen	LOS	S95,FCR	Saranac Lake
Gregory	Allen		LG92	Hadley
Kurt	Allen		LG92	Hadley
L.	Allen	DIC	W	
Marvin M.	Allen	ONC	RG27	Woodgate
W. D.	Allen	SAC	S81,FCR	St. Regis Falls
William	Allen	OSW	W	
William D.	Allen	FRC	RG20	Santa Clara
Henry F.	Amadon	HAC	RG42	Piseco
Daniel	Ames	RAB	FCR	
William	Ames	RAB	FCR	
Frederick C.	Anderson		RG42	Watertown
George	Anderson	LUZ	FCR	
Mark	Anderson		LG92	Blue Mt. Lake
Nancy	Andrews		LG92	Lake Placid
L. R.	Anibal	HAC	RG42	Piseco
H.	Annis	LOS	W	
Willard	Ansback	BEL	FCR	
Fred	Apple	SLC	RG27	Hammond
George	Apple	SLC	RG27,RG42	Hammond
Roy W.	Apple		RG42,RG27	Hammond
Irving	Arbuckle	WAC	RG20	Stony Creek
Edgar W.	Arid	HAC	RG27	Lake Pleasant
George	Armstrong	WAC	RG27	Johnsburg
Ed.	Arnold	FUL	S81	Fulton Chain
Frank	Arnold	HAC	RG20	Northville

George W.	Arnold		RG42	Star Lake
Otis	Arnold	FUL	S81,W	Fulton Chain
Ronald	Ashe	KVL	AL	Presently Gdg.
Charles	Austin	UPS	S95,FCR	Saranac Inn
Duke E.	Austin	HAC	RG20	Long Lake
Farrand	Austin	LGL	S81,FCR	Long Lake
Henry D.	Austin	LGL	FCR	
S. B.	Austin	LGL	S95	Long Lake
Scott	Austin		LG92	North Creek
William	Austin		LG92	Glens Falls
Lyman A.	Avery	HAC	RG20	Green Lake
Sanford	Avery	FRC	S81	Whiteface Mountain
Douglas	Azaert		LG92	Warrensburg
Richard	Azaert		LG92	Warrensburg
Edison	Backus		RG42	Star Lake
Frederick M.	Bailey	FRC	RG20,RG42	Saranac Lake
Harold	Bailey		LG92	Keeseville
Jim	Bailey	KVL	AL	1930s-1940s
Roger	Bailey	KVL	AL	1950s-1960s
Wilbur	Bailey		RG42	St. Regis Falls
A. J.	Baker	LOS	S81,W	Saranac Lake
Andrew	Baker	LOS	FCR	
Arthur	Baker	HAC	RG42	Stony Creek
F.	Baker	STR	S74	St. Regis
Joseph	Baker	STR	S81,W	St. Regis Lake
Janattram	Baldwin	POT	S81,W	Raquette River
Edward	Ball	FUL	FCR	
John E.	Ball	FUL	S95,BTG	Fulton Chain
Milo	Ball	BGM	FCR	
John	Ballantine	IND	S81	Indian Lake
George	Ballard	HEC	RG20	Old Forge
George C.	Ballard	FUL	W	
William	Ballard	RAQ	FCR	
Ernest E.	Bancroft	SLC	RG20	Colton
George	Bancroft	CRA	FCR	
Bernard	Barber	ESC	RG27	Bloomingdale
Wm. K.	Barborer	SLC	RG27	Russell
David	Barcomb		LG92	Lake George
J. C.	Barker		RG42	Old Forge
J. Chase	Barker	HEC	RG27,RG42	Old Forge
John C.	Barker		RG42	Old Forge
Fred.	Barnes	STR	S74,S81	St. Regis
Fred.	Barnes	MEA	S81	Meacham Lake
Frederick	Barnes	BLM	FCR	
Isaac	Barnes	FUL	W	
M. H.	Barnes	LGL	W	
Warren	Barnhart		RG42	St. Regis Falls
Fred	Barns	MEA	W	
Eugene	Barrett	BVR	FCR	
Ralph	Barrett	SLC	RG27	Cranberry Lake
Frank P.	Barrow	FUL	BTG,FCR	Boonville
Frederick	Bartholomew		RG42	Childwold
Leslie	Bartholomew	LEC	RG27	Harrisville
Arthur	Bartlett		RG42	Saranac Lake
Charles O.	Bartlett	LOS	S95,FCR,S81	Saranac Lake

Daniel	Bartlett	LOS	S95,S81	Saranac Lake
George R.	Bartlett	SLC	RG20	Childwold
Gillette W.	Bartlett		RG42	Sabbath Day Point
John	Bartlett		RG42	Arietta
Samuel	Bartlett	GRS	FCR	
James	Bartley	BMT	S81	Blue Mountain Lake
Samuel M.	Barton	ESC	RG20,FCR	Lake Placid
Peter	Bashau	SLC	RG27	Piercefield
Wesley	Bates	BMT	S95,FCR	Blue Mountain Lake
Fred H.	Bauman	HEC	RG27	Old Forge
James	Bayse		LG92	Chestertown
Leslie T.	Beach	HEC	RG27	Thendara
Louis E.	Beach	HEC	RG20	Beaver River
Patrick	Beamish		LG92	Lake Placid
James	Bean	STR	S74	St. Regis
James H.	Bean	MEA	S81,S95,FCR	Meacham Lake
Lester W.	Bean		RG42	Lake Placid
Elmer J.	Beany		RG42	Paul Smiths
George F.	Beck	HEC	RG20	Old Forge
Edgar	Beckman		RG42	Childwold
E.	Beebe	KVL	FCR	
Charles	Beede	KVL	AL,FCR	1870s-1920s
Cyrus	Beede	KVL	AL	
Edward	Beede	KVL	AL	1890s-1930s
Ferdinand	Beede	KVL	AL,FCR	1870s-1933
Fletcher	Beede	KVL	AL	1880s-1900s
George F.	Beede	KVL	S81,AL	Keene Valley
Harry	Beede	KVL	AL,FCR	1870s-1920s
Noel	Beede	KVL	AL	1911-1950s
Orlando	Beede	KVL	AL,W,S74	1860s-1900s
Smith	Beede	KVL	AL,S74,W	1840s-1880s
Walter	Beede	KVL	AL	1900s-1950s
Horace L.	Beers		RG42	Long Lake
Wesley	Beers		RG42	Long Lake
Robert	Begley	FRC	RG27	Saranac Lake
Aaron	Beh		LG92	North Creek
Brock	Beh		LG92	North Creek
James	Belcer		LG92	Star Lake
Abner	Belden	NEW	S81	Newcomb
R. A.	Bell	FRC	RG27	Burke
Frank M.	Bellinger	SLC	RG20	Stark
John A.	Bellinger	ONC	RG27	Forestport
Walter J.	Bellinger	ONC	RG27	Forestport
C. W.	Bellows	CHA	FCR	
Hiram	Bellows	CHA	S81	Chateaugay Lake
Hiram	Benham	LOS	S95,FCR	Saranac Lake
John	Benham	LOS	S74,W	Saranac Lake
Melvin	Benham	LNL	FCR	
Solomon	Benham	POT	S81,FCR	Raquette River
W.	Benham	LOS	W	
Joel	Benjamin	SCH	FCR	
Alva A.	Bennett	STR	S95,RG27	Paul Smiths
Charles	Bennett	BMT	S81	Blue Mountain Lake
Chas.	Bennett	ALA	S81	Olmsteadville
Dick	Bennett	BMT	S81	Blue Mountain Lake

Ed.	Bennett	BMT	S81	Blue Mountain Lake
Edwin	Bennett		RG42	Indian Lake
George	Bennett		RG42	Indian Lake
Henry	Bennett	MOO	FCR	
Henry	Bennett	ESC	S81	Tahawus
Henry W.	Bennett	WAC	RG27	North River
J.C.	Bennett	NOR	FCR	
Lee	Bennett		RG42	Indian Lake
Nate	Bennett	NOR	S81	North River
Richard	Bennett	RAQ	FCR	
Silas	Bennett	NOR	S81	North River
George	Bentley	BMT	FCR	
Henry L.	Benton		RG42	Parishville
John L.	Benton		RG42	Parishville
Lori	Benton		LG92	Indian Lake
Julius	Berggren	LEC	RG27	Croghan
John	Bernardi		LG92	Saranac Lake
Emilia	Bernd		LG92	North River
Nancy	Bernstein		LG92	Gabriels
Wm. C.	Berry	HEC	RG27	Thendara
Mark	Bertsche		LG92	Warrensburg
U. Grant	Bethel	HEC	RG27	Beaver River
James	Betters	STR	FCR	
Levi	Betters	FRC	RG27	Paul Smiths
Otis	Betts	LGL	S95,FCR	Long Lake
John	Beuhler, Jr.		RG42	Saranac Lake
J. O. A.	Beyere	RAQ	FCR	
Addison	Bickford		LG92	Rainbow Lake
Chas. P.	Bigelow	FRC	RG27	Paul Smiths
Merrill W.	Bigelow		RG42	Keene Valley
W. E.	Bill		BTG	Inlet
Albert	Billings	PLD	S81,FCR	North Elba
George	Billings	PLD	S74,S81,W	North Elba
Richard	Birch	NOR	S81	North River
DeForst	Bird	BMT	FCR	
Edward	Bird	BMT	FCR	
F. J.	Bird	BMT	S95	Blue Mountain Lake
Harold	Bird		RG42	Raquette Lake
Joseph	Bird		RG42	Raquette Lake
Charles A.	Bisett	WAC	RG27	Glens Falls
James	Bisnaw	SLC	RG20	Ogdensburg
C. A.	Bissell	NEW	W	
Charles	Bissell	NEW	W,S74	
James	Bissell	LNL	FCR	
James	Bissell	NEW	S74,W	Newcomb
Joe	Bissell	NEW	W,S74	
Nelson	Bissell	NEW	W,S74	
Ozias	Bissell	NEW	S74,W,S81	Newcomb
Abner	Blakeman	FUL	FCR	
Frederick	Blakeman	FUL	FCR	
Geo. A.	Blakeman	HAC	RG27	Inlet
Arthur	Blanchard	BMT	FCR	
C. H.	Blanchard	BMT	S81	Blue Mountain Lake
Charles W.	Blanchard	BMT	FCR	
Charley	Blanchard	LGL	S74	Long Lake

Ernest C.	Blanchard	HAC	RG27	Blue Mountain Lake
Frank	Blanchard	STR	FCR	
Geo. H.	Blanchard	LNL	S81	Loon Lake
Marcello	Blanchard	LNL	S81	Loon Lake
Tammy	Blanchard		LG92	Blue Mt. Lake
Aiken R.	Blinn	KVL	S81	Keene Valley
Robert L.	Blinn	KVL	S81	Keene Valley
Edwin	Bliss	FRC	S81	Whiteface Mountain
Wallace A.	Blood	ESC	RG27	Ticonderoga
Marian	Bodine		LG92	Bloomingdale
	Bogle	KVL	AL	
George W.	Bohling		RG42	Port Leyden
Robert F.	Bolton		RG42	Old Forge
Ralph	Bombard	FRC	RG27	Saranac Lake
Ralph	Bomburd	FRC	RG20	Moody
Charles	Bomyea	FRC	RG27	Saranac Lake
Emmett H.	Booth		RG42	Hammond
Eugene A.	Bordeaux		RG42	North Bangor
Carl	Borgh		LG92	Diamond Point
Fred J.	Bosworth		BTG	Forestport
H. Aldrich	Bouta	HAC	RG27	Inlet
Clarence A.	Bowen	HEC	RG27	Cold Brook
Charles H.	Bowker	SCH	S81	Schroon Lake
Fred	Bowman		RG42	Old Forge
Brian	Boya		LG92	Indian Lake
Lewis H.	Boyce	FRC	RG27	Saranac Inn
Orello	Boyden	LGL	S81	Long Lake
Albert N.	Boyea	FRC	RG27	Malone
Alvin E.	Boyea	FRC	RG27	Whippleville
Eugene W.	Brabon		RG42	St. Regis Falls
William	Brack	HEC	RG27,RG42	Old Forge
Horace	Braiman	KVL	AL	1860s-1880s
Arthur	Braley	NEW	FCR	
Cheney J.	Braley	NEW	S81	Newcomb
Ernest H.	Braley	ESC	RG27	Newcomb
H.	Braman	LOS	W	
Kathleen	Brannon		LG92	Olmstedville
Charles T.	Bratten		BTG	New York
Walter B.	Brayton	WAC	RG27	Glens Falls
Walter P.	Brayton	WAC	RG20	Lake George
David	Breglia		LG92	North Creek
Laura	Breglia		LG92	Lake Clear
Goldie	Breno	SLC	RG20	Ogdensburg
Melissa	Brewer		LG92	Chestertown
Edward	Brewster	PLD	FCR	
Martin	Brewster	PLD	FCR	
Myron	Brewster	PLD	S81	North Elba
James	Bridge	POT	W	
Cornelius	Briggs	FUL	FCR	
Joseph W.	Briggs		RG42	Schenectady
John	Brinkerhoff	FUL	S81,W	Fulton Chain
L. W.	Bristol	SLC	RG27	DeGrasse
Mary Ann	Brody		LG92	Lake Placid
Bill	Broe	KVL	AL	1930s-1970s
Charlie	Broe	KVL	AL	1930s-1970s

Leo N.	Broe	KVL	AL,RG42	1940s-1950s
William	Broe		RG42	Keene Valley
Lewis S.	Brondstatter	HEC	RG27	Rainbow Lake
Archie	Brooks	KVL	AL,RG42	1920s-1950s
Charles	Brooks	WAC	RG20,RG27,RG42	West Stony Creek
A.	Brown	STR	W	
Bert	Brown	HAC	RG27	Indian Lake
Calvin	Brown	LOS	FCR,W,S81	
E. L.	Brown	SAC	FCR	
Ed.	Brown	STR	S81	St. Regis Lake
Ed.	Brown	LOS	W	
Edgar	Brown		LG92	Indian Lake
Edward	Brown	LOS	S74	Saranac Lake
F.	Brown	LOS	W	
Fay J.	Brown	HEC	RG27,RG42	Old Forge
Frederick	Brown		LG92	Glens Falls
Gerald	Brown		LG92	Glens Falls
Harris	Brown	HAC	RG27	Indian Lake
Henry	Brown	IND	FCR	("Comical")
Homer M.	Brown	KVL	AL,RG20,RG27	1909-1930s
James Wm.	Brown	ONC	RG27	Forestport
Jim	Brown	KVL	AL,RG42	1920s-1960s
John K.	Brown	KVL	AL,FCR	1870s-1930s
Josiah	Brown	MOO	FCR	
LeRay	Brown		RG42	Cobleskill
Lowell	Brown	LOS	S95,FCR	Saranac Lake
Mace	Brown	LOS	S95,W	Saranac Lake
Marshall	Brown	LOS	S74,S95	Saranac Lake
Peter C.	Brown	HEC	RG27	McKeever
W. J.	Brown	FRC	RG27	St. Regis Falls
W. T.	Brown	BTG		Old Forge
William	Brown		LG92	Lake Placid
William J.	Brown	HAC	RG27,RG42	Indian Lake
Frank L.	Brownell		RG42	Eagle Bay
Hiram	Brownell		RG42	Cambridge
Adnor	Bruce	FRC	RG27	Santa Clara
C.F.	Bruce	GRS	FCR	
Edward	Bruce	POT	W	
Esra	Bruce	BLM	FCR	
Ezra	Bruce	STR	S81,S95	St. Regis Lake
Harry	Bruce		RG42	Schroon Lake
M.	Bruce	SCH	S81	Schroon River
Albert Geo.	Brucker	HAC	RG27	Blue Mountain Lake
Samson H.	Brucker	ONC	RG27	Forestport
Charles	Brumley		LG92	Saranac Lake
Wayne	Brunie	KVL	AL	Late 1960s
Russell	Brust		LG92	Corinth
Warren	Bryan	LOS	FCR	
Charles	Bryant	LOS	FCR	
Dayton	Bryant	RAW	FCR	
Warren	Bryant	LOS	S95	Saranac Lake
Patrick	Buckley	LNL	FCR	
Milo E.	Bull	FUL	BTG,S95	Old Forge
Fred	Bullard		RG42	Indian Lake
John N.	Bullard		RG42	Severance

Warren	Bullock	CRA	FCR	
Allen	Bump	SCH	FCR	
Charles	Bump	SCH	FCR	
Harold	Bump		RG42	Adirondack
William	Bump	FRC	RG20,RG27	St. Regis Falls
Richard	Burch	NOR	FCR	
Elmer	Burdick	WAC	RG20	Stony Creek
Geo. A.	Burdick	HEC	RG27,BTG	Big Moose
George H.	Burdick		BTG	Inlet
James	Burgess		LG92	Saranac Lake
Charles	Burke	BVR	W	
Fred	Burke		BTG	Old Forge
James	Burke	IND	FCR	
Nan	Burke		LG92	Old Forge
Robert	Burke		LG92	Old Forge
William H.	Burke	FUL	BTG,S85	Old Forge
Free	Burley	WAC	RG27,RG20	North River
Alanson D.	Burlingame	SLC	RG20	Dryden
Jennie	Burnap		LG92	Thendara
James E.	Burnett		RG42	South Colton
John	Burnett	HEC	RG27	Old Forge
Geo. W.	Burnham	WAC	RG27	Lake George
George W.	Burnham		RG42	Conklingville
Melvin S.	Burnham	BMT	S95	Blue Mountain Lake
Howard N.	Burnmark		RG42	Little Valley
Bernard	Burns	CRA	FCR	
Erin	Burns		LG92	Lake Placid
Kevin	Burns		LG92	Lake Placid
Peter	Burns		LG92	Athol
William	Burns	SLC	RG27	Russell
All. G.	Burr	MEA	W,S81	
Bert	Burr	FRC	RG27,RG42	Malone
Bert	Burr	MEA	S95	Meacham Lake
Josha	Burt	ONC	RG27	Forestport
A. M.	Burtch	HEC	RG27	Big Moose
George	Burton	LKP	FCR,S81	
Henry	Burton	LKP	S81	Lake Pleasant
William	Burton	HAC	RG27	Speculator
Anthony I.	Bush	LEC	RG27	Number Four
Harley	Bushey	FRC	RG27	Saranac Lake
William	Buskirk	POT	W	
Jno.	Bustin	HEC	RG27	Clearwater
Cecil E.	Butler	ESC	RG27,RG42	Olmstedville
Elmer H.	Butler	ESC	RG27	Olmstedville
James	Butler	TUP	FCR	
John	Butler	TUP	FCR	
John	Butler	HAC	RG20	Long Lake
Polly	Butler		LG92	Lake Placid
Alanson	Butterfield	BEL	FCR	
Andrew	Butterfield	BEL	FCR	
Andrew	Butterfield	FRC	RG27	Owls Head
Lanson	Butterfield	FRC	S81	Ragged Lake
Lorenzo	Butterfield	FRC	S81	Ragged Lake
M.	Butterfield	FRC	RG27	Owls Head
Madore	Butterfield	FRC	S81	Ragged Lake

Oliver G.	Butterfield	WAC	RG20	Lake George
Myron	Buttles	ESC	S81	Tahawus
Geo.	Butts	STR	S74	St. Regis
John N.	Buyee	HAC	RG20	Lake Pleasant
Jno. P.	Byrne	ESC	RG27	Minerva
Edward W.	Cady, Jr.		RG42	Saranac Lake
Ed.	Cagle	LOS	S95	Saranac Lake
Edward	Cagle	LOS	FCR	
Hugh	Call	LKP	FCR	
John	Cameron		LG92	Wilmington
William	Cameron		LG92	Stony Creek
Elijah	Camp	IND	S81	Indian Lake
David	Campbell		LG92	Saranac Lake
George	Campbell	SAC	FCR	
George	Campbell	SAC	S81	St. Regis Falls
Geo. W.	Campbell, Jr.	HEC	RG27	Ilion
Geo. W.	Campbell, Sr.	HAC	RG27	Inlet
E.	Canada	PLD	W	
Floyd	Carbary		RG42	Childwold
James	Carberry	GRS	FCR	
William	Carlozzi		LG92	Adirondack
Richard	Carlson		LG92	North River
Charles	Carlton	PLD	S81	North Elba
James	Carney	STR	S95	Paul Smiths
C.	Carter	OSW	W	
Arthur	Cary	LNL	FCR	
Berton O.	Cary	HAC	RG20	Long Lake
George	Cary	LGL	S74	Long Lake
Nelson	Cary	LGL	S74,S81,W,FCR	Long Lake
Reuben	Cary	LGL	W,FCR,S74,S81	
Peter	Casamento		LG92	Willsboro
Anthony	Catana		LG92	Star Lake
Herbert	Catlin	SLC	RG27	Hammond
Ed.	Cerbin	STR	S81	St. Regis Lake
Duane	Chadwick	LUZ	FCR	
Carl	Champagne		LG92	South Colton
Herbert W.	Champney	SLC	RG27	Bay Pond
Nelson	Chandler	HEC	RG27	Old Forge
O. E.	Chapman	FRC	RG27	Owls Head
David	Charbonneau	FUL	S95	Fulton Chain
David T.	Charbonneau		BTG	Old Forge
Raoul	Charbonneau		LG92	Bolton Landing
David T.	Charbonneau, Sr.	HEC	RG27	Old Forge
Henry E.	Charlebois		RG42	Forestport
Caleb I.	Chase	NEW	S74,W	Newcomb
Caleb J.	Chase	NEW	S81	Newcomb
Edmund J.	Chase	NEW	S81	Newcomb
Ele	Chase	NEW	W	
Elis C.	Chase	NEW	S74	Newcomb
F.	Chase	NEW	W	
Floromond C.	Chase	NEW	S81	Newcomb
Franklin C.	Chase	NEW	FCR,S74,S81	
Halsey	Chase	KVL	AL,RG42	1932-1950s
Henry	Chase	STR	S74	St. Regis
J.	Chase	DIC	W	

Jeff	Chase	NEW	W	
Jefferson	Chase	NEW	S74,S81	Newcomb
Judson	Chase	NEW	S81	Newcomb
Lorenzo	Chase	RAW	FCR	
Madison H.	Chase	ONC	RG27	Syracuse
Theo. F.	Chase	ESC	RG27	Newcomb
Walsey E.	Chase	ESC	RG27	Keene Valley
Washington	Chase	NEW	S74,W	Newcomb
Willis H.	Chase	NEW	S81	Newcomb
David	Cheney	NEW	S74	Newcomb
Fred	Cheney	FRC	RG20	St. Regis Falls
John	Cheney	NEW	W	
L.	Cheney	DIC	W	
S.	Cheney	HAC	RG27	Blue Mountain Lake
Sherry	Cheney		RG42	Blue Mountain Lake
David	Cherboneau	FUL	FCR	
Milton	Chesmore	CHA	FCR	
Frank A.	Christman	HEC	RG27	Ohio
John H.	Christy	HEC	RG27	Old Forge
Philip	Christy	FUL	FCR,BTG	Old Forge
Philip	Christy		RG42	Old Forge
Philip Henry	Christy	HEC	RG27	Old Forge
A. M.	Church	FUL	S95,BTG	Fulton Chain
Arthur N.	Church	FUL	FCR	
Harvey B.	Church	SLC	RG20	Wanakena
Ray	Churco		LG92	Tupper Lake
David	Cilley		LG92	Lake Clear
Augustus	Ciphert	FUL	S81	Fulton Chain
Chester H.	Clark	HEC	RG27	Old Forge
Cliff	Clark	LOS	S81	Saranac Lake
Geo.	Clark	FRC	RG27	Saranac Lake
Glenn	Clark		LG92	Parishville
Herbert J.	Clark		RG42	Saranac Lake
Joe	Clark	MEA	W	
John R.	Clark	ESC	RG27	Saranac Lake
Leon J.	Clark	FRC	RG20	Faust
Lloyd M.	Clark	FRC	RG20	Saranac Lake
Rans.	Clark	CHA	S81,W	Chateaugay Lake
Sealon	Clark	LKP	FCR	
Thomas	Clark	STR	S81,FCR,S95	St. Regis Lake
William E.	Clark		RG42	Bolton Landing
Edmund	Clement		RG42	Long Lake
John T.	Clement	HAC	RG27	Long Lake
Robert G.	Clifford	KVL	RG42,AL	Keene Valley
Edward J.	Clohosy	FRC	RG20,RG27	Tupper Lake
Mark	Clough	LOS	S74,W	Saranac Lake
George	Clunis	LUZ	FCR	
George W.	Cobb	ESC	RG20	Paradox
Geo.	Codner	WAC	RG27	Stony Creek
Frederick	Colbath	LOS	FCR	
Hosea	Colbath	LOS	S74,FCR,S81,W	Saranac Lake
Bernard	Colburn		LG92	North Hudson
Alba	Cole	LGL	S81,W,S95	Long Lake
Alfred W.	Cole	HAC	RG27	Long Lake
Alva	Cole	LGL	FCR	

Att.	Cole	LGL	S74	Long Lake
Charles	Cole	LGL	S95	Long Lake
Charles B.	Cole	LGL	FCR	
Charles E.	Cole	LGL	FCR	
Clayton	Cole	LGL	S95,FCR	Long Lake
Douglas	Cole		LG92	Wevertown
James S.	Cole	HAC	RG27	Long Lake
Ralph A.	Cole		RG42	DeKalb Junction
S.	Cole	LGL	W	
Simeon	Cole	LGL	S74,S81,FCR	Long Lake
W. W.	Cole	LGL	S95	Long Lake
Warren	Cole	LGL	S81	Long Lake
William	Cole	LKP	FCR	
O.A.	Cole,Jr.	CED	FCR	
William	Cole,Jr.	OSW	FCR	
Anthony J.	Coleman	ONC	RG27,RG42	Forestport
Harold A.	Coleman	ONC	RG27	Forestport
Frank P.	Collard		RG42	Minerva
David	Collins		LG92	Glens Falls
John	Collins	CHA	W	
Nathaniel	Collins	CHA	FCR	
Wayne	Collins	BVR	W	
Vernon	Colton		RG42	Russell
Harvey	Combs	WAC	RG20	Stony Creek
Jules	Comeau		LG92	Tupper Lake
John	Commerford	WOD	BTG,FCR,S95	Boonville
William	Commerford		BTG	Boonville
Wm.	Commerford	ONC	RG27	Forestport
John H.	Conken	HEC	RG27	Ohio
Carson	Conkey	BTG		Raquette Lake
Roscoe	Conklin	HEC	RG27	Ohio
Alfred F.	Conroy		RG42	Ogdensburg
Leon	Conway		RG42	Wells
Dennis	Cook		RG42	Palmyra
George	Cook	CHA	FCR	
James	Cook	POT	W	
George	Coolin	BLM	FCR	
Benjamin F.	Cooper		BTG	Port Leyden
Roy	Cooper		LG92	Old Forge
Edson C.	Corbin	FRC	RG27,S95	Paul Smiths
Philip	Corell		LG92	Cadyville
Alambert	Corey	LOS	S81	Saranac Lake
Charles	Corey	LOS	S74,W	Saranac Lake
Jesse	Corey	LOS	W	
Sem.	Corey	LOS	S74	Saranac Lake
William	Cornell	RAQ	FCR,S95	
John	Corti		LG92	South Glens Falls
William	Coryer		LG92	Peru
Frederick	Coughman	LKP	FCR	
Chauncey	Courtney	LKP	FCR	
Edwin	Courtney	LKP	S81,FCR	Lake Pleasant
Geo. Henry	Courtney	HAC	RG27	Piseco
Warren	Courtney	LKP	S81,FCR	Lake Pleasant
Wm. N.	Courtney	HAC	RG27	Piseco
Charles	Covel	LOS	FCR	

Lewis A.	Covell	HEC	RG20	Beaver River
Earl W.	Covey		BTG	Big Moose
H. H.	Covey		BTG	Big Moose
O. A.	Covill	LOS	S95	Saranac Lake
O.	Coville	STR	W	
Paul	Crago	FUL	S81	Fulton Chain
Richard	Crago	FUL	S81,FCR	Fulton Chain
Chris	Crandall	MEA	W,S81	
Fred B.	Crandall	LEC	RG27	Brantingham Lake
Warland E.	Cranson	FRC	RG27	Tupper Lake
Douglas	Crary		LG92	Tupper Lake
Archie	Crawford	KVL	AL,W	1870s-1900s
Paul	Crego	FUL	W	
Richard	Crego	FUL	BTG,S95	Boonville
Roy G.	Crego	BTG	RG42	Boonville, Old Forge
Basil J.	Croft, Jr.		RG42	Thendara
Harold F.	Crofut	HEC	RG27	Old Forge
John	Crogan	RAQ	FCR	
Leonard	Cronin		LG92	South Glens Falls
Bert	Cronk	UPS	S95	Saranac Inn
D.	Cronk	LOS	W	
Geo.	Cronk	LOS	S81	Saranac Lake
Clarke	Cross	IND	FCR	
James	Cross	STR	S74,S81,FCR,W	St. Regis
Orrin	Cross	IND	FCR	
Oscar	Cross	IND	FCR	
Will	Cross	STR	S95	Paul Smiths
Clayton	Crossman	SLC	RG20	Otter Lake
Schuyler	Crouse	HAC	RG27	Wells
Harvey D.	Crowinshield	FRC	RG27	Moody
Edward	Cullen	LGL	FCR	
William	Cullen	LGL	FCR	
Wm.	Cullins	LGL	S81	Long Lake
Joseph	Cummins		LG92	Blue Mt. Lake
Patrick	Cummins		LG92	Blue Mt. Lake
David	Cunningham		LG92	Glens Falls
Patrick	Cunningham		LG92	North Creek
Patrick	Cunningham Jr.		LG92	Glens Falls
G. Michael	Currie		LG92	Bolton Landing
Arthur J.	Curtis		RG42	DeGrasse
Earl	Curtis		RG42	DeGrasse
George	Dague		RG42	Port Kent
Gregg	Dahlen		LG92	Bloomingdale
James	Dalton	HEC	RG27,BTG	Old Forge
Robert	Dalton	FUL	FCR	
Steven	Daly		LG92	North Creek
Hubert	Danforth	LEW	FCR	
Raymond	Danforth		RG42	Speculator
William	Danforth	MEA	S81,W	Meacham Lake
Abner P.	Daniels	FUL	S81,W	Fulton Chain
Dyer	Daniels	IND	S81,FCR	Indian Lake
Oliver	Daniels("Ginshang")ALA		FCR	
Oliver	Daniels	ESC	RG27	Newcomb
E. J. F.	Danmark	BMT	S95	Blue Mountain Lake
Geo.	Darling	HAC	RG27	Northville

Burt	Darrow	HEC	RG20	Beaver River
William	Dart	BGM	FCR,BTG,S81	
Harry	Davidson		RG42	Woodgate
Charles	Davis	OSW	FCR	
Elmer M.	Davis	FRC	RG27	Owls Head
Frank	Davis	LOS	FCR,S95,RG20	
George	Davis	TUP	FCR	
Gordon R.	Davis		RG42	Wells
H.	Davis	POT	W	
Henry	Davis	LOS	S95,FCR	Saranac Lake
Hugh	Davis		RG42	North River
J. W.	Davis	CHA	FCR	
M.B.	Davis	ELZ	FCR	
Martin B.	Davis	ELZ	S95	Elizabethtown
Morton H.	Davis	ELZ	S95,FCR	Elizabethtown
N. M.	Davis	NOR	S81	North River
Grant J.	Dawley	HEC	RG27	Old Forge
Guy W.	Dawson	FRC	RG27	Dickinson Center
Chester	Day	POT	S81,W	Raquette River
Darwin R.	Day	FRC	RG20	Gile
Earl F.	Day	FRC	RG20	Gile
H. Walter	Day	SLC	RG20	Hollywood
Henry	Day	POT	S81,W	Raquette River
Robert D. J.	Dayton		RG42	Otter Lake
Lyman	De Bar	MEA	S81,FCR,W,S95	Meacham Lake
Olie	De Mun	HAC	RG20	Beaver Dams
Geo.	DeBar	FRC	RG27	Duane
Michael	DeDivitis		LG92	Rainbow Lake
Lyman	Debar	MEA	S95	Meacham Lake
Emery	Decker	WAC	RG20	Silver Bay
Tony	Deepe		RG42	North River
Ivan	Delair		RG42	Hammond
E. Phillip	Delarm Jr.		LG92	Paul Smiths
Jennifer	Delcore		LG92	Indian Lake
Archie	Delmarsh	FUL	FCR,BTG,S95	
E. S.	Delmarsh	BTG		Inlet
---	"Denmark"	NEW	FCR	(no last name in 1893 report)
Charles	Densmore	SCH	S81	Schroon River
Duck	Derby	UPS	S95	Saranac Inn
Earl	Derby	UPS	FCR	
Earl	Derby	UPS	S95	Saranac Inn
Fred	Derby		RG42	Tupper Lake
John	Derby	UPS	FCR	
Millard	Derby	UPS	FCR	
John	Devaney	FRC	RG27	Saranac Lake
Aloney	Dewey		RG42	Dickinson Center
Albert	Dezalia	KVL	AL,RG27	1930s-1940s
Raymond	DiLorenzo		LG92	Corinth
Michael	DiPalma		LG92	Queensbury
George M., Jr.	Dillon	OSW	W	
John L.	Dimick		RG42	St. Regis Falls
Edward	Dimmock	NEW	FCR	
Jed	Dingham	SLC	RG27	Chippewa Bay
Joseph	Disotell		LG92	Tupper Lake

L. F.	Disotell	FRC	RG27,RG42	McColloms
Jody	Dixon		LG92	Northville
Jay	Dizacomo III		LG92	Lake Placid
Austin	Dobson		RG42	Harrisville
Elmer	Dockum	LOS	S95,FCR	Saranac Lake
William	Dodd		LG92	Westport
Brian	Donohue		LG92	Bolton Landing
George E.	Donohue		RG42	Long Lake
Ormon	Doty	FRC	RG20,RG42	Rainbow Lake
Homer J.	Dougall	HEC	RG20	Ohio
D'Avignon	Douglas		RG42	Hawkeye
H.	Douglas	LOS	W	
Wm.	Douglas	FRC	RG27	Upper Saranac
Henry	Douglass	LOS	S74	Saranac Lake
Otis	Dow	STR	S81	St. Regis Lake
John	Downey		LG92	Saranac
Edward	Dows	SAC	FCR	
Ira	Dox	GRS	FCR	
Stephen	Doxzon		LG92	Lake Placid
Uwe	Dramm		LG92	Lake Placid
Frederick	Drescher		RG42	Stony Creek
Jack	Drury		LG92	Saranac Lake
Thomas	DuBois		LG92	Glens Falls
Lewis A.	Duane	HAC	RG27	Long Lake
Rebecca	Dubay		LG92	Queensbury
Robert	Dubay		LG92	North Creek
A. W.	Dudley	LOS	S81,S95,W	Saranac Lake
Clarence S.	Dudley	FRC	RG27	Bloomingdale
Clyde	Dudley	FRC	RG27	Saranac Lake
John C.	Dudley		RG42	Diamond Point
L.	Dudley	LOS	W	
Allen	Duell		LG92	Corinth
John	Duell	WAC	RG27	Horicon
A. W.	Duelley	LOS	S74	Saranac Lake
Michael	Duggan		LG92	Lake Placid
Cowden	Duke		LG92	Rainbow Lake
John	Dukett	LOS	W	
William	Dukett	UPS	S95,FCR	Axton
Samuel	Dunakin	FUL	FCR,W,S81	
James C.	Dunbar	BVR	FCR	
Jessica	Duncan		LG92	Queensbury
John	Duncan		LG92	Queensbury
Lester	Dunham	HAC	RG20	Wells
Daniel	Dunlap	ALA	S81	Olmsteadville
Alva	Dunning	BMT	S81,FCR	Blue Mountain Lake
D.	Dunning	LOS	W	
Douglas	Dunning	ELZ	FCR	
H. E.	Dunning	HAC	RG27	Piseco
R.J.	Dunning	LGL	FCR	
Samuel	Dunning	LOS	W	
Orrin	Duphney	HEC	RG27	Old Forge
Oliver	Dupre	LNL	FCR	
Paul	Durling		LG92	Schroon Lake
Harry	Duso	FRC	RG27	Saranac Lake
Ed	Dustin	STR	S95,S81	Paul Smiths

Charles	Dwight	STR	S74,S81,W	St. Regis
Roy	Early Jr.		LG92	Scotia
James	Eccles	FRC	RG27	McDonald
Mark	Eddy		LG92	Old Forge
Edwyn C.	Edgar	LEC	RG27	Petries Corners
Boyd	Edwards	BVR	W	
C. Sylvester	Edwards	BVR	W	
Charles	Edwards		RG42	Childwold
Jeffrey	Edwards		LG92	Lake Placid
John	Edwards	SAC	FCR	
William	Edwards	DIC	W	
Douglas	Egeland		LG92	Dickinson Ctr
Sanford N.	Egloff	LEC	RG27	Croghan
Don P.	Eighmy	HEC	RG27	Beaver River
Dominic	Eisinger		LG92	Lake Placid
William	Eldridge		LG92	Lake Placid
Charles	Ellerby	HEC	RG20	Fulton Chain
Frank	Elliott	NOH	FCR	
Alvin S.	Ellis	FRC	RG27	Duane
Jackson	Ellis	OSW	W	
William	Ellis	DIC	W	
Gordon	Ellis, Jr.		LG92	North Creek
James	Ellsworth		LG92	Lake George
George	Elthorp	HEC	RG27,RG42	Thendara
B. F.	Emerson	LGL	S74,W,FCR	Long Lake
Franklin	Emerson	LGL	S81	Long Lake
John	Emerson	HAC	RG27	Long Lake
Wallace	Emerson	LGL	FCR,S95	
Wallace F.	Emerson	HEC	RG27	Long Lake
Josoph	Emmett	ELZ	FCR	
Thomas	Eno		LG92	Stillwater
Byron	Estes	KVL	AL,S74,W	1947-1950s
Daniel	Estill		LG92	Stillwater
Karen	Estill		LG92	Stillwater
Lawrence	Estill		LG92	Stillwater
John	Evans		LG92	Eagle Bay
Lucius "Lute"	Evans	LOS	S74,S81,W,FCR	Saranac Lake
Marc	Evans		LG92	Fort Ann
William	Ewing		LG92	Lake Placid
Harvey K.	Exford	SLC	RG27	DeGrasse
Joey	Fabin		LG92	Indian Lake
James	Fagan		RG42	Indian Lake
Louis J.	Fagan	HEC	RG27	Ohio
Wayne	Failing		LG92	Lake Placid
E. C.	Falconer	SAC	FCR	
Ervin	Falconer	SAC	S81	St. Regis Falls
W.	Falconer	SAC	S81	St. Regis Falls
Bernard J.	Falls	SLC	RG27	Mount Arab
Charles E.	Fancher	HAC	RG20	Sabattis
John F.	Far	NEW	S74	Newcomb
Charlie	Far, Jr.	NEW	S74	Newcomb
Frank	Fardelt	ONC	RG27	Forestport
Silas K.	Farley		BTG	Boonville
Arthur	Farmer		RG42	St. Regis Falls
Clark	Farmer	LGL	W	

Fred	Farmer	FRC	RG27	Moody
James L.	Farmer	FRC	RG20,RG42	St. Regis Falls
Lindon	Farmer		RG42	St. Regis Falls
Michael	Farmer		LG92	Old Forge
John	Farmer, Jr.	SAC	FCR	
A.	Farr	DIC	W	
Allen	Farr	SAC	S81	St. Regis Falls
Charles E.	Farr	NEW	S81	Newcomb
J.	Farr	DIC	W	
Richard	Farrell		RG42	Indian Lake
D.E.("Rat")	Farrington	IND	FCR	
Erastus	Farrington	NOR	S81	North River
Herbert	Farrington	IND	FCR	
J. M.	Farrington	FRC	RG27	Saranac Lake
Justin	Farrington	UPS	FCR	
Paul	Fawthrop		LG92	Schroon Lake
George	Fayzett	TUP	S81	Tupper Lake
George	Fayzette	LOS	S95	Saranac Lake
Karen	Fedder		LG92	Wilmington
Michael	Feldman		LG92	Northville
William S.	Fenner		RG42	Raquette Lake
James	Fennessey	ESC	RG27,RG42	Newcomb
Albert	Fenton	BVR	W	
Charles	Fenton	BVR	W	
Larry	Ferrazzano	LG92	Remsen	
Justin	Ferrington	UPS	S95	Saranac Inn
Michael	Ferris	SLC	RG27	DeGrasse
Hamilton	Ferry		RG42	Childwold
Hubert	Ferry	GRS	FCR	
James M.	Ferry	SLC	RG20	Childwold
John	Ferry	POT	W	
Warren	Ffield	CHA	FCR	
James	Fifield	FUL	S81	Fulton Chain
Tracy M.	Figary		RG42	East Syracuse
James	Filbrooks	LOS	W	
James C.	Finch	HEC	RG20	Albany
John	Finegan	STR	S81	St. Regis Lake
Clifford	Finkle		RG42	Bolton Landing
Geo. H.	Finkle	WAC	RG27	Bolton Landing
Harry W.	Finkle		RG42	Bolton Landing
Wesley	Finkle		RG42	Bolton Landing
Mark	Finley		LG92	Indian Lake
Paul W.	Finley		RG42	Gouverneur
Frank J.	Finn		RG42	Saranac Lake
Bert	Fish	HAC	RG27	Indian Lake
Grant	Fish	HAC	RG27	Indian Lake
Howard	Fish		RG42,RG27	Indian Lake
Orla	Fish	ESC	RG20	Moriah
Selden	Fish	ESC	RG20	Port Henry
Andrew	Fisher	LGL	FCR	
Bert	Fisher		RG42	Arietta
Ernest E.	Fisk	HAC	RG27	Sabael
William	Fitzgerald		LG92	Lake Clear
Vogan	Fitzhugh	WAC	RG27	North Creek
Arlo C.	Flagg	LOS	S95,FCR	Saranac Lake

Edward	Flagg	LOS	FCR,S74,S81	
Silas	Flagg	LOS	S95,S81,FCR	Saranac Lake
Eugene	Flanders	STR	S95	Paul Smiths
Warren	Flanders	STR	S74,S81	St. Regis
Earl	Fletcher	FRC	RG27	Upper Saranac
James F.	Flick	LEC	RG27	Croghan
Zenas	Flicke	HEC	RG20	Ohio
Michael	Flora	BMT	S95	Blue Mountain Lake
Michael	Flory	BMT	FCR	
John	Fontana		LG92	Tupper Lake
Williams	Forbes	NOH	FCR	
A. P.	Ford		BTG	Inlet
Harold L.	Ford		RG42	DeGrasse
Harry E.	Ford		BTG	Inlet
Sim.	Forence	STR	8S74⁻	St. Regis
Robert	Forster		LG92	Lake Placid
John	Forsythe		RG42	Hammond
Fred E.	Fosgate	HEC	RG20	Ilion
Fred	Foster		LG92	Lake Placid
Garry	Foster		LG92	Morrisonville
John	Foster	LOS	FCR	
John	Foster	RAB	FCR	
H. Fred	Fountain	ESC	RG27	Lake Placid
Henry H.	Fountain	FRC	S81	Ragged Lake
C. L.	Foy	FRC	RG27	Saranac Lake
Dennis	Franla	FUL	FCR	
Jamie	Frasier		LG92	Olmstedville
Wakley	Frasier	WAC	RG20	Hadley
Dana A.	Fraula		BTG	Fulton Chain
Daniel J.	Frayne	ESC	RG27,RG42	Lake Placid
William J.	Frayne		RG42	Lake Placid
John	Frazier	PLD	S81	North Elba
Vern L.	Freebern	WAC	RG27	North River
Robert	Freeborn		RG42	North River
Harry	Freeman	UPS	S95	Axton
Harvey	Freeman	TUP	FCR	
James	Freeman	TUP	S81	Tupper Lake
Ross	Freeman		RG42	Corey's
Albert D.	French		RG42	Ohio
Harold	French		RG42	Morristown
Paul H.	French		RG42	Schroon Lake
Robert	Frenette		LG92	Tupper Lake
Christopher	Frettoloso		LG92	Olmstedville
Herman	Frey		RG42	St. Regis Falls
John	Friauf, Jr.		LG92	Racquette Lake
Wm. W.	Froher	SLC	RG27	Winthrop
Arthur	Fuller	HAC	RG27	Indian Lake
Arthur J.	Fuller	WAC	RG20	Stony Creek
Clifford	Fuller		RG42	Stony Creek
Duane	Fuller	NOR	S81	North River
Duane	Fuller	BMT	S95,FCR	Blue Mountain Lake
Emmett	Fuller	HAC	RG27	Long Lake
Fremont	Fuller	MEA	FCR	
George	Fuller	BMT	S95	Blue Mountain Lake
George H.	Fuller	HAC	RG20	Wells

George W.	Fuller	BMT	FCR	
Harold L.	Fuller		RG42	Saranac Lake
Wyatt	Fuller	WAC	RG20	Stony Creek
Gary	Gagnon		LG92	Plattsburgh
Albert F.	Gale	SLC	RG20	Gale
Alrin	Gale	POT	S81	Raquette River
Alvan	Gale	GRS	FCR	
Arthur	Gale	GRS	FCR	
Charles H.	Gale	GRS	FCR	
Chas.	Gale	POT	S81	Raquette River
Chas. H.	Gale	SLC	RG27	Piercefield
Emery	Gale	POT	S81,W	Raquette River
Frank	Gale	GRS	FCR	
Howard O.	Gale		G42	Childwold
Henry	Gallagher	ONC	RG27	Forestport
Joseph	Gallagher	ONC	RG27	Forestport
Joseph M.	Gallagher		RG42	Forestport
Patrick	Gallagher		LG92	Lake Placid
Lynn	Galusha		RG42	Indian Lake
Patrick	Gannon		LG92	Old Forge
L. O.	Gardner	WOD	FCR	
Lowell D.	Gardner		BTG	Old Forge
Richard	Garfield		LG92	Lake Placid
Dick	Garone	ESC	RG27	Lake Placid Club
Marshall	Garrow		LG92	Stony Creek
Arthur C.	Garwood		RG42	Saranac Lake
Munro	Gaskell	UPS	S81	Upper Saranac Lake
Gary	Gazaille		LG92	Hadley
George	Gedney		LG92	South Glens Falls
Craig	Genier		LG92	Port Henry
Edward	Gerard	CED	FCR	
James	Gereau		LG92	North Creek
William	Gereau		LG92	Glens Falls
Alfred	Gero	ESC	RG20	Blue Ridge
Carl B.	Getman	HEC	RG27	Ilion
Mark	Getman	HEC	RG27	Otter Lake
Wm. F.	Getman	HEC	RG27	Frankfort
Paul	Gibaldi		LG92	Warrensburg
Archie	Giffin		RG42	Russell
Harvey H.	Gill	SLC	RG27	Crary Mills
Peter	Gill		LG92	Keene
William	Gillies	LGL	FCR	
William H.	Gillis	LGL	S95	Long Lake
Charles	Gillman	KVL	AL,RG42	1930s-1950s
Frank	Gillmore	STR	S81	St. Regis Lake
Peter	Girard		RG42	Wells
Toddy	Girou		BTG	Old Forge
Charles M.	Goodrich		BTG	Old Forge
Christopher	Goodsell	FUL	FCR	
George	Goodsell	FUL	BTG,FCR	Old Forge
Robert	Goodsell	HEC	RG20,RG42	Old Forge
Wallace	Goodspeed	FRC	S81	Whiteface Mountain
Robert	Gosson		LG92	Piseco
Cecil	Gotts	HAC	RG27	Piseco
Charles	Gould	ESC	RG27,RG42	Olmstedville

Duane	Gould		LG92	Saranac Lake
Geroge	Gould		LG92	Lake Placid
Edward	Goulet		RG42	Indian Lake
William	Goulet		RG42	Indian Lake
Theodore	Goutos		LG92	Diamond Point
Harold	Graham		RG42	Speculator
Eric	Granger		LG92	Jay
Dwight	Grant	FUL	W,S95,BTG	
Hoyt	Grant		LG92	Bakers Mill
Leon F.	Graves	ONC	RG27	Rome
Mary Lou	Graves		LG92	Fort Ann
Perley J.	Graves	LOS	S95,FCR	Saranac Lake
Walter	Graves		RG42	Waddington
Robert	Graves, Jr.	BTG	Big Moose	
B. H.	Gray	FRC	RG27	Upper Saranac
H. A.	Green	SAC	S81	St. Regis Falls
Jack	Green		LG92	Olmstedville
Larmon W.	Green		RG42	Greenwich
Charles	Greeno	LOS	S74	Saranac Lake
Charles	Greenough	LOS	S74	Saranac Lake
Fred	Greenough		RG42	North Hudson
Murray	Greenwood	HAC	RG27	Long Lake
Fred	Gregory	ESC	RG20	Boreas River
Archie	Griffin	SLC	RG27	Russell
John	Griffin	NEW	FCR	
Edwin L.	Griffiths		BTG	McKeever
Charles	Griffths	BVR	FCR	
Robert	Griffths	BVR	FCR	
H. D.	Groat	BGM	FCR	
John	Grover	LOS	S74,S81,W	Saranac Lake
Gordon F.	Guile	ESC	RG20	Schroon Lake
McKinley	Guinell	ESC	RG27	Lake Placid Club
Harold L.	Guire	ESC	RG20	Paradox
Edwin J.	Guthrie	FRC	RG27	St. Regis Falls
Clarence	Gutliph	HAC	RG27	Blue Mountain Lake
Augustus	Guyette	WAC	RG27	Glens Falls
J. H.	HIgby	BVR	S81	Booneville
Joseph	Hackett		LG92	Lake Placid
David	Hale	KVL	AL	1850s-1870
Fred	Hale	KVL	AL,RG27	1900s
LeGrand	Hale	KVL	AL,S81	1870s-1900s
Mason	Hale	KVL	AL,RG42,RG27	1900s
Morris	Hale	HAC	RG27,FCR,S95	Blue Mountain Lake
Barton	Haliday	FUL	S81	Fulton Chain
Asa B.	Hall	HAC	RG27,RG42	Long Lake
Benjamin	Hall	LGL	FCR	
Curtis	Hall	LGL	FCR	
E.	Hall	STR	W	
E. S.	Hall	ESC	RG27	Keene Valley
Earl	Hall	KVL	AL	1900s
Ed	Hall	KVL	AL	1900s-1920s
Everett	Hall	KVL	AL	1930s-1950s
Harrison E.	Hall	NEW	S81,S74,FCR,W	Newcomb
Herbert	Hall	LGL	S81,S74	Long Lake
Howard	Hall	KVL	AL,RG27,RG42	1930s

J.	Hall	STR	W	
J. Everett	Hall		RG42	Keene Valley
James	Hall		RG42	Long Lake
James	Hall	NEW	S74,W	Newcomb
James C.	Hall	HAC	RG27	Long Lake
John	Hall	STR	S74,S81	St. Regis
John E.	Hall	NEW	S81,FCR	Newcomb
L.	Hall	LGL	W	
Lias	Hall	STR	S74,S81	St. Regis
Lysander	Hall	LGL	S74,S81	Long Lake
Marshall	Hall		LG92	Glens Falls
Ronald	Hall	KVL	AL,LG92	Present, Keene Valley
Ronald	Hall		LG92	Keene Valley
Rowland	Hall	LGL	S81	Long Lake
Valorous	Hall	NEW	S74,W,S81	Newcomb
Wesley	Hall	KVL	AL	1900s
William	Hall	BGM	FCR	
Fitz Green	Hallock	LOS	S81,S74	Saranac Lake
Charles	Halloran		LG92	Olmstedville
Albert G.	Hamberger	FRC	RG27	Saranac Lake
Caroline	Hambley		LG92	Rainbow Lake
George	Hamblin	HEC	RG27	Cold Brook
William H.	Hamblin	HEC	RG20	Herkimer
Ann	Hamilton		LG92	North Creek
Edward	Hammer	HAC	RG27	Long Lake
Wm. H.	Hammer	ESC	RG27	Lake Placid
A. M.	Hammond	BMT	S95,FCR	Blue Mountain Lake
John	Hammond	BVR	S81	Beaver River
Sherman	Hammond		RG42	Edward
C. B.	Hamner	LGL	S81,S74,W	Long Lake
Geo.	Hamner	SCH	S81	Schroon Lake
George	Hamner	KVL	AL,FCR("Hamer")	1880s-1890s
Joseph	Hamner	LOS	S74	Saranac Lake
Walter	Hamner	LGL	S81	Long Lake
Charles	Hamner, Jr.	LGL	S81	Long Lake
Drew	Hanchett		LG92	Severance
Michael	Hanely		LG92	Queensbury
James	Hanley		LG92	Glens Falls
Charles E.	Hanmer	LGL	FCR	
Ernest J.	Hanmer		RG42	Blue Ridge
Henry	Hanmer	PLD	FCR	
Howard J.	Hanmer	LGL	FCR	
J.	Hanmer	LOS	W	
John	Hanmer	PLD	FCR	
John	Hanmer		RG42	Schroon Lake
Joseph	Hanmer	LGL	FCR	
Joseph	Hanmer	NOH	FCR	
Henry A.	Hanson		RG42	Chippewa Bay
James	Harrington	RAQ	FCR	
John	Harrington		LG92	Old Forge
Wm. F.	Harrington	ESC	RG27	Jay
E.	Harris	WAC	RG27	Katskill Bay
Gordon J.	Harris	WAC	RG20	Stony Creek
Joseph	Harris	CHZ	FCR	
Tyler	Harris	CHA	FCR,W	

Winfield	Harris	CHA	S81	Chateaugay Lake
James	Harrison		LG92	North Creek
Elmer	Hart		RG42	St. Regis Falls
H.	Hart	DIC	W	
Henry	Hart	FUL	FCR	
Henry	Hart	FUL	S95,FCR	Fulton Chain
Ira	Hart	FUL	FCR	
Mike	Hartson	KVL	AL	Present
Rob.	Hartson	LGL	S81,FCR,S95	Long Lake
Harold	Harvey	HEC	RG20	Ohio
L. D.	Harvey	SAC	S81	St. Regis Falls
S. Roy	Harvey	ONC	RG27	Utica
C. M.	Haskins	FRC	RG27	Duane
Charles M.	Haskins	MEA	S95,FCR	Meacham Lake
Jeffrey	Hastings		LG92	Willsboro
Albert J.	Hathaway		RG42	Tupper Lake
Chas. H.	Hathaway	ESC	RG27	Newman
Mel	Hathaway	KVL	AL,FCR,S81	1880s
Ralph J.	Hawkins	FRC	RG27	Malone
Ray	Hawksby		LG92	Plattsburgh
Ahaz	Hayes	BLM	FCR,S81	
Albert A.	Hayes	ESC	RG20	Bloomingdale
Arthur	Hayes	PLD	FCR	
Charles	Hayes	FRC	S81	Whiteface Mountain
Charles	Hayes	LOS	S95	Saranac Lake
Chas. F.	Hayes	FRC	RG27	Saranac Lake
Ellsworth	Hayes	PLD	FCR,S81	
J.	Hayes	STR	W	
Jacob	Hayes	BLM	FCR	
Jacob	Hayes	STR	S81,S95	St. Regis Lake
Millard	Hayes	LOS	S95	Saranac Lake
Rawson L.	Hayes	BLM	FCR	
Ross	Hayes	STR	S81,S95	St. Regis Lake
T.	Hayley	LOS	W	
A. K.	Haynes	HAC	RG27	Piseco
E. D.	Hays	FRC	S74	Whiteface Mountain
M. F.	Hays	FRC	S74	Whiteface Mountain
Herbert	Hazelton	LOS	S95	Saranac Lake
Frank L.	Heald		RG42	St. Huberts
Harold	Heald	KVL	AL,LG92	Present
Henry	Heald	KVL	S81	Keene Valley
Jay O.	Heald		RG42	St. Huberts
Michael	Healey	LNL	FCR	
Thomas	Healy	LOS	S95,FCR	Saranac Lake
Charles	Heaton	POT	W	
C.	Hecox	LOS	W	
Carl	Heilman		LG92	Brant Lake
Dawn	Heilman		LG92	North River
Donald	Helmbrecht		LG92	Saranac Lake
Josiah	Helmer	FUL	W	
D.	Helms	LGL	W,FCR,S95,S74	
David G.	Helms	HAC	RG27	Long Lake
H.	Helms	LGL	W	
James	Helms	FRC	RG27	Malone
John	Helms	LGL	S81,FCR	Long Lake

John M.	Helms	FRC	RG27	Malone
Rouse	Helms	MEA	W	
William	Helms	LGL	S74,S81,W	Long Lake
Henry	Henderson	HAC	RG27	Long Lake
Den	Hennessey	LOS	S95	Saranac Lake
Daniel	Hennessy	TUP	FCR	
Kathryn	Henry		LG92	Indian Lake
David	Hertzner		LG92	North River
Doris	Herwig		LG92	Queensbury
Daniel	Hess	FUL	FCR	
Frederick	Hess	FUL	FCR	
William J.	Heverly		RG42	Waddington
A. F.	Hewitt	FRC	S81	Whiteface Mountain
Clarence	Hewitt	FRC	S81	Whiteface Mountain
George S.	Hewitt	FRC	S81	Whiteface Mountain
Shirley	Hewitt		LG92	Olmstedville
Hiram	Hewitt, Jr.	FRC	S81	Whiteface Mountain
Bob	Hickey	KVL	AL	Present
Charles	Hickok	STR	S81	St. Regis Lake
J. H.	Higby	BGM	FCR	
James	Higby	FUL	S81,W	Fulton Chain
William	Higby	BVR	W	
John E.	Higgins	BMT	S81	Blue Mountain Lake
Charles	Hikock	LOS	S74	Saranac Lake
Roger	Hikok	ESC	RG27	Bloomingdale
Chauncey	Hill	IND	FCR	
John	Hill	HEC	RG27	Old Forge
Arthur	Hinkson	SLC	RG20	South Colton
Daniel	Hinkson	TUP	FCR,S95	
Edward	Hinkson	STR	S81	St. Regis Lake
Ernest	Hinkson	MCC	FCR	
John W.	Hinkston	GRS	FCR	
Herman	Hissink		LG92	Saranac Lake
Beacher	Hitchcock		RG42	Bakers Mills
Bernard	Hitchcock		RG42	Lowville
Harry	Hitchcock	WAC	RG27	Sodom
Jesse	Hitchcock	BVR	W	
John	Hitchcock	BVR	FCR,S81,W	
Merrill	Hitchcock		RG42	Bakers Mills
Wilber	Hitchcock		RG42	Bakers Mills
William	Hitchcock	WAC	RG20,RG27	Bakers Mills
Edgar	Hobart	HEC	RG27	Big Moose
Frank	Hobert	STR	S74,S81	St. Regis
John	Hockenberger III		LG92	Lake Placid
Frederick A.	Hodges	ONC	RG27	Utica
Arthur E.	Hodgkins, Jr.		RG42	Severance
Walter	Hoerning III		LG92	Glens Falls
Charles	Hoffmeister	MOR	FCR	
F.	Holbert	STR	W	
Donald	Holdridge		LG92	Keeseville
Josiah	Holladay	FUL	W	
Myrl W.	Hollenbeck		RG42	Corey's
Bernice	Holly	SCH	FCR	
Frank M.	Holmes		BTG	Old Forge
Timothy	Holmes		LG92	Saranac Lake

Frank	Holt	KVL	AL,FCR	1870s-1900s
Harvey	Holt	KVL	AL,S74,W	1830s-1870s
Hiram	Holt	KVL	AL,S74,S81,W	1870s-1900s
Legrand	Holt	KVL	FCR	
Monroe	Holt	KVL	AL,S81,S74,W	1870s
William Henry	Holt	KVL	AL	1860s
Fred P.	Hood		RG42	Saranac Lake
R. E.	Hopson		RG42	Dolgeville
William E.	Horton		RG42	Utica
Amos	Hough	LGL	FCR,W	
C. D.	Hough	LGL	S74,S81	Long Lake
David	Hough	LGL	FCR,S95	
O.D.	Hough	LGL	FCR,W	
W.	Hough	LOS	W	
Hamor	Houghton		RG42	Long Lake
Clarence E.	House	SLC	RG27	Hammond
Eugene M.	House		BTG	Big Moose
Reuben	Howard	LGL	S74,W	Long Lake
Reuben	Howard	BMT	S81	Blue Mountain Lake
H. S.	Howe	SAC	S81	St. Regis Falls
Arthur	Howland	SLC	RG20,RG27	Cranberry Lake
Fred	Howland	SLC	RG27,RG42	Cranberry Lake
John	Howland	SLC	RG20	Cranberry Lake
Nelson	Howland	SLC	RG27,FCR	Cranberry Lake
Richard S.	Howland		RG42	Cranberry Lake
Spencer	Howland	SLC	RG27,RG42	Cranberry Lake
Willard	Howland	CRA	FCR	
Robert	Hudak		LG92	Lake Placid
J.	Hughes	LOS	W	
John W.	Hughes	HEC	RG27	Old Forge
Leland L.	Hull		RG42	Russell
Aaron	Humes	OSW	FCR	
Warren	Humes	OSW	FCR	
Peter	Hunkins		LG92	Lake Placid
Watson	Hunkins	FRC	S81	Ragged Lake
Alexander	Hunter	ESC	S81,FCR	Tahawus
David C.	Hunter	NEW	S74,S81	Newcomb, Tahawus
George B.	Huntington	FRC	RG20,S95,FCR,RG27	Moody
Elmer	Huntley		RG42	Schroon Lake
Harry S.	Huntley	ESC	RG27,RG42	Olmstedville
George	Hurburlt	CHA	W	
Thomas	Hurlburt	CHA	W	
Thomas	Huryn		LG92	Cadyville
Earl	Hussen	HAC	RG27	Indian Lake
Arvin	Hutchins	IND	FCR	
Carl	Hutchins	HAC	RG27	Indian Lake
Carlos	Hutchins	CED	FCR	
Charles	Hutchins	POT	W	
G. Thomas	Hutchins		LG92	Glens Falls
Hiram	Hutchins	GRS	FCR	
Nancy	Hutchins		LG92	Indian Lake
Oliver	Hutchins	HAC	RG27	Indian Lake
William	Hutchins	IND	FCR	
Harry	Hyatt	ESC	RG20	Boreas River
William	Hyatt		RG42	Ogdensburg

Elbridge	Hyde	MEA	S81,W	Meacham Lake
Edward	Imler		LG92	Plattsburgh
Herbert I.	Ingraham	WAC	RG20	Athol
Giles	Irish	OSW	W	
Jesse	Irish	OSW	W	
Reuben	Irish	OSW	W	
Frank	Irwin		LG92	Hoffmeister
Brent	Isham	KVL	AL	Present
Clint	Isham	KVL	AL	
Edward C.	Isham		RG42,AL	Keene Valley, 1900's
Ted	Isham	KVL	AL	
Stuart	Jackson	SLC	RG27	Forestport
Brent	Jacques		LG92	Gloversville
Peter	Jacques		LG92	Willsboro
George	James	ELZ	FCR	
John	James	ELA	FCR	
E.	Jamison	NEW	FCR	
John	Janack	SLC	RG20,RG42	Wanakena
William	Janeway		LG92	Lake Placid
James	Jaques	STR	FCR	
Emon	Jaquish	STR	S74	St. Regis
Erwin	Jaquish	STR	S81	St. Regis Lake
Elton M.	Jardine		RG42	Waddington
Wm.	Jarvis	HEC	RG27	Big Moose
Alexander	Jeffers	BVR	W	
Edward	Jencks	SCH	FCR	
Frederick	Jencks	SCH	FCR	
Michael	Jencks	SCH	FCR	
Nathan	Jencks	SCH	FCR	
William	Jencks	SCH	FCR	
George S.	Jenkins	RAQ	S95,FCR	Raquette Lake
Sam B.	Jenkins	HAC	RG27,FCR	Raquette Lake
Walter	Jenkins	LOS	S95	Saranac Lake
Ed.	Jenks	SCH	S81	Schroon Lake
W. D.	Jennings	LGL	2S74,S81,W	Long Lake
Amos	Jessie	FRC	RG20	Derriek
Amos J.	Jessie	FRC	RG27,RG20	Derrick
Roger	Jette		LG92	Lake Placid
Charles	Johnson	FUL	FCR	
Dyneley P.	Johnson	HAC	RG20	Sabattis
Edward	Johnson	NOH	FCR	
Elton	Johnson		RG42	Saranac Lake
Elton H.	Johnson	HEC	RG27	Ilion
Ernest	Johnson	LOS	S81	Saranac Lake
Ernest	Johnson	TUP	S81,S95,FCR	Tupper Lake
Frank	Johnson	TUP	FCR,S81	
Frank	Johnson	FUL	S81	Fulton Chain
Frank	Johnson	LOS	S81	Saranac Lake
George E.	Johnson	LOS	S95,FCR	Saranac Lake
Gordon C.	Johnson		RG42	Keeseville
H. D.	Johnson	POT	W	
J. S.	Johnson	TUP	S95	Moody
J. Walter	Johnson	ONC	RG27	Forestport
John M.	Johnson	ESC	RG20	Newcomb
Matthew	Johnson	MEA	FCR,S81,S95	

T. Walter	Johnson		RG42	Forestport
Timothy	Johnson		LG92	Herkimer
Walter E.	Johnson	ESC	RG27	Saranac Lake
William	Johnson	TUP	S81	Tupper Lake
Wm.	Johnson	ONC	RG27	Woodgate
Wm.	Johnson	LOS	S81	Saranac Lake
Barbara	Jones		LG92	North Creek
Charles	Jones	BEL	FCR	
Everett	Jones		RG42	Bakers Mills
Freeland	Jones	RAQ	S95	Raquette Lake
H. P.	Jones	SCH	S81	Schroon River
Hiram	Jones	POT	W	
James F.	Jones	WAC	RG20,RG27	Pottersville
John	Jones	HAC	RG27	Sabbatis
John A.	Jones	RAQ	S95,FCR	Raquette Lake
Maureen	Jones		LG92	Lake Luzerne
Paul	Jones	FUL	S81,W	Fulton Chain
Albert	Jordan	ESC	RG20	Schroon River
Alonzo	Jordan	NOH	FCR	
George	Jordan	NOH	FCR	
Frank	Joscelin	FUL	FCR	
Andrew	Joseph		RG42	Long Lake
Daniel	Josephson		LG92	Old Forge
Clarence V.	Joslin		BTG	Big Moose
F. S.	Joslin		BTG	Old Forge
Charles F.	Joy		RG42	Old Forge
John P.	Joyce	HAC	RG27	Blue Mountain Lake
William J.	Karlan	HAC	RG27	Raquette Lake
A. Linn	Kathan	BMT	S95	Blue Mountain Lake
John S.	Kathan	HAC	RG27	Blue Mountain Lake
Lenuel	Kathan	BMT	FCR	
Schuyler	Kathan	BMT	S95,FCR	Blue Mountain Lake
John	Kays		RG42	Minerva
Eugene	Keet	STR	S81	St. Regis Lake
Eugene	Keith	LNL	FCR	
William	Keith	UPS	FCR	
John	Kellar	LGL	S95	Long Lake
C. R.	Keller	LGL	S74,S81,W	Long Lake
Charles A.	Keller		RG42	Hammond
D.	Keller	LGL	W	
David	Keller	LGL	S74,FCR,S81	Long Lake
Howard L.	Keller		RG42	Hammond
Daniel	Kelley	BMT	FCR	
Diana	Kelley		LG92	Raquette Lake
William	Kelley	BMT	S95	Blue Mountain Lake
John	Kellogg	FUL	W	
James	Kelly	PLD	FCR	
William	Kelly	BMT	FCR	
Paul	Kemp		RG42	Ausable Forks
Henry	Kempton	UPS	FCR	
Henry E.	Kempton	FRC	RG27	Malone
Robert	Kempton	FRC	RG27	Malone
David	Kenison	NEW	FCR	
Bonnie	Kennedy	FRC	RG27	McColloms
Carol	Kennedy		LG92	Tupper Lake

Ed.	Kennedy	PLD	S81,FCR	North Elba
Melvin	Kennedy	PLD	FCR	
Miles	Kennedy	PLD	FCR,S95	
Edwin	Kenney	PLD	S74	North Elba
H.	Kent	LOS	W	
Henry	Kent	STR	S74,S81	St. Regis
Wellington	Kenwell		BTG	Inlet
Clayton V.	Kenyon	WAC	RG20	Athol
Dudley M.	Kenyon	WAC	RG20	Stony Creek
Stanley L.	Kerr		RG42	Oswegatchie
Wm. B.	Kerst	HAC	RG27	Indian Lake
Daniel	Keyes		LG92	Queensbury
Guy	King		RG42	Indian Lake
John	King	LOS	W,FCR,S74	
Joseph	King	HAC	RG27	Indian Lake
Leo E.	King	ESC	RG27	Newcomb
Lester	King		RG42	Indian Lake
Otis Y.	King		RG42	Lake Placid
Phil.	King	STR	S74,W,S81	St. Regis
Robert	King	LOS	S95,FCR	Saranac Lake
Rodney	King		LG92	Old Forge
Stuart	King		RG42	Speculator
Douglas	Kingman	LOS	FCR	
Charles D.	Kirche		BTG	Inlet
Fred	Kirche	FUL	S95	Fulton Chain
Charles	Kirschner	OTT	FCR	
Edward	Kirschner	OTT	FCR	
Charles	Klughart		LG92	Lake George
Frederick C.	Knapp	FRC	RG20	Moody
Geo. H.	Knight	ESC	RG27	Lake Placid Club
Danford	Knowlton	BVR	S81,W	Beaver River
Scott	Knowlton		RG42	Stony Creek
Byron	Knox	SCH	FCR	
John	Knox		LG92	Lake Pleasant
N. B.	Knox	SCH	S81	Schroon Lake
Otto A.	Koenig	ONC	RG27	Rome
Stephen	Koop-Angelicola		LG92	Elizabethtown
Lubomir	Kral		LG92	Lake Placid
Thomas	Kravis		LG92	Northville
Seymour	Kreds	HAC	RG27	Hoffmeister
Henry	Kreutzer	MOR	FCR	
Fred W.	Kreuzer		BTG	Honnedaga
Geo. W.	Kreuzer	HAC	RG27,RG42	Morehouseville
Burt	Kronk	UPS	FCR	
David	Kronk	UPS	FCR	
Nathan	Kullman		LG92	Indian Lake
N. Vivian	La Casse	ESC	RG27	Newcomb
Jos. J.	La Fleur	SLC	RG27	Wanakana
George	La Fountain	TUP	FCR	
Meadore	La Fountain	MEA	W	
"Cal"(Alex.)	La Prairie	RAQ	FCR	
"Doc"(Francis)	La Prairie	RAQ	FCR	
Joseph	La Prairie	MOO	FCR	
Anne	LaBastille		LG92	Big Moose
William	LaBeau	FRC	RG20	Saranac Lake

Harold E.	LaBounty		RG42	St. Regis Falls
Louis S.	LaClair	HEC	RG27,RG42	Old Forge
Jos.	LaFlair	SLC	RG27	Lisbon
Moses H.	LaFountain	SLC	RG20	Conifer
William E.	LaFountain	TUP	S95	Tupper Lake
Charley	LaMay	MEA	W	
Carl	LaMont		BTG	Fulton Chain
James	LaMont		BTG	Fulton Chain
Alfred	LaPell	HAC	RG27	Long Lake
John	LaPelle	LGL	S95	Long Lake
Oren B.	LaPelle	LGL	S95	Long Lake
Wales	LaPelle	HAC	RG27,RG42	Long Lake
Alphonse	LaPlante		RG42	Faust
David	LaPointe		LG92	Olmstedville
Robert	LaPointe		LG92	Hudson Falls
Ernest	LaPrairie		LG92	Blue Mt. Lake
Charles	LaVarnway		RG42	Ogdensburg
A.	Labounty	STR	W	
T.	Labounty	STR	W	
Theodore	Labourly	STR	S81	St. Regis Lake
M.	Labrake	STR	S81,S74	St. Regis Lake
Mark	Lacek		LG92	Wells
Robert A.	Ladd	MEA	S95,FCR	Meacham Lake
Roderick	Lagoy		RG42	Bolton Landing
Arthur	Laiacona		LG92	Glens Falls
C. W.	Lamb	ESC	RG27,RG42	Keene Valley
Cecil E.	Lamb	WAC	RG27,RG42	Bolton Landing
Edward L.	Lamb		RG42	Bolton Landing
Franklin C.	Lamb	FRC	RG27	Malone
Fred	Lamb	KVL	AL,FCR	1890s-1900s
George W.	Lamb	KVL	AL,RG42	1914-1950s
Levi S.	Lamb	KVL	AL,W,S74,S81	1870s-1916
Wesley "Pete"	Lamb	KVL	AL,FCR	1870s-1900s
Levi T.	Lamon	FRC	RG20	Moody
Justin	Lamos	LGL	FCR	
Maurice B.	Lamos		RG42	Long Lake
Stephen D.	Lamos	NEW	FCR	
"Cash"	Lamoy	PLD	FCR	
Brainerd	Lamoy		RG42	Moody
Henry	Lamoy	FRC	S81	Whiteface Mountain
Joseph	Lamoy	LOS	S95,FCR	Saranac Lake
Kenneth W.	Lamoy		RG42	Moody
Lorie	Lamoy	FRC	RG27	Moody
Marshall	Lamoy	PLD	S95,FCR	Lake Placid
McDonough	Lamoy	RAB	FCR	
Peter	Lamoy	PLD	S74	North Elba
Richard	Lamoy		RG42	Tupper Lake
Stephen B.	Lamoy	FRC	RG20,RG27	Moody
Gerald M.	Lamphear		RG42	Raquette Lake
Orrin	Lamphear		RG42	Raquette Lake
Claudius R.	Lamy	FRC	RG20	Saranac Lake
Desmond	Lance		RG42	Long Lake
John	Lando		LG92	Wilmington
Albert A.	Lansing		RG42	Hollis
Eric	Lanthier		LG92	Tupper Lake

Geo.	Lanz	ONC	RG27	Boonville
Charles	Lapell	LGL	FCR,S81	
Orin B.	Lapell	LGR	FCR,S81	
John	Lapell,Jr.	LGR	FCR	
Calvin	Laprairie	NOR	S81,S95	North River
Dock	Laprairie	NOR	S81	North River
Joseph	Laprairie	NOR	S81	North River
Will	Laprairie	NOR	S81	North River
Clarence	Laramay	FRC	RG27	Faust
Ray	Larkin		RG42	Syracuse
Bob	Lashaway	KVL	AL	1952-1956
Will	Lashaway	KVL	AL,RG27	1920s
Dan	Lathrop	MEA	W	
Edward J.	Latray		RG42	Cranberry Lake
John H.	Lauther	HEC	RG20,RG27	Old Forge
Allen	Laverty	ELZ	FCR	
James	Laverty	ELZ	FCR	
William	Laverty	ELZ	FCR	
Wilmer	Lavoy		RG42	Faust
George	Laware	MEA	FCR	
Abe	Lawrence	HAC	RG27	Speculator
Abram	Lawrence	LKP	FCR	
Brett	Lawrence	KVL	AL	Present
Smith	Lawrence		LG92	Keene Valley
Smith Beede	Lawrence	KVL	AL	1940s-1950s
Moes	Lawyer	STR	S81	St. Regis Lake
Justin	Laymas	LGL	S81	Long Lake
Carl	LeBeau	FRC	RG27	Saranac Lake
David	LeBlanc		LG92	Tupper Lake
David	LeClair	KVL	AL	Present
Wm. B.	Lee	FRC	RG27	Malone
William	Leege		LG92	Morrisonville
Chas. L.	Lees	ESC	RG27	Lake Placid Club
Minot C.	Legacy		RG42	Hammond
Benjamin	Lehey	NEW	FCR	
John	Leies	FRC	RG27	Saranac Lake
Milo	Leitch	HAC	RG27,BTG	Inlet
Joseph	Lemere	FRC	RG27	Tupper Lake
James	Leonard		LG92	Warrensburg
John	Leonard	POT	W	
Michael J.	Leonard		RG42	Tupper Lake
Christine	Leskovec		LG92	Bloomingdale
Abraham	Lester	BEL	FCR	
Charles	Lester	TUP	S95,FCR	Moody
Matthew	Levenson		LG92	Lake Placid
Gary	Lewandrowski		LG92	Poland
E.	Lewis	PLD	W	
Edward	Lewis	LOS	FCR	
George F.	Lewis	HAC	RG20	Long Lake
James	Lewis	BVR	FCR,S81,W	
Leon	Liberty	ESC	RG27	Newcomb
Lawrence	Liddle	ONC	RG27	Forestport
Walter	Linck		LG92	Lake Pleasant
Frank	Lindsay	POT	W	
Clarence D.	Lints	SLC	RG27	Hammond

Geo. Irving	Little	LEC	RG27	Croghan
Leslie O.	Lloyd	WAC	RG27	Diamond Point
Daniel	Locke		LG92	Indian Lake
Hosea G.	Locke	IND	FCR	
J. Orvis	Locke	HAC	RG27	Indian Lake
Joseph	Locke	IND	FCR	
Kurt	Locke		LG92	Glens Falls
Marvin T.	Locke	IND	FCR	
Nathaniel	Locke	IND	FCR	
Willard	Locke	IND	S81,FCR	Indian Lake
Mark	Lockwood		LG92	Cold Brook
William	Long		LG92	Plattsburgh
Norman	Lord	POT	S81	Raquette River
Jacob	Loritson	LOS	S81	Saranac Lake
Frank	Loson		BTG	Inlet
Henry	Lotman	BVR	FCR	
Fred.	Loveland	ALA	S81,FCR	Olmsteadville
Harry	Loveland	ALA	FCR	
John	Loveland	ALA	FCR	
Morris	Loveland	ALA	FCR	
P.	Loverin	MER	W	
Arthur H.	Lucas	HAC	RG27	Inlet
Sumner J.	Lucas		RG42	Parishville
Vernie	Lucier	FRC	RG27	Tupper Lake
J.	Lunt	LOS	W	
J. H.	Lunt	STR	S81	St. Regis Lake
Geo. N.	Lycett	ESC	RG27	Schroon Lake
Seth	Lyon	FRC	RG27	Paul Smiths
Harry W.	Lyons		RG42	Ausable Forks
M.	Lyons		BTG	McKeever
Harrison F.	MacCarter	SLC	RG20,RG27,RG42	Potsdam
A. Hector	MacDonald		RG42	Ogdensburg
C.	MacDougall	FRC	RG27	Saranac Lake
Clinton	MacDougall		RG42	Saranac Lake
A.	MacEdward	HEC	RG27	Big Moose
Roderick L.	Mackenzie	KVL	S81	Keene Valley
Frank	Macy		RG42	Paul Smiths
Paul	Mader		LG92	Saranac Lake
Kevin	Magde		LG92	Remsen
Timothy	Mahoney		LG92	Indian Lake
Charles H.	Mallott		RG42	Hammond
Rudolph	Malmberg		RG42	Piseco Lake
Daniel	Malone		LG92	Plattsburgh
Fillmore	Maloney	STR	FCR	
G.	Maloney	STR	W	
Gard.	Maloney	STR	S74,S81	St. Regis
Gardner	Maloney	BLM	FCR	
R. H.	Manard	MEA	FCR	
Basil	Mandigo	SLC	RG27	Hammond
John	Mandigo	SLC	RG27	Hammond
J.	Manley	STR	W	
Benj.	Manning	FRC	RG27	Lake Clear Junction
Peter	Manning	ESC	RG27	Wilmington
Ransom	Manning	LOS	FCR	
Rant	Manning	LOS	S95	Saranac Lake

William	Manning	LOS	FCR	
illiam	Manning	UPS	S95	Saranac Inn
Edgar	Mantle	OSW	FCR	
William	Mantle	OSW	FCR	
Charles	Manwaring		RG42	Baldwinsville
Bert	Marcellus		RG42	Wells
Gary	Marchuk		LG92	Lake Placid
H. B.	Marden	GRS	FCR	
Hector	Marden	POT	S81	Raquette River
S. H.	Marden	GRS	FCR	
Walter	Marden	POT	W	
Fred	Marino		RG42	Watertown
E. L.	Marks		BTG	Old Forge
Camelia	Maroun		LG92	Tupper Lake
Charles	Marsh	OSW	W	
John	Marsh	FRC	RG27	Dickinson Center
David	Marshall	FRC	S81	Whiteface Mountain
John	Marshall		LG92	Lake Placid
C.	Martin	STR	W	
Cal	Martin	RAQ	S95	Raquette Lake
Charles	Martin	LOS	FCR,S81,S95	
Charles	Martin		BTG	Big Moose
Charles	Martin		RG42	Lake Placid
Douglas E.	Martin	STR	FCR,W,S74,S81,S95	
Edward	Martin	RAQ	FCR	
Frederick E.	Martin	STR	FCR,S74,S81,W	
George	Martin	BLM	FCR,W,S74,S81	
George N.	Martin		RG42	Oneida
George W.	Martin		RG42	Hawkeye
Henry H.	Martin	STR	FCR,W,S74,S81	
Leander	Martin		RG42	Gabriels
Stephen C.	Martin	LOS	S74,W,FCR,S81	Saranac Lake
W.	Martin	LOS	W	
Walter	Martin	FRC	RG27	Saranac Lake
Wilbur G.	Martin		RG42	St. Regis Falls
William J.	Martin	MEA	S95	Meacham Lake
Victor	Mason	STR	S81	St. Regis Lake
Greg	Mather		LG92	Olmstedville
John	Matthews	RAW	FCR	
Nicholas	Mauro		LG92	Wells
Nick	Mauro III		LG92	Wells
Colin	Maury		LG92	Pottersville
Floyd L.	Maxam	WAC	RG20	Garnet
Frank	Maxam	NOR	FCR	
Fred	Maxam	HAC	RG27	Raquette Lake
George W.	Maxam	WAC	RG20	Stony Creek
Frank H.	Maxim	WAC	RG20	Garnet
George	May	KVL	AL	1900s
M.	Mayhue	LOS	W	
Ashley	Maynard	ESC	RG27	Lake Placid
James	Maynard		RG42	Lake Placid
John	Maynard	DUA	FCR	
R. H.	Maynard	MEA	S95	Meacham Lake
W. J.	McAleese	SLC	RG27	Cranberry Lake
Wm. J.	McAleese, Sr.		RG42	Cranberry Lake

Martin	McAveigh		RG42	Long Lake
Charles	McBride	TUP	FCR	
James	McBride	TUP	FCR	
James	McBride	TUP	S95	Moody
John	McBroom	OSW	FCR	
Walter	McCabe		RG42	Oswegatchie
Charles	McCaffery	UPS	FCR,S81	
Chester	McCaffery	STR	FCR,S81	
Charles	McCaffrey	UPS	S95	Saranac Inn
Chester	McCaffrey	LOS	S74	Saranac Lake
Harry	McCane		RG42	Indian Lake
Wm.	McCarthy	STR	S81	St. Regis Lake
James	McClellan	LOS	S74,W	Saranac Lake
Cornelius	McCloskey	NEW	FCR	
A. C.	McCollum	STR	S74,S81,W	St. Regis
Byron	McCollum	OSW	FCR	
James	McConnell	OTT	FCR	
James	McCormic	LEW	FCR	
Frank	McCormick	FUL	S81	Fulton Chain
James	McCormick	IND	S81	Indian Lake
P. H.	McCormick	FRC	RG27	Coreys
Cecil R.	McCoy	ESC	RG27	Newcomb
Charles	McCoy	LOS	FCR	
Allen	McCuen	POT	W	
Lewis	McCuen	POT	W	
Robert	McCuen	GRS	FCR	
Warren	McDoner	STR	S81	St. Regis Lake
Brian	McDonnell		LG92	Saranac Lake
William	McDonough		LG92	Port Henry
A. L.	McEwen	SLC	RG27	Childwold
William	McGill		LG92	Lake Clear
Bruce	McGinn		LG92	Olmstedville
Timothy	McGinn		LG92	Olmstedville
Michael	McGuire	IND	S81	Indian Lake
Michael	McGuire	BMT	S95,FCR	Blue Mountain Lake
Dennis M.	McHugh	LEC	RG27	West Leyden
Harry Paul	McIntyre	HAC	RG27,RG42	Long Lake
Andrea	McKee		LG92	Johnsburg
Keith	McKenney		LG92	North River
A.	McKensie	LOS	W,S74,S81	
J.B.	McLaughlin	BMT	FCR	
John	McLaughlin	STR	FCR,W,S74,S81,S95	
Agnus	McLean		LG92	North Creek
Alvin	McLean Jr.		LG92	Willsboro
W. B.	McLear	SLC	RG27	Chippewa Bay
James	McLelland	LOS	S81	Saranac Lake
Stephen	McNally		LG92	Olmstedville
Susan	McNally		LG92	Olmstedville
Dan.	McNeil	SAC	S81	St. Regis Falls
Daniel	McNeil	MCC	FCR	
J.	McNeil	DIC	W	
John	McNeil	SAC	FCR	
Orlo W.	McNeil		RG42	Ogdensburg
D.	McNeil, Jr.	DIC	W	
James	McPhail		RG42	Alexandria Bay

E.	McPherson	CHA	W	
George	McPherson	CHA	W	
Peter W.	McRea	KVL	S81	Keene Valley
Daniel	Meacham	FRC	RG20	Rochester
James J.	Meacham	FRC	RG20	St. Regis Falls
Charles	Mead		LG92	Glens Falls
Greg	Meader		LG92	Lake George
Samuel	Medema		LG92	Long Lake
William	Meehan		LG92	Fort Ann
John	Meek	FUL	W	
Nina	Meiselman		LG92	Saranac Lake
Don	Mellor		LG92	Lake Placid
Theodore	Melvin	LOS	S95,FCR	Saranac Lake
Ed	Mendus		LG92	Gloversville
Peter J.	Merkes	HEC	RG27	Forestport
Peter W.	Merkes	HEC	RG27	Old Forge
Geoffrey	Merrett		LG92	Glens Falls
C. A.	Merrill	SAC	S81	St. Regis Falls
Charels E.	Merrill	CLC	RG20	Merrill
Charles E.	Merrill	CHA	FCR	
D. S.	Merrill	CHA	FCR	
D. W.	Merrill	CHA	W	
E. M.	Merrill	LNL	FCR	
Shepard	Merrill	CHA	FCR	
W. P.	Merrill	CHA	FCR	
William	Merrill	UPS	FCR	
O.	Merrills	DIC	W	
B.F.	Merwin	BMT	FCR	
R. L.	Merwin	BMT	S95	Blue Mountain Lake
Ralph	Merwin	BMT	FCR	
Mark	Meschinelli		LG92	Plattsburgh
Grace	Michelin		LG92	Saranac Lake
Reuben C.	Mick		RG42	Long Lake
Reuben M.	Mick	HAC	RG27,RG42	Raquette Lake
V.	Mihills	FRC	S74	Whiteface Mountain
Wm.	Mikills	FRC	S81	Whiteface Mountain
Raymond	Milks		RG42	Ohio
George R.	Miller		RG42	Kalurah
J. H.	Miller	LOS	S95	Saranac Lake
J. W.	Miller	STR	W	
James	Miller		LG92	Bolton Landing
John	Miller	BMT	S81	Blue Mountain Lake
John H.	Miller	LOS	FCR	
Sandra	Miller		LG92	Gloversville
Jack	Minder		LG92	North Creek
Ronald	Miner		LG92	Keene Valley
Moses	Minie	CHZ	FCR	
Napoleon J.	Minney	FRC	RG27	Lake Clear Junction
Michael	Minor	KVL	AL	1900s
Chas.	Mitchell	BMT	S81	Blue Mountain Lake
Jno.	Mitchell	HAC	RG27	Indian Lake
Jos. C.	Mitchell	ESC	RG27	Minerva
Joseph	Mitchell	IND	S81	Indian Lake
Edward C.	Mitchell, Jr.		RG42	Indian Lake
Alonzo L.	Mix	LGL	S74,W,S81	Long Lake

David	Mix	LGL	S74,W,S81,S95	Long Lake
Vere R.	Mix		RG42	Gabriels
William	Mix	LGL	S95	Long Lake
Michael	Mollica		LG92	Warrensburg
John	Monaghan	OSW	FCR	
Arthur	Monegan	FRC	S81	Ragged Lake
Donnie	Monroe		LG92	Chestertown
Ben	Monty	STR	S81,S74	St. Regis Lake
"Clev"	Moody	LOS	FCR	
"Tidd"	Moody	LOS	FCR	
A. H.	Moody		RG42	Saranac Lake
Abram	Moody	FRC	RG27	Saranac Lake
Adel	Moody	LOS	S81	Saranac Lake
Alric B.	Moody	LOS	S95,S81,S74	Saranac Lake
Benjamin R.	Moody	LOS	FCR,W,S74,S81	
Charles	Moody	KVL	AL	1900s
Charlie	Moody	TUP	S81	Tupper Lake
Cleveland	Moody	LOS	S95	Saranac Lake
Cort	Moody		RG42	Saranac Lake
Cort	Moody	LOS	W	
D.	Moody	LOS	W	
D. L.	Moody	LOS	W	
Daniel S.	Moody	LOS	S81,S74	Saranac Lake
Edmund	Moody		RG42	Saranac Lake
Fayette	Moody	LOS	S74,W,S81,S95	Saranac Lake
Fred J.	Moody	TUP	FCR	
Fred W.	Moody	TUP	S95	Moody
Fred.	Moody	TUP	S81	Tupper Lake
George W.	Moody	STR	S81,FCR	St. Regis Lake
Harvey	Moody	LOS	W	
Hiram	Moody	LOS	S95	Saranac Lake
James	Moody	LOS	FCR	
James W.	Moody	FRC	RG27	Upper Saranac
John	Moody		RG42	Saranac Lake
L.	Moody	LOS	W	
Loney	Moody	STR	S74,S81	St. Regis
Martin	Moody	TUP	S81	Tupper Lake
Martin	Moody	LOS	W	
Milo M.	Moody	ESC	RG27,RG42	Saranac Lake
Richard	Moody	LOS	S74,W	Saranac Lake
Robert S.	Moody	LOS	S95,FCR	Saranac Lake
Tid	Moody	LOS	W	
W.	Moody	STR	W	
William	Moody	LOS	S74	Saranac Lake
Charles D.	Mooney	LEC	RG27	Lyons Falls
John	Moore	ESC	S74	Tahawus
Loring F.	Moore	SLC	RG27	Benson Mines
Clarence J.	Morcy		RG42	Old Forge
Edith	Morcy		RG42	Old Forge
Arthur	Morehouse	HAC	RG27	Bakers Mills
Douglas	Morehouse	HAC	RG27	Bakers Mills
F.	Morehouse	LOS	W	
Florian J.	Morehouse		RG42	Bolton Landing
Lewis J.	Morehouse	WAC	RG20	Bakers Mills
Mike	Morehouse		LG92	Glens Falls

W.	Morehouse	LOS	W	
Walter	Morehouse	HAC	RG27,RG42	Indian Lake
Warren W.	Morehouse	LOS	S81	Saranac Lake
Wm.	Morehouse	LOS	S81	Saranac Lake
J. W.	Morris		BTG	Big Moose
George	Morrison	KVL	AL,RG27,RG42	1911-1950s
Tom	Morrison	KVL	W	
Frank	Morse	ESC	RG20	Minerva
Kevin	Morse		LG92	North River
Richard	Morse		LG92	Warrensburg
Clifford	Mossey		LG92	Plattsburgh
Wm. B.	Mott	SLC	RG27	Cranberry Lake
Arvin	Moulton		RG42	Indian Lake
Howard A.	Moxan	WAC	RG27	Garnet
Paula	Mroz-Rubinstein		LG92	Gloversville
Jamer	Mucle	FUL	FCR	
George	Muir	CRA	S81,FCR	Cranberry Lake
John	Muir	CRA	S81	Cranberry Lake
H. N.	Mullen	OSW	FCR	
Ben.	Munsil	STR	S74	St. Regis
Edward	Murphy		LG92	Glens Falls
William	Murphy		LG92	Chestertown
Carl A.	Murray	SLC	RG20	Stark
George	Mussen	MEA	S81	Meacham Lake
George	Mussen	LOS	S95,FCR,W,S74	Saranac Lake
Leonard	Mussen		RG42	Saranac Lake
Kathleen	Myer		LG92	Lake Placid
Wm.	Myers	SLC	RG27	Star Lake
John	Nabet	HAC	RG27	Long Lake
Gerald	Narron	FRC	RG27	Tupper Lake
William	Nash	ONC	RG27	McKeever
Wm.	Nash	FRC	RG27	Lake Clear
Roy J.	Neely	HEC	RG27	Old Forge
John	Negus	OSW	W	
George U.	Neil, Jr.	MCC	FCR	
Albert	Nejmeh		LG92	Paul Smiths
Joseph	Newell	STR	S74	St. Regis
Joseph L.	Newell	STR	S81	St. Regis Lake
Joseph W.	Newell	STR	S81	St. Regis Lake
Lovel	Newell	STR	S74,S81,S95	St. Regis
Sylvester	Newell	STR	S74,S81	St. Regis
George	Newton	HAC	RG27	Raquette Lake
Robert	Nicholas	ESC	RG27	Lake Placid
Paul	Nichols		LG92	Glens Falls
R. W.	Nichols	LOS	S74,W,S81,FCR	Saranac Lake
Bob	Nicholson	KVL	AL	Present
F.	Nicholson	LOS	W	
Jamie	Nile		LG92	Raquette Lake
J.	Niles	DIC	W	
Kerry	Noble		LG92	Warrensburg
Joseph K.	Noel		RG42	Lyon Mountain
Edward	Norman	SLC	RG20	Stark
John	Norman		LG92	Weavertown
Orvile L.	North	WAC	RG20,RG27	North River
A.	Norton	STR	S74	St. Regis

B. A.	Norton	ONC	RG27	Forestport
E. J.	Noyes	STR	S74	St. Regis
Ed.	Noyes	STR	S81	St. Regis Lake
George	Nunn	OSW	FCR	
William J.	Nurney		RG42	Parishville
Herbert J.	Nye	LEC	RG27	Lowville
Hubert	Nye	KVL	AL	1920s-1980s
W.	Nye	LOS	W	
Wm. B.	Nye	PLD	S74,W	North Elba
Thomas	O'Brien		LG92	Olmstedville
Timothy	O'Brien		LG92	Lake Placid
Bill	O'Connor	KVL	AL	Present
Walter	O'Connor	ALA	FCR	
James	O'Malley	UPS	FCR	
Peter	O'Malley	UPS	S95,FCR	Saranac Inn
Pete	O'Mallie	STR	S81	St. Regis Lake
Patrick H.	O'Neil	STR	FCR,S95	
George	Oaster		RG42	Number Four
David	Olbert		LG92	Newcomb
Glenn	Oldak		LG92	Lake Luzerne
M. J.	Oley		BTG	White Lake Corners
John	Olsen	SLC	RG27	Massena Springs
John	Olson	SLC	RG27	Wanakena
Malcolm	Orcutt		RG42	Dickinson Center
John	Ormsby	PLD	FCR	
Stanley	Ormsby		RG42	Bolton Landing
Crary	Orvis	FRC	RG27	Paul Smiths
Sherrell	Osborn		LG92	Lake Placid
Elmer	Osgood	LEW	FCR	
Eugene	Osgood	IND	S81	Indian Lake
Levi	Osgood	IND	S81	Indian Lake
Edward	Ostberg		LG92	Lake George
Albert S.	Otis	STR	FCR,S81	
Alfred H.	Otis	STR	FCR,S95	
Charles Wesley	Otis	KVL	AL	
Ed.	Otis	LOS	S74,W	Saranac Lake
Edward	Otis	UPS	FCR,S81	
Frank	Otis	STR	FCR	
Fred.	Otis	STR	S81,S74	St. Regis Lake
George	Otis	UPS	FCR,S81,S95	
George	Otis	LOS	W	
J.	Otis	LOS	S74	Saranac Lake
J. Wesley	Otis	KVL	AL	1870s-1900s
John	Otis	KVL	AL	Present
John	Otis	STR	S74,S81	St. Regis
John W.	Otis	ESC	RG27	St. Huberts
Joseph	Otis	UPS	S81,FCR	Upper Saranac Lake
Millard	Otis	UPS	S81	Upper Saranac Lake
Myron	Otis	STR	FCR,S74,S81	
Myron J.	Otis	FRC	RG27,S95	Paul Smiths
Orrin	Otis	BLM	FCR,S74,S81,S95	
Oscar J.	Otis	FRC	RG27,RG42	Paul Smiths
Oscar J.	Otis		RG42	Paul Smiths
S.	Otis	STR	W	
Sylvester	Otis	FRC	RG27,S74,S81	Paul Smiths

Verian D.	Otis	HAC	RG20	Long Lake
James	Owens	KVL	AL,FCR	1870s-1913
Will	Owens	KVL	AL	1890s-1920s
Floyd H.	Oxner	SLC	RG27	Cranberry Lake
Henry	Packard	FRC	S81,FCR	Whiteface Mountain
Benajah	Page	LKP	FCR	
David L.	Page		RG42	Speculator
Perry	Page	LKP	FCR	
Ralph	Page	LKP	FCR	
Ernest A.	Paige		RG42	Ogdensburg
Ann	Palen		LG92	Keene
Edward	Palen		LG92	Keene
Fred	Palmater	HEC	RG27	Little Falls
C. H.	Palmer	LGL	W,FCR	
Cyrus	Palmer	LGL	S81	Long Lake
Cyrus	Palmer	LGL	S95	Long Lake
George	Palmer	LGL	S95,FCR	Long Lake
Leslie	Palmer	LGL	S95	Long Lake
Leslie A.	Palmer	HAC	RG27,RG42	Deerland
Lester	Palmer	LGL	FCR	
Mark	Palmieri		LG92	Stillwater
Jeanne	Panek		LG92	Wilmington
Jno. F.	Paquin	FRC	RG27	Mountain View
Lawrence	Paquin		RG42	Duane
A.	Parker	NEW	W	
Abner S.	Parker	ESC	RG27,RG42	Newcomb
Adelbert	Parker	NEW	S74	Newcomb
Alvin	Parker	IND	S81	Indian Lake
Capt. Calvin	Parker	LGL	W,FCR	
Elbert	Parker	NEW	S81	Newcomb
Frank C.	Parker	KVL	S81	Keene Valley
George	Parker	WOD	FCR	
Henry	Parker	NEW	S74,W	Newcomb
Peter	Parker	HAC	RG20	Lake Pleasant
Ralph E.	Parker	ESC	RG27	Newcomb
Sam	Parker	NEW	W,FCR,S81	
Thomas	Parker	KVL	S81,W	Keene Valley
Kenneth	Parks		RG42	St. Regis Falls
Archie L.	Paro		RG42	DeGrasse
Horace C.	Paro		RG42	Canton
Henry E.	Parslow	HAC	RG20	Lake Pleasant
Anselm	Parsons	FRC	RG27	Saranac Lake
Anson	Parsons	LOS	FCR	
Ben	Parsons		BTG	Old Forge
Ben	Parsons	HEC	RG27,RG42	Old Forge
Ben	Parsons	FUL	S95,FCR	Fulton Chain
Ira H.	Parsons	HEC	RG27,FCR,S95	Old Forge
George	Partlow	OSW	FCR	
Webster	Partlow	OSW	FCR	
Frank "Pat"	Partridge	KVL	AL,RG42	1932-1950s
Geo.	Pashley	HAC	RG27,FCR	Indian Lake
R. Douglas	Paterson		LG92	Warrensburg
E.L.	Patterson	BLM	FCR	
Elverdo	Patterson	STR	S74,W,S81,S95	St. Regis
Fred	Patterson	UPS	S95	Saranac Inn

James	Patterson	BLM	FCR	
James	Patterson	STR	S81,S74,W	St. Regis Lake
Robert	Patterson		LG92	Brasher Falls
Susan	Patterson		LG92	Lake Clear
Bradley	Paye		LG92	Willsboro
Ben	Payne	HAC	RG27	Indian Lake
Lawrence	Payne		RG42	Inlet
Louie H.	Payne		RG42	Glens Falls
Louis	Payne	HAC	RG27	Inlet
Richard C.	Payne		RG42	Inlet
Wm. H.	Payne	HAC	RG27	Inlet
Thomas H.	Peacock	FRC	RG20	Saranac Lake
Tom	Peacock	PLD	S81,FCR	North Elba
Agness	Peak	CHA	W	
Robert	Pearsall		RG42	Old Forge
Harlow	Pearsons	POT	W	
Warren N.	Peck		RG42	St. Regis Falls
Burton	Peck IV		LG92	Paul Smiths
Mark	Peduzzi		LG92	Jay
Charles H.	Peer		RG42	Bolton
George	Pelleren	TUP	FCR	
Ephram	Pelon	HAC	RG27,RG42	Indian Lake
John	Peltier	LKP	S81	Lake Pleasant
Thos.	Pennie	BVR	S81	Chases Lake
Donald W.	Perkins	HEC	RG27,RG42	Old Forge
E. P.	Perkins	MEA	S95,FCR	Meacham Lake
Ezekiel P.	Perkins	FRC	RG27	Duane
Isaiah	Perkins	HAC	RG20	Speculator
J. J.	Perkins		BTG	Old Forge
Sidney	Perkins Jr.		LG92	Boonville
Harry	Perry		RG42	Hammond
John H.	Perry	TUP	S95	Tupper Lake
Moses	Perry	FRC	S81	Whiteface Mountain
Wm. R.	Perry	SLC	RG27	Edwardsville
Jason	Persons		LG92	Bakers Mills
Joseph	Persons		RG42	Brant Lake
Joseph L.	Persons	WAC	RG20,RG27	Horicon
Kenneth R.	Persons		RG42,RG27	Brant Lake
John Edw.	Peterson	HEC	RG27	Ilion
Wm. E.	Petty, Jr.		RG42	Corey's
A. A.	Phelps	SAC	FCR	
Ed	Phelps	KVL	AL,S74,W,S81,FCR	1860s-1930s
Frederick	Phelps	OSW	FCR	
Orson S.	Phelps	KVL	AL,W,S74	1840s-1880s
James	Philbrook	LOS	S74,S81	Saranac Lake
Clifford	Pierce	BMT	S81	Blue Mountain Lake
Clifton	Pierce	RAQ	FCR	
E. C.	Pierce	RAQ	S95	Raquette Lake
Seth	Pierce	BMT	S81,S95	Blue Mountain Lake
Seth M.	Pierce	RAQ	FCR	
Seth M.	Pierce,Jr.	RAQ	FCR,S95	
Harlow	Piersons	POT	S81	Raquette River
George	Pillerin	TUP	S95	Moody
George	Pittenger	TUP	FCR	
Melvin	Place		RG42	Albany

Edward	Plimpton		RG42	Alexandria Bay
Frank	Plimpton		RG42	Alexandria Bay
Henry J.	Plumadore		RG42	Clayburgh
J. D.	Plumbley	LGL	W	
John E.	Plumbley	LGL	S74,W	Long Lake
Levi	Plumby	HAC	RG27	Long Lake
Charles	Plumley	FRC	RG27	Bloomingdale
Daniel	Plumley		LG92	Keene Valley
Frank*	Plumley	LGL	FCR,S81	*sons of "Honest John" Plumley
Handy*	Plumley	LGL	FCR,S95	
J.D.*	Plumley	LGL	FCR	
Jeremiah	Plumley	LGL	S74,S81	Long Lake
Jerry D.	Plumley	LGL	S95	Long Lake
John E.	Plumley	LGL	S81,S95	Long Lake
John E.*	Plumley	LGL	FCR	
R. D.	Plumley	HAC	RG27	Long Lake
Riley*	Plumley	LGL	FCR,S95	
Wallace	Plumley	LGL	S81	Long Lake
Louis	Pollock		RG42	Massena
A. W.	Pond	FRC	S81	Ragged Lake
Frank G.	Pond	FRC	S81	Ragged Lake
George	Pond	MEA	W	
Eric	Poole		LG92	Saranac Lake
"Allie"	Porter	IND	FCR	
Lewis	Porter		RG42	Inlet
Samuel	Porter	HAC	RG27	Long Lake
Carl L.	Poser		RG42	Saranac Lake
Henry	Potter	POT	S81,W	Raquette River
Lee	Potter	WAC	RG27	Glens Falls
J. H.	Powell	FRC	RG27	Dickinson Center
Arthur	Pratt	WAC	RG27	Diamond Point
Harvey	Pratt	ESC	RG27	Ticonderoga
Ralph H.	Pratt		RG42	Ogdensburg
Russell	Pray		LG92	Keeseville
James R.	Prellevitz	FRC	RG27,RG42	Rainbow Lake
Mark	Prendeville		LG92	North River
Julia	Preston		RG42	Higgins Bay
Francis	Prevere	SLC	RG27	Hammond
Burt	Proctor	UPS	FCR	
Asa	Puffer	FUL	8W	
Charles	Puffer	BVR	S81	Watson
Charles	Puffer	FUL	S81	Fulton Chain
G. D.	Puffer		BTG	Big Moose
Orlin	Puffer	BVR	S81	Watson
Sylvester	Puffer	FUL	S81	Fulton Chain
Mary	Purcell		LG92	Saranac Lake
Patrick	Purcell		LG92	Saranac Lake
Albertus	Purdy	FRC	S81	Ragged Lake
Nelson	Purdy	FRC	S81	Ragged Lake
Charles	Quartiers	STR	FCR,W	
Robert	Rafferty		LG92	Lake Placid
Richard	Railton		LG92	Wilmington
Ralph E.	Raine	HAC	RG27	Long Lake
Emile P.	Ramie		RG42	Ogdensburg

D. Frank	Randall	WAC	RG27,RG42	North Creek
Ernest	Randall	HAC	RG27	Piseco
Harry W.	Randall	WAC	RG27	North Creek
Anthony	Randazzo		LG92	Indian Lake
A. A.	Rarick		BTG	Inlet
John J.	Rarick		BTG	Inlet
Harrison	Rasbach	CRA	FCR	
William	Rasbach	CRA	FCR	
John	Rawson		LG92	Lake George
Jeanne	Ray		LG92	Fort Ann
Nathaniel	Ray	IND	S81	Indian Lake
Bernard	Rayder	WAC	RG20	West Stony Creek
Fred.	Raymond	ALA	S81,FCR	Olmsteadville
George	Raymond	CED	FCR	
George	Raymond	MOO	FCR	
William	Raymond	ALA	FCR	
Fred H.	Reams	HEC	RG27	McKeever
John	Redwood	STR	S95,FCR	Paul Smiths
Thomas	Redwood	STR	S81,FCR,S95,S74	St. Regis Lake
Charles H.	Reece	HAC	RG27,RG42	Wells
Pete	Reed	KVL	AL	Present
Clarence G.	Rennie	LEC	RG27	Lowville
Paul	Repak		LG92	Boonville
Theodore	Reymonda	MOR	FCR	
Fred.	Reynolds	LOS	S74,S81,W	Saranac Lake
George	Reynolds		RG42	Raquette Lake
J.	Reynolds	LOS	W	
R.	Reynolds	LOS	W	
Ransom	Reynolds	LOS	S74	Saranac Lake
Rant	Reynolds	LOS	W	
Reuben	Reynolds	LOS	S74,S81	Saranac Lake
Ricky	Reyor		LG92	Saranac Lake
Edgar W.	Rheome		RG42	Hammond
C. W.	Rice	ESC	RG27	Newcomb
Fred M.	Rice		RG42	Saranac Lake
John	Rice	LGL	S74,S81	Long Lake
Alfred	Richards	SCH	FCR	
John J.	Richards	RAQ	FCR	
Edward M.	Richardson	FRC	RG20,RG27	Tupper Lake
Iver W.	Richardson	FRC	RG27	Faust
Reuben W.	Rickard		RG42	Morristown
John	Rickertson	LGL	FCR	
Elbridge G.	Ricketson	STR	S81,S95	St. Regis Lake
John	Ricketson	LGL	S95	Long Lake
John H.	Ricketson	ESC	RG27	Olmstedville
Albert	Rider		RG42	DeGrasse
Garey	Riggs	FUL	S95	Fulton Chain
Garie	Riggs		BTG	Boonville
Garrett	Riggs	BGM	FCR	
Gerrie	Riggs	FUL	S81	Fulton Chain
George H.	Ring	LOS	S74,W	Saranac Lake
Wm. E.	Ring	LOS	S74,W	Saranac Lake
A. F.	Risley		BTG	Old Forge
Ernest D.	Rist	ESC	RG27	Newcomb
Ralph	Ritter		RG42	Old Forge

Frank C.	Ritz		RG42,RG27	Old Forge
John	Rivers	KVL	AL	1920s-1930s
John R.	Rivers		RG42	Upper Jay
Thomas	Rivers	ESC	RG27	Jay
Peter	Rivet	HEC	RG27,S95	Old Forge
Frederick	Rivett	FUL	FCR	
Peter	Rivett	FUL	FCR	
George A.	Rivette		BTG	Old Forge
Zebulon	Roabare	MCC	FCR	
Loney	Roarke	FRC	RG27	Saranac Lake
Halsey	Robare	FRC	RG27	Gabriel
Ed.	Robarge	STR	S74,W	St. Regis
Albert P.	Robbins	LOS	S74,S81,W	Saranac Lake
Bert	Robbins		RG42,RG27	Sodom
Clark	Robbins	LOS	S81	Saranac Lake
Clark	Robbins	TUP	S81	Tupper Lake
P.	Robbins	LOS	W	
David	Robear	STR	S81	St. Regis Lake
Frank	Robear	STR	S81	St. Regis Lake
Zeb	Robear, Jr.	STR	S74	St. Regis
Zeb.	Robear, Sr.	STR	S74,S81	St. Regis
C.	Roberts	LOS	W	
C.	Roberts	PLD	W	
J. Elton	Roberts		RG42	Old Forge
R. W.	Roberts	FUL	S95	Fulton Chain
Robert	Roberts	BGM	FCR	
Rufus	Robertson	CHA	S81	Chateaugay Lake
A. C.	Robinson	LGL	W	
Amos	Robinson	LGL	S74,S81,FCR	Long Lake
B. C.	Robinson	LGL	S95	Long Lake
Boyden	Robinson	LGL	FCR,S81	
Charles	Robinson	NEW	FCR	
Charles C.	Robinson	LGL	S95	Long Lake
Isaac B. C.	Robinson	LGL	S74,S95,FCR,W,RG20	Long Lake
John	Robinson	LGL	FCR,W,S74,S81,S95	
Leo J.	Robinson	SLC	RG27	Colton
Ray H.	Robinson		RG42	Bolton Landing
Rufus	Robinson	CHA	W	
William	Robinson	LGL	S74,W,FCR,S81,S95	Long Lake
Rufus	Robinsson, Jr.	CHA	FCR	
Gary	Rock		LG92	Keeseville
Thomas	Rodwell	GRS	FCR	
Andrew	Rogers	MEA	S81,FCR,S95	Meacham Lake
J.	Rogers	STR	W	
L.	Rogers	MEA	W	
M. V.	Rogers	DIC	W	
R. W.	Rogers		BTG	Inlet
W. E.	Rooney	SCH	S81	Schroon Lake
Charles J.	Root	LEC	RG27	Glenfield
Fred	Rork	STR	S95	Paul Smiths
John	Rork	STR	S81	St. Regis Lake
Edward	Rorke	STR	S95,FCR	Paul Smiths
Frederick W.	Rorke	STR	FCR	
John	Rorke	STR	FCR	
Loney	Rorke		RG42	Saranac Lake

J. J.	Rose	BGM	FCR	
J. J.	Rose		BTG	Big Moose
T. J.	Rose	BGM	FCR	
Andrew C.	Rosman	ESC	RG27	Lake Placid Club
Elmer	Ross		RG42	Lyons Falls
James	Ross	WAC	RG27	Bolton Landing
Lester	Ross	WAC	RG20	Garnet
Howard	Rowe	HAC	RG27	Long Lake
Joseph A.	Rowe	HAC	RG20	Long Lake
Charles A.	Royal		RG42,RG27	Inman
Edward F.	Rule	FRC	RG20	Faust
Jacob	Ruoff, Jr.	WAC	RG27,RG42	Chestertown
Arthur	Russell	HAC	RG27	Long Lake
C. J.	Russell	WAC	RG27	Thurman
Gregory	Russell		LG92	Old Forge
Lyman	Russell	LGL	S95,FCR	Long Lake
Robert	Russell		LG92	Old Forge
D. C.	Ruttan		BTG	Port Leyden
Delbert	Ryan		LG92	Harrisville
C.	Sabattis	LGL	W	
Charles**	Sabattis	LGL	FCR,S81,S74	**sons of Mitchell Sabattis
Harry W.	Sabattis	HAC	RG27	Long Lake
Harry**	Sabattis	LGL	FCR	
Isaac**	Sabattis	LGL	S74,W,S81,FCR,S95	Long Lake
Joseph D.	Sabattis	HAC	RG20,W	Long Lake
Mitchell	Sabattis	LGL	W,S74,S81	
A.	Sabin	DIC	W	
A. M.	Sabin	DIC	W	
Millard	Sabin	SAC	FCR	
William H.	Sabin	FRC	RG20	Faust
Sandra	Sabourin		LG92	Keene
Richard	Salmon		LG92	Lake Luzerne
Enos	Sanders	KVL	AL	1900s
S.	Sanders	SCH	S81	Schroon Lake
Gordon	Santor		LG92	Plattsburgh
Merle	Saunders		RG42	Clark Mills
James	Sausville		LG92	Saranac Lake
Jennifer	Sausville		LG92	Saranac Lake
Orion	Savage	LOS	S95	Saranac Lake
Thomas	Savage	IND	FCR	
John	Sawyer	STR	FCR	
Moses	Sawyer	STR	FCR,W,S74,S95	
Wakeman	Sawyer	HAC	RG20	Benson
Eugene L.	Scafford	FUL	S95,FCR	Fulton Chain
Theodore R.	Schenck		RG42	Babylon
Mark	Schiesser		LG92	Essex
Paul	Schiffhauer		LG92	Indian Lake
Mark	Schmale		LG92	North River
Ervie A.	Schryer		RG42	Syracuse
M. V. B.	Schults	CHA	FCR	
Charles	Schuyler	OSW	FCR	
Gary	Scott		LG92	Wilmington
John	Scrafford	FUL	FCR	
Frank	Sears	ESC	RG27	Newman
Dean	Seavey	GRS	FCR	

Martin	Segoves	BVR	FCR	
Robert C.	Selfridge		RG42	Long Lake
Andrew	Selkirk	MEA	S95	Meacham Lake
Charles	Selkirk	MEA	W	
Daniel M.	Selkirk	MEA	S95	Meacham Lake
George	Selkirk	MEA	S95,FCR	Meacham Lake
Harry	Senecal		RG42	Chippewa Bay
Robert	Serpico		LG92	Lake Placid
Dean L.	Sevey	SLC	RG20	Potsdam
Dewitt C.	Sevey	SLC	RG20	Childwold
Jay S.	Shafer		BTG	Old Forge
Daniel	Shambo	ESC	RG27	Ausable Forks
Edward	Shappe		RG42	Long Lake
Michael	Sharp		LG92	North Creek
Jack	Shaw	WAC	RG20	Luzerne
Philander	Shaw	IND	S81,FCR	Indian Lake
John J.	Shea	FRC	RG27	Saranac Lake
Patrick	Sheehy, Jr.	WAC	S95	Adirondack
Kirk	Sheets		LG92	Plattsburgh
Frederick	Sheey, JR.	SCH	FCR	
Arthur	Sheldon	RAQ	S95,FCR	Raquette Lake
Wm.	Sheldon	LOS	S81	Saranac Lake
Guy	Shelton		LG92	North Creek
Oscar	Shens	ESC	RG27	Bloomingdale
Augustus D.	Shepard	HEC	RG27	Old Forge
George E.	Shepard		BTG	Turin
Jack	Shepard	FUL	S81,W	Fulton Chain
Nathan	Sherman	SCH	FCR	
Dolph	Shields	NOR	S81	North River
Mark	Shoemaker		LG92	Forestport
R. M.	Shults	CHA	FCR	
C. H.	Shumway	FRC	RG27	Vermontville
Edwin	Shumway	GRS	FCR	
George	Shumway	GRS	FCR	
George	Shumway		RG42	Childwold
Preston	Shurtliff	GRS	FCR	
Martin	Shutte	CHA	W	
George	Shutts	CHA	S81	Chateaugay Lake
Martin	Shutts	CHA	S81	Chateaugay Lake
Herman	Sibley	ESC	RG27	Newman
Herman	Sibley		RG42	Lake Placid
Howard	Simons	HAC	RG20	Wells
Ira	Simpson		LG92	Bolton Landing
Kenyon	Simpson		LG92	Bolton Landing
Andrew	Sims	BMT	S81	Blue Mountain Lake
Lauran A.	Singer	LEC	RG27	Lowville
George	Skiff	STR	S81,W	St. Regis Lake
Alvah	Slack		RG42	Lake Pleasant
Howard	Slater	LOS	FCR	
Howard	Slater	LOS	S95,FCR	Saranac Lake
John	Slater	LOS	FCR,W,S74,S81	
Warren J.	Slater	LOS	FCR,W,S81,S95	
Mark	Sleinkofer		LG92	Ausable Forks
Charles E.	Smith		RG42	Fort Edward
Charles H.	Smith		BTG,FCR,W	Petrie's Corners

Charles R.	Smith	BVR	S81,W	Beaver River
Douglas L.	Smith		RG42	Dickinson Center
Ed.	Smith	PLD	S74	North Elba
Edward	Smith	CED	FCR	
Edward	Smith	HEC	RG27	Old Forge
Elon L.	Smith		BTG	Beaver River
Eugene	Smith	AKL	FCR	
Eugene	Smith	MCC	FCR	
Eugene	Smith	MEA	FCR	
Eugene	Smith	TUP	S81	Tupper Lake
F.	Smith	MER	W	
Fay	Smith		BTG	Beaver River
Frank W.	Smith		BTG	McKeever
Fred V.	Smith		BTG	McKeever
Fremont	Smith	LNL	S81,FCR	Loon Lake
George W.	Smith	LGL	FCR	
George W.	Smith		BTG	Big Moose
Henry B.	Smith	WAC	RG27,RG42	Bolton Landing
Howard R.	Smith	SLC	RG27	Chippewa Bay
J. D.	Smith	DIC	W	
J. P.	Smith	DIC	W	
James	Smith	CHA	S81	Chateaugay Lake
James N.	Smith	CHA	S81,FCR,W	Chateaugay Lake
Jeffrey	Smith		LG92	Bolton Landing
Jno. W.	Smith	WAC	RG27	Stony Creek
John	Smith		LG92	Hoffmeister
Judson B.	Smith	WAC	RG27	Horicon
Karen	Smith		LG92	Paul Smiths
Malcolm	Smith	LOS	S81	Saranac Lake
Marcus	Smith	BVR	2S81	Beaver River
Mark	Smith	BVR	FCR,W	
Millard	Smith	ONC	RG27,BTG	Hawkinsville
P. D.	Smith	BMT	S95,FCR	Blue Mountain Lake
Peter	Smith	ESC	RG27	Newman
Richard E.	Smith	KVL	AL	Present
Ronald	Smith		LG92	Thendara
William	Smith	BEL	FCR	
William	Smith	CHA	FCR	
William	Smith	BVR	S81	Beaver River
William J.	Smith	WAC	RG20	Horicon
William R.	Smith	BVR	FCR	
Joseph	Snack		LG92	Warrensburg
Henry H.	Snider	NEW	S74	Newcomb
Alfred	Snyder		RG42	Cranberry Lake
Henry	Snyder	NEW	W	
Henry	Solmons	BVR	S81	Beaver River
J.	Solomon	LOS	W	
John	Solomon	LOS	S74	Saranac Lake
Peter	Solomon	LOS	FCR,S81,S95	
H.	Solon	LOS	W	
Henry	Somers	MCC	FCR	
Leslie	Sornberger		RG42	Northville
O. H.	Southwick	HEC	RG27	Old Forge
Silas	Spear	CHA	S81,W	Chateaugay Lake
William	Spear	CHA	S81,W	Chateaugay Lake

D. F.	Sperry		BTG	Old Forge
D. L.	Sperry	FUL	S95	Fulton Chain
Frank	Sperry	FUL	FCR	
Franklin	Sperry	BVR	S81	Chases Lake
William	Sperry	FUL	FCR	
Wm. D.	Sperry	HEC	RG27,BTG	Old Forge
Harold	Spetla, Jr.		LG92	Tupper Lake
Alan	Spieldenner		LG92	Corinth
H. L.	Spinning	FUL	S95,FCR	Fulton Chain
Andrew	Sprague		LG92	Warrensburg
Anthony	Sprague	CHA	W	
Bill	Sprague	MEA	W	
Frank	Sprague	NOH	FCR	
Frank A.	Sprague		RG42	Saranac Inn
Halsey R.	Sprague	MEA	S95,W,FCR	Meacham Lake
John H.	Sprague		BTG,FCR	Old Forge
Richard	Sprague	MEA	S81	Meacham Lake
Warren	Sprague	MCC	FCR	
William	Sprague	DUA	FCR	
William H.	Sprague	MEA	S95,FCR	Meacham Lake
Charles	Spring	BMT	FCR	
Richard	Spring		LG92	Indian Lake
Jack	Springer, Jr.		LG92	Fort Edward
Jack	Springer, Sr.		LG92	Fort Ann
A.	Squires	SCH	S81	Schroon Lake
Pick	Squires	SCH	S81	Schroon Lake
Bert	St. Dennis	FRC	RG20	Tupper Lake
Ben	St. Germain	STR	S81,S74,FCR	St. Regis Lake
Benjamin	St. Germain	CHZ	FCR	
Bonum	St. Germain	STR	S74	St. Regis
Fayette	St. Germain	STR	S74,W	St. Regis
Levi	St. Germain	STR	S74,W	St. Regis
Masie	St. Germain	LOS	S81	Saranac Lake
Moses	St. Germain	GRS	FCR	
Moses	St. Germain	STR	S74,W,S81	St. Regis
Nelson	St. Germain	STR	S74	St. Regis
George	St. Louis		RG42	Saranac Inn
Gary	Staab		LG92	Old Forge
Sherman	Stancliff	MEA	W	
Ed.	Stanton	LGL	S81	Long Lake
Edward	Stanton	LGL	FCR	
Edwin	Stanton	LGL	S95	Long Lake
G.	Stanton	LGL	W	
Geo. B.	Stanton	LGL	S81,FCR,S74	Long Lake
Gilbert	Stanton	LGL	FCR,S74,S81,S95	
Henry	Stanton	LGL	S74,W	Long Lake
James	Stanton	PLD	S95,FCR	Lake Placid
William	Starbuck	IND	FCR	
John A.	Stark		RG42	St. Regis Falls
DeWitt	Starkey		RG42	DeGrasse
Debra	Starling		LG92	Indian Lake
John	Starling		LG92	Indian Lake
Harvey	Staves	FRC	RG27	Tupper Lake
Ahas	Stayes	STR	S74	St. Regis
Jacob	Stayes	STR	S74	St. Regis

Ross	Stayes	STR	S74	St. Regis
William	Stearns	LOS	S95,FCR	Saranac Lake
Chas. E.	Steele	FRC	RG27	Upper Saranac
Hiram	Steers	RAQ	FCR	
Warren	Steers	RAQ	FCR	
John	Stell		BTG	Forestport
John F.	Stell		RG42	Old Forge
William	Stell	WOD	FCR	White Lake Corners
Gardner	Stephens		LG92	Lake Placid
Trina	Stephenson		LG92	Elizabethtown
Charles	Stevens	PLD	FCR	
Shellie	Stevens		LG92	Raquette Lake
Fred.	Stevenson	BMT	S81	Blue Mountain Lake
Tracy	Stevenson		LG92	Lake George
John	Steves	WAC	RG20	Bakers Mills
Warren	Steves	WAC	RG27	Glens Falls
Donald	Stewart	CRA	FCR	
C.	Stickney	MER	W	
Charles	Stickney	LNL	FCR	
Charley	Stickney	MEA	W	
Cyrus	Stickney	LNL	S81,FCR	Loon Lake
David	Stickney	FRC	RG27	Malone
George	Stiefel, Jr.		LG92	Plattsburgh
George	Stiff	MCC	FCR	
James	Stiff	MCC	FCR	
Howard	Still	ONC	RG27	Forestport
George H.	Stoddard		BTG	McKeever
Karen	Stolz		LG92	Keene
Robert	Stolz		LG92	Keene
Isaac	Stone	BVR	FCR,W,S81	
Bertie L.	Storrs	FRC	S81	Whiteface Mountain
Charles	Storrs	CHZ	FCR	
George	Storrs	CHZ	FCR	
Georgie C.	Storrs	FRC	S81	Whiteface Mountain
William H.	Storrs	GRS	FCR	
Fred	Straight		RG42	North River
Henry	Straight	NOR	FCR	
Elmer	Streeter	WAC	RG20	Horicon
Willard	Streeter	AKL	FCR	
Charles	Strickland		RG42	Newcomb
John A.	Strong	LOS	S81	Saranac Lake
Sheri	Stuart		LG92	Tupper Lake
James	Sturges	LEW	FCR	
James	Sturges	LKP	FCR	
John	Sturges	LEW	FCR	
John	Sucharski		LG92	Keeseville
James	Sullivan	FRC	RG27	Paul Smiths
John M.	Sullivan	HAC	RG20	Long Lake
Joseph	Sullivan	LEC	RG27	Martinsburgh
E. E.	Sumner	LOS	S95	Saranac Lake
Reubens E.	Sumner	LOS	FCR	
Julius	Susice	FRC	RG27	Santa Clara
DeWitt Clinton	Sutton		RG42	Long Lake
E. R.	Sutton	NEW	W	
M. R.	Sutton	NEW	S74	Newcomb

Willard	Sutton	LGL	S95,FCR	Long Lake
Amos	Swanson	WAC	RG20	Stony Creek
James	Swedberg		LG92	Long Lake
Ed.	Sweeney	STR	S81	St. Regis Lake
Geo.	Sweeney	LOS	S81,FCR,S74	Saranac Lake
Henry	Sweeney	CHZ	FCR	
Henry	Sweeney	STR	S81	St. Regis Lake
Mitch.	Sweeney	STR	S81	St. Regis Lake
Ransom	Sweeney	UPS	FCR	
D.	Sweeny	STR	W	
George	Sweeny	LOS	W	
Andrew	Syms	RAQ	FCR,S95	
Kirk	Synder		LG92	Saranac Lake
Augustus	Syphert	FUL	FCR,W	
William	Tabor	BMT	S95	Blue Mountain Lake
William	Taher	BMT	FCR	
Loren	Taintor	OSW	FCR	
Robert	Takacs		LG92	Bloomingdale
Archie	Talbot	LGL	FCR	
Roy	Tallman	KVL	AL	1930s-1970s
Aaron	Taylor	POT	W	
B. Cyrus	Taylor	ESC	RG27	St. Huberts
Earl	Taylor		RG42	Lowville
Harold	Taylor		LG92	Warrensburg
Henry	Taylor	BMT	FCR	
Henry	Taylor	RAQ	S95	Raquette Lake
Nathan	Taylor	KVL	AL,RG27	1920s
T.H.	Taylor	LUZ	FCR	
William	Taylor	SCH	FCR	
Wilmot J.	Taylor	HEC	RG20	Hamilton
Anna	Telfer		RG42	Lake Pleasant
John	Thaiauldt	ESC	RG27	Keene Valley
Gordon	Tharrett		LG92	Dickinson Ctr.
John	Theriault	KVL	AL	1920s-1930s
Henny	Thilo	NOH	FCR	
Charles	Thomas	CRA	S81	Cranberry Lake
Ezra	Thomas	CRA	S81	Cranberry Lake
Ezra	Thomas	OSW	W	
Morris	Thomas	CRA	S81	Cranberry Lake
Richard	Thomas	OSW	W	
Albert	Thompson	CRA	FCR	
Claude B.	Thompson		RG42	Potsdam
Harry	Thompson	STR	S81	St. Regis Lake
Frederick	Thornley		LG92	Paul Smiths
Eric F.	Thornton	HAC	RG20	Long Lake
Howard	Thornton		RG42	Newcomb
Rob.	Thornton	LGL	S81	Long Lake
William	Thurber	CHA	S81	Chateaugay Lake
Paul	Tibbets	RAQ	FCR	
Frank L.	Tiffany		BTG	Inlet
John	Tinder	SLC	RG27	Wanakena
Albert R.	Titcomb		RG42	Corey's
Wm. H.	Titus	FRC	RG27	Paul Smiths
Vivian	Tompkins	SLC	RG27	Edwardsville
Joseph	Topping	WAC	RG27	North Creek

William	Toran		LG92	Lake Luzerne
Simeon	Torrance	LOS	FCR,W,S81	
Clark	Town	OSW	W	
Herbert	Town	STR	S81	St. Regis Lake
John	Town	OSW	W	
Richard	Town	OSW	W	
Calvin	Towns	LGL	FCR	
Lorenzo	Towns	LGL	FCR	
Ren	Towns	LGL	S81	Long Lake
James	Tracy		LG92	Old Forge
Max	Tredo	KVL	AL,S74,S81	1870s-1900s
Will	Tredo	KVL	AL,S74	
Lucien	Trim	MEA	FCR,RG27,S95	
Edwin	Trimm		RG42	Tupper Lake
Dave	Trine	MEA	W	
M.	Trude	KVL	W	
W.	Trude	KVL	W	
John M.	Trudo	HAC	RG20	Long Lake
Arthur	Trumbull	KVL	AL,FCR,S81	1880s-1900s
C.W.	Trumbull	KVL	FCR	
Charles	Trumbull	KVL	AL,S81	1870s-1920s
John	Trumbull	KVL	AL,RG20	1910s
John H.	Trumbull	ESC	RG20	Keene Valley
Mel J.	Trumbull	KVL	AL,W,S81,FCR,S74	1860s-1920s
A. N.	Tupper	POT	W	
William R.	Tupper	CHA	W	
Edwin	Turk	WOD	FCR	
Arza	Turner	CHZ	FCR	
Charles	Turner	CHZ	FCR	
Frank	Turner	CHZ	FCR	
John	Turner	LOS	S95,FCR	Saranac Lake
Stephen	Turner	STR	S81,W,S74	St. Regis Lake
Lottie E.	Tuttle	HEC	RG27	Old Forge
Orley C.	Tuttle		RG42,RG27	Old Forge
Abner	Tyler	STR	FCR	
Wayne C.	Tyler		RG42	Saranac Lake
Wort	Tyler	STR	S95	Paul Smiths
Leonard J.	Tyrell	ESC	RG27,RG42	Lake Placid
Leonard J.	Tyrell		RG42	Lake Placid
Frank	Umber		RG42	Lake Placid
George	Umber		RG42	Saranac Lake
John	Umber	ESC	RG27,RG42	Lake Placid
John	Umber		RG42	Lake Placid
William H.	Umber		RG42	Lake Placid
Stephen	Uzdavinis		LG92	Old Forge
Dale	Vallier		RG42	Star Lake
Peter	Valois		RG42	Ogdensburg
Arthur	Van Aernun	LEC	RG27	Greig
E. J.	Van Arnam		BTG	Inlet
Herman	Van Dusen	WAC	RG20,RG27	Stony Creek
Willis C.	Van Skoik	HEC	RG27	Big Moose
John	Van Valkenburgh	FUL	S81	Fulton Chain
F. A.	Van Wert	DUA	FCR	
Fred A.	Van Wert	MEA	S95	Meacham Lake
Carlton	VanKirk, Sr.		LG92	Fort Ann

Jno. R.	Vandecar	SLC	RG27	Wanakena
Garry	Vandenburgh	FRC	RG27	Saranac Lake
Joseph	Vanderhoof		LG92	Port Henry
Lee J.	Vanderwalker		RG42	Schroon Lake
George	Vandyning		RG42	Rossie
Foster	Vansant		RG42	DeGrasse
Clayton	Vantine	SLC	RG27	Star Lake
Orson	Vassar	ESC	RG27	Lake Placid
James	Vianna		LG92	Stillwater
Oscar	Vibber	POT	W	
Michael	Vickerson		LG92	Caroga Lake
Richard	Villeneuve, Jr.		LG92	North Creek
George	Villers		BTG	Old Forge
Clayton	Villiere		RG42	Old Forge
Geo.	Villiere	HEC	RG27,RG42	Old Forge
Reginald	Villiere		RG42	Old Forge
William	Visscher		LG92	Lake Luzerne
Hermanus	Vos		LG92	Lake Placid
Frank	Vosburgh	LOS	S95	Saranac Lake
Jason	Vosburgh	LOS	S74,S81,W	Saranac Lake
Stanley C.	Vroman		RG42	Hammond
David B.	Vrooman		RG42	Wells
Marie Kay	Wade		LG92	Saranac Lake
Charles F.	Wagner		RG42	Wanakena
Christspher	Wagner	BVR	FCR	
Elmer B.	Wagner	FRC	RG42	Buffalo
Jos.	Wagner	ONC	RG27	McKeever
Michael J.	Wagner		RG42	Schenectady
Mark	Wagstaff		LG92	Saranac Lake
John	Wait	POT	W	
George	Wake	LOS	S74,W	Saranac Lake
John	Wake	STR	S74	St. Regis
William	Wakley		RG42	Indian Lake
Lester	Waldron	WAC	RG27	North Creek
Wm. M.	Waldron		RG42	Phoenix
Stearns	Walker		RG42	Saranac Lake
Emerson	Walker, Jr.		LG92	Glens Falls
I. A.	Walton	FRC	RG27	Saranac Lake
Alonzo	Wandover	HEC	RG20	Remsen
John	Ward	OSW	W	
Spencer	Ward	OSW	W	
Stephen	Ward	CRA	S81	Cranberry Lake
Stephen	Ward	OSW	W	
Frank M.	Wardner	RAW	FCR	
Seth	Wardner	STR	S74	St. Regis
Seth	Wardner	MER	W	
Seth	Wardner, Jr.	STR	S81	St. Regis Lake
Charlie	Warner	KVL	AL,RG27,RG42	1930s-1940s
Daniel	Warren	FRC	RG27	Saranac Lake
Frank H.	Warren	WAC	RG20	Bakers Mills
James	Warren	LEC	RG27	Lake Bonaparte
A.	Washburn	MER	W	
Amasa	Washburn	LNL	S81	Loon Lake
Frank	Washburn	LEW	FCR	
Perry	Washburn		RG42	Indian Lake

S.	Washburn	MER	W	
Simeon	Washburn	LNL	S81,FCR	Loon Lake
Leonard B.	Waterman	HEC	RG27	Big Moose
Elmer L.	Watson	SLC	RG20	Stark
John R.	Watson	SLC	RG27	Stark
Lloyd	Watson	KVL	AL	1960s
Terry	Watson		LG92	Lake Placid
Thos. T.	Watson	ESC	RG27	Ausable Forks
William	Watson		BTG	Old Forge
A.	Weatherby	NEW	W	
Jeffrey	Weaver		LG92	Blue Mt. Lake
Kathryn	Weaver		LG92	Chestertown
Oscar	Webber	POT	S81	Raquette River
Harvey J.	Webster	ESC	RG27	Keene
Huley	Webster	KVL	AL	
R. G.	Webster	FRC	S81	Ragged Lake
Warren J.	Webster		RG42	Huletts Landing
Wellington	Weedmark		BTG,FCR	Old Forge
Edward C.	Wehl	ONC	RG27	Utica
Julie	Weinstein-Churco		LG92	Lake Placid
Ernest	Welch	FRC	RG27	Tupper Lake
Frank	Welch	FRC	RG27	Tupper Lake
Jos.	Welch	LGL	S95	Long Lake
Fayette N.	Weller	IND	FCR	
Henry	Weller	STR	S81,S74	St. Regis Lake
Frank E.	Wells	ONC	RG27	Prospect
Gilbert J.	Wells		RG42	Ausable Forks
Joseph	Welsh	LGL	FCR	
Thomas	Welsh		LG92	Minerva
Augustus F.	Werner	HEC	RG27	Beaver River
Joseph F.	Wesley		RG42	Long Lake
Dennis	West		LG92	Warrensburg
Lawrence V.	West		RG42	North Creek
Chauncey	Westcott	CRA	FCR	
Clayton A.	Westcott	FRC	RG20	Mountain View
Nicholas	Weston	FUL	FCR	
Alonzo	Wetherbee	NEW	S74,S81	Newcomb
Daniel	Wetherbee	NEW	FCR	
Ezra	Wetmore	BVR	FCR	
William	Wharton, Jr.		LG92	Lake Pleasant
John	Wheeler	FUL	FCR	
LeRoy	Wheeler		RG42	Dickinson Center
John	Whicher	STR	S81	St. Regis Lake
Jeffrey	Whisher		LG92	Bloomingdale
Fred.	Whitcomb	IND	S81	Indian Lake
Eugene	White	STR	S74,W	St. Regis
Merrill M.	White	HEC	RG20,BTG,FCR,S95	Old Forge
Peter	White	HEC	RG27,RG42	Old Forge
Theodore	White	KVL	AL,W,S74	1860s-1870s
Michael	Whiting		LG92	Glens Falls
Robert	Whitman		LG92	Tupper Lake
Eleazer	Whitmarsh	OSW	W	
Carlos	Whitney	LOS	FCR,S74,S81	
Don	Whitney	KVL	AL	1950s-1980s
Joseph	Whitney	BMT	S81	Blue Mountain Lake

Joseph	Whitney	POT	W	
Judson	Whitney	KVL	AL	1960s
Reginald	Whitney	KVL	AL	1966-1976
Tom	Whitney	KVL	AL	Present
Benjamin F.	Wickham	SCH	S95,FCR,S81	Schroon Lake
George W.	Wickham	SCH	S81,FCR	Schroon Lake
Paul W.	Wigley	WAC	RG27	Pottersville
Calvin H.	Wilber	HAC	RG20	Speculator
James	Wilcox	NEW	FCR	
Malvin	Wilcox	ESC	RG27	Newcomb
Samuel	Wilcox	FRC	S81	Whiteface Mountain
James H.	Wilder	LEC	RG27	Lowville
Wayne	Wilkins		LG92	Plattsburgh
Donald	Williams		LG92	Gloversville
Ernest	Williams	FRC	RG27	Moody
Evan H.	Williams	FRC	RG20	Saranac Lake
Frank	Williams	FUL	S95	Fulton Chain
Harrison H.	Williams	NEW	S81	Newcomb
Harry	Williams	LGL	FCR	
Henry	Williams	FRC	RG27	Moody
James	Williams	LNL	FCR	
Sterns	Williams	STR	S81	St. Regis Lake
W.	Williams	NEW	W	
Warren	Williams	NEW	FCR	
William	Williams	FRC	RG27,RG42	Inman
Eben	Willis	POT	W	
J.	Willson	LOS	W	
Earl W.	Wilson		RG42	Tupper Lake
J. Arthur	Wilson		RG42	Syracuse
James F.	Wilson		RG42	Parishville
Michael	Wilson		LG92	Raquette Lake
William	Wilson	LGL	FCR	
Asher N.	Winch	ESC	RG27	Upper Jay
Larry	Winslow		LG92	Glens Falls
John	Witcher	BLM	FCR	
John	Witcher	STR	S95	Paul Smiths
A.	Wood	LGL	W	
Alonzo	Wood	FUL	FCR	
Alonzo	Wood	FUL	W	
Alvin W.	Wood		BTG	Old Forge
Bert J.	Wood	HEC	RG27,RG42	Old Forge
Charles	Wood	AKL	FCR	
Charles D.	Wood		BTG	Point Rock
Charles N.	Wood		BTG	Old Forge
Charles N.	Wood	LEC	RG27	Lowville
Chas. D.	Wood	HEC	RG27	Big Moose
Cyrus	Wood	BGM	FCR	
Ervin	Wood	FRC	RG27	Malone
Frank	Wood	CED	FCR	
Fred	Wood	FRC	RG27	Newark
Henry	Wood	LOS	S74,W,S81	Saranac Lake
J.	Wood	LGL	W	
J. A.	Wood		BTG	Old Forge
J. Scott	Wood		LG92	Diamond Point
James	Wood	SCH	S81	Schroon River

Jerome	Wood	RAQ	FCR	
Jerome	Wood	LGL	S74,S81	Long Lake
Jerome	Wood	RAQ	W	
Logan	Wood		RG42	Lowville
Oscar	Wood	FUL	S95,FCR	Fulton Chain
Wesley	Wood	UPS	S95	Saranac Inn
William J.	Wood	WAC	RG20	Athol
William J.	Wood		RG42	Raquette Lake
C. Ben	Woodard		LG92	Constableville
Alan	Woodruff		LG92	Woodgate
Dick	Woodruff	MEA	W	
Judson	Woodruff	FRC	S81	Whiteface Mountain
Richard	Woodruff	MEA	S81,S95,FCR	Meacham Lake
Spenser E.	Woodruff	GRS	FCR	
William	Woodruff	FRC	S81	Whiteface Mountain
Wesley	Woods	UPS	FCR	
Warren	Woodward	NOR	FCR	
Charles L.	Wright	HEC	RG20	Fulton Chain
Frank	Wright	ESC	RG27	Keene Valley
Loyal S.	Wright		RG42	Chazy
Michael	Wright	POT	W	
John	Wrolsen		LG92	Keene
William	Wyman	FUL	FCR	
Ben	Yancey	LEC	RG27	Lowville
Edward	Young	OSW	FCR	
George	Young	OSW	FCR	
Harlo C.	Young	HEC	RG27	Lowville
Irvin	Young		LG92	Saranac Lake
Randy	Young		LG92	Saranac Lake
Sheila	Young		LG92	Saranac Lake
Frank	Yule	FUL	FCR	
Frank L.	Yule	HEC	RG27	Old Forge
Bernard	Ziolkowski		LG92	Saranac Lake
Milford	Zufelt	WAC	RG27	North River

Note: The following guides are not in the sources cited above.

First Name	Last Name	Area	Source	Residence
Byron Pond	Ames	RAB, HAC		
Daniel	Ames	RAB		Ray Brook
Giles	Becraft	FUL		
Dell	Bellinger	ONC		Forest Port
Frank	Benham	LOS		Saranac Lake
Jesse	Boula	LOS		Saranac Lake
Richard	Brady			LaFargeville
Benjamin	Brewster	PLD		
Charles	Brown	LOS		
Reuben	Brownell	HEC		Twitchell Lake
Joseph O.A.	Bryere	RAQ		Raquette Lake
Clifford	Burlingame	HAC		
Francis N.	Coburn	NOH		North Hudson
Jim	Coughlin	LOS		Saranac Lake
Lyman	Epps, Sr.	AKL		North Elba
John	Fleury	ESC		Westport
Robert	Gallagher	FRC		Paul Smiths

John	Galusha	NEW	Thurman, Minerva
Art	Gates	BMT	Blue Mountain Lake
Jim	Goodwin	KVL	Connecticut
Albert Lyman	Graves	WAC	Hague
Ira	Gray		Harrisburg
Frank	Grey		
Elmer	Grimshaw	KVL	Keene
Les	Hathaway	LOS	Saranac Lake
Chauncey	Hathorne	RAQ	Raquette Lake
Bert	Hinds	ESC	
Will	Isham	KVL	Keene Valley
Fordinand	Jennsen	TUP	Tupper Lake
Gerald	Kenwell	FUL	Sixth Lake
Beecher	LaPrarie	BMT	Blue Mountain Lake
William	LeBeau	LOS	Saranac Lake
Frank	Lucas	SLC	Hopkinton
Sanford	McKenzie	PLD	Lake Placid
"Uncle Bill"	McLaughlin	TUP	Tupper Lake
Jonathan	Meeker	FUL	Fourth Lake
Loyal A.	Merrill	PLD	
Jacob	Moody	LOS	Saranac Lake
Wilfred	Morrison	CRA	Cranberry Lake
Wallace	Murray	LOS	Saranac Lake
Marshall E.	Mussen	STR	
Bill	Nye	AKL	North Elba
John	O'Connor	STR	
Arthur L.	Otis	STR	Paul Smiths
Harry G.	Otis	STR	Paul Smiths
Enos	Perry	CLC	Lyon Mountain
Sanford	Perry	FUL	
William	Pohl	OSW	
William D.	Pond	SLC	Childwold
Beecher	Roblee	BMT	b. North Creek
Jed	Rossman	AKL	Lake Placid
Louis "French Louie"	Seymoure	HAC	West Canada Lake
James	Short	ALA	Minerva
Elijah	Simonds	ELZ	Elizabethtown
Edward G.	Slaven	STR	Brighton
Leslie	Smith	LOS	Saranac Lake
Perly J.	Squires	SLC	Saranac Lake
Hyland	Steves	RAQ	Raquette Lake
Mitchell	Swinyer	FRC	Vermontville
Henry	Thompson	ESC	
John H.	Titus, Jr.	STR	Keese Mills
James	Umber	UPS	Jay
Jay "Zeke"	Vandenburgh,Jr	LOS	b. Tupper Lake
James Edgar	Weaver	HAC	b. Wells
Raymond E.	Weaver	HAC	
James E.	White	LOS	Saranac Lake
Francis	Young	HEC	Petrie's Corners
William B.	Young	ESC	b. Black Brook

Appendix B: Some Quotations by and about Guides

"Charlie (Dwight) was a guide, his favorite by-word, Crr-ist-on-the-mountain!'" -- Lem Merrill.

"These old-time guides created characters for themselves." --Mary MacKenzie, Lake Placid and North Elba Historian.

"The early guides saw the sportsmen as a cash crop -- they'd have their wives cook for them and kick their kids out of their bedrooms into the barn." -- Warder Cadbury, Adirondack historian.

"... that rapidly disappearing type, the true Adirondack guide, than whom no other woodsman is likely to be more elusive, or more interesting for his nature lore, his skill, and his philosophy of life." -- from Peaks and People of the Adirondacks, by Russell Carson, 1927.

"I have always looked upon John (Cheney) as a necessary appendage to the Adirondacks, almost as necessary as Mt. Marcy itself. He has left a good name behind him -- and this, (as the Biblical book of) Solomon says, is better than precious ointment." -- Professor Farrand Benedict, in 1877, on learning of Cheney's death.

"With such men as Elijah Cowles, Burr Sturges, and Alvah Dunning, for guides, no one, if anything of sportsman, visiting Hamilton County, at the proper season, can fail to meet with good success." -- from "A Deer Hunt in Hamilton County, N.Y.," February 19, 1883, "Spirit of the Times", by "Y."

"But I learned one thing during this my first experience with an Adirondack guide, which I will hand on for the benefit of others: namely, not allow him to drink whiskey from a bottle!" -- J.H. Hunt, in Three Runs in the Adirondacks and One in Canada, 1892.

"They (old guides) were a wealth of information if they wanted to talk to you, but they weren't worth a darn if they didn't." -- Ed "Bud" Betters, former guide, 1991.

Saranac guide, I have yet to know it." -- Alfred B. Street, in <u>Woods and Waters: or, The Saranacs and Racket</u>, 1860.

"... the man who has followed the occupation of guiding becomes prematurely aged, and notwithstanding his life in the woods, with all the benefits supposed to be attached thereto, many a bronzed fellow presents the appearance of an old man before he has yet reached his prime." -- "The American Angler," No. 12, Vol. IV.

"(Old Mountain) Phelps was a guide because, in addition to a guide's equipment of woodcraft and knowledge of topography, he had the soul of a philosopher and poet, and a fine appreciation of the beauties and sublimities of nature." -- Russell Carson, <u>Peaks and People of the Adirondacks</u>, 1927.

"Most everyone did some guiding when they weren't farming. But I suspect they did more farming than guiding." -- Marvin H. Bissell, Newcomb.

"In my long career in the woods I have never killed a deer." --Ed Bennett, nineteenth-century Raquette Lake guide.

"I can hardly bring myself to add that when I shot that buck, my guide had him by the tail." -- Dr. Eggleston, guided by Lysander Hall.

"Many a time I have returned to camp, late in the evening, after a difficult trip, to find that Mr. Murray had, with his own hands, prepared for me a warm supper. God bless the man who is kind to guides!" -- John Plumley, guide to William H. H. Murray, who wrote <u>Adventures in the Wilderness</u>, 1869.

"I have never known an amateur whose efforts could compare with the feats performed by such men as (guides) Charlie Beede and Wesley Lamb, in the course of their hunting, logging, and trapping." -- Newell Martin, remembering 1895, in July, 1931, "High Spots."

"Myth and reality combined to make the guide the most attractive figure in Adirondack life and literature." -- Paul Jamieson, Adirondack author.

"When I find myself spending more time reading and writing about Adirondack guides than being one, I get worried and depressed."
-- Chuck Brumley, part-time writer, part-time guide.

"The average guide now admits that a deer's track to him, when the pleasure season is on, is worth more than a caracass."-- Ferd Chase, Proprietor, Loon Lake House, 1895.

"This network of lakes and ponds is a wonderful and attractive feature of the great wilderness, adding a rare diversity to the scenery. They are so closely connected that trips of one hundred miles can be made in guide-boats; water journeys broken only by short carries that seldom exceed two miles in length. These water-routes, combined with mountain trips and Adirondack stage rides, make this region a perpetual delight to the summer tourist. Nowhere in the world is there such a combination of wild, grand scenery, and delightful, easy travel, lying at the very threshold of civilization." -- New York Forest Commission Report, 1891.

"The woods kind of faded in Saranac Lake -- they became obsessed with a different kind of clientele -- t.b.; t.b. became the industry." -- Gail Rogers Rice, Saranac Lake, 1991.

"Many individuals not hunters, but who were anxious to have a hunt, if it were only to be able to say that they had been in the woods and camped out with a master hunter; used to urge their company upon Uncle Jock; indeed, not a few of this sort received the tuition of Stoner and Foster." -- from Trappers of New York, by Jeptha Simms, 1850.

"Whether viewed as the last surviving primitive men, true Thoreauvian transcendentalists, or indigenous eccentrics, these backwoodsmen (guides) created a legend of their own ... they embodied the dual qualities of the age as the people most in touch with the spirituality found in nature and as rugged individualists permeated with the spirit of pragmatism." -- Anne G. Russell, "The Adirondacks and the Adirondack Guide."

"Guides do not understand the fun of tramping day after day over rocks and logs and bogs, when you can have a comfortable shanty on a beautiful lake by a cool spring, with plenty of fish and deer within reasonable reach, to take which only a moderate amount of exercise is necessary." The Adirondack; or, Life in the Woods, by Joel T. Headley, 1849.

"In March, 1879, a fine female of this rare owl (Syrnium lapponicum cinereum, the great gray owl) was shot in the Adirondacks by a guide. This is, I believe, the first record of the occurence of this bird in this state." -- Bulletin of the Nuttall Ornithological Club, Vol. V, April, 1880.

"I never worked for a company or business organization in my life, but I made a better living than most people and my family has always had a comfortable home." -- Ernie Blanchard, Blue Mountain Lake guide.

"Brant Lake bass ain't used to living on painted kindlin'." -- "Uncle Jud" Smith, of Horicon, regarding finishing plugs.

"Climb the pole and cut his throat." -- Blue Mountain Lake guide Ernie Blanchard, to a sport who had wound a fish up to the end of his pole and wondered what to do.

"The deer must have (defecated) when it jumped over the stand."-- Guide Buster Bird, to a sport who observed porcupine droppings on a high deer stand and thought they were from a deer.

"There is a good deal that is romantic in their appearance and they are very social and obliging." -- G. M. Payne, a visitor in 1871 from Bath, Maine, about Adirondack guides.

"The old Adirondack guides were most striking personalities and an interesting lot of men, like children about many things, a happy, easy-going lot, who took no care for the morrow and enjoyed life for life's sake." -- Dr. Edward Livingston Trudeau, An Autobiography, 1916.

"There's nothing pretty much to say about them. They're just ordinary men. And they had a job to do and they done it." -- Saranac Lake native Horton Duprey, 95 years old in 1992.

"My guide-boat will go through the water like a snake and climb a wave like a puffball -- six mile an hour an' never sweat a hair!" -- Guide Phil Christy, at 83, of Old Forge.

"One summer Mr. ??????, who lived at Little Rapids, had a young cow to sell, so my father (guide and hotelkeeper James LaMont) bought it, and butchered it, and when it was served to the boarders, they of course thought it was venison, and said what a wild taste the meat had." -- Nina Lee, born 1877.

Keene Valley Howard Hall, on being asked why so many local boys marry local girls: "I dunno. Laziness, I guess. When I decided to get married, I said to myself I'm not going to marry anybody local. I'm going a long ways off for my wife. So I went to Tupper Lake."

"Very fortunate is that person who has secured the services of a good guide, and his lump of gratitude must be undeveloped if he does not thank his lucky stars. The woods are swarming with men who call themselves guides, but few are deserving of the name. The first-class guides always designate those frauds who try to earn an odd penny, by claiming some knowledge of woodcraft, as farmers.

They can chop wood, carry a moderately sized load, but as for performing any of the functions appertaining to woodcraft, one might as well engage the service of a tobacconist's sign. Their short comings in knowledge and experience they strive to neutralize by pretense and swagger. They will make any kind of statement and confirm it, by sticking to it, which, four times out of five is the only confirmation it ever receives.

Giles (Becraft) is a genuine unadulterated back-woodsman, none better, few so good, and not like so many of his class who are as difficult of solution as one of Euclid's problems would be to the average Digger Indian. Guides usually have a mysterious look and manner, seldom vouchsafing any of their woodcraft to outside barbarians, as though telling north from west on a cloudy day, was an impossibility save to those born and educated in the forest, while the faculty of detecting intricate and hidden trails transcends the acquirements and capacities of ordinary mortals. From what few words they condescend to address to you, you must draw your own inferences, for seldom will they enter into details.

Giles is not one of that class. All his knowledge is like himself, at your service." -- From Random Casts, by E.M.E. (Edward Eames Millard), 1878.

INDEX

Note: Names in capitals have separate biographical sketches.

Adirondack Forty-Sixers 2, 27
Adirondack Guides Association 22, 28, 30, 31,
   33, 35, 125, 151
Adirondack Iron Works at Tahawus 148
Adirondack League Club 47, 48, 56, 93, 98,
   111, 123, 146, 160, 166
Adirondack Lodge 141, 152
Adirondack Mountain Club 25, 126
Adirondack Mountain Reserve 47, 48, 126, 144,
   164
Adirondack Park 38
Adirondack Park Agency 241
Adirondack; or, Life in the Woods, The 54, 105
Adirondacks Illustrated, The 103, 141
Adventures in the Wilderness 54, 114
Agassiz, Louis 138
ALFORD, HARVEY 91, 152
Algonquin Hotel 165
Allen, Eugene 29, 91
Alvord 284, 289-293, 295
Alvord, Mr. 281
American Romanticism 57
AMES, BYRON POND 92
AMES, DANIEL E. 92
Ames, Daniel II 92
AMES, WILLIAM 92
Ampersand Hotel 111, 165
Ampersand Mountain 144
Archibald, John 53
Aristocrats, The 166
Arnold, Benedict 157
Arnold, Dave 65
ARNOLD, EDWIN 93
Arnold, Otis 4, 93, 159
Arthur, President 138
Article XIV 39
Atherton, Gertrude 166
Ausable Lakes 27
Avalanche Pass 141
Avery, Lyman 50
Avery's Hotel 50, 51
Bacheller, Irving 54
Bailey, Fred 240
Bailey, Roger 263, 265
BAKER, ANDREW 93
Baker, Jack 51
BALL, JOHN EDWIN 93
Ballard 13
Barber, George 30

Bartlett, Dan 128
Bartlett's Carry 108
BARTON, SAMUEL MERRIFIELD 93, 169
Bay View Hotel 165
Beach, Matthew 3
Bear iii
Beardslee, Lester 21
Bearor, Bob 12
Beaver 31
BECRAFT, GILES 98, 368
BEEDE, CHARLES 98, 130
Beede, Smith 150
BELLINGER, DELL 98
Bellows, Francis 57
Bellows, Jonathan 57
Benedict, Farrand 102
BENHAM, FRANK 98
Benham, Hiram 29
Bennett, Charles 40, 117
BENNETT, ED 98, 100, 112, 160
Bennett's Hotel 21
Berkeley, George A. 100
Betters, Will 273
BIGELOW, CHARLES 98
Billings Landing 99
Billings, A. H. 30
BILLINGS, ALBERT 98, 99
BLAKEMAN, ABNER 99
Blanchard, C. W. 30
BLANCHARD, ERNIE 99
Boardman, William H. 56
Boonville 30
BOULA, JESSE 99
Brace, Charles Loring 161
BRADY, RICHARD 99
Brakey, Sam 64
Braman, Horace 125
Brandreth Park Reserve 101
Brandreth, Dr. Benjamin 168
Brewster, Benjamin 98, 99
BREWSTER, MARTIN 100
Brightside 100
BROWN, CHARLES 100
Brown, Homer 269
Brown, John 142, 144, 146
Brown, Marshall 29
Brown's Tract Guides' Association 28, 30, 31,
   33, 35, 47, 48, 93, 123, 159
Brown's Tract Inlet 117

BROWNELL, REUBEN 100, 168
Brundage 279
BRYANT, WARREN 100
Bryere, Joseph O.A. 100
Buel's patent Spoon 281
Bumpo, Natty 52, 53
Buntline, Ned 114
BURLEY, FREE 101
BURLINGAME, CLIFFORD 101
Burr Sturges 282
Bushnell, Horace 164
Call, Silas 281, 282, 286, 289, 293, 296, 300,
          301, 303
Cameron, Byron 203
Camps and Tramps in the Adirondacks 18
Canada Lakes 287
Canning, Bob 200
Carson, Russell 25, 126, 147, 148
Cary, Reuben 9, 101
Caswell Company 14
Cedar Island 112
Chandler, Nelson 30
Charbonneau, David 32
Chase, C.J. 9
Chase, Caleb 113
Cheney, John 8, 15, 25, 26, 53, 102, 291
Childwold Park Hotel 151
Chittenden, L. E. 65
Chittendon, L. E. 154
Church, Artie 30
Cibeele 303, 304, 309
Cilley, Dave 210, 252
Civilian Conservation Corps 238
Clafin, "Albany Sam" 51
Clark, Herb 26, 27, 108
Cleveland, Grover 114, 136, 138, 144, 159
Clifton 123
Clouthier, Irv 50
Coburn, Bernard 110
COBURN, FRANCIS N. 109
Cohasset 93
Colbath, Hose 125
Colburn, Mace 125
Cole, Warren 30
Coles 296
Coluton, Fred 50
Colvin, Verplanck 26, 29, 141, 144, 147, 150,
          159
Commerford, John 48, 56
Conservation Commission 41
Conservation Department 43, 240
Constable 4
Conway, Pat 50
Cooch 286, 288, 290, 295-297 (see Couch)
CORBIN, EDISON 110

Corey, Jesse 144
Corrados, John 27
Couch 280, 281, 283, 285 (see Cooch)
COUGHLIN, JIM 110
Coulson, Ernest 64
Courtney, Frank 295
Covill, O. A. 30
Cowles, Elijah 7, 62
Craig, Jim 50
CRANDALL, CHRIS 110
Crego, Richard 30
Cripplebrush 109
Crusting 11
Cummerford, John 30
Cummerford, William 30
DALTON, JIM "BROCKIE" 111
Danferd, Les 50
Dart, Bill 31
Davis, Eula 64
DAVIS, HENRY 111
Davis, Nelson 111
De Bougainville, Louis Antoine 2
DeBAR, GEORGE 111
DELMARSH, ARCHIE 112
Department of Environmental Conservation 34,
          44
Dibble, Seth 147
Driving deer 11
Duane, Ernie 64
Dudley, Alonzo 29
DUNAKIN, SAM 112
Dunnigan, Sam 102
Dunning, Alvah 4, 93, 112, 132
Duquette, Will 199, 200
Durant, Dr. Thomas 112, 114
Durant, William West 115
Eighth Lake 117
Emmons, Ebenezer 26, 102
Emperor, Dick 238
EPPS, LYMAN SR. 118
Essex County Republican 149
Estey, George 26
Esty, Peter 293
Evans, Lute 29, 118
Failing, Wayne 233
FARMER, ARTHUR 118
Farmer, Clark 102
Farrington, D. E. 41
Fayette, George 29
Fish Creek 203
FLEURY, JOHN 119
FLEURY, ROY 119
Flower, Governor Roswell 140
Flynn, Michael Francis "Farmer" 59
Forest and Stream 13

Forest Commission 36-39
Forest Commission Report, 1893 viii
Forest Preserve 36, 38, 39, 42
Forge House 147
Fosburgh, Pieter W. viii
Foster, Jeanne Robert 120
Foster, Nat 3, 4
Fountain, Sandy and Fred 244
Frayne, Dan and Bill 223
FRAYNE, DANIEL J. 119
Freeman, Gene 209
FREEMAN, HARRY E. 119, 200
FREEMAN, ROSS C. 119, 209
French and Indian War 1, 3
FULLER, DUANE 119
Fuller, Harold 240
GALLAGHER, ROBERT 120
GALUSHA, JOHN 120
Game Protectors 247
GATES, ART 120
Gereau, Ed 109
GIFFIN, ARCHIE 65, 120
Gillen, Charlie 265
Gilman, John 283
Golden Beach 117
GOODWIN, JIM 121
Grand View Hotel 91
GRANT, DWIGHT 30, 48, 123
GRANT, LEWIS 123
GRAVES, ALBERT LYMAN 123
GRAY, IRA 124
Greeley, Horace 149
Green, Seth 116
Grenno, Charles 128
GREY, FRANK 124
GRIMSHAW, ELMER 124
Guide-boat 4, 8, 61, 63, 213
Hackett, Joe 33, 35
HALE, DAVID 125
HALE, LeGRAND 125
HALL, ASA B. 125
Hallock, Charles 13
HALLOCK, FITZ GREENE 29, 125
Hamilton County 278, 306, 307, 309
Hamilton, Low 168
Hamner, Willard 213, 216, 241
HANMER, HENRY 125
Hanmer, Theodore 111
Haskell, Truman 64
Hathaway, Carl 209, 268
Hathaway, Les 13, 125
HATHAWAY, MELVIN 126
HATHORNE, CHAUNCEY 127
HAYES, ARTHUR W. 127
HAYES, CHARLIE 128

Hayes, Clark 246
HAYES, ELLSWORTH D. 127, 128
HAYES, ROSS 129
Headley, Joel 54, 105
Heald, Dave 150
Heald, Harold 270
HEALY, THOMAS T. 30, 129
Henderson, David 103
Herreshoff Manor 93, 112
Hickey, Billy 270
Hickey, Bobby 270
Hickey, Jimmy 270
Hickok 26
Higby, J.H. 117
Higby, William 4
High Peaks 25
HINDS, BERT 129
Hinkson, J. W. 30
History of the Adirondacks 137
Hoffman, Charles Fenno 26, 52, 102, 106
Holmes 279, 281, 298, 300, 301, 309
Holt, Charles 14
HOLT, FRANK 129
HOLT, HARVEY 26, 129
HOLT, MONROE 59, 129
Homer, Winslow 57, 58
HOOD, FRED 130
Hounding 10, 40, 41, 47, 61
Howland, George 18, 167
Hoyt, Gould 250
Hudson River School 57, 59
Hunter, David 27
Independent Guide Club 28
Indian Lake 305
Indian Pass 141
Indian River 302, 305
Indians 2, 3
Inlet Hotel 139
ISHAM, ED 130
ISHAM, WILL 130
Island Harbor House 124
Ives, H. L. 56, 66
Jacklighting 9, 10, 40, 41
Jacoby, Col. Edward 35
Jamieson, Paul 53
JENKINS, GEORGE 130
JENNSEN, FORDINAND 130
Jessup's River 283, 305, 307, 308
John Camp 303, 304
JOHNSON, ERNEST H. 131, 137
Jones, Freeland 13
Jones, Henry 206
Keene Valley 27
Keene Valley Guides Association 49, 150
KELLY, JAMES 131

KENNEDY, EDWIN W. 131
KENNEDY, MELVIN 132
KENNEDY, MILES 30, 132
KENWELL, GERALD 132
Kenwell, Ike 115
Kenwell, Isaac 132
KENWELL, WELLINGTON 132
Kirby, Will 274
Kirch, Fred 112
Kniffen, Millo 50
Kreisler, Fritz 119
La Bastille, Anne 45
LaCASSE, NOAH 133
Lake Alvord 290
Lake House 124
Lake Lily 167
Lake Piseco Trout Club 6
Lake Placid Club 100
Lake Placid House 100
Lake Placid Inn 100
Lake Pleasant 278-280, 282, 300, 301, 304, 306,
307, 309
Lake Tear of the Clouds 141
Lamb, Pete 130
LaMONT, JAMES 133
LAMOY, CASSIUS 134
LAMOY, JOSEPH B. 134
LAMOY, MARSHALL 134
Lamy, Ed 240
Lanman, Charles 102
LANPHEAR, ORRIN 134
LaPRARIE, BEECHER 134
Last of the Mohicans, The 52
Lawrence, "Pants" 50
Lawrence, Brett 269
LeBEAU, WILLIAM 135
Leege, Bill 12
Lemoy, Bernie 213
Lemoy, Braynard 209
Lemoy, Ken 209
Lewis, Paul 264, 265
Lige 303
Long Lake 2, 9, 58
Louis Lake 305, 307
Lovers of the Woods 56
LUCAS, FRANK 135
Lundy, Reverend John 20
MacKenzie, Mary 6, 140, 146, 147
Man of the Woods 139
Marcy, William Learned 25
Marden, H. B. 30
Marshall, Bob 109
Marshall, George 2, 26, 109
MARTIN, CHARLES 135
MARTIN, DOUGLAS 30, 135

MARTIN, HENRY 135
Martin, Stephen 111
Martin, Steve 29
Martin's 145
Masten 102
Mather, Fred 115
Mattie 167
MAXAM, FRED "MOSSIE" 135
Maynard gun 13
McBride, James 30
McCaffrey, Charles 30
McCormick, Pete 206
McDonnell, Brian 194
McKENZIE, ALBERT 135
McKENZIE, SANFORD P. 136
McKinley, President 123, 133, 143
McLAUGHLIN, 'UNCLE BILL' 136
McLAUGHLIN, JOHN 136
Meacham Lake Hotel 161
MEEKER, JOHATHAN 136
MERRILL, LOYAL A. 136
Michelfelder, Bill 221
MICK, REUBEN 136
Middle Earth Expeditions 233
Miller, J. Herbert 29
Mohawk and Malone Railroad 134
Monroe, Tom 34, 44
MOODY 137
Moody, Ben 29
MOODY, CLEVELAND EUGENE 138
Moody, Cort 61
MOODY, JACOB 137, 138
MOODY, MART 128, 137, 138, 201
Moody, William 63
Moose 31
Morcy, Edith 165
Morrill, Nat 6
MORRISON, WILFRED 139
Morrow, Ralph 217
Mount Marcy 26, 141
Mount Morris House 138
Murray, Lady Amelia 138
Murray, W.H.H. (Adirondack) 114, 125, 138
145, 147, 150, 151
MURRAY, WALLACE 140
MUSSEN, GEORGE W. 140
MUSSEN, MARSHALL EUGENE 140
My Angling Friends 115
Nash, J.V. 141
Nehasane Park 92, 100, 125
Nessmuk 116, 140
New York State Outdoor Guides Association 28
33, 35, 44, 194
New York Tribune 149
Norris, Thaddeus 157

Iorth Woods Club 58, 59, 101, 159
Iorth Woods Walton Club 123
Iorthrup, A. Judd 18, 52
Iorthville 279, 298
Iye, Bill 26, 140
IYE, HUBERT 142
I'CONNOR, JOHN 142
I'MALLEY, JIM 143
Iettinger, Fred 44
Iliver, Almeron 26
ITIS, ALBERT 143
ITIS, ALFRED H. 143
ITIS, ARTHUR L. 143
ITIS, HARRY G. 143
Itis, Matt 240
ITIS, MILLARD 143
ITIS, OREN 143
ITIS, SIDNEY EDWIN 144
ITIS, SYLVESTER 144
IWENS, JAMES 144
ACKARD, HENRY 144
age, Dave 15
arker, Captain Calvin 58
ARSONS, ANSELM 144
arsons, Ira 30
EACOCK, THOMAS 128, 144
eaks and People of the Adirondacks 126, 148
eck, Professor Charles E. 168
ERKINS, DONALD "RED" 146
ERKINS, EZEKIEL "ZEKE" 146
erks, Rufus 228
ERRY, ENOS 147
ERRY, SANFORD 147
erryman, Don 43
ersonal Reminiscences 1840-1890 154
etty, Clarence 198
HELPS, ED 130, 147
HELPS, ORSON 8, 25, 26, 48, 59, 98, 130, 147
IERCE, SETH 150
LUMLEY, JEREMIAH 150
LUMLEY, JOHN E. 54, 151
OHL, WILLIAM 151
OND, WILLIAM D. 151
orter, Bob 51
orter, Noah 164
orter, William 6, 14
orter's Clearing 302
ost, Marjorie Merriweather 244
reston, Julia 8, 13
rospect House 144
adford, Harry 32, 150
andall, William 301
aquette Lake 3, 296
aquette Lake House 132

Rarick, Johnny 112
Ray Brook House 275
Redfield, William 102
Redwood, Thomas 30
Register of Guides 42
Reminiscences of the Adirondacks 56
Revolutionary War 2, 3
Reynolds, Rant 128
Reynolds, Reub 128
Rice, Dr. Gail Rogers 18
Rice, Walter 29
Richard, Ed 50
Riggs, Garry 30
RING, WILLIAM "UNCLE BILL" 151
Riverside Inn 140
Rivett, Peter 30
Roberts, Robert 30
ROBLEE, BEECHER 152
Rockwell, Norman 120
Rondeau, Noah John 204, 238
Rondel, Frederic 57
Roosevelt, Theodore 31, 119, 123, 124, 133, 135, 145
RORK, FRED 152
ROSSMAN, JED 152
Rottner, Bob 250
Round Lake 278, 280, 281, 285, 297
Rustic Lodge 206
Sabattis, Isaac 30
SABATTIS, MITCHELL 2, 65, 152, 157
SABATTIS, PETER 152, 157
Sacondaga river 279
Saranac Inn 203
Savard 238
SAWYER, MOSES 157
Scafford, E. L. 30
Schryers, Will 198
Scott, Philo (Fide) 54
SEARS, FRANK 158
Sears, George Washington 116, 140
SEYMOUR, "FRENCH LOUIE" 158
Shaw, George 105
SHEPARD, NAT 158
SHEPPARD, EDWIN "JACK" 117, 158
SHORT, JAMES 159
Sibley, Herm 228
Silas Strong 54
Simonds, Elijah 107, 159
Simons, Will 200
Skidmore, Tim 6
Skilton's Lodge 100
Slack, Artliss 162
Slater, John 29
Slater, Warren 30
SLAVEN, EDWARD G. 159

SMITH, CHARLES H. 159
Smith, Dutch 51
Smith, Gerrit 118
SMITH, LESLIE 159
Smith, Paul 164
SMITH, PETER 160
Smith, Phelps 158
Solomon, John 128
Solomon, Peter 29, 30, 128
Sperry, Sanford 93
Spirit of the Times 6
Sprague, Anthony 57
Sprague, Halsey 30
SPRAGUE, WARREN H. 160
SQUIRES, PERLY J. 160
ST. GERMAIN, MOSES 56, 160
Stanton, Henry 9
STANTON, JAMES H. 160
State Fish Commission 116
State registration of guides 41
Stearns, Charlie 274
STELL, JOHN H. 160
Stevens House 127
Stevenson, Robert Louis 93, 98
STEVES, HYLAND 160
STEVES, WARREN 160
STICKNEY, DAVID W. 161
Still-hunting 11
Stillman, William 57
Stoddard, Seneca Ray 21, 141
Stoner, Nick 3
Stories the Keg Told Me 166
Story of Adirondac, The 102
Street, Alfred B. 1, 26, 138
Sturge, George 304
Sturges, Burr 300, 301, 307
Sturges, George 305
Sumner, Ed 29, 30
SUTTON, M.R. 161
SWINYER, MITCHELL 161
Tahawus 26, 27
Tahawus Club 120, 133
Tahawus House 102
Tahawus Iron Works 141
Tait, Arthur Fitzwilliam 57, 101, 272
TELFER, ANN 161
Tent platform sites 39
Thatcher, George 98
The Antlers 117
Thirteenth Lake Lodge 101
Thomas and Armstrong Lumber Company 149
THOMPSON, HENRY 144, 163
TITUS, JOHN H. JR. 164
TITUS, WILLIAM H. 164
Todd, John 157

Torrence, Sim 29
Tredo, Max 125
TRIMM, LUCIAN (LUTE) 164
Trout House Hotel 124
Trudeau, Dr. Edward Livingston 29, 125, 135, 138, 151, 158
Trumbull, Arthur 49
TRUMBULL, MELVIN 27, 164
Tupper Lake House 138
Turner, Fred 27
Turner, Gilbert 146
Turner, Phelps 27
Turner, Steve 8
Tuscarora 134
TUTTLE, LOTTIE E. 165
Twitchell, Joseph 164
Tyler, Henry 135
UMBER, JAMES 165
Under the Hemlocks 98, 100, 112, 160
Upper Ausable Lake 48, 148, 263
Van Dyke, Henry iii
Van Hoevenberg, Henry 168, 169
Van Valkenburg, Norm 44
VANDENBURGH, GARRY 165
VANDENBURGH, JAY "ZEKE" JR. 130, 165
Vosburgh, Jake 201, 206, 238
Walker, William 157
Wallace, Rufus 59
Wanakena Ranger School 139
Wapiti 31
Ward, Steve 139
Wardner, Frank M. 272
Wardner, Seth 272
Warner, Charles Dudley 147, 164
Water Lily 167
Waters, Peter 3
Wawbeek Hotel 202
WEAVER, JAMES EDGAR 166
WEAVER, RAYMOND E. 166
Webb, Dr. William Seward 92, 112, 134
Webber, Charles 4
Welds, William 264
WERNER, AUGUSTUS 166
West Canada Creek 281, 289, 298
Westcott, Zeke 64
Westport Inn 119
Wetherby, Lon 65
Wharton, Don 50
Wharton, Jr., Bill 11
WHITE, JAMES E. 166
White, Merril 30
WHITE, PETER 166
WHITE, THEODORE 167
Whiteface 141
Whitehouse 22, 47, 49-51, 166

Whitney, Carlos 204
Whitney, Donald 264
Whitney, Jess 264
Whitney, Reginald 263
WILBUR, CALVIN 167
Williams, Frank 30
WILLIAMS, HARRY 167
Winchester 13
Withe 11
Wood Hotel 132
WOOD, CHARLES 41, 168
Wood, Jerome 30
Wood, William 3
Woods, Fred 203
Wrisley, Loren 228
Yards 11
YOUNG, EDWARD 168
YOUNG, FRANCIS 168
YOUNG, WILLIAM B. 169